D1047114

TRAVEL & LEISURE

Amsterdam

by Carol Winkelman

Macmillan • USA

MACMILLAN TRAVEL
A Simon & Schuster Macmillan Company
1633 Broadway
New York, NY 10019

Find us on-line at **hhtp://www.mgr.com/travel**
or on America Online at Keyword: **Frommer's**

ISBN: 0-02-860698-1
ISSN: 1088-4793

Editors: Suzanne Roe and Alice Thompson
Production Editor: Trudy Brown
Design by Amy Peppler Adams—designLab, Seattle
Maps by Douglas Stallings
Digital Cartography by Ortelius Design
Illustrations on pp. 8, 88, 119, 120, 131, 158, 170, 175, 220,
and 222 by Giselle Simons

SPECIAL SALES
Bulk purchases (10+ copies) of Frommer's and selected
Macmillan travel guides are available to corporations,
organizations, institutions, and charities at special discounts,
and can be customized to suit individual needs. For more
information write to Special Sales, Macmillan General
Reference, 1633 Broadway, New York, NY 10019.

Manufactured in Singapore

CONTENTS

LIST OF MAPS

About the Author

Carol Winkelman is a freelance writer and editor who has adopted Amsterdam as her home-away-from-home. She grew up in Wausau, Wisconsin, but escaped to Bard College, The New School for Social Research, the University of Wisconsin at Madison, and the University of California at Irvine to study social science and literature. For the last ten years she has taught writing at UC Irvine, Duke University, and the University of North Carolina at Chapel Hill.

Her yen for traveling has taken her to Latin America and Europe. Every December she dreams of a cold Dutch winter so she can return to Holland to skate the frozen canals. Meanwhile, she splits her time between California and North Carolina.

An Additional Note

Please be advised that travel information is subject to change at any time—and this is especially true of prices. We therefore suggest that you write or call ahead for confirmation when making your travel plans. The author, editor, and publisher cannot be held responsible for the experiences of readers while traveling. Your safety is important to us, however, so we encourage you to stay alert and be aware of your surroundings. Keep a close eye on cameras, purses, and wallets, all favorite targets of thieves and pickpockets.

Acknowledgments

Many thanks to my editors, Alice Thompson and Suzanne Roe, for their helpful suggestions and good taste, to Nancy Novogrod and Margot Guralnick from *Travel & Leisure* for sending this project my way, and to my publisher, Michael Spring, for his support.

Additional thanks to my research assistants, Hanneke Kemmeling for her humor and willingness to bike in bad weather, Kendall Boyd for all those tram rides and tedious telephoning, and Gerard for his generosity. Much appreciation to Elliot Eisenberg and Fijgje de Boer for their friendship and many fruitful conversations; the Hougans, Weares, and Cusimanos for their encouragement; Eileen Killory for heartening dinners and a crucial ride to the airport; Rodney Bolt for his warm spirit—and that memorable flambé; Rob de Wilde for his Amsterdam savvy and excellent eye; Blair Pollack for his encouragement and reading of the manuscript; Dick Harmsen for his gezellige translations; Willem-Jan and Marijke for their Rotterdam secrets; Allen Goldin for tips on the Amsterdam jazz scene and helpful suggestions; the late Bob LaBrasca for his stories, his skating fever—and for opening that door; Edith Spiegel Winkelman for her continuous support and encouragement; and to Peter (wherever you are) for introducing me to your beloved Amsterdam.

I would also like to thank the Netherlands Board of Tourism (especially Charlotte van Weeghel for her insights and patient assistance and Jelte Bakker, Ineke Haase, Carmen van den Hombergh, and Paola Strijk for all their additional assistance); Els Wamsteker, Odette Taminiau, and Gerrie Davidson for their advice and gezelligheid; Helene Hoofdman for the lovely drive to the Vecht; Wina Born for good talk about good food; Mees Hermes for all those faxes; Menno; Guido Goudsmit and Stans De Jong; Raymond van der Boogaard; Paul van Dijk; Mary M; Yolanda Morales; Debra Weiner; Linda Davis; Benjamin; and the VVV Tourist Offices in Amsterdam, Delft, Enkhuizen, Leeuwarden, Loosdrecht, Rotterdam, Utrecht (Provincial), and Zandvoort.

Thanks also to Derek Blyth for his contributions to the Dining (Cafe section), Sights & Attractions, Rotterdam, and Portraits chapters.

AMSTERDAM . . .
A COSMOPOLITAN
VILLAGE

O N MY FIRST VISIT TO AMSTERDAM, LOOKING OUT the window of a bright-yellow Dutch train running smoothly along its track, I got the feeling I was coming home. I'd had this feeling as a child when, after long car-trips, my parents would turn the corner onto our street, and the familiar patches in the asphalt, the old oaks, and the anticipation of pulling into our driveway, would trigger a deep comfort.

The Dutch call this feeling *gezelligheid*. It is central to the Dutch soul—and my homey experience on the train was a traveler's premonition.

Gezellig, literally translated, means cozy, snug, homey. But it is more than that. Gezelligheid (the state of being gezellig) is at the heart of everything Dutch— from child-rearing to beer drinking. Dutch parents tell their quarreling or whining children to "Keep it gezellig"—keep it cozy. Bartenders find it their social duty to keep it gezellig and will throw out anyone whose behavior is *ongezellig* (*not* gezellig).

Gezellig is an aesthetic as well as a mood—and it has a long history in Holland. Jan Vermeer, Pieter de Hooch, and other Dutch painters were obsessed with cozy interiors and domestic scenes, and during the golden age wealthy merchants and farmers put their best energy and money into lovingly decorating their homes with fine imported furniture and familiar Dutch art. Nowadays, moving into a new apartment includes "making it gezellig" by hanging paintings, bringing fresh flowers, and arranging furniture.

There are, however, significant differences in taste when it comes to Dutch gezelligheid. What is gezellig for some may be *tegezellig*—too cozy or cute—for others. The old-fashioned style—with perfectly pressed white lace curtains, a house filled with knickknacks, or window sills lined with plants and porcelain figurines—can be oppressively cute for urbane Amsterdammers.

"While gezelligheid is bound up with a love of home, family, and friends," says Dutch-American novelist Hans Koning, "it is also rooted in the Amsterdammers' restlessness, their desire to be part of the wide world with all its possibilities." Amsterdammers go out to meet the world and exercise their finely honed social and conversational skills in "brown" cafes that some affectionately call "living-room cafes" because they feel like a second home. Fortunately, feeling at home and socializing are forms of Dutch gezelligheid easily accessible to travelers. Joseph Conrad, novelist and world traveler, experienced this conviviality in a cafe his first night in Amsterdam. In *The Mirror of the Sea,* Conrad describes "a gorgeous cafe in the center of town" that was "upholstered in red plush, full of electric lights, and so thoroughly warmed that even the marble tables felt tepid to the touch. The waiter who brought me my cup of coffee bore, by comparison with my utter desolation, the dearest aspect of an intimate friend."

My personal theory about this Dutch delight in living is that a city built on stilts and protected by dikes from a threatening sea copes with its precarious situation by amusing itself whenever possible. It is an interpretation of Calvin with a hedonistic twist: Eat, drink, smoke, smell the roses, and be merry—for tomorrow may bring the Deluge.

My purpose in writing this guide is to help you feel at home in Amsterdam—to take you *inside* Dutch culture and help you find and appreciate its unique spirit. The book is also a guide for discovering the city's cosmopolitan possibilities, its whimsical humor, hidden courtyards, and simple pleasures. My bias is toward simple pleasures: exploring the canal neighborhoods, bicycling through the patrician countryside, visiting favorite van Goghs, sipping *koffie verkeert* in a brown cafe. Although this guide shows you the well-known hotels, restaurants, tourist attractions, and nightlife options, it also leads you to the offbeat and unconventional. My aim is to take you inside Amsterdam to the small streets between the canals—vestiges of golden-age abundance—that are crammed with exotic specialty shops much as they were 300 years ago when Dutch voyagers brought home silks, spices, and other treasures. And I will bring you to my adopted "Prinsengracht neighborhood"—the home I slip off to whenever I'm in Amsterdam—to show you the canalside cafés, the peaceful rhythm of bicycles pedaling by at dusk, and the quirky, witty ship windows and gable stones that Amsterdammers have amused themselves with for centuries.

In this guide, I try to give you the good without glossing over the bad, to help you make informed choices about hotels, restaurants, getting around, and where to walk or not walk at different times of day or night.

Amsterdam Today

Amsterdammers like to describe their city as "the world's largest village," where people still chat regularly with the local baker, bicycle to work, and value time for family and friends. But it's a cosmopolitan village— a center for the arts with a world-class orchestra, concert hall, and museums. As it was in the golden age, Amsterdam is a vibrant center of international trade whose small shops are packed with exotic goods from around the world: everything from African musical instruments to Indonesian shadow puppets and Turkish tapestries. What Baudelaire once wrote of a mythical European city could aptly be said of Amsterdam today: "Every corner, every crack, every drawer and curtain's fold breathes forth a curious perfume, a perfume of Sumatra whispering back."

It is also a city of small, hidden places where what lies behind a seemingly ordinary door on a narrow street can hold intriguing surprises: secluded gardens, hidden courtyards, or clandestine churches. Open such a door in the Jordaan or on the Spui square and you might find a *hofje*—a cluster of almshouses surrounding a peaceful courtyard garden. Walk through an arched passageway between Kloveniersburgwal and Oude Zijds Achterburgwal and you may find the Oudemanhuispoort, where old men sell used books and antiquarian drawings from wooden stalls.

Alongside the exotic is the quirky. Amsterdam is a storehouse of offbeat curiosities: a floating flower market, a houseboat for homeless cats, a royal palace standing on 13,659 wooden piles, cartoons and abstract art splashed across bright-yellow trams, and ingenious bicycle contraptions for everything from carrying children to hauling furniture. The city has approximately half a million bicycles, a thousand bridges, 2,500 houseboats, and 7,000 protected monuments. This combination, along with countless architectural masterpieces, makes Amsterdam one of the most visually dynamic cities in Europe.

What is most unique is the city's visual humor, manifested in everything from 17thC gable stones to contemporary "window art," where playful displays in shop and residential windows are designed to amuse passersby. The oldest form of gable-stone humor can be seen in stones that pun on the name or occupation of a building's owner. The newer gable jokes tend toward the offbeat, such as depicting a playful interpretation of life on the canals.

You will find the most whimsical examples of window art in the Jordaan and along the small streets between the Singel and Prinsengracht canals. Here, for example, in a shop devoted to dental care, colorfully painted toothbrushes sit like people on a whirling miniature Ferris wheel. In another window a lineup of goofy porcelain pigs gently mocks the kitsch aesthetic of old-timers who take their porcelain figurines seriously.

Aesthetics—whether serious or irreverent—are always important in Amsterdam. Almost every year there is a special exhibit at one of the city art museums of such native luminaries as van Gogh, Rembrandt, or Vermeer. But art is also frequently playful and participatory, such as the Buddha sculptures afloat in a Vondelpark pond that became art-in-progress as local artists paddled out by boat to the meditating figures to add such colorful—and irreverent—touches as flamboyant neckties.

It is in this irreverent humor that the spirit of the 1960s and 1970s can still be felt in Amsterdam—once a mecca for hippies and the politically radical sixties youth culture. In the 1970s, this humor took a form called *ludiek*—funny things that break with tradition and custom with an original style or artistic flair. Ludiek humor was used by the Provos, a provocative group of activists, to raise serious political and ecological issues in a playful way. The unorthodox Provos staged frolicsome protests against pollution, war, and tobacco. They painted their faces, published fanciful articles, and brandished sticks of rhubarb to "defend" themselves from the police. The Kabouters, or "Gnomes," a later splinter group, maintained the ludiek tradition by choosing gnomish red hats as their official uniform. But the

Kabouters took their politics seriously enough to get 5 Gnomes elected to the 45-seat Municipal Council in 1970.

In the 1980s and early 1990s, this progressive, anarchistic spirit has turned from taunting provocation to a gentle jostling of social and political conventions. What remained of sixties' thinking grew into left/liberal political sentiments with a strong environmentalist bent. Provo/Kabouter idealism—combined with European social-democracy and the preexisting Dutch traditions of tolerance and charity—pushed the Netherlands further in the direction of social welfare, egalitarianism, and government support of artists and the arts.

But times are changing. Though still comfortably liberal, Amsterdam politics are slowly moving to the right. Today, the Netherlands no longer supports artists in the style to which they had become accustomed in the 1980s, and the country is considering changing the laws regulating soft drugs to curb "drug tourism" and to comply with the wishes of European trading partners who hold less liberal views on marijuana and hashish.

Amsterdam is trying to change its image from that of the hippie mecca of the 1970s to a sophisticated 1990s center of the arts and international business. Hotels have added business centers, conference halls, and state-of-the-art gyms. Consequently, the city has become a desirable spot for trade shows and medical and academic conferences; and at times, impeccably dressed conventioneers inundate the city and the surrounding towns. The chemistry and constituency of the city has changed, too. Several scruffy neighborhoods once frequented by junkies and prostitutes have been renovated. Although the red-light district still attracts its share of unsavory characters, the district is well-regulated and self-policed by bouncers who are bulkier and nastier than most Amsterdam police.

Although Amsterdam is no longer a hippie mecca, it still attracts hordes of neohippie international youth who gather freely at Dam Square, the Leidseplein, and Vondelpark. And despite its interest in business and banking, Amsterdam still has a vital bohemian/intellectual community that draws artists, writers, and musicians from all over the world.

Despite Amsterdam's interest in further restrictions on soft drugs, the city is still a haven of tolerance compared to most large American and European cities. Since the 16thC Amsterdam has been known for its tolerance and humanism, attracting successive waves of Jews, Huguenots, and Armenians fleeing religious or political persecution. The city even gave asylum to a group of Pilgrim Fathers before they left for America.

Nowadays, Amsterdam tolerates cultural and sexual differences as well as political and religious ones. The city gracefully accepts gay relationships (a popular Dutch television comedy focuses on the life of a gay couple) and is a place where the gay community need not be defensive or clandestine. Amsterdammers also tolerate cultural differences and benign eccentricity: Street musicians perform at both public squares and chi-chi cafes, and fire-eaters, belly dancers, and mimes wend their way from Leidseplein to Vondelpark, Dam Square, and Centraal Station. Locals fondly greet a well-known Salvation Army worker as she goes from table to table in fashionable restaurants asking for donations. And the Amsterdam City Council tolerates a mind-boggling array of political parties and diverging opinions.

The Dutch open-mindedness goes along with their zest for enlightened social experiments and charitable organizations. Historically, Amsterdam has spent impressive sums of money on social improvements such as houses of correction, orphanages, almshouses, and municipal housing projects. At the root of this concern for the disadvantaged is Dutch humanism combined with Calvinism and its attitude toward wealth and the expenditure of money. For the religious Protestant, charity was a way around Calvin's warnings about the dire consequences of worldly indulgence. Wealthy Dutch merchants offset their purchases of palatial houses and expensive furnishings with donations to the poor and oppressed.

In the Netherlands, charity remains a Christian, as well as a social-democratic, way to come to terms with personal and collective wealth. In the 1960s and 1970s, with the help of the era's prevalent idealism, the Netherlands became a welfare state, using its vast wealth to subsidize the disabled and unemployed. Despite growing conservatism with regard to government spending, the Dutch still subsidize health care, the arts, and education. And every Nederlander is entitled to at least 1 month of paid vacation.

Amsterdammers, however, are not all humanism and tolerance. While one side of Dutch tolerance is grounded in a commitment to religious and political liberty, the other side is purely practical. They believe in "Live and

Let Live" out of self-interest as well as altruism. In the case of soft drugs and prostitution, Amsterdammers feel it is wise to let in a little evil—which can be closely regulated—in order to prevent a larger evil from finding its way into Dutch society. Decriminalizing—but carefully regulating—brothels and hashish coffee shops gives Dutch authorities control, and curbs the power of the underworld. The Dutch also believe that soft drugs, the "little evil," do not lead to hard drugs when the world of pot coffee shops and soft drugs like marijuana and hashish is set apart from the criminal world of hard drugs like cocaine and heroin.

Amsterdam's rough edges—the alleys of the red-light district and the junkies hovering around Dam Square and Nieuwemarkt—are buffered, though not entirely smoothed over, by permissive Dutch policies. Junkies may well be waiting for the Methadone truck—not their connection—and prostitutes are unionized and provided with some of the best HIV education and preventive health-care in the Western world.

Amsterdam's seamier sides are easily avoided, and they rarely intrude on the quieter parts of town. Because the city is neatly divided into districts, you can simply decide on the "Amsterdam experience" you wish to have—and to go to the parts of town where you can have it. If you're looking for the crowds and intensity of the big city—for street musicians, trolleys, fast food, clubs, casinos, and cafes—head for Leidseplein. If you're seeking the genteel side of city bustle, the Amstel and Museum neighborhoods will give you nightlife and cafes as well as some peace and quiet. And if you want enchantment, tranquillity, convivial cafes, and the flavor of golden age Amsterdam, slip off to the canals where the gentle chiming of church bells and whirring of bicycle wheels will lull you into a trance.

Whichever "Amsterdam" you choose, in order to experience the soul of the city, go to a cafe. Amsterdam's cafe scene is uniquely specialized, and somewhere in the city there is a cafe for you. The challenge is to find it amidst the daunting selection: elegant designer cafes, opulent grand cafes, neighborhood brown cafes, avant-garde cafes, theater cafes, lefty cafes, media cafes, yuppie cafes, music cafes. Your cafe is a place where you can relax, feel at home, converse with polyglot Amsterdammers, and dip into Dutch gezelligheid—the balm that keeps such a diverse, opinionated, and individualistic city rolling harmoniously along.

Cafes on the Leidseplein

Customs, Etiquette & Some Aspects of Dutch Culture

Amsterdammers are, in many respects, "citizens of the world." American jazz and blues pour out of traditional brown cafes, cozy canalside restaurants serve French-international cuisine, and Delftware, made in Makkum, was originally modeled on Chinese porcelain. Despite this melding of things Dutch with things foreign, Amsterdammers have rules of etiquette and customs that are unmistakably Dutch. Their etiquette is straightforward. Their customs are quirky and their values sometimes contradictory, but matters are always resolved practically—which is typically Dutch.

Some Aspects of Dutch Culture

Kopje Koffie   Translated literally, this means a little cup of coffee, but it really means a cup of coffee presented in a friendly, *gezellig* way. To be invited for a *kopje koffie*, whether it's at someone's kitchen table or at a grand cafe, is the essential stuff of Dutch social life. The Dutch will offer you coffee at job interviews, business meetings, and friendly visits. Coffee is served black accompanied by *koffie melk* (thick evaporated milk), sugar, and a small cookie (*koekje*) unless you specify that you want *koffie verkeerd*—coffee with milk (literally translated as "coffee made the wrong way").

Smoking   Since Dutch traders brought tobacco to Amsterdam hundreds of years ago, the cigarette has taken hold. Amsterdammers are smokers—a fact made absolutely clear by the smoke-stained walls of brown cafes (that's why the cafes are dubbed "brown"). Few cafes,

Rules of Dutch Etiquette

1. Be gezellig.
2. Behave in a way that's good for business (trade before all).
3. Tolerate the cultures, religions, and sexual preferences of other people. (It's gezellig—and good for business.)
4. Never tell a Nederlander that the Dutch language sounds or reads a lot like German: The Dutch do not take this well.
5. Wear the right shoes (preferably leather, and definitely not clunky ones unless you are doing something athletic, in which case they *are* the right shoes).
6. Bring flowers or wine when invited to dinner.
7. Never forget a birthday.
8. Don't stare into, breathe on, or in any way mar the cleanliness of windows.
9. Offer your guests coffee—at least 2 cups. (This applies at both the office and at home.)
10. Address bosses and elders with the formal thank you, *dank u,* instead of the informal, *dank je.*
11. Greet acquaintances with a solid handshake and friends with 3 kisses on alternating cheeks (kiss the air if you are not close friends).
12. Do not, upon first meeting, immediately ask a Dutch person what he/she does for a living or promptly tell them what you "do." They are more interested in who you are, which can best be revealed in a relaxed, sociable way, while sipping a *kopje koffie.*
13. Do not mention how much money you make or flaunt your new Rolls or, for that matter, have the audacity to buy a new Rolls.
14. If you are in Amsterdam for professional reasons, do not hang out in pot coffee shops—they're for tourists and not the best places to be seen.

restaurants, or hotels cater to nonsmokers. Although the larger hotels have nonsmoking rooms, the smaller hotels do not. Few restaurants have nonsmoking sections, and cafes are often thick with smoke. Even when restaurants do have nonsmoking sections, the smokers get the better tables. Most trains have nonsmoking cars, and the platforms in between cars are often designated nonsmoking preferred, leaving decisions about smoking to the good judgment of passengers. This "smoke if you want to, but think of your neighbors" attitude is very Dutch.

The Open Drape Policy The Dutch leave their living room drapes open wide (even at night, when the whole room is illuminated by lamp light). Their usual explanation for this behavior: to show that they have nothing to hide and to affirm their sense of living in a friendly community. But there is also a hidden agenda: to display their well-furnished homes and their material wealth (Calvinist no-no's) in a modest, respectable way. You are expected to look—but not too closely. The Dutch respect for privacy is as strong as their curiosity; Amsterdammers may glance into windows as they pass by, but you will not find them stopping to stare.

Cleanliness The Dutch are clean, obsessively clean—a fact frequently mentioned in travelogues of the Netherlands. What William Aglionby, a 17thC social chronicler, observed is as true now as it was 300 years ago: "They have a great care of their House, and keep all their Cupboards, Cabinets, even the Floors, extream neat: some of them are so curious, as to not let you come into their Rubb'd Rooms, without putting on a pair of Slippers, or making your Shooes very clean."

Dutch homes, shops, and even budget hotels are almost always tidy and squeaky clean. The only exceptions are the crowded tourist squares like Leidseplein and Dam Square, and the streets in the fashionable "DINK" (Double Income–No Kids) canal neighborhoods. The otherwise lovely—and pricey—canal neighborhoods make up for their childlessness by an abundance of well-scrubbed and well-loved dogs. There are, however, no curb laws—a notable inconsistency in the preoccupation with cleanliness. Another exception are the canals that are sometimes the receptacles for broken bicycles and flotillas of cans and plastic bags.

Flowers In the Netherlands, flowers are a staple—a weekly necessity. A Dutch home has fresh-cut flowers in the living and dining rooms and women friends exchange flowers on special occasions. Flowers are also big at national festivals and memorials. Tulips are a national passion which, in the 17thC, reached a feverish peak in the Great Tulip Mania. In the 1620s, tulips were the expensive flowers of the elite and within 10 years prices increased by tenfold. The demand grew, as did a futures market that created dizzying profits. The mania ended finally, in 1637, with a panic and a market collapse.

The price of tulips returned to normal, but the passion remained—and became infectious. Now the Dutch tulip is an international cliché (along with wooden shoes and windmills). Every tulip season draws an international wave of tourism that boosts the already healthy Dutch economy.

Dogs are People, too   Amsterdammers treat pets like members of the family. Amsterdam has a large population of clean and generally well-behaved cats and dogs who are permitted in most restaurants and cafes— as long as they don't bother anybody. Consequently, it is not unusual to see the cafe cat asleep on the bar or curled up on the chair next to yours. You'll find dogs, belonging to customers or owners, resting comfortably under tables and counters.

Skating   In the Netherlands, skating is not merely a sport or recreation—it is a passion. There are skating customs, skating drinks, skating heroes, and a skating race that stops the nation in its tracks (which occurs infrequently, only about every 8 or 10 years, since the canals seldom freeze hard or long enough for the 200km race to take place).

Despite the infrequency these days of frozen canals (due, perhaps, to pollution and warmer temperatures), the Dutch keep their skating traditions alive at the ice rinks, teaching their children to skate on old-fashioned *Friesedoorlopers* (wood-and-steel strap-on skates); it is customary for beginning skaters to hold on to wooden chairs for support as they stumble around the rink. The true fanatics train for marathon races, which will take place on either artificial or "nature" ice.

National media focus on ice texture and depth as measurements—taken daily by skating experts— determine if the natural ice is strong enough for the *Elfstedentocht* (Eleven Cities Tour), a much awaited marathon skating race through 11 cities in Friesland. If the race is called, the country is taken with *Elfstedenkoortz* (Eleven Cities Fever). People either watch the race on TV, cheer at the sidelines, or join the race as competitors or "tourists" (in either case aspiring skaters can spend 15 years on a waiting list training passionately for a race that hardly ever occurs).

An Overview of the City

Amsterdam is a compact city with a distinctive pattern of canals and streets which, once mastered, is never forgotten. There are 3 major squares in the city that will be "hubs" during your visit. **Dam Square** is the heart of the city and site of the dam across the Amstel River that gave the city its original name. Today it is encircled by the Koninklijk Paleis (Royal Palace), the Nieuwe Kerk (New Church), several department stores, hotels, and restaurants. The **Leidesplein,** with the streets around it, is in many ways the heart of the city—and tourist central. It bustles with restaurants, nightclubs, theaters, the city's casino, and a few major hotels. **Muntplein** is essentially a transportation hub—one of the busiest in the city—identified by the Mint Tower (Munttoren).

The most fruitful area for exploring is the 17thC ring of canals known as the **Grachtengordel** (canal girdle), which encloses the old city in a sweeping arc. The main canals, **Herengracht, Keizersgracht,** and **Prinsengracht,** offer an endless parade of architectural styles from Renaissance to postmodern. The main museums are located beyond here in the 19thC ring, which extends in a broad arc around the old city, whose boundary is marked by **Singelgracht.** The architecture in this area ranges from opulent to utilitarian, and the streets tend to lack the animation of the central area. The 20thC ring and the outlying suburbs are of considerable interest architecturally, but are otherwise somewhat dull and suburban.

Neighborhoods in Brief

The following list gives an idea of the distinctive character of each of Amsterdam's different areas.

The Historic Center   The oldest part of the city, around Dam Square and the Centraal Railway Station, includes major shopping areas and such attractions as the Royal Palace, the Amsterdam Historical Museum, and the canal-boat piers.

The Canal Area   This semicircular network of canals was built around the old part of the city during the 17thC. It includes elegant, gabled houses, many restaurants and cafes, fascinating shops, and small hotels. A few of the sightseeing attractions here include the Anne Frank Huis and the Westerkerk.

The Jordaan   This maze of streets and canals lies west of the Center, beyond the major canals. Once a working-class neighborhood, it's fast becoming a fashionable residential area. It possesses a charm that Amsterdammers find irresistible, and it's jammed with small studios and businesses ranging from the bohemian to the bizarre. It's also home to some good cafes and intimate restaurants.

The Museum Quarter The Museum Quarter (Museumplein) is home to Amsterdam's 3 major art museums: the Rijksmuseum, the Vincent van Gogh Museum, and the Stedelijk Museum of Modern Art. It is mostly a residential area, and also includes Vondelpark, the Concertgebouw concert hall, and Amsterdam's most upscale shopping streets, P.C. Hooftstraat and Van Baerlestraat.

Jewish Quarter The Jewish Quarter (Jodenbuurt), established in the 1600s, contains relics of Amsterdam's once-flourishing Jewish community. Attractions here include the Joods Historisch Museum and the Portuguese Synagogue. With the completion of the Muziektheater, the area has at last begun to recover from the bitter memory of the war, and streets such as Staalstraat and Oude Doelenstraat are increasingly fashionable.

Amsterdam South This exclusive, modern residential area is the site of a number of hotels, including the Okura and Hilton.

DINING

Dining Out in Amsterdam

Until recently, Amsterdam was noted for few culinary delights besides *rijsttafel* (a banquet of Indonesian dishes), herring, *pannekkoeken* (large pancakes with sweet or savory toppings), chocolate—and a few fine restaurants. But in the last 10 years that has changed. Amsterdammers have become foodies and eating out is in. New restaurants have popped up all over town, especially in the trendy Jordaan and Prinsengracht neighborhoods.

You will find a wide selection of restaurants to choose from—French, Dutch, Indonesian, Thai, Chinese, Indian, and even Surinamese. Although some restaurants specialize in classic French cuisine, others take a more adventurous, creative approach. The Dutch have continued their tradition of bringing spices and products from all over the world to Amsterdam. Much of the new cuisine has a French base with quality Dutch products and a hint of international flavors. Expect mango, figs, saffron, curry, and thyme to subtly influence everything from duck to sorbet.

Many of the popular new restaurants are distinguished by a relaxed, cozy atmosphere, otherwise known as *gezelligheid*. To best appreciate Dutch restaurants, especially the small ones in the Prinsengracht and Jordaan neighborhoods, it helps to understand *gezelligheid*. *Gezelligheid* (the noun, or *gezellig*, the adjective) is a many-faceted thing—an aesthetic as well as a mood. Candles illuminating an artfully set table is *gezellig*—even if the table is made of rough wood. Some of the best restaurants are simply furnished, with wood floors and bare wood tables. This may seem inelegant by American standards, but if you adopt the Dutch attitude, you're likely to relax and enjoy the food more.

You'll also find sociable, relaxed table service. This, too, is *gezellig* to the Dutch, although sometimes service is so slow that the dining experience is, for Americans at least, no longer *gezellig*. I suggest that when in Holland, do as the Dutch do: Place atmosphere before speed, and set aside ample time for dinner ($1\frac{1}{2}$ to 2 hours). Ask for the check when you are ready to leave; don't expect the waitstaff to bring you the check, since rushing dinner guests is considered rude.

A particularly gezellig form of Amsterdam dining takes place in **brown cafes:** These are traditional cafes named for their dark wood bars and paneling, bare wooden floors, and wood tables that are either bare or covered with a Turkish rug. For more information on these establishments, see the section "Amsterdam's Cafes" later in this chapter.

If you prefer dining with tablecloths and efficient service, try more traditional French, Dutch, and Indonesian restaurants such as La Rive, Excelsior, Ciel Bleu, De Goudsbloem, Dynasty, or Brasserie van Baerle. Less conventional but equally efficient are Christophe, Beddington's, Halvemaan, and Van Harte.

For those who like exotic food and good service, Indonesian *rijsttafel* is a must. *Rijsttafel* (rice table) is a sampling of dishes from all of Indonesia, which is a huge country with many regional cuisines (and since Indonesia is the melting pot of Asia, these regional cuisines also have Japanese and Chinese influences). During the colonial period, Dutch plantation owners started serving a combination of dishes from various regions. And this is what is served in Amsterdam—colonial *rijsttafel*.

Lunch & Eetcafés

For lunch or an inexpensive dinner, try the convivial **eetcafés.** You may find the *dagschotel* (dish of the day) surprisingly sophisticated and well prepared. Van Puffelen, a brown cafe on the Prinsengracht canal, consistently attains gastronomic heights. De Reiger, a brown cafe in the Jordaan, and Café Schiller on Rembrandtsplein are also quite good. Traditional dishes at eetcafés are salmon fillet or *entrecote* (quality sirloin steak cooked rare) or mussels steamed in wine. Meals are often accompanied by a mound of french fries, a side of mayonnaise (not catsup), and a salad. The degree of mayonnaise in salad dressings varies from subtle to overriding, although a few health-conscious kitchens have opted for vinaigrette. Eetcafé menus are usually written on blackboards. The main drawbacks of

Theater Menus, Fixed-Price Meals & Tipping

Some restaurants offer fixed-price meals designed for pretheater dining. Patrons are sometimes asked to present theater tickets and to depart by 8pm. Others are more casual and require neither tickets nor time deadlines. Prices vary considerably. A theater menu at Indonesia may bring you a small *rijsttafel* at Dfl. 30, whereas one at La Rive may bring you a gourmet meal for Dfl. 87.50. Restaurants and cafe-restaurants most likely to have theater menus are those near the theaters of the Leidseplein, Nes, and Muziektheater neighborhoods. For atmospheric dinner in a cafe adjoining one of Amsterdam's small theaters, try De Smoeshaan near Leidseplein and Frascati, De Brakke Grond, and Blincker near the Dam (see "Amsterdam's Cafes" below).

Some restaurants serve fixed-price dinners offering 3, 4, or even 7 courses, while others have a fixed-price *dagschotel* (dish of the day), which may be a 3-course dinner that includes salad (or appetizer), main course, and dessert. The *dagschotel* is substantial enough to satisfy most appetites and is usually a good value.

Dutch restaurants and cafes include sales taxes and the customary 15% service charge in the price. Although many may tell you it is not necessary to tip, it is a good idea, especially if the service is good and you want to return to that restaurant in the future or if you have taken up a table for an hour or two. Tipping is a sign of appreciation. The Dutch round up to the next guilder or, in the case of a large bill, up to the next 5 or 10 guilders. Some leave a flat 5% to 10% tip.

cafe eating are the noise and smoke, but for some this is part of the charm of such places. See the section "Amsterdam's Cafes," later in this chapter, for more information on eetcafes.

For lunch, Café De Jaren, a grand cafe on the Amstel River, offers simple inexpensive sandwiches and very good soups. Luxembourg, a trendy cafe on the Spui, provides tasty but more expensive sandwiches, Caesar salads, and Dutch croquettes. De Prins and Land Van Walem also serve salads, soups, and the usual ham and cheese.

Price Chart

Price categories are based on the cost of a 3-course meal and do not include beverages, tax, or tip. For the eetcafés, 3 courses means entree, potato, and salad or vegetable.

Symbol	Category	Current Prices
$	Budget	under Dfl. 22
$$	Inexpensive	Dfl. 22–32
$$$	Moderate	Dfl. 33–55
$$$$	Expensive	Dfl. 56–75
$$$$$	Very Expensive	over Dfl. 75

As a rule, cafe kitchens tend to close around 10 or 10:30pm, but the bar stays open late, until 1am on weekdays and 2 or 3am on weekends. Lunch and/or snacks may be served from noon until 3, 4, or 5pm. Some cafes are closed Sundays.

Wheelchair Access

The architecture of Amsterdam does not gracefully accommodate wheelchairs. Most restaurants are small and narrow, and most bathrooms are accessible only by steep, winding stairs. There are some exceptions, however. Large hotel restaurants may have ground or elevator access and bathrooms large enough to let a wheelchair through the door. Some small restaurants and cafes have wheelchair accessible tables and bathrooms on ground level—but small bathroom doors. The most accessible restaurants are Roberto's (Amsterdam Hilton), La Rive (The Amstel Intercontinental), Excelsior (Hotel de l'Europe), Ciel Bleu (Okura Hotel), Bordewijk, and Blincker. Other restaurants such as Kantjil en de Tijger and Haesje Claes have wheelchair-accessible tables but not bathrooms. Many restaurants suggest that people with special needs call in advance in order to reserve an accessible table.

Reservations Policies

Because restaurants in Amsterdam tend to be small and are frequented by both Amsterdammers and tourists, it is a good idea to reserve in advance. The more intimate restaurants may have only 2 seatings per night—one at 6 or 6:30pm and another at 8:30 or 9pm, so you may be out of luck if you have to show up in between.

Recommendations

In the following listings I have used star ratings to denote quality. Highly recommended restaurants have

1 star (★), and really exceptional restaurants have been given 2 stars (★★).

In our selection, price category, reservations policy, cost of a 3-course or average meal, and nearest tram stops are given. Times are specified for when restaurants are closed.

Restaurants by Neighborhood

The Canals
★Chez George. **$$$/$$$$**
★★Christophe. **$$$$$**
★★Grekas. **$/$$**
★De Goudsbloem. **$$$$/$$$$$**
★De Luwte. **$$/$$$**
★Koh-I-Nor. **$/$$$**
Het Land Van Walem. **$$**
★Tout Court. **$$$**
★★Van Harte. **$$$**
★★Van Puffelen. **$$/$$$**

The Jordaan
★At Mango Bay. **$$$**
★Bolhoed. **$$/$$$**
★★Bordewijk. **$$$$**
★★Claes Claesz. **$$$**
★★The Pancake Bakery. **$**
★De Prins. **$/$$**
★De Reiger. **$$**
★★Speciaal. **$$$/$$$$**
★★Toscanini. **$$/$$$$**

The Historic Center
Blincker. **$$**
★Café Schiller. **$/$$**
★Dynasty. **$$$$/$$$$$**
Egg Cream. **$**
Frascati. **$$/$$$**
★Haesje Claes. **$$$**
Kantjil en de Tijger. **$$$**

Lucius. **$$$**
Luden. **$$/$$$**
De Oester Bar. **$$$$**
★★Selecta. **$$$**
★De Smoeshaan. **$$/$$$**
★Het Swarte Schaep. **$$$$$**
★Tempo Doeloe. **$$$**
★Treasure. **$$$$/$$$$$**
★d'Vijff Vlieghen. **$$$$$**

Museum Quarter & Concertgebouw
★★Beddington's. **$$$$**
Bodega Keyser. **$$$$**
★Brasserie van Baerle. **$$$**
★Le Garage. **$$$$**
★★Sama Sebo. **$$$**

Overlooking the Amstel (or nearby canals)
★★Excelsior. **$$$$$**
★Klaes Compaen. **$$/$$$**
★★La Rive. **$$$$$**

Amsterdam South
★★Ciel Bleu. **$$$$/$$$$$**
★★Halvemaan. **$$$$$**
★★De Trechter. **$$$$$**
Umeno. **$$/$$$**
★★Yamazato. **$$$$$**

Restaurants by Cuisine

Belgian/French
★Chez George. **$$$/$$$$**

Chinese
★Dynasty. **$$$$/$$$$$**
★Treasure. **$$$$/$$$$$**

Dutch
Bodega Keyser. **$$$$**
★★Claes Claesz. **$$$**

★Haesje Claes. **$$$**
★d'Vijff Vlieghen. **$$$$$**

Eetcafés and Theater Cafes
Blincker. **$$**
★Café Schiller. **$/$$**
Frascati. **$$/$$$**
Het Land Van Walem. **$$**
★De Prins. **$/$$**
★De Reiger. **$$**

★Smoeshaan. **$$/$$$**
★★Van Puffelen. **$$/$$$**

French
★★Beddington's. **$$$$**
★★Bordewijk. **$$$$**
★Brasserie van Baerle.
  $$$
★★Christophe. **$$$$$**
★★Ciel Bleu. **$$$$/**
  $$$$$
★★Excelsior. **$$$$$**
★Le Garage. **$$$$**
★De Goudsbloem. **$$$$/**
  $$$$$
★★Halvemaan. **$$$$$**
Luden. **$$/$$$**
★De Luwte. **$$/$$$**
★★La Rive. **$$$$$**
★Het Swarte Schaep.
  $$$$$
★★De Trechter. **$$$$$**
★★Van Harte. **$$$**

Greek
★★Grekas. **$/$$**

Indian
★Koh-I-Nor. **$/$$$**

Indonesian
Kantjil en de Tijger. **$$$**
★★Sama Sebo. **$$$**
★★Selecta. **$$$**
★★Speciaal. **$$$/$$$$**
★Tempo Doeloe. **$$$**

Italian
★★Toscanini. **$$/$$$$**

Japanese
Umeno. **$$/$$$**
★★Yamazato. **$$$$$**

Pancakes
★★The Pancake Bakery. **$**

Philippine
★At Mango Bay. **$$$**

Seafood
Lucius. **$$$**.
De Oester Bar. **$$$$**

Thai
★Klaas Compaen. **$$/$$$**

Vegetarian
★Bolhoed. **$$/$$$**
Egg Cream. **$**

Critic's Choice

For a true taste of gezelligheid—the warm, intimate atmosphere the Dutch so prize—try **Claes Claesz** or **Haesje Claes.** Claes Claesz, located in the Jordaan, is a bit more contemporary while the Spui area's Haesje Claes is Old Dutch down to its Delft tiles and traditional sautéed sole. For romance, I recommend either **De Luwte** or **Van Harte,** where you'll find soft lighting, gleaming wood, and beautifully set tables for two. Both restaurants are relaxed, but De Luwte attracts a slightly younger and more casual crowd.

For sheer luxury, nothing beats a night out at **La Rive.** A magical view of the Amstel, chairs you never want to leave, and some of Holland's best French cuisine produce an opulence as heady as the fine wine—it could send a voluptuary straight to heaven. The best spot for adventurous palates and foodies is **Christophe,** where chef Christophe Royer's modernized French cuisine is setting new standards in Amsterdam.

If views are what you're looking for, consider **Excelsior,** overlooking a beautiful stretch of the Amstel, alive each evening with bright reflections. **Ciel Bleu,** perched on the 22nd floor of the Okura Hotel, gives you fine sunsets, dramatic Dutch skies, and all of Amsterdam spread out before you. **De Goudsbloem** offers the city's best wine list, and with a classy atmosphere and inventive French/Asian/Italian cuisine it's a good choice for celebrations and special occasions.

For a sumptuous brunch—very popular on Amsterdam's otherwise quiet Sundays—try what the **Ciel Bleu** refers to as its "Heavenly Brunch" or sample the regal (and expensive) spread at the **Amstel Hotel.** For a brunch in centrally located—and very Dutch—surroundings, try the **Hotel Krasnipolsy.** The **Brasserie van Baerle** offers tasty and affordable brunches that are particularly recommended on warm days when it's served in the restaurant's lovely, secluded garden.

For late-night dining your best bet is trendy **Le Garage.** The kitchen here always has something good to offer, and the restaurant is thoroughly amused with itself for surrounding its see-and-be-seen clientele with a bank of well-lit mirrors. Also in the running for best trendy spot is the Jordaan's bohemian **Bordewijk,** which also happens to be one of the best French/international restaurants in the city.

For a casual atmosphere and excellent value I recommend **Van Puffelen.** Wonderful French/international food in several pleasing surroundings: a canalside terrace, a lively brown cafe, and a quiet back room with marble on the tabletops and angels painted on the ceiling. Even more casual and less expensive is **Grekas**—a Greek deli and take-out restaurant with the best Greek food in town.

Best destination if you have kids in tow is **The Pancake Bakery.** Amsterdam's best pancakes—both sweet and savory—are served for lunch and dinner at this roomy canal-house restaurant with indestructible furniture. The fanciful umbrellas and colorful thingamajigs that appear on desserts add up to happy—and frisky—children. **Bolhoed** bills itself as a "child-friendly restaurant" and promises to "love your child," which is enough to relax any parent. The vegetarian food couldn't be healthier or tastier;

it's up to you to decide if it's a bit too adventurous for members of the smaller set. The canalside location also allows for some necessary stretching of legs. When it comes to adult tastes, Bolhoed is clearly the best vegetarian restaurant in town.

Puccini gets the nod for best pastries, from fresh fruit tarts to exotic cakes. No trip to Amsterdam would be complete without sampling those typically Dutch street-treats sold at **fish stands:** *haring* (herring), smoked *paling* (eel), and a very pink and mayonaissey version of salmon salad. The best stands are the ones across from Centraal Station and in front of Westerkerk.

Indonesian rijsttafel is also a must for those with exotic tastes. Sama Sebo, Selecta, and Speciaal all serve excellent rijsttafel.

Amsterdam's Restaurants A to Z

★At Mango Bay
Westerstraat 91.
☎ 20-6381039. AE, DC, MC, V. Reservations recommended on weekends. Closed: lunch. Tram: 10 to Marnixstraat. Canal Bus to Westerkerk. 3-course dinner: Dfl. 33–40. PHILIPPINE. **$$$**.
A bright facade in the Jordaan marks a Philippine restaurant that is well worth the trek. Situated in the former front room of a gable house, At Mango Bay conjures up the tropics with its bouquets of colorful flowers and a Gauguinesque mural of women on a tropical beach. The cooking is based on delicate touches of ginger, coriander, and lemongrass. Try the beef marinated in honey and soya sauce, or prawns simmered in coconut milk with spices. Cocktails come with cheeky names such as "Imelda's Shoes Plus or Minus 3,000 Ingredients," which contains mango puree, passion fruit, brandy, and lemon juice. Service is Jordaan-gezellig. The restaurant is located near Noorderkerk and the picturesque Brouwersgracht canal.

★★Beddington's
Roelof Hartstraat 6-8.
☎ 20-6765201. AE, DC, MC, V. Reservations recommended for Fri and Sat. Closed: Sun. Tram: 3, 5, 12, 24, 25 to Roelof Hartsplein. 3-course dinner: Dfl. 65; 4-course dinner: Dfl. 80. FRENCH. **$$$$**.
The very original food here is prepared by chef/owner Gene Beddington, a British woman who brings French and Japanese culinary experience to her kitchen. Expect modern eclectic French cuisine with a unique blend of international influences. Flavor combinations like wild duck with tamarind and tomato sauce, Japanese-inspired presentation, and heavenly English sweets are the chef's hallmarks.

Blincker
St. Barberenstraat 7.
☎ 20-6271938. No credit cards. Reservations not necessary but recommended on weekends.

Wheelchair accessible. Tram: 4, 9, 16, 24, 25 to Dam. Dagschotel Dfl. 18. 3-course dinner Dfl. 35. EETCAFÉ. **$$**.

Large leafy plants dangle from the ceiling, softening the hard edge of a metallic winding staircase that leads upstairs.

The food is French with an international twist—good by eetcafé standards. The lamb with garlic sauce or entrecote with red-wine sauce are good buys, as are the vegetable pies. During warm weather, the restaurant's sidewalk cafe takes over a protected courtyard/alley that is sunny at noon and festively lit at night. You can count on an arty crowd at Blincker since it adjoins the Frascati theater (see "Amsterdam's Cafes" below, and "The Arts" on page 216).

★Bolhoed

Prinsengracht 60-62. ☎ 20-6261803. No credit cards. Reservations required for more than 3 persons and recommended on weekends. Tram: 13, 14, 17 to Westermarkt. Canal Bus: to Westerkerk or Keizersgracht. 3-course dinner: Dfl. 28-33. VEGETARIAN. **$$/$$$**.

One of the best vegetarian restaurants in Amsterdam, Bolhoed is health conscious, creative, and hippiesque.

At Bolhoed, fresh, organic food is prepared thoughtfully, sometimes artfully, so that vegetables retain their taste and texture. Try the pumpkin terrine with its combination of vegetables, or the fried seitan (a textured soy protein that tastes like meat). Bolhoed also serves fish stew (a nonvegetarian entree typical of Amsterdam's vegetarian restaurants) and a variety of breads and cheeses, quiches, salads, and soups.

Unlike most Amsterdam restaurants and cafes, there is a nonsmoking section.

The decor—benches with zebra stripes, whimsical paintings—matches its young, arty, international clientele. And the staff, demonstrating the *gezelligheid* of the younger generation, promote a "child-friendly restaurant" and promise to "love your child."

★★Bordewijk

Noordermarkt 7. ☎ 20-6243899. AE, EC, MC, V. Reservations strongly recommended. Closed: Mon. Wheelchair accessible. Tram: 3, 10 to Marnixstraat. Canal Bus: to Westerkerk or Keizersgracht. 3-course dinner: Dfl. 56. FRENCH. **$$$$**.

Some say this is one of the best restaurants in Amsterdam. The food is French with Asian and Italian influences. Expect fresh homemade pasta with serrano ham and fruit marinated in wine, vinegar, and mustard seed, or chicken and pigeon from Bresse, or Japanese-style fish—marinated or raw. Bordewijk also aspires to serve "honest food" such as rib roast cooked in sea salt and served with Bordelais sauce. Menus change frequently, which is part of the restaurant's local appeal. An array of cheese and wines are also available.

The restaurant's outdoor terrace, a pleasant place on warm summer evenings, faces Noorderkerk and the Prinsen-gracht canal.

★Brasserie van Baerle

Van Baerlestraat 158. ☎ 20-6791532 or 20-6622090. AE, MC, V. Reservations strongly recommended, especially on nights when concerts are given in the Concertgebouw. Closed: Sat. Tram: 5, one stop past Concertgebouw. Breakfasts

Dfl. 15–27; brunch Dfl. 21–39; lunch Dfl. 45; 3-course dinner Dfl. 55–68. FRENCH. **$$$**.
The Brasserie serves an excellent and reasonably priced Sunday brunch with fresh baked bread, luscious jams, choice smoked salmon, American-style scrambled eggs, and beautifully diced mango. Try "the hedonist breakfast" with all the Dutch/continental delicacies.

The garden terrace, shaded by hanging vines, is a relaxed, inviting oasis on a sunny afternoon. Conveniently located a few blocks away from P. C. Hooftstraat, the shopping street, and the Museum Quarter, the Brasserie is also a good place for weekday lunch, especially if you want more than a small Dutch sandwich.

★Café Schiller

Rembrandtplein 26. ☎ 20-6249846. No credit cards. Reservations not necessary. Tram: 4, 9, 14 to Rembrandtplein. Dagschotel: Dfl. 19–22. EETCAFÉ. **$/$$**.
Café Schiller's original owner was a "Sunday painter" who invited his customers to pose for paintings. These paintings still decorate the walls, paying tribute to Mr. Schiller and the former habitués of his 1920s theater cafe—actors, singers, and theatergoers. Nowadays, people come for dinner or drinks before ballet and opera performances at the Stopera, musicals at the Carré, or movies at the Tuschinski Cinema, a beautiful Art Deco building only a few blocks away.

As an eetcafé, Café Schiller is both good and inexpensive with a standard *dagschotel* of meat or fish, potatoes (scalloped, mashed, or french fried), and a salad or vegetable

for Dfl. 19 to Dfl. 22. The cuisine is French/international eclectic, with vegetarian dishes such as homemade Italian pasta with saffron, or rich entrees like stingray with egg butter cream sauce, or sirloin steak with a sweet garlic reduction glaze. Not surprisingly, the desserts are rich. Try the cafe's own homemade ice cream. Service is friendly and reasonably efficient. The cherry-wood paneling is warm and polished, the booths and tables cozy, the seats soft, and the overall effect is a bit cushier than many eetcafés and other larger, noisier cafes on Rembrandtsplein.

★Chez Georges

Herenstraat 3. ☎ 20-6263332. AE, DC, MC, V. Reservations required. Tram: 13, 14, 17 to Westerkerk. 5-course dinner: Dfl. 56; 7-course dinner: Dfl. 75. BELGIAN/FRENCH. **$$$/$$$$**.
A jovial Belgian/French restaurant on a street between the canals, Chez George is a small, snug restaurant that cooks for large, continental appetites. Belgian beer forms the base for some sauces and is used to marinate meat. Beer even appears in soup, such as the soup of Belgian beer, red wine, truffles, and vegetables. Expect quality meats in interesting combinations: Angus beef served with goat cheese and Provençale vegetables, or venison served with pear. The only constant on the menu is (thankfully) a lower calorie item: smoked salmon with a salad of 6 lettuces topped with hazelnuts.

★★Christophe

Leliegracht 46. ☎ 20-6250807. AE, DC, MC, V. Reservations strongly recommended. Closed: lunch and Sun. Tram: 13, 14, 17

Dining in Central Amsterdam

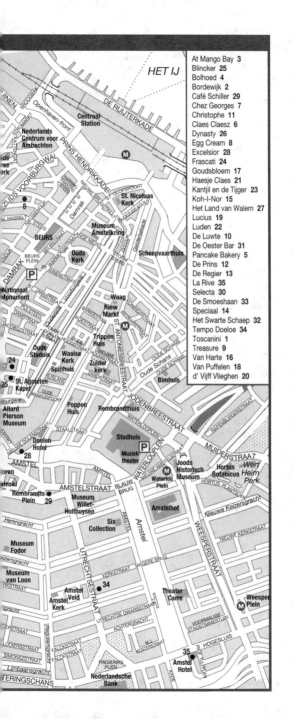

HET IJ

At Mango Bay 3
Blincker 25
Bolhoed 4
Bordewijk 2
Café Schiller 29
Chez Georges 7
Christophe 11
Claes Claesz 6
Dynasty 26
Egg Cream 8
Excelsior 28
Frascati 24
Goudsbloem 17
Haesje Claes 21
Kantjil en de Tijger 23
Koh-I-Nor 15
Het Land van Walem 27
Lucius 19
Luden 22
De Luwte 10
De Oester Bar 31
Pancake Bakery 5
De Prins 12
De Regier 13
La Rive 35
Selecta 30
De Smoeshaan 33
Speciaal 14
Het Swarte Schaep 32
Tempo Doeloe 34
Toscanini 1
Treasure 9
Van Harte 16
Van Puffelen 18
d' Vijff Vlieghen 20

to Westermarkt. Canal bus: to Westerkerk or Keizersgracht. 4-course dinner Dfl. 75–95; entrees Dfl. 45–80. FRENCH. **$$$$$**.

French-trained, Michelin-starred chef Christophe Royer set new culinary standards in Amsterdam with his classic French cooking modernized with accents from the Mediterranean—notably Italy, Spain, North Africa, and Southern France. Christophe describes his food as "simple—with 2 or 3 main tastes" and cites as examples his lobster roasted with sweet garlic and potatoes (the house specialty) and the lamb marinated in olive oil with a touch of cumin. His wine menu is similarly offbeat, but good. Service is gracious and professional.

The interior of the canalside restaurant is as original as the cooking. Christophe made the lampshades from rice papier mâché and designed his restaurant to be "sober, elegant yet comfortable" with soft carpets, rich cherry wood, and the graceful floral paintings of contemporary Dutch artist, Martin van Vreden.

★★Ciel Bleu

Okura Hotel, Ferdinand Bolstraat 333. ☎ 20-6787111. AE, DC, MC, V. Reservations strongly recommended. Closed: lunch. Wheelchair accessible. Tram: 12, 25 to Cornelis Troostplein. 3-course menu Dfl. 60–90; brunch Dfl. 75. FRENCH. **$$$$/$$$$$**.

This highly rated French restaurant situated on the top floor of a 23-story Japanese hotel offers the twin attraction of a panoramic view and Michelin-star cuisine. French food delicately prepared with Dutch and Japanese products is presented with Japanese artistry. The salmon tartar is

served with a dressing of a traditional Dutch liqueur called "Roses without thorns." The sesame sweet-sour sauce and vegetable tempura add a Japanese touch to the roasted duck.

Ciel Bleu's "Heavenly brunch" is an uplifting and sumptuous way to start a Sunday with salmon, sole, ray, pâté, salads, cheese, and wine—but it's pricey at Dfl. 75.

The view is stunning, but don't take the name Ciel Bleu too literally: Dutch skies are seldom blue, and their fascination, as the 17thC landscape painters discovered, lies in dramatic cloud formations and sudden rainstorms. To enjoy the full spectacle, choose a bright, changeable day or an evening before sunset. Reserve a window table.

★★Claes Claesz

Egelantiersstraat 24-26. ☎ 20-6255306. DC, MC, V. Reservations strongly recommended, especially Sat–Sun. Closed: Sat–Sun lunch. Tram: 13, 14, 17 to Westermarkt, or tram 3, 10 to Marnixstraat. Canal Bus: to Westerkerk or Keizersgracht. 3-course dinner special Mon–Wed Dfl. 28. DUTCH. **$$$**.

Claes Claesz gives its patrons traditional Dutch dishes prepared for the contemporary palate. Such Dutch staples as carrots, potatoes, roast duck, and apple compote are artfully arranged and prepared for those who like their vegetables tender (but not overcooked), their duck rare, and their compote tangy. (If you want your meat medium or well done, tell your waiter.)

The restaurant serves local Jordaan liqueurs (from the only

remaining distillery) bearing such whimsical names as "Bride's tears," a wedding liqueur with floating "tears" of gold and silver leaf, and "Lift up your shirts," a smooth citrus drink served in a tiny glass accompanying delicate desserts. An even older vestige of Amsterdam culture, a *hofje*—a hidden, protected courtyard encircled by homes for the widowed or disadvantaged, lies just behind Claes Claesz.

★Dynasty

Reguliersdwarsstraat 30.
☎ 20-6268400. AE, DC, MC, V.
Reservations necessary.
Closed: Tues. Tram: 1, 2, 5 to
Koningsplein or tram 4, 9, 14, 16,
24, 25 to Muntplein. 3-course
dinner: Dfl. 70–100. CHINESE.
$$$$/$$$$$.
Dynasty serves Thai and Cantonese cuisine with unusual spices, and tantalizing names such as Promise of Spring. Dishes like duck with jellyfish and century-old egg are not for everyone, but other exotic yet less intimidating combinations include lobster with duck and watercress or the succulent mixture of duck, pigeon, and lamb. Crispy Duck, a Chinese dish, is the house specialty.

The decor is luxurious Far Eastern, with silk hangings, Buddhas, orchids, and Chinese parasols. The Dynasty is often crowded, so reservations are essential. Prices are high, like many of the upscale Chinese restaurants in Amsterdam. (For less expensive but good Chinese food in far-from-luxurious surroundings, try the Chinese restaurants near Nieuwemarkt, Amsterdam's Chinatown.)

Egg Cream

St. Jacobstraat 19.
☎ 20-6230575. No credit cards.
Reservations not accepted.
Closed: Tues. Tram: 1, 2, 3,
13, 14, 17 to Nieuwe Zijds
Voorburgwal. Dinner Dfl. 17;
breakfast Dfl. 13. VEGETARIAN. **$**.
Like many of Amsterdam's vegetarian restaurants, Egg Cream is not exclusively vegetarian. Although it offers a selection of vegetarian dishes, 3-egg omelets, soups, sandwiches, and salads, the breakfast special includes bacon with the eggs and coffee. Prices for this typical American breakfast are reasonable, and, at Dfl. 12.50, about half the price of similar hotel breakfasts.

Egg Cream is small, casual, popular with a youngish crowd, and simply done in wood tables, benches, and a few wall posters. Service is quick and efficient—an influence of the no-nonsense British owners.

★★Excelsior

Hotel de l'Europe, Nieuwe
Doelenstraat 2-8. ☎ 20-
6234836. AE, DC, MC, V.
Reservations strongly
recommended. Closed: Sat
lunch. Jacket required.
Wheelchair accommodating if
given advanced notice. Tram: 4,
9, 14, 16, 24, 25 to Muntplein.
Canal Bus: to City Hall. Water
taxi: to hotel terrace. 4-course
dinner: Dfl. 90–130. FRENCH.
$$$$$.
One of the most elegant places to eat in Amsterdam, this Michelin-star–rated restaurant overlooks the Amstel River and Muntplein. The atmosphere is Old World, the style is genteel (and a bit stiff), the service is excellent, and the food is classic French with a modern twist, using French and Dutch products with subtle international influences. In the codfish with oriental rice, for instance, the cod is

Dutch, the rice is Asian, and the preparation is French.

Frascati

Nes 59. ☎ 20-6241324. No credit cards. Reservations not Closed: lunch. Tram: 4, 9, 16, 24, 25 to Dam. Dinner: Dfl. 35. EETCAFÉ. **$$/$$$**.

The dark and dingy Nes, tucked away behind Rokin near Dam Square, is a surprising setting for a handsome cafe like Frascati. Fortunately, the Nes has been cleaned up, illuminated with festive lights at night, and made into an attractive spot for theater- and cafe-goers (still it's not wise to wander these streets alone after dark). The cafe belongs to the Frascati Theater, a small production theater, as does Blincker, which is just around the corner. Whereas Blincker is casual and bright and full of plants, Frascati is dark, snug, and classy: The glass is frosted, the lighting soft, and the wood rich and polished. The pasta pesto is divine—but generally, the menu is French/Dutch fare, with entrees of lamb, entrecote, or fish.

★Le Garage

Raysdaelstraat 54-56. ☎ 20-6797176. AE, DC, MC, V. Reservations strongly recommended. Closed: Sat–Sun lunch. Tram: 3, 5, 24, 25 to Roelof Hartplein, or tram 16 to Ruydaelstraat. 3-course dinner: Dfl. 69.50. FRENCH. **$$$$**.

Le Garage, located in a quiet neighborhood near the Concertgebouw, is a good place to eat late since many entrees are still available after 10pm. The cuisine tends to be country French, but Le Garage aims for an international kitchen that includes Thai, Portuguese, and Japanese dishes. Menus change monthly, but the catch of the day (fish grilled, baked, or poached according to individual tastes), Mediterranean fish soup, carpaccio, and crème brûlée are always available. Monthly offerings range from terrine of rabbit to Italian-style raw salmon.

The food is good, but not exceptional. The atmosphere is another matter. Le Garage is a festive, trendy, unusual restaurant frequented by TV and fashion people who go to be seen and see themselves being seen—since the chef/owner (a TV cook) has paneled the restaurant with mirrors. The restaurant can become a bit noisy, but never dull.

★De Goudsbloem

The Pulitzer Hotel, Reestraat 8. ☎ 20-6253288. AE, DC, MC. V. Reservations necessary on Sat. Closed: lunch and Sun–Mon. Tram: 13, 14, 17 to Westermarkt. Canal Bus: to Westerkerk or Keizersgrcht. Water taxi: to Pulitzer Hotel dock. 4-course tourist menu: Dfl. 72.50. FRENCH. **$$$$/$$$$$**.

De Goudsbloem (The Marigold), has one of the best wine cellars in Amsterdam and a cozy atmosphere rich in history. A recipient of a Wine Spectator Award, the restaurant has the best wines from the best years (the selection is one of the biggest in Holland) as well as a nice choice of modest wines at reasonable prices.

The food is light, not-too-rich French with Asian and Italian influences, such as scallops with sesame oil and oyster sauce or Italian oyster soup with oyster stuffed ravioli, and is good although not as exceptional as restaurants at the Amstel Hotel or Hotel de l'Europe. But the atmosphere is choice: classy, romantic, and a great place for special occasions. The service is quick and cordial.

★★Grekas

Singel 311. ☎ 20-6203590. No credit cards. Reservations not accepted. Closed: Mon. Tram: 1, 2, 5 to Spui. Average dinner: Dfl. 12–20. GREEK. **$/$$**.

Grekas would be a rare find in any city, except maybe a Greek one. This is authentic, carefully prepared Greek cuisine—the kind you might find in Athens or Crete. The moussaka is baked with enough meat to balance the eggplant and topping. The list of on-target Greek dishes goes on: fresh spanokopita, hummus with just enough garlic, tzatziki, grape leaves, pastitchio, souvlaki, and yogurt. And all is beautifully displayed on colorful Greek platters. Retsina is available by the glass and by the bottle.

The only downside to this cozy Greek deli is that there is not enough of it; there are only 3 tables since the restaurant is geared primarily to take-out customers. Be sure to arrive early, before supplies are depleted.

★Haesje Claes

Spuistraat 273-5. ☎ 20-6249998. AE, DC, MC, V. Reservations recommended. Tram: 1, 2, 5 to the Spui. Tourist 3-course set menu Dfl. 25; other 3-course dinners Dfl. 35–75. DUTCH. **$$$**.

Atmosphere is the house specialty. The textured wallpaper, wood paneling, exposed brick, and painted tiles are typical of Old Holland. The smoked salmon and "new" herring (pickled, not raw) are also traditional Dutch, as are the mounds of country-style carrots, potatoes, and green beans that are sometimes boiled to taste-lessness and sometimes firm,

tasty, and subtly seasoned, depending on the day. Meats are automatically cooked rare unless you specify otherwise.

For dessert, try the *appel bol*—a peeled, tangy apple baked in a pastry shell and served with rich ice cream. Since the food is heavy, and the portions enormous, and the floor plan close and cozy, both food and atmosphere can best be appreciated in cool weather.

★★Halvemaan

Van Leyenberghlaan 20. ☎ 20-6440348 or call toll free 06-0224477. AE, DC, MC, V. Reservations recommended. Closed: Sat–Sun. Tram: 5 to Neyerode. 4-course dinner: Dfl. 95. FRENCH. **$$$$$**.

Known as a culinary "citizen of the world" and as one of the most original chefs in Amsterdam, John Halvemaan adds Chinese spices to his simmered duck—and minced oysters (and a fried egg) to the steak tartar. His kitchen is mostly French but with Asian, Mediterranean, and English influences (like the English bread and butter pudding). He is also known for creating surprising combinations with ordinary foods like potatoes, sausage, and beans.

The atmosphere is relaxed—a refuge from the tourist bustle of the city center. Halvemaan overlooks lawns, gardens, and a small lake in southern suburban Amsterdam.

Het Land Van Walem

Keizersgracht 449. ☎ 20-6253544 or 3444. No credit cards. Reservations not necessary. Tram: 1, 2, 5 to Keizersgracht. Dinner: Dfl. 20–27. EETCAFÉ. **$$**.

Café Walem is best known for its coffee, Sunday breakfast, style, scenic terrace on the Keizersgracht canal, and good selection of foreign newspapers. The cooking is international: fettuccini with smoked salmon, fish, or meat with sauces of basil or saffron, and a selection of quiches, soups, and salads. Breakfast, at Dfl. 12.50, is a particularly good value considering the location and atmosphere—you can pay twice as much in an upscale hotel. Service is slow.

Designed by Rietveld in the spirit of "de Styl" group (Café De Jaren was designed by a different architect along similar lines), van Walem is modern and spacious but not cold, with comfortable wicker chairs encircling round metallic tables. In the summer, you can choose between garden and canalside terraces.

★Kantjil en de Tijger

Spuistraat 291. ☎ 20-6200994. AE; DC, MC, V. Reservations recommended. Tram: 1, 2, 5 to Spui. Average dinner Dfl. 40; rijsttafel for two Dfl. 73–93. INDONESIAN. **$$$**.

Kantjil is a good place for the uninitiated tourist to sample an exotic Indonesian dish or two for dinner, although you can, if you want, order an entire rijsttafel. Ask the waiters to explain the menu and to point out the hot and spicy dishes. The menus also carefully spell out the contents of each dish. Specialties include satays and grilled goat on skewers.

This is a spacious, casual Indonesian restaurant with polished wooden tables and waiters wearing fashionable black. Big tables are available for groups and small ones for solo diners. The restaurant is popular with students and tends to be crowded, so allow some time for dinner.

★Klaas Compaen

Raamgracht 9. ☎ 20-6238708. No credit cards. Reservations

recommended. Tram: 4, 9, 16, 24, 25 to Muntplein. Canal Bus: to City Hall. Average dinner entree: Dfl. 30. THAI. **$$/$$$**.

This Thai restaurant, named after a 17thC Dutch seaman, is as dark and cramped as a ship's galley. There are few tables, but, perched at the bar, you can watch the cooks shell shrimp and conjure up exquisite dishes featuring coconut and spices. The sweet and sour fish is particularly good—lightly fried, flaky, ample and not too sweet. For dessert, try the Klaas Compaen Surprise—if you like to be surprised. When I asked the waiter what it was, he wouldn't tell me. "Don't order it if you don't want to be surprised," he said. The cooks and waiters/waitresses in the open kitchen demonstrate Zen-like concentration. However, it is the food, not the customer, that absorbs them, and you need to clamor for their attention.

★Koh-I-Nor

Westermarkt 29. ☎ 20-6233133. AE, DC, EC, V. Reservations recommended. Tram: 13, 14, 17 to Westerkerk. Canal Bus: to Westerkerk or Keizersgracht. Tourist menu Dfl. 21; fixed menu combination plates Dfl. 29–50. INDIAN. **$/$$$**.

For years, Koh-I-Nor has consistently offered North India curries and tandooris at very reasonable prices. The soups, breads, yogurt drinks, and desserts are graciously presented and carefully prepared. The meats are tender, the breads fresh, the sauces spicy but not excessive, and the desserts subtle and refreshing. Try the lamb vindaloo and the ice cream with fresh, ripe, beautifully sliced mango. After a busy day on the town, Koh-I-Nor is a soothing little place:

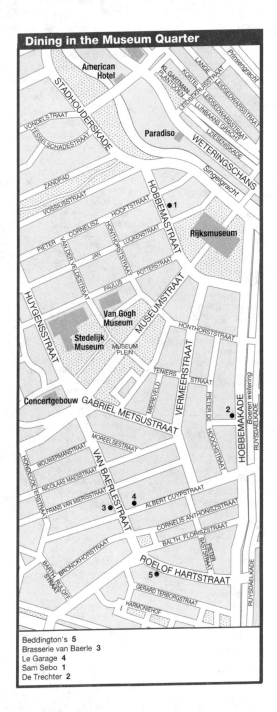

Dining in the Museum Quarter

Beddington's **5**
Brasserie van Baerle **3**
Le Garage **4**
Sam Sebo **1**
De Trechter **2**

The music is hypnotically Indian, the chairs cushy soft, and the service quick yet gezellig. As to the decor, it helps to like pink.

Lucius

Spuistraat 247. ☎ 20-6241831. AE, DC, MC. V. Reservations recommended. Closed: lunch and Sun. Tram: 1, 2, 5 to Spui. 3-course dinner: Dfl. 47.50. SEAFOOD. **$$$**.

This seafood restaurant on Spuistraat offers a wide choice of dishes: salmon, oysters, mussels, and lobsters from northern waters and fresh bass and John Dory from the Mediterranean. If you like shellfish, try the seafood plate, which features an impressive line-up: oysters, clams, mussels, shrimp, and lobster. The decor is down to earth; menus are written up on large blackboards and the tables are simple wood. The only colorful touch are the tropical fish that swim past you on the wallside aquarium.

Luden

Spuistraat 304. ☎ 20-6228979. AE, MC, V. Reservations necessary for dinner (at 6 and 9pm). Tram: 1, 2, 5 to Spui. 3-course dinner: Dfl. 42.50. FRENCH. **$$/$$$**.

Luden is divided into 2 parts— an informal and popular brasserie on one side and a chic French restaurant next door. You can sit on Spartan wooden benches in the brasserie to eat simple Italian pasta, or you can order a 3-course French meal in the restaurant. The French fare is *bourgandisch*—relaxed, not stiff. Expect a changing menu of fresh fish or meat, salads, and soups—but carpaccio with parmesan and capers, broiled salmon with creamy white-wine sauce, sliced beef with mushrooms, and French fish soup rich with a variety of fish and shellfish are always available.

In the summer, the outside terrace is one of the most inviting on Spuistraat, a street lined with sidewalk restaurants and cafes.

The Dutch are not big on lunches, and Luden is one of a few places in Amsterdam with a good full lunch. The wine list includes 40 wines— most reasonably priced.

★De Luwte

Leliegracht 26-28. ☎ 20-6258548. No credit cards. Reservations not accepted. Closed: lunch. Tram: 13, 14, 17 to Westermarkt. Canal Bus: to Westerkerk or Keizersgracht. Salads Dfl. 14–26; 3-course dinner Dfl. 50. FRENCH. **$$/$$$**.

A romantic, offbeat French restaurant on a small canal in the Jordaan/Prinsengracht neighborhood, De Luwte is a popular place for special occasions, especially for couples. Salads are the specialty; smoked salmon with Roquefort cheese and walnuts, duck liver with prunes, and Dutch shrimp with apple/celery salad are three of the eight salads on the menu. Main courses are simple, the tastes distinct, the sauces light—veal fillet with wine sauce, lamb chops with rosemary sauce. The menu offers the option of full or half orders, making it possible to sample different items for reasonable prices.

Fanciful murals illustrating Old Holland decorate the walls. This small, gezellig, canal-house restaurant is a local favorite—reservations are recommended. Service is relaxed.

De Oester Bar

Leidseplein 10. ☎ 20-6263463. AE, DC, MC, V. Reservations recommended. Tram: 1, 2, 5, 6, 10 to Leidseplein. Canal Bus: to Leidseplein. 3-course dinner: Dfl. 70. SEAFOOD. **$$$$**.

A classy, expensive, and somewhat touristy restaurant done in white and decorated with a huge tank housing large fish that may haunt your dinner, De Oester Bar is elegant but comfortable. The house specialties are traditional Dutch fish dishes: fried Dover sole, grilled salmon, and a fish platter with smoked eel, smoked salmon, and shrimp. People-watching through the large picture windows that overlook Leidseplein is interesting since the Leidseplein is a favorite haunt of street musicians, jugglers, and mimes from all over the world.

★★The Pancake Bakery

Prinsengracht 191. ☎ 20-6251333. AE, MC, V. Reservations necessary for more than 10 persons. Tram: 13, 14, 17 to Westermarkt. Canal Bus: to Westerkerk or Keizersgracht. Pancakes Dfl. 8–19. PANCAKES. **$**.

The best and widest selection of pancakes in Amsterdam are served in The Pancake Bakery, an atmospheric canal house. You have a choice of many unusual toppings, sweet or spicy, such as chicken with Cajun sauce, curried turkey with pineapple and raisins, or ice cream with Grand Marnier. These pancakes fill a dinner plate and are intended as lunch, dinner, or a major dessert. Consequently, like many other pancake restaurants, the bakery does not open until noon. The restaurant is a favorite with children who like the special small desserts topped with colorful clowns and umbrellas. The spacious 2-story restaurant also allows active children room to move.

In the summer, long wooden tables lined up in front of the restaurant provide pleasant views of the Prinsengracht canal—and attract a crowd of hovering, syrup-drunk yellow jackets (late Aug and early Sept is their season). Although the hornets are surprisingly docile, you may be more comfortable sitting inside the restaurant—a charming canal house with exposed beams, winding staircases, and windows overlooking the canal.

★De Prins

Prinsengracht 124. ☎ 20-6249382. No credit cards. Reservations not accepted. Tram: 13, 14, 17 to Westermarkt. Canal Bus: to Westerkerk or Keizersgracht. Dinner: Dfl. 22–29. EETCAFÉ. **$/$$**.

De Prins serves up tangy fondues, large salads, vegetarian lasagna, and typical Dutch French entrecote. The food is unusually good for a brown cafe, especially one as small and crowded and unassuming as De Prins. Try the tomato soup, the salad with smoked trout and shrimp, or the cheese fondue with blue cheese and white wine. The house specialty, Cheese Fondue "de Prins," is Swiss cheese with a kick of kirsch and white wine. (I suggest letting some of the liquor boil down unless you like strong brews.)

Lunch at De Prins offers more variety than most eetcafés: mountainous salads (which are very un-Dutch), vegetarian tacos, and sate as well as the usual Dutch bitterballen (meat croquettes) and ham broodjes.

Both bar and restaurant areas are packed—which only contributes to gezelligheid since people share tables (and therefore conversations) with strangers. Consequently, it is an excellent place for solo travelers to eat without feeling alone. The only drawback is that quarters sometimes become too cramped and noisy, and that service is so relaxed (or otherwise distracted) that you must resort to flagging down waiters or inching your way to the bar. A convivial brown cafe in an 18thC canal house with beamed ceilings, yellow walls, modern paintings, antique clocks, and a mixed clientele, De Prins is quintessential Amsterdam.

★De Reiger

Nieuwe Leliestraat 34.
☎ 20-6247426. No credit cards. Reservations not accepted. Tram: 13, 14, 17 to Westermarkt. Canal Bus: to Westerkerk or Keizersgracht. Dagschotel Dfl. 23–30; 3-course dinner Dfl. 40. EETCAFÉ. **$$**.
Café De Reiger is better than it looks or, I should say, better than it looks at first. Like many eetcafés, De Reiger is divided into 2 parts—a bar and a cafe-restaurant. The bar—a typical "brown bar" with funky wooden tables and chairs, smoke-yellowed walls, a glossy bar, and a neighborhood clientele—is neither beautiful nor physically comfortable. The cafe-restaurant is cozy but simple. At 6pm the kitchen opens, the candles come out, and the atmosphere transforms. Waitresses put candles everywhere—on tables, sideboards, window sills. Within an hour the restaurant fills with young professionals who have become

relatively recent neighbors in the once working-class, now trendy, Jordaan. Two professional cooks provide better than average cafe cuisine: steamed salmon in soya sauce, loin of lamb with sundried tomatoes and basil, venison steak with cranberry sauce, or grilled entrecote with truffle butter. In mussel season you can order mountains of fresh, tender Zeeland mussels steamed in white wine.

★★La Rive

The Amstel Intercontinental Hotel, Professor Tulpplein 1.
☎ 20-6226060. AE, DC, EC, V. Reservations required. Closed: Sat–Sun lunch. Tram: 4, 6, 7, 10 to Weesperplein or Frederiksplein. Canal Bus: to City Hall. Water taxi: to Amstel Hotel. 3-course dinner: from Dfl. 125. FRENCH. **$$$$$**.
A Michelin-star restaurant in the Amstel Hotel, Le Rive is classy, comfortable, and considered one of the best French restaurants in Holland, with a chef known for an inventive, subtle culinary style. The cooking is French/Mediterranean, using reductions and natural juices instead of heavy sauces—and no cream. Many dishes include fish that is smoked or grilled. The house specialty, the lean back of salmon, is "home-smoked" on the premises. The dessert special is rich and unexpected—hot chocolate cake, with hot liquid filling, topped with ice cream.

Reserve a window seat: The restaurant provides a mesmerizing view of the Amstel River. In the summer, the restaurant opens onto a quiet, protected terrace. You can have a private party in the cozy wine room, stacked floor to ceiling with exceptional wines, or at the "chef's table" in the middle of the kitchen.

Despite the Amstel's grandeur, La Rive is surprisingly comfy and relaxing. Service is impeccable.

★★Sama Sebo

P.C. Hooftstraat 27.
☎ 20-6628146. AE, DC, MC, V. Reservations recommended. Closed: Sun. Tram: 2, 5 to Rijksmuseum, or tram 10 to Marnixstraat. Canal Bus: to Rijksmuseum. Rijsttafel for one: Dfl. 48. INDONESIAN. **$$$**.
Although the prices are high for a full rijsttafel, you can find a tasty à la carte meal at a reasonable price and enjoy pungent, refined, and not-too-spicy Indonesian cuisine. The rijsttafel may not be the biggest in town, but it is one of the most fragrant and carefully prepared, with sauces that are dark and full-bodied yet never too heavy. The decor, batik tablecloths and Indonesian masks, is exotic but not overdone.

If you are in Amsterdam for a day or two and want an introduction to Indonesian food after a day in the museums, Sama Sebo is convenient—and a local favorite (so reserve a table).

★★Selecta

Vizelstraat 26. ☎ 20-6248894. AE, DC, MC, V. Reservations recommended. Tram: 16, 24, 25 to Vizelstraat. Rijsttafels: vegetarian Dfl. 30; others: Dfl. 48–56. Sates Dfl. 34; dinner for two Dfl. 30. INDONESIAN. **$$/$$$**.
This is a family run Indonesian restaurant with a personal touch, despite the numerous tour buses that pull in for large group meals. The restaurant is also sufficiently authentic and reasonably priced to attract an Indonesian clientele. The serving staff, students from Indonesian hotel schools, work in the kitchen to learn the cuisine before they wait tables. Consequently, service is both gracious and well informed.

The satays are tender, the tofu transcendent, if that is possible for bean curd, and the sambel spicy, but sweet and not explosive (but do not treat it like salsa—always dip with moderation in red Indonesian sauces).

Decor is simple, authentic, and carefully chosen. Shadow puppets and paintings, chosen by owner/chef Mr. Liam, illustrate stories from Indonesian folktales, and delicate white orchids, cultivated by Mrs. Liam, brighten the window sills.

★De Smoeshaan

Leidsekade 90. ☎ 20-6250368. AE, EC. Reservations necessary upstairs for 6:30 or 8:30pm dinner; not necessary in the downstairs cafe. Tram: 1,2, 5, 6, 7, 10 to Leidseplein. Canal Bus: to Leidseplein. Dinner: approx-imately Dfl. 35. EETCAFÉ. **$$/$$$**.
De Smoeshaan is a find—if you can find it. Most Americans don't—unless a helpful concierge at Hotel American sends them to this stylish theater cafe and restaurant within feet of the hotel.

The cafe and restaurant differ in atmosphere but not cuisine, since you can get restaurant entrees in the cafe. The brown cafe has beamed ceilings, soft lighting, and a cozy, sheltered-from-the-street atmosphere. It is crowded and a nice place for solo travelers to eat without feeling alone—if they can tolerate the smoke.

The upstairs restaurant is another world—quiet, digni-fied, and luxurious, with padded leather chairs, a bar with shiny copper and brass, and an à la carte menu (which is also available downstairs). The menu is international with an Indonesian bent since the cook is Indonesian. Expect Indonesian specialties such as grilled jumbo shrimp in garlic sauce or grilled pork with hot chili sauce as well as the usual French/international cafe cuisine—entrecote, lamb chops, and fish. But as with many Amsterdam restaurants, the menu changes frequently. De Smoeshaan is known for having good wines, mostly French, with 5 house wines available.

The restaurant adjoins the Theater Bellevue.

★★Speciaal

Nieuwe Leliestraat 142.
☎ 20-6249706. AE, EC, V. Reservations recommended. Closed: lunch. Tram: 13, 14, 17 to Marnixstraat. Canal Bus: to Westerkerk. 3-course dinner: Dfl. 50. INDONESIAN. **$$$/$$$$**.

The Speciaal is situated on a quiet street in the otherwise lively **Jordaan,** and many say it's the best Indonesian restaurant in town. From the outside, the restaurant looks tiny, but it opens out at the back into an attractive bamboo-lined room with slowly revolving ceiling fans. A tropical heat builds up as the restaurant fills, and ziggurats of rijsttafel dishes are piled precariously onto the plate-warmers. In addition to a choice of 2 rijsttafels, the menu offers an interesting selection of Indonesian meat, chicken, and fish dishes—simple, old-fashioned Indonesian cuisine. The helpings are big and meant to fill. The spices are appropriately authentic: hot but not painfully so, but *do not* chomp down on those cute

little red or green chile peppers.

★Het Swarte Schaep

Korte Leidsedwarsstraat 24.
☎ 20-6223021. AE, DC, MC, V. Reservations recommended. Tram: 1, 2, 5, 6, 7, 10 to Leidseplein. Canal bus: to Leidseplein. 3-course dinner Dfl. 75; 4-course dinner Dfl. 90. FRENCH. **$$$$$**.

Until a few years ago there were several excellent French restaurants around Leidseplein, but one by one they have packed up and moved, leaving only one, appropriately named The Black Sheep, as a lonely outpost of good French cuisine. The Black Sheep is known for fine wines and traditional French cooking, offering such dishes as rabbit stewed in beer, duck with sweet-and-sour blackcurrant sauce, smoked salmon with truffle dressing, and parfait of goose liver with peaches and lavender. The 3-course menu changes daily. The building dates from 1687 and is cozily furnished with heavy dark wood and polished brass. The old-fashioned atmosphere and service place Het Swarte Schaep in sharp contrast to the nearby Bulldog Cafe, a pot cafe (otherwise known as a coffee shop), and the neon lights of the Leidseplein.

★Tempo Doeloe

Utrechtsestraat 75.
☎ 20-6256718. AE, DC, MC, V. Reservations recommended. Closed: lunch. Tram: 4 to Keizersgracht. 3-course dinner: Dfl. 42.50+. INDONESIAN. **$$$**.

The Javanese, Balinese, and Sumatran dishes at Tempo Doeloe make no concessions to the wimpy Westerner palate: When a dish is described as *pedis* (sharp), it is hot. Tempo Doeloe is a good find if you

like authentic—and spicy—
Indonesian food. The
restaurant's specialties include
the chili-strewn nasi koening.
To buffer the effect, have
pickled vegetables, tea, or beer
on hand. The porcelain plates
and refined decor hardly
prepare you for the intensity
of the spices.

★★Toscanini

Lindengracht 75.
☎ 20-6232813. No credit
cards. Reservations strongly
recommended. Tram: 10 to
Marnixstraat. Canal Bus: to
Westerkerk. Main courses:
Dfl. 24–27. ITALIAN. **$$/$$$$**.
A small restaurant in the
Jordaan, Toscanini is known for
its Southern Italian country
dishes such as *fazzoletti* (fresh
green pasta) stuffed with
ricotta, mozzarella, and
mortadella—and its convivial
atmosphere. The food is fresh
and the pasta homemade on
the premises. Try the pasta
dishes, especially the extra-
ordinary lasagna made with
ground veal. The fish dishes
are less consistent, sometimes
tender, sometimes dry.

The restaurant looks like
an Italian grotto, bakery, and
country kitchen all rolled into
one. Service is friendly but
relaxed—which in this case
means slow. Toscanini is
popular with the young artists
and professionals who live in
the Jordaan.

★Treasure

Nieuwe Zijds Voorburgwal 115.
☎ 20-6260915. AE, DC, MC, V.
Reservations recommended.
Closed: Wed. Tram: 1, 2, 5, 9,
13, 14, 16, 17, 24, 25 to Dam.
3-course meal Dfl. 60–125;
4-course meal Dfl. 125.
CHINESE. **$$$$/$$$$$**.
The extensive menu of this
friendly Chinese restaurant on
Nieuwe Zijds Voorburgwal

includes curiosities such as
squirrel fish, Charlie Chaplin
duck, and a certain dish
known as Pun Fan Pei, which
the menu tantalizingly claims
is a mysterious Chinese dish
indescribable in Western
terms. Classic Peking Duck
is available by special order.
Treasure also offers Peking-
style dim sum lunches.

Along with exotic Asian
decor, the restaurant has a
personal touch: The paintings
are done by the owner, Ho
Man King, an artist and
calligrapher who studied in
China.

★★De Trechter

Hobbemakade 62-63.
☎ 20-6711263. AE, DC, EC.
Reservations recommended.
Closed: lunch; Sun–Mon; mid-
July to early Aug. Tram: 16, 24.
25 to Albert Cuyp Market. 4-
course dinner: Dfl. 93. FRENCH.
$$$$$
De Trechter (called The Funnel
because of its unusual shape),
has only 10 tables. It's small
and intimate enough for a
dinner party. The food is both
classic and modern French
with dishes such as smoked
fillet of sole in vinegar sauce
from lavender served with
mushrooms, or wild duck from
the Bresse region. The wine
list is good, and the service
attentive. This Michelin-star
restaurant is consistently
excellent and always full, so it
is wise to reserve well in
advance.

Umeno

Agamemnonstraat 27.
☎ 20-6766089. No credit cards.
Reservations recommended.
Closed: Sun dinner; Mon. Tram:
24 to Olympiaplein. Main course:
Dfl. 25–49. JAPANESE. **$$/$$$**.
This small, traditional Japanese
restaurant near Olympialein
offers fragrant, colorful fish

and meat dishes as well as fresh sushi and sashimi presented with consummate art and delicacy. Its business lunch, served at a breathtaking pace, is eagerly devoured by Japanese executives attending trade fairs at the nearby RAI exhibition center. Decor is typically simple and sleek Japanese. Prices are more reasonable than at the elegant Restaurant Yamazato located in the Amsterdam Hilton.

★★Van Harte

Hartenstraat 24. ☎ 20-6258500. AE, DC, V. Reservations strongly recommended. Closed: lunch; Tues. Tram: 1, 2, and 5 to the Spui or 13, 14, 17 to Westerkerk. Daily special Dfl. 30; 4-course dinner Dfl. 57. FRENCH. **$$$**. A simple romantic restaurant with a fetching terrace, Van Harte has an inviting candlelit interior, polished wood tables, good wines, and an excellent French kitchen with Dutch, Mediterranean, and Japanese influences. You can order sashimi (tuna or salmon) as well as pasta or, for a sumptuous feast, try the venison with mushroom sauce served with braised pear, red cabbage cooked with raisins and cinnamon, and scalloped potatoes. For dessert, Van Harte's specialty is traditional Dutch macaroon pudding served with macaroon ice cream. The well-schooled and accommodating staff can help you choose your wine.

★★Van Puffelen

Prinsengracht 377.
☎ 20-6246270. MC, V. Reservations strongly recommended. Tram: 13, 14, 17 to Westermarkt. Canal bus: to Westerkerk or Keizergracht. Water taxi: to the Pulitzer dock. 3-course dinner Dfl. 47; daily special Dfl. 27. EETCAFÉ. **$$/$$$**.

I have had some of my most relaxed dinners in Amsterdam at this canalside brown cafe. The quality is surprisingly consistent: No matter the time of day or season, I have always been presented with moist fish, tender entrecote, subtle and imaginative sauces, the best french fries in town, and a wide variety of beer. Try the salmon with beurre blanc sauce or the suckling pig cutlets with coriander pesto. Meals here are a terrific buy, considering Van Puffelen's stylish address. Daily specials come with fries, salad, and vegetables for Dfl. 27.

Service is friendly, relaxed, and sometimes slow, providing ample time to take in the atmosphere—ceiling frescoes, candlelight, 17thC canal houses, fanciful houseboats, and the placid Prinses canal. Others have discovered this unusual cafe—and they reserve their tables in advance. Reserve a table for the terrace or front room, especially in the summer. After dinner, the restaurant becomes a lively cafe with an educated, stylish clientele. The only drawback is the level of noise and smoke, especially if you are sitting inside.

★d'Vijff Vlieghen

Spuistraat 294-302.
☎ 20-5546015. DC, MC, V. Reservations recommended. Closed: lunch. Tram: 1, 2, 5 to Spui. 3-course dinner: Dfl. 55–300. DUTCH. **$$$$$**. Commonly known as "The Five Flies," this restaurant is an Amsterdam institution—a cozy, candlelit, and atmospheric shrine to Old Holland. The food is fanatically organic, Dutch, fresh, and sophisticated. Expect good Dutch veal and duck (and sometimes wild boar) and

small, tasty vegetables at disconcerting prices. But foremost here is atmosphere. The restaurant is comprised of 17thC houses full of nooks and crannies and architectural surprises and complete with Old Dutch wallpaper and an impressive array of antiques: tiles, liquor kegs, plates, cooking utensils, and, they say, original Rembrandt etchings. More recent history includes visits from Orson Welles and Walt Disney; some dignitaries even have chairs named after them. The Five Flies was once a main tourist attraction and is still a place where Amsterdammers take foreign visitors. The collection of Dutch geneevers and antiques along with the atmosphere are a greater draw than the food, which is good but not as popular as the French/European cuisine of some of the newer restaurants.

★★Yamazato

Okura Hotel, Ferdinand Bolstraat 333. ☎ 20-6787111. AE, DC, MC, V. Reservations recommended. Closed: lunch. Tram: 12, 25 to Cornelis Troostplein. 3-course Dinner: Dfl. 80. JAPANESE. **$$$$$**

Yamazato is situated in Amsterdam's only Japanese hotel, the **Okura** on Ferdinand Bolstraat. It offers a wide range of traditional Japanese dishes such as sashimi (raw fish), tempura (deep-fried delicacies), and seaweed soup. Fish and vegetable dishes are beautifully arranged shrines to Japanese cooking—with fresh sushi, grilled lobster, and various incarnations of bean curd. But you pay for the fresh food and the artistry. Dinners range from Dfl. 80 to Dfl. 130. Lunches, at Dfl. 30, are more affordable. Service is excellent.

Amsterdam's Cafes

Cafes are an integral part of Amsterdam's social and cultural life. Socializing in a cafe is a ritual built into the day, especially for those under 40, although the middle-aged and elderly still find time to stop in for a *kopje koffie* (little cup of coffee) and a warm hello to neighbors and friends. In the evening, Amsterdammers arrive on bicycles (sometimes with briefcases) to meet with friends before going home. They often stop in for congenial, inexpensive dinners at the eetcafés (see above), or they drop by for a late-night *pilsje* (a little glass of beer), which is often served in a *fluitje,* a fluted little glass. Because of their central role, many cafes are open long hours—from 11am to 1am weekdays and 11am to 2 or 3am weekends.

The term cafe applies to a wide range of establishments—traditional brown cafes (named for their dark wood paneling and bar, bare wooden floors, and wood tables that are bare or covered with a Turkish rug), modern designer cafes, grand cafes, or special interest cafes that are foyers for theaters, cinemas, concert halls, or political institutes.

If you are looking for the soul of Amsterdam, you are as likely to find it in one of the city's many brown cafes as you are in a Rembrandt painting. In fact, if you miss out on the cafes—brown or otherwise—you haven't really experienced Amsterdam.

Cafe Culture

Amsterdam cafes combine the neighborly feeling of London pubs, the bohemian spirit of Paris cafes, and the gezelligheid of a Dutch living room. The cafes are quiet places where you can meet with friends, read the newspaper, or sip an exotic beer without being rushed. In all but the most brusque establishments, you can spend a long rainy afternoon reading a book from beginning to end without being disturbed. Some cafes even provide Dutch and foreign newspapers and a well-lit reading table. Most will offer filled rolls (*belegde broodjes*) or apple cake (*appeltaart*) as well as traditional Dutch snacks such as *bitterballen* (meatballs) and various types of *worst* (sausage). Unless you only have 1 drink, it is customary to keep a running tab and pay for everything at the end.

Beer is central to this culture, partly because it was once safer than the water, but also because the Dutch have elevated beer to a ritual and art form. Amsterdammers drink beer in glasses of varying sizes and shape depending on the kind of beer. There are about 100 different beer glasses which, the breweries claim, enhance the "life" and flavor of each beer.

Pils, or plain lager, is the most commonly served beer and is served cold, in small glasses—with 2 fingers of foam on top that the bartender flattens with a plastic *spatel* to keep "the life" in the beer. Amsterdammers balk at beer that is too warm or that lacks the standard 2 fingers of foam. They hate to look at foamless, British beer because it is "dead in the glass." To further their beer aesthetic, the Dutch hold yearly beer drafting competitions to see who can draft the most consistently beautiful glasses of beer from 1 barrel.

Pils comes in a common, straight *stapelglas.* It also comes in a *fluitje* (a fluted glass—tiny by American standards), which is currently the hippest and most popular way to order pils. You can also order pils by the *emmertje* or "little bucket" (which is the sign of a no-nonsense drinker—or an American tourist). Belgian beers, of which there are many, tend to come in their own glasses provided to cafes by the individual breweries, creating a complex protocol for bartenders and a fond ritual for beer connoisseurs. De Koninck, a dark Belgian beer, comes in its own fluitje or bell shaped glass. Duvel, a highly yeasted Belgian beer, comes in a slender bell. Westmalle (a Trappist beer made by Belgian monks) comes in a "grail shaped" glass, whether or not you order the dark beer (*dubbel*) or the light beer (*trippel*). *Bokbier*, a heavy, rich beer that is both Dutch and Belgian, comes in its own glass—and its own season: spring bok or autumn bok. *Witbier* (Belgian or Dutch white beer), a fresh, sour summer beer, is served with a slice of lemon and is a popular drink on cafe terraces.

Each cafe is allied with a brewery, and that brewery supplies it with beer and specialized glasses. So if you see a Grolsch sign outside, or Grolsch coasters at the bar, do not expect Amstel on tap.

Do not underestimate the alcohol level of the Belgian beers; they are more alcoholic than the lagers, and 4 or 5 glasses can get you completely drunk. In this case, expect the "good" Dutch bartender to refuse to serve you any more—and to offer you soda, coffee, or a cab ride home. This is part of good cafe etiquette and is expected of appropriately affable and protective bartenders.

Traditional Brown Cafes Some brown cafes, with their dark wood wainscoting, mustard-colored walls, and haphazard selection of tables and chairs, are themselves antiques. They have been in business since the 17thC, and their dark, candlelit interiors evoke the atmosphere of Old Holland. Occasionally, there is a hint of former splendor in an ornate lamp, stained glass window, beautiful copper tap, or calligraphic detail, but the overwhelming look is one of gentle decline.

The best brown cafes are the daily neighborhood bars—*stemkroeg*—that offer far more than nostalgia for the past. They serve as a home away from home for Amsterdammers, many of whom live in cramped apartments (especially if they live in the Jordaan). These are bars that resemble old Amsterdam living rooms in both decor and atmosphere: There are antique prints or paintings on the wall, creaky but comfortable wooden tables and chairs, newspapers, soft music, congenial conversation, and, somewhere, a sleeping cat.

Modern Cafes In the 1980s, young Amsterdammers made a decisive break with tradition when they began to frequent bright white, architect-designed cafes with zinc tables, walls of mirrors, and postmodern architecture. Although in the beginning these ultramodern cafes sent a shiver of dismay through the old brown cafes, they now have settled into the fabric of the city, bending to the dominant culture by offering their own version of gezelligheid. Het Land Van Walem is one of the warmer designer cafes, and Blincker has its own offbeat high-tech charm.

Grand Cafes Amsterdammers currently favor a new generation of spacious, high-ceilinged cafes modeled on the "grand cafes" of the 19thC. Some of these establishments have no justification for describing themselves as grand, but De Jaren, De Kroon, and Luxembourg possess a certain splendor and cosmopolitan allure. Café Américain, with its Deco fixtures, murals, and stained glass, is grand indeed.

Specialized Cafes Another relatively recent trend— one that sets Amsterdam's cafes apart from those of Paris, London, and Berlin—is the emergence of specialized cafes. These include theater cafes such as De Smoeshaan and Frascati, film cafes like Desmet and Kriterion, music cafes like Odeon and De IJsbreker, chess cafes such as **Het Hok** (Lange Leidsedwarsstraat 134), women-only cafes such as **Saarein** (Elandsstraat 119), specialized beer cafes such as **Gollem** (Raamsteeg 4), "Old Amsterdam" karaoke cafes, marijuana cafes, gay cafes, and even a political/cultural cafe, Café De Balie. For more information on some of these cafes, refer to "Amsterdam After Dark."

Proeflokalen An entirely different Amsterdam drinking institution is the *proeflokaal,* or tasting house. Originally these were attached to *jenever* (Dutch gin) distilleries and allowed customers to sample the product before they purchased a bottle. Although the licensing laws now prohibit them from selling jenever in bottles, the proeflokaals still retain the atmosphere of a shop rather than a cafe. These are ideal spots in which to have an apéritif, most being situated in attractive 18thC buildings in the old part of the city. Among the most genial proeflokalen are De Drie Fleschjes, behind the Nieuwe Kerk, and De Admiraal and Het Hooghoudt.

Eetcafés An increasing number of Amsterdam's cafes, particularly some of the student brown cafes and modern cafes, have begun to offer complete meals at reasonable prices. The menu, which is usually chalked on a blackboard, often includes a dish of the day (*dagschotel*) and a vegetarian dish (*vegetarische schotel*). The cuisine usually consists of sustaining Dutch fare, although a few eetcafés such as Van Puffelen, Frascati, De Reiger, De Smoeshaan, Café Schiller, and Het

Molenpad offer French/international cuisine. Some of these cafes are open for both lunch and dinner. Food may be ordered at the bar or tables. Tipping is appreciated, although not necessarily expected. Many Amsterdammers tip a flat 5%, or they round up to the nearest guilder for an inexpensive meal or up to the nearest 5 or 10 guilders for more expensive meals.

Breakfast, Brunch & Dessert

Amsterdam cafes generally do not open early in the day, and few places serve breakfast. However, Het Land Van Walem and Morlang, both on the Keizersgracht canal, serve full breakfasts, and De Prins and Luxembourg serve brunchlike items such as salads and quiches. Despite its cramped interior, **Café Puccini** (Staalstraat 21, ☎ 20-6265474; tram 9, 14 or metro to Waterlooplein) is favored by the young and fashionable. It serves beautiful, freshly baked European desserts.

Terraces

Cafe terraces are a fine way to enjoy a summer afternoon and dip into local culture at the same time. Amsterdammers flock to cafe terraces at the slightest hint of sunshine, to drink a fashionable Belgian Witbier, fresh-squeezed orange juice, or lukewarm Coke (bars are not equipped for hot weather, and you will be lucky to find ice). Café Américain's terrace offers sun or shade and some of the liveliest people-watching in town. They put out a few metal chairs in front of Het Land Van Walem and Het Molenpad (both off Leidsestraat) or a slew of well-used wood or wicker ones at 't Smalle, Twee Prinsen, or Van Puffelen (all on or near the Prinsengracht) to catch the afternoon sun, but most of the big cafe terraces are away from the 17thC canal ring.

De Jaren has 2 terraces on the Amstel waterfront that catch the sun most of the day. The spacious terrace of Café Dantzig, in front of the opera house on the Amstel, is another alluring spot. But De IJsbreker's terrace on the grassy, tree-lined banks of the Amstel and Café Vertigo's 2-tiered terrace facing a lake on Vondelpark are the 2 most peaceful spots to spend a summer afternoon.

Cafe-Hopping by Neighborhood

Cafe-hopping is a fine way to discover Amsterdam and to sample the flavors of its neighborhoods since the city is so compact and a fair variety of cafes are usually within easy walking distance.

The canals, especially the Prinsengracht and Keizersgracht, offer a variety of cozy brown cafes (Het

Molenpad, Van Puffelen) and modern cafes (Het Land Van Walem, Felix Meritis) with canalside terraces and an educated, under-fortyish, somewhat artsy clientele. The **Jordaan** cafes tend to draw an alternative crowd of artists, writers, and youngish professionals or a middle-aged to elderly bunch of down-home, accordion playing, karaoke singing Jordaaners. **The Spui,** near the city's Historic Center, is the heart of a lively cafe scene that accommodates the young and trendy (Café Luxembourg), the older and affluent (Hoppe), the intellectual and offbeat (De Zwart). Beer aficionados of all ages and nationalities flock to Gollem. Also in the Center, tucked in the narrow streets and alleys behind Rokin and **Dam Square,** are some well hidden and surprisingly charming theater cafes—Blincker, Frascati, and De Brakke Grond. However, due to the potential late-night scruffiness of such dark alleys, it is best not to wander here alone after 10pm (see "Safety" in "The Basics"). The area around **Centraal Station** just down Damrak offers some of the oldest (Karperskoek) and newest (Oibibio) of the city's cafes.

For more sophisticated cafes, try the **Leidseplein:** De Smoeshaan if you like theater people, Café Américain if you like Art Deco or gorgeous desserts, and Café De Bali if you like humor with your progressive politics. The areas around the **Amstel River** and the **University of Amsterdam** harbor an attractive array of offbeat cafes—De Engelbewaarder and Staalmeesters on the Kloveniersburgwal canal, De IJsbreker and De Jaren on the Amstel. On the nearby **Rembrandtsplein,** you will find the comfortable, cozy Café Schiller or the grand and noisy Café De Kroon. For lively, late-night gay cafes and restaurants, Reguliersdwarsstraat and Amstelstraat (see "Amsterdam After Dark") lie just around the corner.

Amsterdam has over 1,500 cafes for you to discover. What follows is a list of some special ones categorized by both neighborhood and type (grand cafe, brown cafe, etc.) to make a cafe tour of Amsterdam an easy and relaxing activity for a few hours some afternoon or evening.

Cafes by Type

Brown Cafes
De Doffer
De Engelbewaarder
Gollem
Hoppe
Karpershoek

Het Molenpad
1E Klas
Papeneiland
De Pels
De Prins
De Reiger

Scheltema
't Smalle
De Staalmeesters
Thijssen
De Twee Prinsen
De Twee Zwaantjes
Van Puffelen
De Zwart

Buitenlandse Bierencafes (Wide Selection of Foreign Beers)

De Brakke Grond (Belgian)
Gollem
In De Wildeman
Van Puffelen

Film Cafes

Desmet
Kriterion
Vertigo

Grand Cafes

Américain
De Jaren
De Kroon
Oibibio

L'Opera
Vertigo

Modern Cafes

De Jaren
Het Land Van Walem
Luxembourg
Morlang

Music Cafes

De Engelbewaarder
De IJsbreker
Odeon

Political/Intellectual Cafes

Café De Balie

Proeflokaal

De Drie Fleschjes

Theater Cafes

Blincker
De Brakke Grond
Café Cox
Felix Meritis Foyer
Frascati
Grand Café Dantzig
De Smoeshaan

Cafes by Neighborhood

Leisdseplein

Américain

Leidseplein 28. ☎ 20-6245322.
Tram: 1, 2, 5, 6, 7, 10 to
Leidseplein. Open: Sun–Wed
11am–midnight; Thurs–Sat
11am–1am.

The Américain Café, overlooking Leidseplein, was once a famous meeting place for writers and intellectuals, although in recent years the literati have been replaced by musicians performing in the nearby Paradiso and Melkweg. The terrace still functions as a popular meeting place for tourists, conventioneers, and Amsterdammers. The cafe and the American Hotel of which it is a part (see "Accommodations") were designed by Willem Kromhout in 1902, combining elements of Venetian Gothic, Art Nouveau, and Art Deco. With its magnificent vaulted ceilings, stained-glass windows, and deco lamps, the cafe brought new grandeur to Amsterdam, and is still the most beautiful—and most Deco—cafe in town. Prices can be steep, but the aesthetic experience along with coffee and first-class people-watching makes spending an hour or two in the cafe worthwhile. You are not obliged to order more than coffee, but if you like sweets, try the tempting desserts, especially the mousse shaped like flower petals or the huge, whimsical ice-cream creations—large

enough for 2 adults or 3
children.

Café De Balie

Kleine Gartmanplaantsoen 10.
☎ 20-6243821. Tram: 1, 2, 5,
6, 7, 10 to Leidseplein. Open:
Sun–Thurs 11am–1am, Fri–Sat
11am–2am.

The 30-something intellectual
clientele of Café De Balie, part
of The Cultural and Political
Center, provides a sharp contrast to the young, touristy
throngs of Leidseplein. It is
not a pasty, academic crowd
at Balie but a feisty, progressive
one. On Saturdays, the entire
building (a former courthouse
divided into separate offices
and discussion rooms as well
as the cafe) becomes a "news
magazine" with each room
housing a discussion on
anything from war crimes in
the former Yugoslavia to the
state of the arts in Holland.
Balie also hosts a literary TV
show of Dutch authors talking
about their work as well as
cross-cultural events featuring
the music and poetry of
African immigrants. Some
Balie events are offbeat and
off-the-wall, like the Barbie
doll competition, the goal
of which was to redesign
Barbie. Stop at Balie for good
cappuccino and lively political
debate. The bartenders are
smart and amiable, and, like
everyone else in the place,
good conversationalists.

Café Cox

Marnixstraat 429.
☎ 20-6207222. Tram: 1, 2, 5,
6, 7, 10 to Leidseplein. Open:
Sun–Thurs 10am–1am, Fri–Sat
10am–2am.

Café Cox, the theater cafe
for the municipal theater, De
Stadsschouwburg, and sharing
the same 19thC building, has
high ceilings, large tables, and
a restaurant on the 2nd floor.

It is particularly comfortable,
quiet, and relaxed during the
day—and far less expensive
than Café Américain, which
is just across the street. The
downstairs cafe looks up onto
the street and is a good spot
for people-watching, meeting
with friends, or reading the
paper on a rainy day. At night,
the cafe is popular as an "in-
between cafe"—a place for
people of all ages to go before
or after movies, theater, or
music events on Leidseplein.
Café Cox is also a good place
to eat late, since the restaurant
serves dinner until 11:30pm.

De Smoeshaan

Leidsekade 90. ☎ 20-6250368.
Tram: 1, 2, 5, 6, 7, 10 to
Leidseplein. Open: Tues–Thurs
11am–1am, Fri–Sat 11am–2am,
Sun 1–5pm.

De Smoeshaan, a sheltered-
from-the-street brown cafe
with beamed ceilings, soft
lighting, and a gezellig
atmosphere, was named after
a play that was forbidden in
1975 by the mayor of Harlaam
because it featured props that
he regarded obscene. The
group of players was housed
in this building, part of the
Bellevue Theater, which then,
and now, performs offbeat
modern and postmodern
plays. Actors and actresses,
technicians, and production
people gather in this dark, arty,
and comfortable brown cafe
to launch new productions and
mourn those that have died. A
painting by artist and musician
Herman Brood of artists at the
De Smoeshaan bar hangs on
the wall, commenting on past
and present clientele. There is
a good and inexpensive cafe
menu, and a slightly more
expensive restaurant upstairs
(see listing above). The
atmosphere is friendly and
relaxed.

Historic Center

Blincker
St. Barberenstraat 7.
☎ 20-6271938. Tram: 4, 9, 16, 24, 25 to Dam. Open: Mon–Thurs 10am–1am, Fri–Sat 10am–2am.
A tiny 16thC alley behind Dam Square on the Nes is a surprising spot for the 2-tiered sunlit theater cafe Blincker. The cafe is attached to the Frascati Theater (see "The Arts") and tends to fill with avant-garde theatergoers, choreographers, dancers, and artists as the evening wears on. The masks and plaster noses attached to the wall provide a touch of whimsy and the Frascati theater's well-designed posters contribute lively touches of color. In the summer, the alley becomes a pretty outdoor patio lit up at night by a string of lights. The cafe offers inexpensive and good food for lunch and dinner (see listing above).

De Brakke Grond
Nes 43. ☎ 20-6260044. Tram: 4, 9, 16, 24, 25 to Dam. Open: Mon–Thurs 11am–1am, Fri–Sat 11am–2am, Sun 1–5pm.
This peaceful, classy little cafe is attached to the Vlaams Cultureel Centrum (Flemish Cultural Center), which exists to promote the culture of Dutch-speaking Belgium. The cafe's contribution is to offer a range of potent Belgian beers in a somewhat formal modern Belgian setting. Try the creamy-topped Grimbergen from the tap; or one of the many bottled beers, each of which is meticulously poured into its proper glass. Duvel and Wittekop are pleasant light beers, while Geuze Lambiek from the Brussels area is a darker and sweeter brew. The upstairs restaurant offers a taste of the culinary culture of

Belgium, featuring several unusual dishes prepared in beer, as well as waterzooi, the traditional fish stew.

De Drie Fleschjes
Gravenstraat 18.
☎ 20-6248443. Tram: 1, 2, 4, 5, 9, 13, 14, 16, 17, 24, 25 to Dam. Open: Mon–Sat noon–8:30pm, Sun 3–7pm.
A convivial proeflokaal (a tasting house for Dutch gin) dating from 1650, De Drie Fleschjes (The Three Jars) is located in a bell-gabled house behind the **Nieuwe Kerk.** The green and cream wooden interior is softly lit by lamps in old brass fittings, and a solitary candle flickers romantically on top of the beer tap. Occasionally, the bartender will ascend a stepladder to fill a glass from one of 43 padlocked casks, each marked with the name of a local business.

Frascati
Nes 59. ☎ 20-6241324. Tram: 4, 9, 14, 16, 24, 25 to Spui. Open: Mon–Sat 10am–1am, Sun 5pm–1am.
With its frosted glass, rich wood, and gleaming brass fittings, Frascati is a haven of gezelligheid on the dark and narrow Nes. The cafe belongs to the Frascati Theater (see "The Arts"), as does the Blincker, which is just around the corner, and an arty crowd gathers here to read Volkskrant theater reviews, fill in applications for grant money, and gorge on enormous slices of apple cake.

Karpershoek
Martelaarsgracht 2.
☎ 20-6247886. Tram: 1, 2, 5, 13, 17 to Martelaarsgracht. Canal Bus: to Centraal Station. Open: Daily 7am–1am.
The scruffy, nostalgic, Karpershoek—a typical brown

cafe with sawdust on the floor and smoke stains on the walls—has stood on the old harbor front since 1629 and claims to be the oldest cafe in Amsterdam. The cafe is conveniently close to Centraal Station, and its clock is set 5 minutes fast to ensure that regulars don't miss the last train to Purmerend or Paris. However, the cafe's history is more charming than its current neighborhood or clientele.

1E Klas

Centraal Station (spoor 2b).
☎ 20-6250131. Tram: 1, 2, 4, 5, 9, 13, 16, 17, 24, 25 to Centraal Station. Canal Bus: to Centraal Station. Open: Mon–Sat 9:30am–11pm, Sun 10:30am–11pm.
The handsome neo-Gothic interior of the former first-class cafe-restaurant at Amsterdam's principal rail station has been restored to its 19thC style. With its heavy, dark wooden furniture and mellow light filtering through stained-glass windows, the interior evokes the warmth of a Breitner painting. There are newspapers on wooden handles for patrons to read, and the coffee is excellent. This is an atmospheric place to meet someone arriving by train and yet avoid the crowded chaos of the station.

Grand Café Oibibio

Prins Hendrikkade 20.
☎ 20-5539323. Tram: 1, 2, 4, 5, 9, 13, 16, 17, 24, 25 to Centraal Station. Canal Bus: to Centraal Station. Open: Sun–Thurs 8:30am–12:30am, Fri–Sat 9:30am–1:30am. Sauna: Mon–Sun 11am–midnight; tea garden 1pm–8pm. Wheelchair accessible.
Oibibio is a comfortable grand cafe popular with a young crowd—and with anyone who likes saunas or

beautifully converted old buildings. It combines stately 19thC Amsterdam architecture with New Age sensibilities to create a 4-story haven complete with cafe-restaurant, bookstore, gift shop, Japanese tea garden, and rooftop sauna. The cafe is divided into sections with different lighting and atmosphere—an airy window cafe overlooking the street, a well-appointed bar, a reading area next to the magazine rack, a cozy nook on a lower level in the back, and a restaurant on the 2nd floor. Although the restaurant serves both lunch and dinner, the food is often mediocre, especially the vegetarian dishes in which vegetables are doused with soy sauce and cooked to tastelessness. The salads, how-ever, are reasonably good.

Smits Koffiehuis

Stationsplein 10.
☎ 20-6233777. Tram: 1, 2, 4, 5, 9, 13, 16, 17, 24, 25 to Centraal Station. Canal Bus: to Centraal Station. Open: Mon–Sat 8am–8:30pm, Sun 9am–8:30pm.
Stepping out of Centraal Station into the confusion of trams, bicycles, and street musicians, the first building to catch your eye is the ornate, wooden Smits Koffiehuis, formerly a tram station and now a tourist information office (VVV) upstairs. What is less obvious is that the downstairs houses an attractive Old Dutch–style koffiehuis that serves good coffee and reasonably priced food and is a pleasant place to catch your breath after a long trip or to recover from waiting in line for hotel information upstairs. It is a bit touristy, as is almost every restaurant in the neigh-borhood, but peaceful compared to the circus of the

station and Damrak. In summer, the cafe spills out onto a floating terrace overlooking the former harbor front.

In De Wildeman

Kolksteeg 3. ☎ 20-6382348. Tram: 1, 2, 5, 13, 17 to N. Z. Kolk. Open: Mon–Thurs noon–1am, Fri–Sat noon–2am.

The Dutch Association for the Protection of Historical Monuments, which occupies a nearby 17thC corn exchange, should be proud of its local *bierproeflokaal* (beer-tasting house). Located in a medieval alley that is stubbornly resistant to change, In De Wildeman is a handsomely restored shop with lofty windows, wood-paneled walls, and magnificent brass lamps. The neat rows of jars on the shelves behind the counter and the gleaming tiled floor create something of the air of a pharmacy, but the regulars generally take the chill off the place. Young Amsterdammers come here to sample distinguished Belgian beers.

Canals

De Doffer

Runstraat 12. ☎ 20-6226686. Tram: 1, 2, 5 to Spui. Open: Sun–Thurs noon–2am, Fri–Sat noon–4am.

Candles flicker invitingly into the early hours at this popular student brown cafe. During the afternoon, De Doffer is a quiet, relaxed place for coffee and conversation, but after 6:30pm students pour in and the place becomes crowded, lively, noisy, and filled with smoke. This is a young crowd, and one of a handful of student cafes where the grunge look is in. The decor is typical Amsterdam youth culture—lots of candles, posters for

movies and plays, and simple wood tables and chairs. The food is average but reasonably priced, and the selection impressive for a student eetcafé—eggrolls, bitterballen, jumbo shrimp, grilled lamb chops, poached catfish, and rabbit stew.

Felix Meritis Foyer

Keizersgracht 324. ☎ 20-6262321. Tram: 13, 14, 17 to Westermarkt. Canal Bus: to Keizersgracht. Open: Tues–Fri noon–midnight, Sat 4pm–2am.

Located in an 18thC canal house attached to the Felix Meritis Theater, this cafe consistently attracts an intense, articulate crowd of composers, musicians, and dancers. Despite the modern, black, angular tables and mint-green decor, the neoclassical high ceilings and tall windows set the tone. You can enjoy the splendid view of the Keizersgracht canal from inside this stately golden-age house and take in the peaceful evening rhythm of life on the canals.

Het Land Van Walem

Keizersgracht 449. ☎ 20-6253544. Tram: 1, 2, 5 to Keizersgracht. Open: Sun–Thurs 8:30am–1am, Fri–Sat 9am–2am.

Cafe Walem is best known for its coffee, canalside terrace, wide selection of international newspapers, rear garden complete with classical teahouse, and modern interior design by Rietveld. If you want to sit on the outdoor terrace, get here early—by noon the chances of finding an unoccupied seat are slim. Walem attracts a mixed crowd including students, journalists, and people living or working in the neighborhood. The cafe-restaurant serves good and reasonably priced French/

international cuisine (see listing above).

Het Molenpad

Prinsengracht 653.
☎ 20-6259680. Tram: 1, 2, 5 to Prinsengracht. Open: Sun–Thurs noon–1am, Fri–Sat noon–2am.

A cozy, nicely polished brown cafe on **Prinsengracht** where you can sit and read a book undisturbed or relax on the tiny canalside terrace—at least until 6pm when the cafe becomes impossibly packed with a well-heeled dinner crowd due to its reputation for high quality, reasonably priced French/international cuisine.

The mill path (*molenpad*) that ran just south of here until it was swallowed up by the Fourth Expansion of 1609 is depicted in a painting by the window.

Morlang

Keizersgracht 451.
☎ 20-6252681. Tram: 1, 2, 5 to Keizersgracht. Open: Sun–Thurs 10am–1am, Fri–Sat 10am–2am.

With its fine view of the Keizersgracht, the 2-level Morlang (cafe upstairs, restaurant downstairs), situated in a stately 18thC canal house, offers a pleasant alternative to the overcrowded Het Land Van Walem next door. But there is a reason Walem is crowded and Morlang is not. Despite the fanciful New Age ceiling mural of frolicking whales and angels or the tall windows overlooking the canal, Morlang seems cold and hard compared to the soft wicker furnishings and overall gezelligheid of Walem. However, the food is good, and the menu offers a wide variety of choices including scrambled eggs, vegetarian dishes, pastas, and the usual French/international cafe cuisine.

Odeon

Singel 460. ☎ 20-6249711.
Tram: 1, 2, 5 to Koningsplein.
Cafe open: daily 10pm–4am.
Music: Pop music, daily 10pm–5am; jazz, Fri and Sat 10pm–5am; 60s and 70s music, Thurs–Sat 10pm–5am.

Set in a 17thC neck-gable house designed by Phillips Vingboons, Odeon offers 3 floors of music—jazz in the basement, sixties and seventies music on the top floor, and contemporary pop (everything from house to hip hop) in the middle—to Amsterdammers in their 20s, 30s and 40s. These assorted folks come together for pils, coffee, and conversation in Odeon's brown cafe, with 17thC murals on the ceiling and windows overlooking the Singel canal. Odeon is one of the best places in town to dance if you're 40-something. The Paradiso, a brief walk from Café De Balie, is another (see "Amsterdam After Dark").

De Pels

Huidenstraat 25.
☎ 20-6229037. Tram: 1, 2, 5, to Spui. Open: Sun–Thurs 10am–1am, Fri–Sat 10am–3am.

A small, weathered, bohemian brown cafe, De Pels has a faithful daytime clientele of sardonic artists, journalists, writers, and hipsters. At night, the crowd gets somewhat younger, more affable, and less sardonic. But during the day, expect gezelligheid—with an edge. In the 1960s, De Pels was a Provo (radical environ-mentalists and politicos) cafe full of lively discussions on culture, politics, and art. According to its owner/bartender, it attracted "the people who made Amsterdam the town it is." These folks still drop in from time to time.

Pieper

Prinsengracht 424.
☎ 20-6264775. Tram: 1, 2, 5
to Prinsengracht. Open: weekdays noon–1am, weekends
noon–2am.

Pieper is a snug old brown
cafe on Prinsengracht
possessing that nonchalant
shabbiness that Amster-
dammers cultivate in their
cafes. The photographs and
press cuttings on the wall
remind you that this
unassuming wooden interior
is one of Amsterdam's most
venerable institutions, and the
soft light that falls through the
stained-glass windows invokes
nostalgia in the most hardened
of citizens.

Van Puffelen

Prinsengracht 377.
☎ 20-6246270. Tram: 13, 14,
17 to Westermarkt. Canal Bus: to
Westerkerk. Open: Mon–Thurs
3pm–1am, Fri 3pm–2am, Sat
12pm–2am, Sun 12pm–1am.

The main reason that
fashionable Amsterdammers
flock to this brown cafe,
located on the western rim of
the main canals, is to sample
the exceptional cuisine in the
restaurant at the back, where
the portions are more
substantial and less expensive
than in some of the more
precious French establishments
on the canals (see "Amsterdam's Restaurants A to Z"
above). But Van Puffelen draws
its fashionable, educated
crowds for reasons other than
dinner—it is a lively brown
cafe with a terrace overlooking the Prinsengracht, a bar
serving a wide selection of
Dutch and foreign beers, and a
charming back room with
angel frescoes on the ceiling,
marble tables, and candles
everywhere. In the evening,
the best tables are frequently
reserved. For a good seat,

reserve a table for dinner or
arrive well before 6pm. The
only drawback is the level of
smoke and noise, especially if
you are sitting inside.

Amstel/ Koveniersburgwal/ Waterlooplein

Grand Cafe Dantzig

Zwanenburgwal 15.
☎ 20-6209039. Tram: 9, 14 or
metro to Waterlooplein. Canal
Bus: to City Hall. Open: Mon–
Thurs 10am–1am, Fri–Sat
10am–2am.

A spacious, modern, and
somewhat cold cafe in a
corner of the new Stadhuis/
Muziektheater complex,
Dantzig features a lovely view
of the Amstel River. The broad
terrace facing the Amstel is
packed at the first hint of
spring.

Desmet

Plantage Middenlaan 4a.
☎ 20-6273434. Tram: 7, 9, 14
to Plantage Kerklaan. Open:
6pm–1 or 2am nightly; Sun
before and after film screenings.

The Desmet cafe is a simple,
relaxed brown cafe where you
can sip coffee or beer before
going to the movies and then
return to your table to talk
until 1 or 2am. It is the film
cafe attached to the Art Deco
Desmet movie theater. The
theater shows classics as well as
noncommercial art films and
premieres of new films with
lectures by visiting directors
and actors. On Sunday
afternoons the theater presents
special programs of theme
movies or documentaries. On
Saturday nights and Sunday
afternoons there is also gay
cinema. The cafe serves drinks
and snacks but no full meals.
The clientele are film buffs of
all ages.

De Engelbewaarder

Kloveniersburgwal 59.
☎ 20-6253772. Tram: 4, 9, 16, 24, 25 to Muntplein. Canal Bus: to City Hall. Open: 11am–1am.

This is a quiet, spacious brown cafe near Amsterdam University and Waterlooplein with monstrous Amsterdam School–style iron lamps casting pools of soft light. De Engelbewaarder (The Guardian Angel) maintains its reputation as a literary cafe with regular readings and art exhibitions, and it attracts a mixed clientele of journalists, writers, and students of all ages. On Saturday afternoons, particularly peaceful in this part of town, you can quietly read the newspaper; on Sunday, however, jazz sessions draw considerable crowds. Filling cafe food, a sunlit front room with windows overlooking the canal, a pleasant canalside terrace, and a tempting range of beers make this one of Amsterdam's finest brown cafes.

De IJsbreker

Weesperzijde 23.
☎ 20-6653014. Tram: 6, 7, 10, sneltram 51, or metro to Weesperplein. Open daily 10am–1am.

Mirrors, murals, arched ceilings, and Art Nouveau lamps decorate this elegant fin de siècle cafe. The terrace—on a grassy, tree-lined bank of the Amstel River—is one of the prettiest in town and a fine place to spend a summer afternoon. On winter days, the IJsbreker's excellent hot chocolate is wonderfully warming. The coffee is also good, but the food is otherwise mediocre and the service amazingly slow. The cafe is attached to a concert hall and center for contemporary music (see "The Arts")

and is a popular gathering place for artists and musicians.

De Jaren

Nieuwe Doelenstraat 20-22.
☎ 20-6255771. Tram: 4, 9, 14, 16, 24, 25 to Muntplein. Canal Bus: to City Hall. Open Sun–Thurs 9:30am–1am, Fri–Sat 9:30am–2am.

Both the young and old are drawn to this former bank building, which has been transformed into an airy 2-tiered grand cafe. The interior is fashionably bare, while the Amstel waterfront terraces on both floors are constantly crowded on sunny days. The reading table with its variety of foreign newspapers insures a constant influx of journalists and academics from the nearby university. The cafe is known more for its atmosphere than its food. Soups and sandwiches are good and the salad bar is one of the few in town, but the pastas and other dinner entrees are average at best. The beer list, however, is impressive and includes Grolsch, Columbus (from Amsterdam's small 't IJ brewery), and the Belgian summer brew, Hoegaarden Grand Cru.

Kriterion

Roetersstraat 170.
☎ 20-6231708. Tram: 6, 7, 10 to Roetersstraat. Open: Sun–Thurs 11am–1am, Fri–Sat 11am–3am.

The cafe attached to the Kriterion movie theater is cozy, attractive, and full of students discussing movies, studying for exams—and running the show. For the last 50 years, the cinema has been democratically run by students, a tradition that began in 1945, after World War II, when students who were members of the Dutch Resistance movement started Kriterion.

Before the war, the Art Deco/ Amsterdam School structure had been a Jewish diamond factory—until the Nazis took it over and made it a German theater.

The movie theater and cafe now draw film buffs of all ages, although the cafe tends to attract a youngish crowd. Kriterion considers itself a commercial cinema with "better movies"—everything from *Dangerous Liaisons* to art films by Australian, Italian, or South African directors. Many films are in English or with English subtitles.

Rembrandtsplein

Café De Kroon (Royal Cafe)

Rembrandtsplein 17.
☎ 20-6272011. Tram: 4, 9, 14, to Rembrandtsplein. Open: weekdays 10am–1am, weekends 10am–2am.

This is a posh grand cafe with a big city atmosphere, expensive decor, and a yuppie clientele. Its parquet floors, oriental rugs, overstuffed chairs and sofas, classy ceiling fans, and potted palms are unusual for Amsterdam—and more typical of some grand old hotel in the tropics. Somehow, the loud pop music doesn't quite fit, and it makes normal conversation virtually impossible.

L' Opera

Rembrandtsplein 27.
☎ 20-6275232. Tram: 4, 9, 14 to Rembrandtsplein. Open: weekdays 11am–1am, weekends 11am–2am.

An Art Deco grand cafe, L'Opera has a large terrace on the commercial and sometimes touristy Rembrandtsplein. Sunday afternoon the cafe has live piano music—classical, pop, and jazz. The cafe is becoming increasingly popular with a young, affluent crowd and with summer tourists. But if you want a true sampling of Amsterdam's cafe life, do not spend your whole evening here. Move on—to Café Schiller across the street, De Jaren a few blocks away, and then a brown cafe or two.

Café Schiller

Rembrandtsplein 26.
☎ 20-6249846. Tram: 4, 9, 14 to Rembrandtsplein. Open: weekdays 4pm–1am, weekends 4pm–2 or 3am.

Café Schiller is too small to be a grand cafe, and too upholstered to be a brown cafe. Although it's rumored to be a Deco cafe, only the hand-painted mosaic overlooking the bar is truly Deco. But Schiller's is most definitely a comfortable and charming cafe with an atmosphere more gezellig than most on Rembrandtsplein. In the 1920s and 1930s, the cafe attracted cabaret artists who stopped at Schiller. Paintings of these former customers, done by Mr. Schiller on Sunday afternoons, still decorate the walls. Nowadays people come to Café Schiller for dinner or drinks before ballet and opera performances at the Stopera, musicals at the Carré, and films at the Tuschinski Cinema. It offers good cafe food and homemade desserts at rea-sonable prices (see listing above).

Spui

Gollem

Raamsteeg 4. ☎ 20-6266645. Tram: 1, 2, 5 to Spui. Open: Sun–Thurs 4pm–1am, Fri–Sat 4pm–2am.

This snug brown cafe tucked away in a narrow street near the Spui was the first "beercafe" in the Netherlands and the first to serve Bok beer on a commercial scale. Gollem is internationally famous for its selection of Dutch and Belgian beers; it has 200 varieties of beer and eight on tap. The cafe also has an excellent selection of American jazz and blues tapes played softly enough to not drown out conversation. In fact, Gollem is designed to promote conversation since the semicircular brown bar is small enough for all the people sitting at it to talk to one another. For more privacy, you can climb a flight of stairs and retreat to a cozy room in the back with comfortable tables, beamed ceilings, and lots of brown wood. Gollem is a cafe steeped in Amsterdam beer culture, and, not surprisingly, the decor is devoted to beer: A variety of beer bottles, coasters, and labels decorate the walls, and a long list of available beer is written on the blackboard behind the bar.

Hoppe

Spui 20. ☎ 20-6237849. Tram: 1, 2, 5 to Spui. Open: "sit" bar weekdays 8am–1am, weekends 8am–2am; "stand bar" weekdays 11am–1am, weekends 11am–2am.

Dating from 1670, the Hoppe claims to be the second oldest bar in Amsterdam (Cafés Chris and Karpershoek both claim to be the oldest). Hoppe is an institution—a traditional old brown cafe complete with sawdust on the floor, old Dutch paintings on the walls, and traditionally conversational and artful bartenders (some of whom win beer drafting competitions). Into Hoppe's smoke-choked sawdust-strewn interior are crammed a curiousbundle of people: professors of literature, politicians, unemployed

seamen, tourists. The crush is almost always suffocating and noisy, although on sunny days it eases slightly as the hordes of drinkers spill out into the street, conversing in any of up to 6 languages. After 6pm in the summer it's particularly busy as the briefcase crowd arrives for after-work socializing.

Luxembourg

Spui 22-24. ☎ 20-6206264. Tram: 1, 2, 5 to Spui. Open: weekdays 10am–1am, weekends 10am–2am.

A handsome cafe with plump chairs, dark woodwork (à la brown cafe), and artfully distressed walls that create an impression of antiquity, Luxembourg is in fact modern and relatively new. Café Luxembourg is best in the morning when you can quietly read the international press at the large reading table or sit in the back room watching the boats go by on the Singel canal. It is overcrowded by the late afternoon and impossibly packed on a Saturday with a fashionable beautiful-people set who are very much on display. The front terrace is directly across from the historic statue of Het Lieverdje, the "little darling" who figured in some of the 1960s happenings on the Spui.

De Zwart

Spuistraat 334. Tram: 1, 2, 5 to Spui. Open: weekdays 11am–1am, weekends 11am–2am.

De Zwart is an old brown cafe with yellowed walls and thick rugs for tablecloths; it is crowded, sociable, more bohemian and less businesslike than the Hoppe across the alley. The terrace is a pleasant place to sit late on summer afternoons to people-watch as the popular Spui cafes come to life. Since The Athenaeum Bookstore and Newsstand are directly across the street, De Zwart is also a convenient spot to read the paper.

Jordaan

Nol

Westerstraat 109.
☎ 20-6245380. Tram: 13, 14, 17 to Marnixstraat. Open: weekdays 9pm–3am, weekends 9pm–4am. Closed: Tues.

Cafe Nol is both touristy and authentic. Amsterdammers and foreign tourists alike come to Nol to experience "the quintessential Jordaan" in a friendly cafe gaudily done in red neon, fringed red lampshades, and porcelain figurines. Expect knee-slapping accordion music, jolly singalongs, and women with blonde bouffants, leopard skin stretch pants, and gold lamé pumps. The Jordaan taste in music, furnishings, and clothes somehow holds firm despite the influx of trendy young artists and yuppies. Nol features karaoke music on Wednesdays with typical Jordaan "Amsterdam music" and popular local singers stopping by to sing along. Unfortunately, Nol no longer has live bands.

Papeneiland

Prinsengracht 2.
☎ 20-6241989. Tram: 3 to Haarlemmerplein. Canal Bus: to Westerkerk. Open: Sun–Thurs 11am–1am, Fri–Sat 11am–2am.

A cozy brown cafe on the edge of the Jordaan, occupying a 17thC step-gable house blessed with a picturesque view of Brouwersgracht and Prinsengracht. The cafe's name is inscribed in ornate calligraphy on the exceptionally tall windows,

while the interior is evocative of a Dutch Old Master, with Delft tiles and antique brass hanging lamps. The view from the front window was captured by Breitner on a cold winter's day in 1901 in a painting that now hangs in the **Amsterdams Historisch Museum.**

De Prins

Prinsengracht 124.
☎ 20-6461547. Tram: 13, 14, 17 to Westermarkt. Canal Bus: to Westerkerk. Open: weekdays 11am–1am, weekends 11am–2am.

Set in an 18thC canal house, this brown cafe has beamed ceilings, smoke-stained walls, modern paintings, soccer trophies, lively conversation, and tasty dinners. Its tall sash windows overlook a particularly nice part of the Prinsengracht canal. In the summer, its doors are open and customers spill into the street. In the 1970s, a far-thinking cafe owner realized that people liked the old brown cafes, so he decided to create some. He rented vacant cafes, painted them brown, and gave them names that began with P such as De Prins, De Princess, and De Pels. These bars became well-known for their comradery, their bohemian clientele, and their soccer clubs. One of the original "P" cafes, De Prins still participates in soccer with its surviving "P" comrades. Soccer team photos, a few trophies, and a neon "P" won in a match are proudly displayed behind the bar. The De Prins aims to "keep it gezellig" for solo cafe-goers, especially women, and unduly aggressive men are asked to leave the bar. De Prins also serves inexpensive and good cafe food (see listing above).

De Reiger

Nieuwe Leliestraat 34.
☎ 20-6247426. Tram: 13, 14,
17 to Westermarkt. Canal Bus: to
Westerkerk. Open: Mon–Thurs
11am–1am, Fri–Sat 11am–2am,
Sun noon–1am.

De Reiger, a typical brown cafe in the Jordaan, is divided into 2 parts: the bar and the cafe-restaurant. The bar has the usual funky wooden tables and chairs, smoke-yellowed walls, friendly bartenders, and neighborly clientele, which gives it the feeling of an extended "living room" for the young professionals and stock brokers who have recently moved into the neighborhood. The cafe-restaurant, with its larger tables and magazines neatly stacked on the window sill, is comfortable for sipping coffee, reading the paper, or eating dinner. The cafe food is quite good (see listing above) and attracts a regular dinner crowd.

't Smalle

Egelantiersgracht 12.
☎ 20-6239617. Tram: 13, 14,
17 to Westermarkt. Canal Bus:
to Westerkerk. Open: weekdays
11am–1am; weekends 11am–
2am.

This popular cafe occupies an ivy-covered 18thC house just a few blocks from De Prins on the edge of the Jordaan. The interior—originally the distillery and tasting house of Pieter Hoppe—has been tastefully restored, and the golden light that filters through the stained-glass windows evokes the mellow hue of a Rembrandt painting. 't Smalle is especially attractive on dark winter evenings, with candles flickering at every table, or on summer evenings when the canalside terrace is a relaxing spot to pull up a chair and watch the ducks swim by.

The only drawback is that such a congenial—and tiny—cafe is almost invariably bursting at the seams. Most of the customers are an alternative crowd in their 30s and 40s.

Thijssen

Brouwersgracht 107.
☎ 20-6238994. Tram: 13, 14,
17 to Marnixstraat. Open: Sun–
Thurs 10am–1am, Fri 10am–2am,
Sat 8am–2am.

Named after the socialist writer Theo Thijssen, an educator who wrote of his youth in the Jordaan in his novel *Kees de Jongen,* Thijssen is a brown cafe that attracts a younger, more fashionable crowd than either De Prins or 't Smalle. Thijssen is large and pretty with plenty of tables inside, a long bar, and a terrace overlooking a square in which there is a statue of Thijssen—and a lively Saturday morning produce market. This is a nice spot to stop when walking through the Jordaan (see "Amsterdam Walks") or visiting the nearby markets.

De Twee Prinsen

Prinsenstraat 27.
☎ 20-6249722. Tram: 13, 14,
17 to Westermarkt. Canal Bus:
to Westerkerk. Open: weekdays
10am–1am, weekends 10am–
2am.

The Twee Prinsen is a low-key "living-room bar," one of those small, gezellig brown cafes with an extended family atmosphere. On a given night, people may be riveted to the soccer game while others are reading the paper or talking. The customers, ranging from their 20s to 50s, are largely a blue-jeaned, alternative crowd—unlike the younger scene across the street at the more modern and less casual De Vergulde Gaeper. Both cafes have extensive canalside terraces, making them popular on summer evenings.

De Twee Zwaantijes

Prinsengrac3ht 114.
☎ 20-6252729. Tram: 13, 14, 17 to Westermarkt. Canal Bus: to Westerkerk. Open: Sun–Thurs 8pm–1am, Fri–Sat 8pm–3am.
This is a neighborhood Jordaan brown bar with a traditional working class Jordaan clientele that still plays the old "Amsterdam music" to which the regulars burst into song.
The cafe brings in some first-class—and well-known—local singers. If you want to experience gezelligheid Jordaan-style in a more modest setting than Café Nol, this is the place to go—especially if you like down-to-earth sing alongs. (See "Walk 2: The Jordaan" in "Amsterdam Walks.")

Museum Quarter/ Vondelpark

Bodega Keyser

Van Baerlestraat 96.
☎ 20-6711441. Tram: 3, 5, 12, 16 to Museumplein. Open: noon–midnight. Closed Sun.
This is a popular hang-out for classical musicians and for music lovers of all ages before and after concerts at the Concertgebouw across the street. It's a traditional cafe (in operation since 1905) with dark wood interior, Turkish rugs covering the bar tables, and years of accumulated gezelligheid. Keyser is also a good cafe after a day of museums, browsing in antique stores, or shopping on P. C. Hooftstraat, the exclusive shopping street. It is convenient if you are staying in the Museum Quarter or in Amsterdam South.

Vertigo

Vondelpark 3A. ☎ 20-6123021. Tram: 1,2, 5, 6, 7, to Leidseplein. Canal Bus: to Leidseplein. Open: Sun–Thurs 11am–2am, Fri–Sat 11am–3am. Outdoor terrace is open 11am–11pm in good weather.
Cafe Vertigo, attached to the Film Museum, has a lovely and extensive 2-tiered terrace overlooking a lake in Vondelpark. The upper deck is sunny while the ground-level terrace is pleasantly shaded by large, leafy trees. Cafe Vertigo attracts a mixed, but generally sophisticated bunch, drawing in joggers, bicyclists, movie- and museum-goers, shoppers, intellectuals, students, aspiring actors, and a handful of tourists lucky enough to wander in. The ground-level terrace serves only drinks and light snacks, except in the summer on Friday nights when Vertigo serves a tempting outdoor fish-fry.

ACCOMMODATIONS

Choosing the Accommodation That's Right for You

The selection of hotels in this guide has been made not only to give a wide choice of price and location, but also with such priorities in mind as hospitality, comfort, and atmosphere. I have used 1 star (★) to indicate recommended hotels and 2 stars (★★) for highly recommended hotels.

Note that many of the larger hotels now have **non-smoking** rooms as a courtesy to American tourists. Also, some Amsterdam hotels do not charge for **children** under 12 as long as they stay in their parents' room, although some hotels will charge from Dfl. 15 to Dfl. 30 to bring in an extra bed or crib.

Hotel Neighborhoods

For many people a visit to Amsterdam would not be complete without staying in a historic house on one of the **canals.** Here you can move away from the crowds and neon of tourist streets and see how Amsterdammers live. You'll find havens of *gezelligheid* in small neighborhood shops, restaurants, and cafes within a 10-minute tram ride and easy walking distance of major sights. The main drawbacks—steep staircases, small rooms, and impossible parking—are offset by the charm of oak-beamed ceilings, peaceful canals, and 17thC gables. Of the canalside hotels, the Ambassade, Pulitzer, and Canal House are the most luxurious and reminiscent of the golden age. Even the small, inexpensive canal-house hotels may have cozy lobbies done up with oriental carpets, Dutch tiles, and European antiques; they may also have terrific canal views, although the guest rooms might be surprisingly stark and small.

Another popular location is the **Museum Quarter** near the **Rijksmuseum, Van Gogh Museum, Stedelijk Museum, Concertgebouw,** and **Leidseplein.** The **Vondelpark,** an oasis of lawns, ponds, weeping willows, and biking/running trails, is also nearby. Hotels in this area are often situated in 19thC mansions influenced by Cuypers (designer of the Rijksmuseum), the Amsterdam School, and Art Nouveau architecture. Neighborhoods are quiet and residential; parking is easy.

A hotel **overlooking the Amstel** puts you in the midst of history and grandeur, especially if you stay at the Amstel Hotel or Hotel de l'Europe. This is a neighborhood where historical sites from different periods converge: the Munttoren (Mint Tower, 1490 and 1618), Amstel Hotel (1867), Hotel de l'Europe (1895), Rembrandt House (mid 1600s), the old Jewish neighborhood with the Portuguese Synagogue (1675), the Jewish Historical Museum (made up of three 17th to 18thC Ashkenazi synagogues), and the new Statehouse and Muziektheater (1986). Oudekerk (1565) and what remains of medieval Amsterdam are a 10-minute walk away, as is the red-light district and shopping streets.

Another option is to rent a **houseboat on the Amstel River,** which allows you to experience Amsterdam from an entirely different perspective—from the water. Amsterdam House (Amstel 176a, 1017 AE Amsterdam, ☎ 20-6262577), an agency offering nightly, weekly, or monthly houseboat rentals, has 6 surprisingly spacious and tastefully decorated houseboats on the Amstel in a historic and fashionable neighborhood near Hotel de l'Europe. The furniture is modern, the kitchens and bathrooms well equipped, and the picture windows delightful. The dining and living room areas are roomy and bright, while the bedrooms are small and cottagelike, with white-wood paneling and river views. You can open your windows and throw bread crumbs to passing families of ducks or, if you're lucky, swans. The only drawbacks to on-the-water living are the mosquitoes, especially in the hot summer months, and an occasional flotilla of beer cans.

Leidseplein is at the center of Amsterdam's nightlife, where theaters, cinemas, and live music can be found. The Lido, with its casino and dinner theater, is just off the square. Although the Leidseplein attracts young neohippies, street musicians, and mimes, it also draws a sophisticated older crowd and is the home of a repertory theater, fine restaurants, and a thriving cafe scene.

Only a 10-minute walk from the museums and Vondelpark and 10 minutes from popular canalside cafes, this is a good home base for those who like to feel at the center of things—and who can tolerate the convergence of trolleys, bicycles, taxis, and bewildered pedestrians on the busy streets.

Another area worth considering is the **Historic Center,** close to Centraal Station and convenient for those making excursions outside Amsterdam. However, a good hotel in this area does not come cheap and parking is again virtually impossible, although many larger hotels have their own garages. Another drawback is that the neighborhoods near Dam Square and Centraal Station tend to be scruffy, especially late at night. Damrak, the busy tourist street, is well lit and crowded even past midnight, but Dam Square is not. Although Amsterdam is safe compared to most American and European cities, you should avoid walking through the Dam alone at night. When in doubt—take a cab.

Hotels in **Amsterdam South** are popular with businesspeople visiting the World Trade Center or RAI exhibition center and are also close to suburban rail stations with frequent services to Schiphol airport, Leiden, The Hague, Delft, and Rotterdam. They are also good choices for anyone with a car since parking is easy and hotel lots are large. The main drawback of the area is that it is somewhat removed from the principal sights, although the city is really quite compact and the Concertgebouw and museums are closer than they may seem—5 minutes by tram, 10 to 15 minutes by bicycle.

Chain Hotels

Although branches of most international hotel chains can be found in Amsterdam, including a Hilton in the wealthy Amsterdam-Zuid neighborhood (Apollolaan 138, 1077 BG, ☎ 20-6780780, fax 20-6626688), a Holiday Inn Crowne Plaza in the old town (Nieuwe Zijds Voorburgwal 5, 1012 RC, ☎ 20-6200500, fax 20-6201173), and a Marriott near Leidseplein (Stadhouderskade 21, 1054 ES, ☎ 20-6075555, fax 20-6075511), they reflect scarcely any Dutch character. However, these hotels guarantee travelers a high standard of service, hairdryers, minibars, large rooms, and few unpleasant surprises. But they lack an essential component of the Dutch atmosphere, an ingredient both visual and tactile, both personal and social—*gezelligheid*. To find it, you must venture outside most international hotel chains (with the exception of the Pulitzer). I suggest trying a hotel on the canals or near Vondelpark to find a lobby that feels like a living room, a *kopje koffie* (little cup of coffee) amiably poured for you at breakfast, and a plump cat asleep on the bar.

Reservations

The standard influx of summer tourists plus an international conference or two can fill all the hotels in Amsterdam and send last-minute travelers to surrounding towns like Leiden and Haarlem, so it is wise to book a month or two in advance for a July or August visit, especially over weekends. Even if you are an experienced go-with-the-flow traveler, book 2 to 3 weeks in advance unless you are willing to stay in budget hotels, share a bath, and climb 3 to 4 stories of steep, winding stairs. Easter, the Queen's Birthday, the Christmas holidays, and tulip season are also very busy times in the city. This is not to say that last minute bookings are impossible—just unpredictable.

To Book in Advance   If you already know where you would like to stay, I recommend calling or faxing the hotel directly. If you don't know, the Netherlands Board of Tourism in Chicago (☎ 312-819-0300) can send you a list of hotels and help you choose one. The Netherlands Reservations Center (P.O. Box 404, 2260 AK Leidschendam, ☎ 70-3202500, fax 70-3202611) provides a free reservations service throughout the Netherlands; you can reserve by letter, telephone, or fax.

Winging It   For last-minute reservations during high season, try calling hotels around checkout time (11am) to see about cancellations or early check-outs. In a pinch, try the hotel reservation services of the **VVV** (tourist office) at Schiphol airport or across from Centraal Station. The VVV checks hotel availability and makes reservations when possible (for a 5-guilder booking fee). At Centraal Station in high season, expect a daunting line and a 1-hour wait.

Prices

The price categories quoted for each hotel in this book are intended as a rough guide to what you can expect to pay. There are 5 categories: budget (**$**), inexpensive (**$$**), moderate (**$$$**), expensive (**$$$$**), and very expensive (**$$$$$**). The very expensive hotels are luxurious, offering all the usual amenities plus huge tubs, good restaurants, and conference facilities; many have saunas and fitness centers. Expensive and moderately priced hotels may be comfortable, architecturally interesting—and more *gezellig* than the luxurious ones. Inexpensive hotels often have cozy breakfast rooms and lobbies, tidy gardens, and clean but bland bedrooms. Cheap hotels vary widely, although they are almost always clean and neat, with winding stairs and cotlike beds.

Many hotels offer significantly lower rates during the low season—October through March. Some hotels add beds for a 3rd person at surprisingly reasonable rates, and many hotels let children under 12 share their parents' room for no extra charge, which can represent a considerable saving for a family.

Breakfast

Breakfast is often, but not always, included in the price in the less expensive hotels. Typical Dutch hotel breakfasts consist of fruit juice, cold meats, a boiled egg, sliced Gouda cheese, various breads, jam, and coffee. The luxury hotels offer ample American-style breakfasts at about Dfl. 24 to Dfl. 30, although breakfast is sometimes complimentary. If breakfast is not included, try a cafe for less expensive and equally tasty breakfasts (see "Amsterdam's Cafes" in "Dining" for suggestions) or sample Sunday brunch Dutch-style at the Amstel Hotel or the Brasserie van Baerle. Pancakes may seem like a good option for breakfast, but the Dutch think of them as lunch or dinner; consequently, pancake restaurants tend to open at noon.

Parking

Some of the larger hotels have parking lots of their own, while smaller ones sometimes make paid parking arrangements with lots nearby. Street parking is relatively easy in Vondelpark and the Museum Quarter, but this is often metered parking.

Price Chart

Price categories are based on the cost of a 3-course meal and do not include beverages, tax, or tip. For the eetcafés, 3 courses means entree, potato, and salad or vegetable.

$ = less than Dfl. 120
$$ = Dfl. 120–Dfl. 210
$$$ = Dfl. 211–Dfl. 310
$$$$ = Dfl. 311–Dfl. 410
$$$$$ = over Dfl. 410

Transportation to Your Hotel

The free **KLM Hotel Bus** will take you directly to most of the larger hotels, and it will also drop you off at a large hotel which may be convenient if you are staying at a small hotel nearby. If you are staying at a hotel far from a major drop-off point, you can take the train to Centraal Station and then catch a bus, tram, or cab to your hotel. With heavy luggage, you might consider springing for a cab. See "Getting Around" in **Basics** for more information.

Hotels by Neighborhood

*Overlooking the
Amstel River*

★★Amstel Inter-Continental
Hotel. **$$$$$**
★Amsterdam House.
$$/$$$
Doelen Karena. **$$$$**
★★Hotel de l'Europe.
$$$$$

On the Canals

Agora. **$$**
★★Ambassade. **$$$**
★★Canal House. **$$/$$$**
Estheréa. **$$$**
Hotel Hegra. **$/$$**
Prinsenhof. **$$**
★★Pulitzer. **$$$$$**
Seven Bridges. **$$**
Van Onna. **$**
★Wiechmann. **$$**

The Historic Center

Aspen. **$**
Grand Hotel Krasnapolsky.
$$$$/$$$$$
★Holiday Inn Crowne Plaza.
$$$$$

Ramada Renaissance.
$$$$$
RHO. **$$**
Roode Leeuw. **$$$**
SAS Royal Hotel. **$$$$$**
Swissotel Amsterdam
Ascot Hotel. **$$$$/
$$$$$**
★★Victoria Hotel. **$$$$**

Leidseplein

Barbizon Centre. **$$$$$**
★Hotel American. **$$$$$**

*Museum Quarter/
Vondelpark*

Atlas. **$$**
★Europa '92. **$$**
★★De Filosoof. **$$**
★★Jan Luyken. **$$$**
Owl. **$$**
Piet Hein. **$$/$$$**
★Prinsen. **$$**
★★Toro. **$$**
Wijnobel. **$**

Amsterdam South

Amsterdam Hilton. **$$$$$**
Okura. **$$$$/$$$$$**

Critic's Choice

Although there are many appealing hotels in Amsterdam, some stand out from all the rest. For *gezelligheid* in a historic canal house, try the **Canal House** or the **Ambassade Hotel.** The Ambassade is the most private and romantic, while the Canal House is best for those traveling alone (the management encourages social gatherings by serving tea all day). The **Pulitzer** is the most historic, located in 24 canal houses dating from the 17th and 18th centuries. For traveling in grand style, the **Amstel Hotel** is the most regal, and **Hotel de l'Europe** the most chic. Of the small, Museum Quarter hotels, the **Jan Luyken** is the most elegant. **Hotel American,** the most Deco, is perfect for hipsters, rock and rollers, and business types with bohemian tendencies. **De Filosoof,** the most intellectual and offbeat hotel, is not surprisingly the least likely roost for conventioneers. The best accommodations for conventioneers are at the **Okura** and **l'Europe** hotels. The **Victoria** is the most *gezellig* business hotel; for the moment, it also has the best gym, although the Okura may outdo it within the year. For backpackers who can do stairs, the best deals are **Seven Bridges, Wijnobel, Van Onna,** and **Aspen.** And the best place for frisky kids is the **Toro,** and other hotels near the playgrounds of Vondelpark. For women traveling alone, the best places (in a variety of price ranges) are the **Canal House, De Filosoof, Van Onna,** and the **Pulitzer.**

Amsterdam's Hotels A to Z

Agora

Singel 462, 1017 AW Amsterdam. ☎ 20-6272200; fax: 20-6272202. 16 rooms, 12 with bath. Tram: 1, 2, 5 to Koningsplein. AE, DC, MC, V. Breakfast included. **$$**.

This recently renovated 16thC canal house has a comfortable lounge and a cheerful breakfast room overlooking a garden. Both the breakfast room and lounge are very Dutch, with overstuffed chairs, vases of flowers, oriental carpets, and antique-style furniture. Guest rooms are small and not nearly as cozy; those at the front overlook lively university buildings on the Singel canal, while back rooms have a view of the garden. The location is lovely, on a canal near the flower market, the Spui, and the Amstel, but traffic from a busy cross street nearby makes the hotel noisy during the day.

★★Ambassade

Herengracht 341, 1016 AZ Amsterdam. ☎ 20-6262333; fax: 20-6245321. 52 rooms, all with bath. Canal Bus: Westerkerk or Keizersgracht. AE, DC, MC, V. Breakfast included. **$$$**.

Those who rank romance and ambiance above modern amenities and parking garages should try for a room in this privately owned hotel. Located in a row of 17th and 18thC merchants' houses on the stately and quiet Herengracht—the gentleman's canal—a stay at the Ambassade will make you feel like a house guest in Old Amsterdam. The regal canal houses are furnished with beautiful antique clocks, chairs, and paintings, and the owner's personal collection of china is displayed in the lounge adjoining the airy breakfast room. Each guest room is spacious, perfectly lit by a combination of sunlight and well-placed lamps, and provided with several comfortable chairs and a desk. The only drawback is that a few of these rooms, like those of many houses from this period, are only accessible by winding, narrow stairs designed for the surefooted. Ask for a room with elevator access if this is a concern. Suites are a bargain— traditional Dutch charm at half the price of a luxury hotel. Some suites have 2 stories—a sitting room with steps winding up to a sleeping loft with broad oak rafters. For the summer season, book a room months in advance. Try for a view of the Herengracht from the 2nd or 3rd story. First floor and ground level rooms put you close to street sounds. *Amenities:* In-room safes.

★★Amstel Inter-Continental Hotel

L Professor Tulpplein 1, 1018 GX Amsterdam. ☎ 20-6226060; fax: 20-6225808. 79 rooms, all with bath. Tram: 6, 7, 10 to Oosteinde; sneltram 51 or metro to Weesperplein. Canal Bus: Waterlooplein. AE, DC, MC, V. **$$$$$**.

This grand palace hotel, built in 1867 by the dynamic entrepreneur Samuel Sarphati, is the most splendid place to stay in Amsterdam, with its magnificent entrance hall and view of the Amstel and its rooms with antique furniture, rich mahogany woodwork, and oriental rugs. The hotel was recently restored throughout in a bid to retain the loyalty of the monarchs and rock stars who have stayed here in the past, and it worked. The Rolling Stones stay here, with Mick Jagger in the Royal Suite. All rooms come equipped with towel heaters, telephones with private answering machines, video and CD players, and a classy incarnation of the minibar— a tray with fine liquors set out in crystal and glass decanters. The Amstel is *gezellig* in a regal sort of way. Some, however, might find the atmosphere here a bit much, the chandeliers too overwhelming, the staff too studied and hushed. The Amstel takes class seriously, and a protective concierge may greet your casually dressed friends with an *ongezellig* (unfriendly) response.

A good time to experience the full grandeur of the Amstel Inter-Continental is at its Sunday brunch served in the glittering Spiegelzaal (reservations essential, Sun 11am–2pm). *Amenities:* Jacuzzi, sauna, Turkish bath, massage, beauty salon, 2 restaurants (one with a Michelin star), boat tours via antique boat available, conference facilities, 1 room wheelchair accessible.

★Amsterdam House B.V.

Amstel 176a, 1017 AE Amsterdam. ☎ 20-6262577; fax: 20-6262987. 30 apartments, 6 houseboats. Tram: 4, 9, 14, 16, 24, 25 to Muntplein. Canal Bus: City Hall. AE, DC, MC, V. **$$/$$$**.

If you want to feel like an Amsterdam insider, or if you need to stay in Amsterdam for an extended period of time, you can rent a houseboat or riverside apartment on the Amstel—at privileged, lovely locations. Amsterdam House rents 6 houseboats on the Amstel River in a scenic and historic neighborhood near Hotel de l'Europe, Muntplein, and the Muziektheater. Thirty apartments are also for rent at locations on the Amstel and on Spuistraat (near the Amsterdam Historical Museum). Considering the locations—and the hardwood floors, tasteful furniture, fully equipped kitchens and bathrooms, and beautiful views—these apartments are a real find. The management is accommodating and friendly, and the apartments are generally clean and well kept, but at least one splendid apartment—with terrace, fashionable furniture, and stunning view—could use new linoleum in the bathroom and a paint job on the bedroom ceiling.

One-, two-, and three-bedroom apartments and houseboats are available. Apartments rent by the night, week, or month. *Amenities:* Some apartments have sauna, grand piano, and/or compact disc player. All apartments and boats have fully equipped kitchens. Linens and house-cleaning are provided.

Aspen

Raadhuisstraat 31, Amsterdam. ☎ 20-6266714; fax: 20-6200866. 8 rooms, 4 with bath. Tram: 13, 14, 17 to Westerkerk. Canal Bus: Westerkerk or Keizersgracht. No credit cards. **$**. This is a small, friendly, privately owned hotel in the architecturally interesting arcade buildings (designed by A. L. van Gendt), with a manager who lives in an enviable apartment on the 2nd floor. The carpets are new, the rooms impeccably clean, the atmosphere more cheerful than many budget hotels, and you'll often find a room available here when other hotels are booked. However, the furniture is minimal, and the staircase steep, winding, and a real challenge with heavy

luggage (expect to carry your own). Breakfast is not available at the hotel, but can be found at cafes down the street. Another advantage is the location—2 blocks from Westerkerk and the lively cafes of the Jordaan. To avoid the early morning traffic noise on Raadhuisstraat, ask for a back room with a garden view.

Atlas

Van Eegenstraat 64, 1071 GK Amsterdam. ☎ 20-6766336; fax: 20-6717633. 23 rooms, all with bath. Tram: 2 from Centraal Station to Willems Parkway. AE, DC, MC, V. Breakfast included. **$$**. A small, comfortable family-owned hotel with intriguing Art Nouveau brickwork, stained glass, and carved wooden door on the building's exterior. But a graceful mahogany staircase and a few lamps are all that remain of the Art Nouveau interior since the hotel has been thoroughly modernized on the inside. The modern furniture is simple but comfortable and the atmosphere personal and relaxed. Mrs. Lensink prepares breakfast and coffee behind a small bar in the light, cozy breakfast room while Gerard Lensink, who refers to the Atlas as "the smallest 4-star hotel in Amsterdam," manages the front desk. Views are unremarkable, but the location on a quiet street bordering the Vondelpark is convenient for joggers, shoppers, and museum-goers. *Amenities:* Small bar, room service.

Barbizon Centre

Stadhouderskade 7, 1054 ES Amsterdam. ☎20-6851351; fax: 20-6851611. 239 rooms, all with bath. Tram: 1, 2, 5 to Stadhouderskade or 6, 7, 10 to Leidseplein. Canal Bus:

Leidseplein. AE, DC, MC, V.
$$$$$.
Contemporary art exhibits
and cozy restaurants make the
Barbizon more *gezellig* than
most American-style hotels.
The bedrooms are tastefully
furnished in modern decor,
although the hotel is currently
renovating all rooms in a
British Victorian style for a
warmer look, with rich wine
upholstery and reproductions
of period furniture. Back
rooms are quiet, with large
windows but nothing much to
look at, while rooms at the
front overlook the bright lights
of the **Leidseplein.** Tickets to
the nearby Lido dinner theater
are free and provided at the
front desk. *Amenities:* Air-
conditioning; in-room safes;
2 restaurants; bar; fitness center
with weight room, sauna, and
Turkish bath (50% discount for
hotel guests); business and
secretarial services available;
conference facilities; 1 room
wheelchair accessible.

★★Canal House

Keizersgracht 148, 1015 CX
Amsterdam. ☎ 20-6225182;
fax: 20-6241317. 26 rooms, all
with bath. Tram: 13, 14, 17 to
Westermarkt. Canal Bus:
Keizersgracht. AE, DC, MC, V.
Breakfast included. **$$/$$$**.
This small, friendly hotel
situated in 2 historic canal-
houses is owned by an
American couple who have
lovingly decorated the rooms
and halls with antiques, period
clothing, hand-painted plates,
photos, paintings, and an
artful variety of visual
surprises. The atmosphere
blends Old Holland canal
house with New England inn.
The bedrooms are small, cozy,
and pretty, with wood or
velvet headboards and
American country quilts.
Rooms on the front, including

a few attic hideaways, offer fine
canal views, while those at the
back overlook a peaceful,
manicured garden, which is
illuminated at night. Some of
the rooms, accessible only by
winding stairs, have exposed
brick or wooden rafters and
beams, and are well worth the
climb. There are no televisions
or radios, but there is conversation and tea and coffee
downstairs in the Victorian-
style bar. Antique furniture
and hand-painted Italian plates
give the breakfast room/
lounge a touch of golden age
opulence, but the leather
armchairs are more worn than
comfy and the carpet has seen
more colorful days. An
excellent place for solo
travelers since the owners and
desk clerks go out of their way
to help guests.

Doelen Karena

Nieuwe Doelenstraat 24, 1012
CP Amsterdam. ☎ 20-6220722;
fax: 20-6221084. 85 rooms, all
with bath. Tram: 4, 9, 14, 16, 24,
25 to Muntplein. Canal Bus:
Waterlooplein. AE, DC, MC, V.
Breakfast included. **$$$$**.
One of the oldest hotels in
Amsterdam, the Doelen is
atmospheric and well located,
but its former grandeur has
somewhat faded (along with
the carpets). Still, the paneled
breakfast room overlooking
the Amstel, the stained-glass
windows, the antiques in the
lobby and hallways, and the
lively staff (including a cook
who sculpts mermaids out of
mussels and butter) make this
an appealing hotel for those
who put history—and
gezelligheid—before pristine
furnishings. It would be hard
to find a better hotel from
which to explore Rembrandt's
Amsterdam since this impressive 19thC neoclassical
building stands on the site of

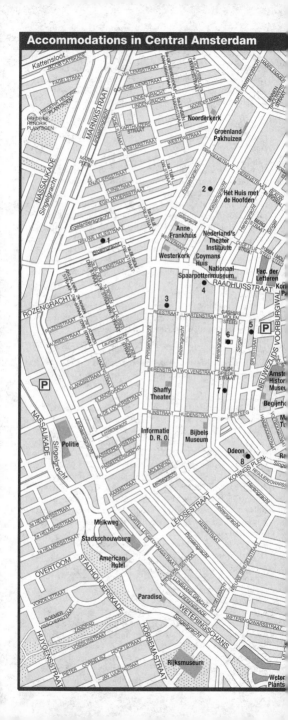

Accommodations in Central Amsterdam

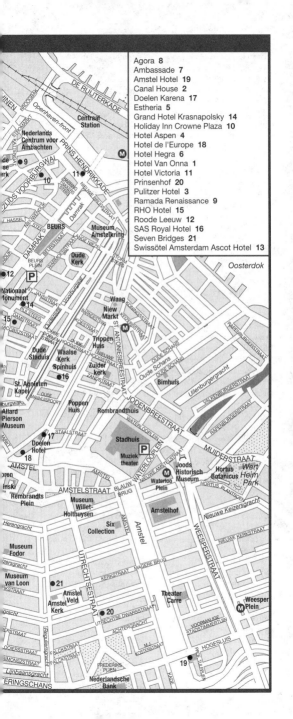

Agora **8**
Ambassade **7**
Amstel Hotel **19**
Canal House **2**
Doelen Karena **17**
Estheria **5**
Grand Hotel Krasnapolsky **14**
Holiday Inn Crowne Plaza **10**
Hotel Aspen **4**
Hotel de l'Europe **18**
Hotel Hegra **6**
Hotel Van Onna **1**
Hotel Victoria **11**
Prinsenhof **20**
Pulitzer Hotel **3**
Ramada Renaissance **9**
RHO Hotel **15**
Roode Leeuw **12**
SAS Royal Hotel **16**
Seven Bridges **21**
Swissôtel Amsterdam Ascot Hotel **13**

the medieval tower where Rembrandt painted the *Night Watch*. Suite 515 offers a fine view down the Kloveniersburgwal canal to the WAAG, the former weigh house where *The Anatomy Lesson of Dr. Tulp* was painted. For modern comfort, ask for a room with a renovated bathroom and tub. *Amenities:* Minibar, safe at reception desk, 2 breakfast rooms, restaurant, 3 conference rooms, private boat landing for water taxis and other boats.

Estheréa

Singel 303-307, 1012 WJ Amsterdam. ☎ 20-6245146; fax: 20-6239001. 75 rooms, all with bath. Tram: 1, 2, 5 to Spui. AE, DC, MC, V. Breakfast included. **$$$**.
This friendly hotel is located near the most beautiful area of the old city, the small specialty shops of the Prinsengracht and Herengracht neighborhoods, and the cafes of the Spui. The charms of this quiet hotel lie in its view of the Singel canal, as well as its cozy lobby and 17thC facade. The rooms are generally bland and small but well-equipped. Ask for a room with a view of the canal.

★Europa '92

1e Constantijn Huygensstraat 103-105, 1054 BV Amsterdam. ☎ 20-6188808; fax: 20-6836405. 32 rooms, all with bath. Tram: 1 to Overtoom. Canal Bus: Leidseplein. AE, DC, MC, V. Breakfast included. **$$**.
One of the prettier moderately priced hotels in the museum district and a very good value, Europa '92 is a family-run hotel with a personal touch and a modern look. The breakfast room, with its pine tables inside and white garden furniture on the terrace outside, is a pleasant place to start the day, especially in

summer. For a hotel in this neighborhood and price range, the rooms have a homey touch, especially the honeymoon suite with its blue wicker bed.

Europa is conveniently located near Leidseplein, Vondelpark, and the Rijksmuseum. The only drawback is noise from the busy street in front. Ask for a room overlooking the back terrace. *Amenities:* Small bar.

★★De Filosoof

Anna Vondelstraat 6, 1054 GZ Amsterdam. ☎ 20-6833013; fax: 20-6853750. 25 rooms, all with bath. Tram: 1, 6 to Constantijn Huygensstraat; or tram 1, 11 from Centraal Station. Canal Bus: Leidseplein. AE, MC, V. Breakfast included. **$$**.
Ida Jongsma studied philosophy and cultural anthropology before she opened this small hotel in a 19thC building bordering Vondelpark. Her enthusiasm is reflected in the naming of the hotel (The Philosopher) and the interior design. In the Eros Room, you'll find cherubs, Degas prints, and the words of Augustine: "Love and then do what you want." There is also a Socrates room and an Egyptian Room. The decor is imaginative—often the work of Amsterdam artists. On Thursday evenings the Philosopher's Café congregates in the hotel's study to discuss topics more practical than abstract: like corporate dilemmas, medical ethics, housing problems, and immigration. Although hotel guests are often a heady crowd of academics and writers, the atmosphere is homey, not stiff. The 3-room lounge provides a comfortable living area, with a glass-enclosed terrace over-looking the garden, a front

room with long wooden reading tables and bar, and the study that looks like a Victorian living room. *Amenities:* Fax available, philosophy and other courses offered 2-3 times a week in winter.

Grand Hotel Krasnapolsky

Dam 9, 1012 JS Amsterdam. ☎ 20-5549111; fax: 20-6228607. 429 rooms, all with bath. Tram: 4, 9, 16, 24, 25 to Dam. Canal Bus: Keizersgracht/Radhuisstraat. AE, MC, V. Breakfast included for groups. **$$$$/$$$$$**.
Named after the Polish emigré who built the hotel in 1883, the Krasnapolsky is a huge, bustling hotel on Amsterdam's main square, with a beautiful 19thC cast-iron and glass Winter Garden, where breakfasts are served. The hotel has recently redone existing rooms, built a new wing, and installed modern conference facilities, including 14 conference rooms capable of accommodating 1,500. The business center provides fax, photocopying, secretarial, and computer services. The hotel also has added a Japanese garden and a Dutch-style roof garden. As a result, the hotel is an intelligent choice for anyone staging a large conference, but individual travelers may feel overwhelmed.

The bedrooms are comfortable and modern, but some of them look out on dingy alleys. Although the busy street in front of the hotel is safe and well-lit, avoid the alleys and side streets after dark. Women alone should avoid walking through Dam Square late at night. (See "Safety" in "The Basics.") During the day, Dam Square is quite safe—and a hub of tourist activity. It is also

convenient—a 5-minute walk from Centraal Station and a 10-minute walk from the Jordaan. *Amenities:* Safe; minibar; air conditioner in each room; special ticket arrangements with the Lido, the new casino/dinner theater near Leidseplein; 7 restaurants; fitness center; 1 room wheelchair accessible.

Amsterdam Hilton

Apollolaan 138, 1077 BG Amsterdam. ☎ 20-6780780; fax: 20-6626688. 271 rooms, all with bath. Tram 16 to Emmastraat, 5 to Apollolaan. AE, DC, MC, V. **$$$$$**.
The Amsterdam Hilton, the first American chain hotel in the city, has made some interesting changes in the last few years. The new management created an inviting riverside terrace, manicured lawn, and marina, as well as a new restaurant, Roberto's, which specializes in Italian food and offers a Friday fish-fry.

The Amsterdam Hilton is, most certainly, a Hilton: the lobby is vast, the guest rooms are spacious and comfortable, and the service is efficient. With the notable exceptions of Roberto's and the antique Dutch and British boats, it is also most certainly American. However, the Hilton did have its brief moment in the international spotlight when John Lennon and Yoko Ono staged their 1969 "bed-in for peace" in one of the large bedrooms upstairs. The bedroom, decorated à la John and Yoko and equipped with Beatles CDs, is available to those who can afford the Dfl. 999 tariff.

The location, the wealthy Amsterdam South neighborhood near RAI and the Okura Hotel, is more convenient than it appears to be. Amsterdam is a compact city; from the Hilton, it is a 10-minute tram ride to the museums and a 10- to 15-minute bicycle ride to Vondelpark. *Amenities:* Minibar, restaurant, garden/ riverside terrace cafe, marina, water taxis and antique boats for hire, 2 rooms wheelchair accessible.

★Holiday Inn Crowne Plaza

Nieuwezijds Voorburgwal 5, 1012 RC Amsterdam. ☎ 20-6200500; fax: 20-6201173. 270 rooms, all with bath. Tram: 1, 2, 5, 13, 17 to Nieuwezijds Voorburgwal. AE, DC, MC, V. **$$$$$**.

This is a friendly and luxurious American-style hotel. The reception staff and doorman are helpful, and the rooms are large and comfortable—just like the ones back home. The furnishings and design are contemporary American, and it is easy to forget that you are in Holland. The neighborhood is convenient, close to tram lines and Centraal Station, but not as charming as the canal or museum districts. *Amenities:* Air-conditioning, minibar in every room, restaurant, whirlpool, swimming pool, sauna/solarium, 1 room wheelchair accessible.

★Hotel American

Leidsekade 97, 1017 PN Amsterdam. ☎ 20-6245322; fax: 20-6253236. 188 rooms. Tram: 1, 2, 5, 6, 7, 10 to Leidseplein. Canal Bus: Leidseplein. AE, MC, V. **$$$$$**.

Hotel American, a towering Art Deco structure built in 1902 by Willem Kromhout, is a landmark and meeting place. The interior, however, was modernized in the 1980s, so many rooms only hint of Deco and no longer reflect the beauty of the original architecture. Although the

rooms are tasteful enough, the pink hallways with their garish lights are not. However, the hotel's splendidly Deco Café Américain (see "Dining") makes up for the aesthetic lapses upstairs. Known as the "rock-and-roll hotel," the American attracts visiting rock stars and music biz personalities who like its location near live music venues like the Paradiso and the Melkweg. On the busy Leidseplein, it is steps away from cafes, theaters, cinemas, and restaurants, and 10 minutes from museums and the Vondelpark. An oasis of calm surrounded by a chaotic convergence of speeding bicycles and trolleys, the hotel is for the agile and quick-witted who enjoy the bustle of the city—and can manage to cross the street. *Amenities:* Bar, cafe-restaurant with terrace, conference facilities.

★★Hotel de l'Europe

Nieuwe Doelenstraat 2-8, 1012 CP Amsterdam. ☎ 20-6234836; fax: 20-6242962. 100 rooms, all with bath. Tram: 4, 9, 14, 16, 24, 25 to Muntplein. Canal Bus: City Hall/Rembrandt House. AE, DC, MC, V. **$$$$$**.

In the heart of Amsterdam, near the Spui and the flower market, this hotel is located in a fashionable old neighborhood. It is elegant in the way only grand European hotels can be. The ceilings are high, the filigree is gold leaf, and the aesthetic is opulent Victorian/ neoclassical. Tall stained glass windows overlook broad 19thC staircases. Hotel Europe is a place for special occasions, for traveling in style, and for pampering yourself with marble tubs, plush robes, luxurious beds, and fine views of the Amstel River. The hotel spa offers a sauna, massage room, solarium, modern lap pool, and exercise room.

Some young Amsterdammers find the atmosphere a bit stiff since the dining room requires formal attire—no jacket, no dinner. The management plans to make the grand but somewhat cold lobby more inviting, but the formal dining policy will hold firm. *Amenities:* Minibar; safe; air-conditioning; vintage boat available by the hour; fax and photocopying services; 2 restaurants; terrace cafe-restaurant; bar; pool, gym, and health spa; golf nearby; private jetty for boats and water taxis; conference facilities.

Hotel Hegra

Herengracht 269, Amsterdam. ☎ 20-6237877; fax: 20-6238159. 11 rooms, 9 with bath. Tram: 1, 2, 5 to Spui or 13, 14, 17 to Westerkerk. Canal Bus: Keizersgracht or Westerkerk. AE, DC, MC, V. Breakfast included. **$/$$**.

A cozy breakfast room, friendly atmosphere, and view of the Herengracht compensate for the cot beds, steep winding staircases, and small, bare rooms. Doubles with a canal view are both bigger and brighter than singles. With breakfast included, this hotel is a terrific buy for the neighborhood. It is also good for budget travelers and for anyone with a lodging crisis since it frequently has vacancies when other hotels don't. A real find considering the location: the Herengracht canal near Westerkerk and the lively cafes of the Prinsengracht and Jordaan neighborhoods.

★★Jan Luyken Hotel and Residence

Jan Luykenstraat 58, 1971 CS Amsterdam. ☎ 20-5730730;

fax: 20-6763841. 63 rooms, all with bath. Tram: 1, 2, 5 to Stadhouderskade. Canal Bus: Leidseplein or Rijksmuseum. AE, DC, MC, V. Breakfast included. **$$$**.

The Jan Luyken is a small, classy, family-run hotel. French windows, marble hallways, stained glass, fresh flowers, baskets of ripe fruit, and subtle Victorian fabrics add to the atmosphere of this beautifully restored 19thC townhouse. Mr. Cok van Schaik, whose wife and 2 daughters still run the hotel, did much of the remodeling himself. The bathrooms are particularly nice, with 2 sinks per bathroom, and tub shapes to match your size and temperament; the hotel has small tubs for those who find the luxuriously large Dutch tubs overwhelming or unsafe. The garden patio is pretty and popular with guests but the lounge, although pleasant enough, is almost always empty. This hotel is an excellent value, especially if you are looking for a quiet retreat on a residential street. If you're looking for nightlife, Leidseplein, with its cafes, theaters, and restaurants, is only 10 minutes away. During the day, activities are much closer since the hotel is minutes away from Vondelpark and P. C. Hooftstraat (the exclusive shopping street). *Amenities:* Minibar, safe in every room; bar and adjacent garden patio; fax services, secretarial services, and electrical outlets for business equipment available; the Jan Luyken Residence across the street rents office space and 5 conference/function rooms.

Okura Amsterdam

Ferdinand Bolstraat 333, 1072 LH Amsterdam. ☎ 20-6787111;

Accommodations in the Museum Quarter

Amsterdam Hilton **12**
Atlas Hotel **10**
Barbizon Centre **2**
De Filosoof **9**
Europa 92 **4**
Hotel American **1**
Jan Luyken **8**
Okura Hotel **13**
Owl Hotel **5**
Piet Hein **7**
Prinsen **3**
Toro **11**
Wijnobel **6**

Informatie D.R.O.
Bijbels Museum
Odeon
Rasphuis
MUNT PLEIN
Munttoren
LIJNBAANSGRACHT
MOLENPAD
KONINGS PLEIN
Singel
Tuschinski
REGULIERSDWARSSTRAAT
RAAMSTRAAT
Leidsegracht
Herengracht
KORTE LEIDSEDWARSSTRAAT
LANGE LEIDSEDWARSSTRAAT
LEIDSESTRAAT
KERKSTRAAT
Prinsengracht
Keizersgracht
Herengracht
Melkweg
VIJZELSTRAAT
Museum Fodor
Stadsschouwburg
1
STADHOUDERSKADE
NIEUWE SPIEGELSTRAAT
Keizersgracht
Museum van Loon
2 ●
Paradiso
LIJNBAANSGRACHT
KERKSTRAAT
● **5**
LIJZENSKADE
WETERINGDWARSSTRAAT
WETERINGSCHANS
Prinsengracht
ZANDPAD
Singelgracht
NOORDERSTRAAT
VOSSIUSSTRAAT
VIJZELGRACHT
● **6**
HOOFTSTRAAT
Lijnbaansgracht
WETERINGSCHANS
7
CORNELIS
HONTHORSTSTRAAT
LUIJKENSTRAAT
Rijksmuseum
8 ●
JAN
POTTERSTRAAT
Wetering Plantsoen
PAULUS
RUYSDAELKADE
NICOLAAS WITSENKADE
Van Gogh Museum
MUSEUMSTRAAT
STADHOUDERSKADE
Stedelijk Museum
HONTHORSTSTRAAT
JACOB VAN CAMPENSTRAAT
Heineken Brouwerij
MUSEUM PLEIN
VERMEERSTRAAT
HANS HALSSTRAAT
QUELLIJNSTRAAT
certgebouw
GABRIEL METSUSTRAAT
HOBBEMAKADE
Boeren wetering
1e VALDE HEIJESTRAAT
SARPHATIPARK
MOREELSESTRAAT
SAENREDAMSTRAAT
VAN BAERLESTRAAT
MIEREISSTRAAT
ALBERT CUYPSTRAAT
FRANS VAN
FERSTRAAT
CORNELIS ANTHONISZSTRAAT
1e JAN STEENSTRAAT
BRONCKHORSTSTRAAT
BALTH. FLORISZSTRAAT
1e JAN VAN DER HEIJDENSTRAAT
ROELOF HARTSTRAAT
CEINTUURBAAN
VAN OSTADESTRAAT
GERARD TERBORGSTRAAT
HOBBEMAKADE
RUYSDAELKADE
RUSTENBURGER STRAAT
HARMONIEHOF
VAN HILLIGAERT STRAAT
VINCENT VAN GOGH STRAAT
APOLLOLAAN
JOSEF ISRAELS KADE
13 ●
Amstel
Kanaal
AMSTEL KADE
SCHELDESTRAAT
CHURCHILLAAN
STADIONWEG
ZWEERSKADE
HERMAN HEIJERMANSWEG
Overtoom
BERNARD
DIEPENBROCKSTRAAT
Kanaal
DEUBLOO STRAAT

fax: 20-6712344. 370 rooms, all with bath. Tram: 12, 25 to Cornelis Troostplein. AE, DC, MC, V. **$$$$/$$$$$**.

Situated in the 20thC ring, close to RAI and the beltway (ring road), this 23-story, Japanese-owned hotel is ideal for business travelers or those with a car who prefer not to get tangled up in the narrow inner-city streets. Not that you feel isolated in the Okura, for the city is easily accessible by tram and bicycle—a fact that is most obvious from the roof. At the Okura, the city spreads out before you.

The hotel is the 2nd-highest building in Amsterdam and offers the most complete view: the modern Amsterdam School architecture of Amsterdam Zuid, the spires of the **Rijksmuseum,** and the cranes at the harbor. Also appealing is the hotel's Japanese flavor, from the shop in the basement selling sake to the Yamazato restaurant that overlooks a small Japanese garden and has the best sushi in town. There are Western features as well, including the award-winning French cuisine of the Ciel Bleu restaurant on the top floor. The guest rooms are a mixture of Western and Japanese aesthetic. The wood is light and sleek, the furniture Eastern-modern, and the fabrics understated. *Amenities:* Minibar; safe; air-conditioning; 4 restaurants; bar; conference facilities for 1,200; fitness center with sauna, massage, and swimming pool.

Owl

Roemer Visscherstraat 1, 1054 EV Amsterdam. ☎ 20-6189484; fax: 20-6189441. 34 rooms, all with bath. Tram: 1, 2, 5, 6, 7, 10 to Leidseplein. Canal Bus: Leidseplein. AE, DC, MC, V. Breakfast included. **$$**.

This quiet hotel, set in a dignified 19thC quarter near Vondelpark, is convenient for visiting Amsterdam's major sights. The bedrooms are clean and pleasant, and the cheerful breakfast room overlooks a garden and terrace. Claustrophobes should take the stairs since the elevator is small and shaky.

Piet Hein

Vossiusstraat 53, 1071 AK Amsterdam. ☎ 20-6628375; fax: 20-6621526. 40 rooms, all with bath. Tram: 2, 3, 5, 12 to Van Baerlestraat. Canal Bus: Leidseplein or Rijksmuseum. AE, DC, MC, V. Breakfast included. **$$/$$$**.

The Piet Hein is a small, congenial hotel situated in a 19thC house overlooking Vondelpark. The bedrooms are plain, but bright and comfortable with modern prints, white wicker furniture, and a vase of Dutch flowers. Ask for a room with a balcony, with a view of Vondelpark— or the honeymoon suite with the waterbed. The proximity to the park makes this a good choice for joggers and families with children, since Vondelpark has running/biking paths, playgrounds, ice-cream stands, and lots of dogs and Frisbees. *Amenities:* Bar.

★Prinsen

Vondelstraat 38 Amsterdam. ☎ 20-6162323; fax: 20-6166112. 41 rooms, all with bath. Tram: 2, 3, 5, 12. Canal Bus: Leidseplein or Rijksmuseum. AE, DC, MC, V. Breakfast included. **$$**.

This privately owned hotel near Vondelpark is comprised of two 1890s Cuyper-style homes. Cuypers, who built the Rijksmuseum, lived across the street in a house he designed. Nellie, the personable manager, and her affable cat, Max, supervise breakfast, which is served in a *gezellig* room furnished in rattan and brightened by large windows overlooking a spectacular garden. Tall pines, thick ferns, and several varieties of flowering trees shelter the garden terrace from the sights and sounds of the city. The bedrooms are small and simple, but peach quilts, blue rattan chairs, and good light make them cheerful enough. Because the hotel has no restaurant, Nellie encourages her guests to bring take-out dinner into the breakfast area. Ask for a room with a garden view. If you need a desk, request it in advance.

Prinsenhof

Prinsengracht 810, 1017 JL Amsterdam. ☎ 20-6231772; fax: 20-6388868. 10 rooms, 2 with bath. Tram: 4 to Prinsengracht. AE, DC, MC, V. Breakfast included. **$$**. This clean, quiet, low-budget hotel is situated in an 18thC canal house on the Prinsengracht. As with many inexpensive Amsterdam hotels, the breakfast room is more attractive than the bedrooms. The breakfast room is appropriately *gezellig*—with framed pictures and cozy tables. The guest rooms have cots—basic, but comfortable. Some have the original beamed ceilings. Front rooms overlook the canal. The neighborhood is close to lively cafes on the Rembrandtsplein and the canals.

★★Pulitzer

Prinsengracht 315-331, 1016 GZ Amsterdam. ☎ 20-5235235; fax: 20-6276753. 240 rooms, all with bath. Tram: 13, 14, 17 to Westermarkt. Canal Bus: Westerkerk or Keizersgracht. Canal taxi to the Pulitzer's Prinsengracht entrance. AE, DC, MC, V. Breakfast included with some packages. **$$$$$**. No other hotel in Amsterdam manages to combine the romantic atmosphere of a canal house with the modern facilities of a business hotel. The Pulitzer is comprised of 24 artfully renovated 16th and 17thC canal houses, complete with gables and colorful old sign posts. Although the interior is modernized, in each room and hallway you discover vestiges of Old Holland—an original beamed ceiling, brick wall, winding staircase, marble hearth. (The connecting of these different houses has resulted in effects both charming and confusing; hallways on the same floor are at different levels, with unexpected stairs and turns.) I recommend rooms overlooking the Keizersgracht canal or those with terraces on the central gardens. Even though the Pulitzer has been owned by 2 corporations—first the Italian CIGA group and, most recently, the Sheraton chain, the hotel still retains a warm, personal atmosphere. However, the recent change in owner-ship may have delayed some home improvements. Some walls are a bit scuffed and in need of paint. A paint job and minor renovations are planned for 1997.

The neighborhood is appropriately charming and historical. Ask Robin van Kooten, the Pulitzer's savvy and amiable concierge for 25 years, for tips about side trips, boat tours, and restaurants. *Amenities:* Air-conditioning, minibar, safe, 2 restaurants, a bar, an award-winning wine cellar,

7 conference rooms (several retain the architectural grandeur of the golden age).

Ramada Renaissance

Kattengat 1, 1012 SZ Amsterdam. ☎ 20-6212223; fax: 20-6275245. 425 rooms, all with bath. Tram: 1, 2, 5, 13, 17 to Martelaarsgracht. Canal Bus: Centraal Station. AE, DC, MC, V. **$$$$$**.

A supermodern luxury hotel, the Ramada Renaissance is situated in a historic quarter of the old city, close to the harbor, and a 5-minute walk from Centraal Station. This large, impersonal hotel offers every creature comfort (large beds, huge tubs, a restaurant and cafe, a health club), as well as live music and dancing in the nightclub downstairs, and a convenient location—but little soul. The reception area is often too busy to have a friendly atmosphere. The modern lobby is sleek, roomy, and cold, although it does have exhibitions by Dutch COBRA artists. It's a good choice for business travelers, but women traveling alone who like to walk around at night may feel more comfortable in the more residential canal or museum neighborhoods. However, the peaceful Singel canal is just around the corner, the protective doormen are comforting, and a taxi stand is a few steps away. *Amenities:* Minibar, safe, restaurant, cafe, nightclub, fitness center, parking garage, conference facilities seating 700, 2 rooms wheelchair accessible.

RHO

Nes 11-23, 1012 KC Amsterdam. ☎ 20-6207371; fax: 20- 6207826. 60 rooms, all with bath. Tram: 1, 2, 4, 5, 9, 13, 14, 16, 17, 24, 25 to Dam. AE, MC, V. Breakfast included. **$$**.

The RHO hotel is situated in a curious building that originally was an old Amsterdam music hall. Bought in 1912 by the gold dealer H. Drijfhout (whose name still appears above the door), the historic building was converted into a hotel in 1989. The spacious music hall now serves as a breakfast room. The bedrooms, which come in various shapes and sizes, have contemporary furniture and fabrics. The Nes neighborhood, just off Dam Square and full of narrow streets and dark alleys, was a place to avoid alone at night a few years ago. But the theaters and popular theater cafes, along with efforts by the city council, have changed the atmosphere. However, women walking alone at night should stick to brighter streets with more pedestrian traffic; after 10 or 11pm take a cab. *Amenities:* Safes and minibars in rooms; bar.

Roode Leeuw

Damrak 93-94, 1012 LP Amsterdam. ☎ 20-6240396; fax: 20-6204716. 78 rooms, all with bath. Tram: 4, 9, 16, 24, 25 to Dam. AE, DC, MC, V. Breakfast included. **$$$**.

The Roode Leeuw is an old-fashioned hotel in a convenient location near trams, Dam Square, and Centraal Station. The rooms at the front are bright, but suffer slightly from the throb of traffic. Some rooms need paint, but the airy breakfast room, small lounge, lively cafe terrace, and adjoining restaurant add a touch of *gezelligheid*. Damrak at night can be *ongezelli*—seedy, though not dangerous. When in doubt after dark, take a cab—especially after 11pm. *Amenities:* Minibar, restaurant with traditional Dutch menu, 1 room wheelchair accessible.

SAS Royal Hotel

Rusland 17, 1012 CK Amsterdam. ☎ 20-6231231; fax: 20-5208200. 247 rooms, all with bath. Tram: 4, 9, 14, 16, 24, 25 to Spui. AE, DC, MC, V. **$$$$$**

Here a row of 18thC gable houses has been incorporated into the new SAS Royal Hotel in an entirely original manner. The traditional facades conceal an extraordinary 7-floor atrium with tropical vegetation and a gurgling waterfall, standing on the site of an old church. To add to the aesthetic confusion, the Scandinavian-owned hotel offers a choice of 3 bedroom decors: Dutch if you are looking for old-fashioned furniture and oak-beamed ceilings, Scandinavian for those who prefer modern pale-wood furniture, or Oriental. The hotel is in the heart of the old city. *Amenities:* Air-conditioning; minibar; 2 restaurants; bar; fitness center with solarium and sauna; business facilities, including computers, faxes, portable phones and an office; conference facilities; 2 rooms wheelchair accessible.

Seven Bridges

Reguliersgracht 31, 1017 LK Amsterdam. ☎ 20-6231329. 11 rooms, 6 with bath. Tram: 4 to Keizersgracht. Canal Bus: City Hall. AE, MC, V. Breakfast included. **$$**

A small, cozy, 17thC canal-house hotel, Seven Bridges is named after a viewpoint where 7 arched bridges can be counted by diligent tourists. The rooms are basic, but the laid-back, homey atmosphere appeals to young Americans on tight budgets. Imaginative

decor—Art Deco antiques and brightly colored bathroom tiles, new hardwood floors, a small garden, and views of the canals make this hotel a charming spot for a good value. It is also close to the cafes of the Rembrandtsplein. Reserve early and ask for the garden room or one overlooking the canal. Breakfast is served in your room.

Swissotel Amsterdam Ascot Hotel

Damrak 95-98, 1012 LP Amsterdam. ☎ 20-6260066; fax: 20-6270982. 110 rooms, all with bath. Tram: 4, 9, 16, 24, 25 to Dam. Canal Bus: Keizersgracht or Westerkerk. AE, MC, V. **$$$$/ $$$$$**.

This is one of the better hotels near Dam Square. Although it's in the midst of tourist throngs on the outside, the hotel's interior is calm, tasteful, and immaculate. It is also just around the corner from the **Royal Palace** and close to shops, restaurants, and cafes of the Jordaan and Prinsengracht neighborhoods. Getting around town is effortless, as most trams stop near the hotel, while excursions can easily be made from Centraal Station, a 5-minute walk away. Rooms are stylish and well-equipped, and although the hotel does not have parking, there is a 24-hour parking garage at the nearby **Grand Hotel Krasnapolsky.** Proximity to Dam Square may be an asset, but not at night, especially for women alone (see "Safety" in "The Basics"). *Amenities:* Minibar, air-conditioning, fax and secretarial services available, restaurant, bar, 2 floors of special business rooms with safes, conference space for up to 50, 1 room wheelchair accessible.

★★Toro

Koningslaan 64, 1075 AG
Amsterdam. ☎ 20-6737223;
fax: 20-6750031. 22 rooms, all
with bath. Tram: 2 to Valeriusplein.
Canal Bus: Leidseplein. AE, DC,
MC, V. Breakfast included. **$$**.
This hotel in a renovated
19thC mansion is cozy, filled
with plants and flowers, and
decorated with an English
country touch. The breakfast
room is furnished with lovely
antique furniture and family
portraits. Both the breakfast
room and adjoining outdoor
garden terrace overlook a small
lake in Vondelpark. Bedrooms
are spacious and comfortable,
and some of them have views
of the **Vondelpark.** Parking
in the area is relatively easy
by Amsterdam standards (but
I suggest bicycle or tram
instead of a rental car if your
destination is Amsterdam's
Historic Center). Proximity
to the park with its concerts,
running paths, and children's
playgrounds make the Toro a
real find. The only drawback is
the longish walk to Leidseplein
and the city center. *Amenities:*
Minisafe, refrigerator.

Van Onna

Bloemgracht 102 Amsterdam.
☎ 20-6265801. 39 rooms,
21 with bath. Tram: 13, 14, 17 to
Westerkerk. Canal Bus:
Westerkerk or Keizersgracht.
No credit cards. **$**.
Hotel van Onna is on a
narrow, quiet canal in the
Jordaan—the "village" in the
midst of Amsterdam. Anthony
Perkins made a movie here and
included the hotel's owner and
manager, Loek van Onna, in
the cast. (He played a hotel
owner.) Loek van Onna was
born in one of these houses
and still lives here. He provides
neighborhood lore, infor-
mation about Amsterdam, and
personal philosophy, as well as

coffee and tea. The hotel is
intended for budget travelers,
so the rooms are basic—cots,
towels, and, if you are lucky, a
view of the canal. The rooms
are Spartan—without
telephones, radios, and TV—
because van Onna believes in
keeping his hotel (and life)
simple and inexpensive (no
one pays more than 60
guilders). "Go out and see the
city," van Onna encourages his
guests. "You don't come to
Amsterdam to watch TV." Ask
for a room overlooking the
canal since the interior rooms
are dark and small. In any case,
ask for a room in the new
building.

★★Victoria Hotel

Damrak 1, 1012 LG Amsterdam.
☎ 20-6234255; fax: 20-
6252997. 305 rooms, all with
bath. Tram, metro, or Canal Bus
to Centraal Station. AE, DC, MC,
V. Breakfast with some bookings.
$$$$.
The handsome Victoria Hotel,
vintage 1890, was renovated
and expanded by the Swedish
Scandic group and later sold to
an Israeli firm. There are now
2 wings: modern Scandinavian
and Victorian/Dutch. If you
want a comfy but dignified
19thC room, ask for the
Victorian Wing where the
wardrobe, working desk, and
large closet are made of dark,
rich wood. Chairs are high
backed and something you'd
want to sink into after a hard
day's work. Every room is
different. In contrast, the
modern wing is symmetrical,
cool, and a bit stark by Dutch
standards. The rooms are
spacious and democratic—
everyone gets exactly the same
thing (good for tour groups).
The staff is unusually efficient
and friendly. Breakfast is both
Dutch and American: the
traditional bread, ham, and

cheese, along with granola, cornflakes, and 4 kinds of yogurt. The Victoria is a good place if you can't do without a gym. The weight room is serious, complete with trainer and state-of-the-art machines. The sauna and steam bath meet the usual high Dutch standards, but the heated pool is tiny.

Since the hotel is opposite Centraal Station (which was once Amsterdam's harbor), you are well located for trips by train or bus from Centraal Station. This also places you in a historic, busy, crowded, and somewhat seedy (though not unsafe) neighborhood. But to transcend all that, visit Amsterdam's New Age Center, the Oibibio, with its restaurant, tea room, bookstore, gift shop, and beautiful sauna, which is 1 block away. *Amenities:* Air-conditioning. Free first-class train travel to and from Schiphol Airport; bar; restaurant; cafe; business center with secretarial, fax, and photocopying services; conference rooms available with space for 150; fitness center with weight rooms and trainers, sauna, Turkish bath, and swimming pool; 2 rooms wheelchair accessible.

★Wiechmann

Prinsengracht 328, 1016 HX Amsterdam. ☎ 20-6263321; fax: 20-6268962. 36 rooms, all with bath. Tram: 1, 2, 5 to Prinsengracht. No credit cards. Breakfast included. **$$**.
The Wiechmann is a well-situated hotel with simple guest rooms done in wicker or in antiques. Some rooms have a canal view, although this sometimes has a downside; the hotel owner warns that late-night cafe-goers sometimes stop out front to "serenade the ducks." The lobby and break-fast room have Old World charm—hardwood floors, oriental rugs, beamed ceilings, and a few well placed antiques. Wiechmann is well-located for cafe life—north of Leidseplein on the edge of the Jordaan.

Wijnobel

Vossiusstraat 9, 1071 AB Amsterdam. ☎ 20-6622298. 12 rooms, 1 with bath. Tram: 1, 2, 5, 6, 7, 10 to Leidseplein. No credit cards. **$**.
This friendly, family-run hotel is best suited for young people or families on a limited budget. The rooms are bright, clean, and spacious; those at the front enjoy a view of the **Vondelpark** and, at night, the golden glow of the floodlit **Hotel American.** The only drawbacks are the hotel's lack of a breakfast room or private bathrooms, but for those who don't mind a bathroom down the hall, this is one of the most pleasant, cheap hotels in the city. It is also conveniently located on a quiet street 5 minutes from the Rijksmuseum.

SIGHTS &
ATTRACTIONS

Taking It All In

Although Amsterdam's famous art museums—most
notably the Rijksmuseum, the Stedelijk, and the Van
Gogh Museum—are every bit as good as their reputation, my strongest impressions of Amsterdam have come
from the smaller things that I discover when rounding
a corner or walking through a seemingly innocuous
gate. The city's peculiar charm lies in hidden courtyards like the Begijnhof, in the narrow, languid canals,
and in the appeal of the *grachtenhuizen* (canal houses)
with their elaborate gables and witty gable stones. Even
if you never set foot in the Rijksmuseum, you still can
experience a form of Dutch art—medieval to modern—in the architecture on almost every block in the
old *grachtengordel,* the 17thC canal ring.

A selection of Amsterdam's most eccentric sights is
given below under "Curiosities." For a bird's-eye view
of Amsterdam, see the recommendations listed in
"Viewpoints." Things to see on or near the canals
and rivers are spotlighted in "Waterways." In addition,
many sights are also mentioned under the area descriptions and in both the "Essential Amsterdam" and
"Jordaan" walks in the "Amsterdam Walks" chapter of
this book.

Organizing Your Time

On a short visit to Amsterdam, try not to cram in too
much sightseeing. Visit one or two museums, of course,
and take a boat trip on the canals, but you would be
missing an important dimension of Amsterdam if you
did not experience a Dutch cafe or while away an hour
or two exploring small specialty shops or appreciating

the 17thC gable houses in the narrow streets near the canals. It is generally a good idea to spend cold or wet days in museums, and hope for sunny weather to explore the canals.

Visiting the Museums

The Netherlands spends lavishly on its museums, and every sizable town has at least one interesting collection. If you plan to visit several museums, it is well worth investing in a **Museumjaarkaart** (1-year museum card), which gives you access to the 300 museums listed on the card (although for some special exhibitions an entrance fee may be charged). The Museumjaarkaart, valid from January 1 to December 31, is sold at VVV tourist offices and in major museums (passport photograph required).

Remember that many museums are closed on Sunday morning (with the exception of the **Anne Frankhuis**), and all day Monday, with the exception of the **Stedelijk Museum, Amsterdams Historisch Museum, Nieuwe Kerk, Willet–Holthuysen Museum,** and **Tropenmuseum.** See individual museums listed below for opening times. You should also be aware that certain departments in the Rijksmuseum are occasionally closed because of staff shortages.

How to Use This Section

In the following pages, Amsterdam's sights are arranged alphabetically, using English or Dutch names according to common English-speaking usage. The sights are listed below by subject and by neighborhood.

Look for the ★ or ★★ symbol to indicate the most important sights or buildings of great architectural interest. For sights and experiences of particular interest to children, refer to the "Amsterdam with Kids" section at the end of this chapter. If you only know the name of a museum, say, in English, and cannot find it in the following A-to-Z listing, try looking it up in the index. Some lesser sights do not have their own entries but are included within other entries: Look these up in the index as well.

For First-Time Visitors

Following is a list of the major attractions and neighborhoods, as well as unusual treats, that shouldn't be missed. Full descriptions of all of these sights are available in the A-to-Z listings that follow.

1. ★★ Amstel River (especially the Blauwgrug, Magere Brug, and the Hogesluis)

2. ★★ Anne Frankhuis

3. ★★ Begijnhof

4. ★★ Grachtengordel (especially the Herengracht and Prinsengracht canals)

5. ★★ Joods Historisch Museum and ★ Jodenbuurt

6. ★ Jordaan

7. ★★ Koninklijk Paleis

8. ★★ Rijksmuseum

9. ★★ Van Gogh Museum

10. ★★ Stedelijk Museum

Orientation Tours

If you don't have the time to get lost in Amsterdam, it pays to take a guided tour in order to get oriented. Once you have your bearings, you can more easily identify where you want to go—and how you want to get there: by boat, tram, bicycle, taxi, or on foot.

Walking Tours

Amsterdam is an ideal city for walking because it is small, compact, and full of subtle architectural details and hidden courtyards that can best be seen on foot. Guided walking tours that take you past small squares and historic monuments, down quiet, narrow canalside streets, and into the Jordaan (the village within Amsterdam) can be arranged from April 1 to October 31 by **Artifex Travel** (Herengracht 342, 1016 CG Amsterdam, ☎ 20-6208112). Another guided walking tour, organized by **Strichting Het Gilde** (☎ 20-6251390), takes you through the historic center, the Jordaan, and a "surprise route." This tour leaves from the Amsterdam Historical Museum daily at 11am. Book several days in advance. For additional information on walking tours, ask the VVV Tourist Offices in Amsterdam for suggestions or turn to the "Amsterdam Walks" chapter of this book.

Bicycle Tours

One of the best ways to tour Amsterdam is by bicycle. You can cover a lot of the city in a short time and see just how small and navigable Amsterdam really is (which makes planning the rest of your trip all the easier). Traveling by bicycle also lets you experience the city as most Amsterdammers do—on two wheels. **The Yellow Bike** (29 Nieuwezijds Kolk, ☎ 20-6206940) offers 3-hour tours by young, affable, and well-informed guides daily at 9:30am and 1pm. The best time to bicycle in Amsterdam is Sunday morning, when you can experience the city free from the distractions (and dangers) of frenetic traffic. Yellow Bike also offers a more specialized 6- to 7-hour tour of the Dutch countryside and small Dutch fishing villages just north of Amsterdam.

Boat Tours

The most peaceful way to see Amsterdam is by boat. Exploring Amsterdam by boat orients you to the system of concentric canals around which the city was built and gives you a unique perspective—the one from the water. In a canal boat, you can simply lean back and take in the architecture of the *grachtenhuizen* (canal houses), admiring the smaller touches—the gables, gable stones, and cornices. You can also see the churches, bridges, historical monuments, and harbor, which you otherwise might never see.

Canal cruises bring you nose to nose with Amsterdam's curious array of houseboats, with their miniature vegetable gardens, potted trees, stylish decks, hanging laundry, and boat-bound pets. The tour boats operate year-round, since they have glass tops and are insulated from all kinds of unpleasant weather. They are an especially good alternative when the weather is too cold or wet to tour on foot or bicycle.

Several companies offer 2-hour candlelight cruises through the canals that include a guided tour, music, cheese, and wine. Candlelight cruises on **Rederij Lovers BV** (☎ 20-6222181) cost Dfl. 42.50 for adults and Dfl. 32.50 for children 3 to 12, while **Rederij Kooi** (☎ 20-6233810) charges Dfl. 35 for adults and Dfl. 17.50 for children 4 to 14. The **Holland International** (☎ 20-6227788) cruise at Dfl. 45 for adults and Dfl. 25 for children 4 to 12 is the most interesting candlelight cruise since it includes a typically Dutch experience: a stop at a cozy bar for Dutch or red-currant gin. Holland International also offers a sumptuous brunch cruise (adults Dfl. 55, children Dfl. 50), which includes a 3-hour tour of the canals and a 3-course feast, and an afternoon tea cruise (adults Dfl. 55, children Dfl. 45).

Amsterdam on Sunday

Even in Amsterdam, the liveliest and most hedonistic Dutch city, Sundays can sometimes be forlorn. The best antidote for Sunday doldrums is an appealing cafe, a sunny terrace, or a sumptuous brunch. I suggest Café De Jaren or De IJsbreker on the Amstel (both have sunny terraces), Walem on the Prinsengracht, or Luxembourg on the Spui. For brunch, the Amstel is regal and expensive whereas Brasserie van Baerle offers an earthier kind of pampering along with a cozy garden terrace and friendly cat.

Those who want to cycle in Amsterdam should find Sundays a welcome opportunity to ride peacefully—and safely—without the anarchy of trams, cabs, bicycles, and cars all vying for the same piece of pavement. Sunday is also ideal for bicycle trips to nearby villages like Oude Kerk or Broek-en-Waterland.

Spui is animated on Sunday mornings, when Amsterdammers and tourists flock to the Athenaeum newspaper shop (Spui 14-16, ☎ 20-6226248) to choose from an international selection of Sunday newspapers and the paintings and drawings of local artists selling their wares. Several Sunday markets have recently started up, aimed mainly at tourists who are at loose ends. Local painters and potters set up stands around the 19thC bandstand on Thorbeckeplein (noon–6pm), and on Spui (10am–6pm). If it rains, you can take shelter in the indoor market De Looier (see "Shopping").

Concerts are often held on Sundays in churches or in Vondelpark (see "The Arts" for listings), and matinees are shown in some of the art houses and mainstream cinemas.

The **Museum Boat** and the dinner, brunch, and candlelight cruises tend to be more expensive than the Canal Bus. But the Museum Boat (☎ 20-6222181) is a good choice if you have limited time in Amsterdam and want to focus on the museums and canals. A day pass (adults Dfl. 20, children Dfl. 17.50) includes unlimited transport to 5 fixed stops near important museums as well as discounts on admission to several museums. These boats, however, attract flocks of museum-goers bearing large shopping bags. If you have more time and flexibility, the **Canal Bus** (☎ 20-6239886) is a less expensive, more relaxed, and surprisingly educational mode of transportation that takes you to fixed stops near key neighborhoods such as the Jordaan, Leidseplein, Waterlooplein, and the Museum Quarter. There are 2 lines, the Red and the Green, with slightly different routes all conveniently located for walks as well as for sight-seeing and shopping (regular stops include Leidseplein, Rijksmuseum, Centraal Station, Anne Frank's House, City Hall, and Keizersgracht/Raadhuisstraat). The Canal Bus is relatively inexpensive (16.50 Dfl), and the pass is sometimes good for 2 days instead of one, making it a viable mode of transportation within the city. It is slower than a tram—but more peaceful.

Canal Bikes (Canal Bike ☎ 20-6265574) are best for adventurous souls or for those who already have their bearings. The advantage is that you can pedal your water cycle through even the narrowest of canals and go places that a conventional tour boat could never take you. You can also stop at cafe terraces and cafe-hop from the water, but be sure to keep an eye on your water bike since it cannot be locked. Cafes with terraces on floating barges are the best bet: Simply park the bike near your table. A chic, relaxing, and far more expensive way to tour by water is the **Water Taxi** (☎ 20-6222181).

Most of these boat services are available on the canal in front of Centraal Station. For other reliable canal cruises, contact **Holland International Canal Cruises** (☎ 20-6227788), **Rederij Lovers** (☎ 20-6234208), or **Rederij Noord/Zuid** (☎ 20-6791370).

Some hotels like **Hotel Pulitzer,** the **Amsterdam Hilton, Hotel de l'Europe,** and the **Amstel Hotel** offer tours of the city in beautiful vintage boats which are smaller, more personal, and far more expensive than the ordinary cruise lines.

Special-Interest Tours

The **VVV Tourist Offices** (pronounced vay vay vay) in Amsterdam offer an assortment of brochures for do-it-yourself theme tours on such subjects as the Jordaan, Jewish Amsterdam, Vincent van Gogh's Amsterdam, and Rembrandt and Amsterdam. You may either send for these brochures in advance or buy them at one of Amsterdam's VVV offices. The main office is located across from Centraal Station at 10 Stationsplein (☎ 06-34034066) and there is another office at Leidseplein 1. For more information on special tours, ask the VVV staff to suggest walking or cycling routes.

Main VVV tourist office

Several tour companies offer tours of the red-light district, but Boom Chicago's (see "Amsterdam After Dark") tour in the **Boom Boat** (☎ 20-4221776) is casual, witty, well-informed—and on the water, which gives you a welcome distance from the scruffy characters hanging out on the streets. The Boom Boat will sometimes arrange other canal tours to suit your interests.

For art and architecture tours, there are 2 good companies in Amsterdam: **Artist Guide Service** (Haarlemmerdijk 94, 1013 JG Amsterdam, ☎ 20-4200840) and **Drs. WH Drenth** (Spuistraat 318, III, 1012 VX Amsterdam, ☎ 20-6227525).

Other local tours include **Archivisie** (architecture), 5 Zaandstraat, ☎ 20-6258908; **Artifex** (art history, cultural tours, museums), 342 Herengracht, ☎ 20-6208112, which is a popular tour; **Van Garderen Amsterdam Tours** (history, architecture, and present-day Amsterdam), 314 Weesperstraat, ☎ 20-6275822; and **Metafoor** (architecture and excursions), 32 Binnengasthuisstraat, ☎ 20-4206238.

Stichting Het Gilde organizes a tour of the old city center and the Jordaan that departs from **Amsterdams Historisch Museum** (Kalverstraat 92, ☎ 20-6251390) at 11am. Book at least 2 days ahead.

Special Moments

Entering the world of the Begijnhof   "Come take a look at this," my friend said as he motioned me toward a nondescript group of 17thC buildings on the Spui. He led me through an arched brick passageway, and we emerged in a peaceful, hidden courtyard—enclosed on all sides by 16th and 17thC houses, insulated from the noisy traffic outside its walls, and seemingly immune to the passage of time. The houses, each with its own tidy flower garden, encircled a small church and a green. On a wall to our left, displayed like paintings on a living-room wall, were an array of colorful 17thC gable stones symbolizing trades and religious themes. It was strangely still for Amsterdam, and no tourists or residents arrived to break the spell. The bicycles (belonging to the older women who live in this *hofje,* a sheltered low-rent community) lined up in neat little racks near the entrance were the only signs of modernity.

A "Last Night" Party in the Jordaan   I walked into a brown cafe in the Jordaan to find myself in the midst of a young woman's "Last Night" Party, a celebration of her last night of single life. Women from the provinces come to Amsterdam for these parties in which the bride-to-be must perform some difficult— but possible—task. But this was an Amsterdammers' party—with their typical irony. The group had taken the term "bachelor's party" to heart and all, except the bride, were dressed in drag: wearing men's suits, hats, and charcoaled five o'clock shadows. One woman wore a moustache. I was clearly out of place, but they waved me into the party, passed me a beer, and chatted with me in perfect English. Within minutes, a policeman arrived, responding to a neighbor's complaint about the noise. When he realized this was a Last Night Party, he was most convivial: He congratulated the bride-to-be, wished everyone good cheer, and left us to our noisy celebration—which was the gezellig thing to do under the circumstances. At least in Amsterdam.

The perennial dog in the bike basket   Amsterdammers put their dogs in bike baskets or side carts where the animals sit quietly as their owners ride them around the city. I have never heard these dogs whine or bark—and have never seen one jump. For years this has puzzled me. Why would Amsterdam dogs behave so differently from American ones? I have 2 feeble explanations: gezelligheid is infectious—or there's something in the water.

Memorials to courage and loss in Jodenbuurt   Amsterdam's Jewish neighborhood, the Jodenbuurt, was decimated in World War II as a result of Nazi round-ups and deportations from which few Jews ever returned. This fact became less abstract, more tangible, and thus more haunting to me as I stood looking at the Muziektheater/Stopera complex, built amidst some local controversy, on a razed portion of what had once been the Jodenbuurt. On the pavement next to the Muziektheater, a white outline marking the former foundation of a Jewish boys orphanage conjured a most powerful sense of loss. The Nazis had sent its young occupants to Sorbibor concentration camp; none survived. Just a few minutes' walk away, in front of the Stopera buildings and overlooking the Amstel, the city of Amsterdam erected a monument (in 1988, after the Stopera was constructed) dedicated to Jewish courage and resistance to the Nazi occupation.

The Herengracht canal on a winter's night
Standing on a bridge over the Herengracht canal, I could see rows of tiny lights outlining the arched bridges in the distance and casting a warm, golden glow on the melting ice. The living rooms of the 18thC canal houses, with drapes pulled open—as is the Dutch habit—were illuminated by soft lights, and I could finally see the interiors of those seemingly impenetrable buildings. They were as beautiful as I'd imagined them, with oak-beamed ceilings, chic couches, wood carvings and sculptures from exotic places, and rows of books.

A cryptic window display on the Singel canal
Mystifying or whimsical window art is "typical Amsterdam." As I passed by a display window on the Singel canal, I saw a thickly feathered white wing, large enough for Pegasus, hovering over a sea of gray pebbles. Included in the background setting were 2 cardboard objects: a cactus and a setting sun. Whether this was a shop, a gallery, or an artist's studio was not made obvious. You had to go inside to find out.

Sights & Attractions by Category

Major Museums
★ Amsterdams Historisch
    Museum
★★ Anne Frankhuis
★ Het Rembrandthuis Museum
★★ Rijksmuseum
★★ Stedelijk Museum
★★ Van Gogh Museum

Other Museums
Allard Pierson Museum
★ Aviodome
Bijbels Museum
Electrische Museum Tramlijn

Informatiecentrum
    Ruimtelijke Ordening
★★ Joods Historisch Museum
Madame Tussaud Scenerama
★★ Nederlands Scheepvaart
    Museum
Nederlands Theater Instituut
NINT Technisch Museum
★ Tropenmuseum

Period Houses
Amstelkring, Museum
★ Van Loon, Museum
Willet-Holthuysen, Museum

Churches & Synagogues

Nieuwe Kerk
★★ Oude Kerk
★ Portuguese Synagogue
  (see Jodenbuurt)
★★ Westerkerk
Zuiderkerk

Other Sights

★★ Begijnhof
★ Beurs van Berlage
Heineken Brouwerij
Hollandse Schouwburg
★★ Koninklijk Paleis
Normaal Amsterdams Peil
Schuttersgalerij
★ Tuschinski Cinema
★ Waag

Canals & Rivers

★★ Amstel River
★★ Herengracht

Keizersgracht
★★ Prinsengracht
Singel

Districts

★★ Grachtengordel
★ Jodenbuurt
★ Jordaan
★ Nieuwe Zijde
Nieuwmarkt
★ Oude Zijde

Parks & Gardens

Amstelpark
★★ Amsterdamse Bos
★ Artis
★ Hortus Botanicus
★★ Vondelpark

Squares

★ Dam
★ Leidseplein
★ Spui
★ Waterlooplein (see Jodenbuurt)

Sights & Attractions by Neighborhood

The Canals

★★ Anne Frankhuis
Bijbels Museum
★★ Grachtengordel
★★ Herengracht
Keizersgracht
Nederlands Theater Instituut
★★ Prinsengracht
Singel
★ Van Loon, Museum
★★ Westerkerk
Willet-Holthuysen, Museum

The Historic Center

Allard Pierson Museum
Amstelkring, Museum
★ Amsterdams Historisch
  Museum
★★ Begijnhof
★ Beurs van Berlage
★ Dam Square
Electrische Museum Tramlijn
★★ Koninklijk Paleis
★ Leidseplein
Madame Tussaud Scenerama
★★ Nederlands Scheepvaart
  Museum
Nieuwmarkt

★ Nieuwe Zijde
★★ Oude Kerk
★ Oude Zijde
Schuttersgalerij
★ Spui
★ Waag
Zuiderkerk

Jordaan

★ Jordaan

Museum Quarter/ Vondelpark

Heineken Brouwerij
Museumplein
★★ Rijksmuseum
★★ Stedelijk Museum
★★ Van Gogh Museum
★★ Vondelpark

Overlooking the Amstel, Waterlooplein, Koveniersburgwal

★★ Amstel River
★ Artis
Hollandse Schouwburg
★ Hortus Botanicus

Amsterdam's Sights A to Z

Air Museum (see Aviodome)

Allard Pierson Museum

Oude Turfmarkt 127. ☎ 20-5252556. Open Tues–Fri 10am–5pm; Sat, Sun, holidays 1–5pm. Admission: Adults Dfl. 5, children Dfl. 2. Tram: 4, 9, 16, 24, 25 to Spui.

The extensive archaeological collection of the University of Amsterdam is located in a neoclassical building that once belonged to the Nederlandsche Bank. The interior has been completely modernized, leaving only the curious 19thC lamps as a memento of the bank. The museum's collection includes unusual Coptic finds, a large selection of Greek relics, and a number of objects from Crete and Cyprus. The museum occasionally organizes excellent temporary exhibitions on classical themes.

★★ Amstel River

Tram 9, 14, sneltram 51, or metro to Waterlooplein; or tram 6, 7, 10 to Oosteinde.

The meandering River Amstel, a remote distributary of the Rhine, once formed the main axis of the city, although now it is a tranquil backwater and a popular place for walks in the afternoons. The finest stretch is south from the 19thC bridge, the **Blauwbrug,** an attempt by the architect W. Springer to copy the Belle Epoque allure of Paris. Look to the south, toward the restored wooden drawbridge known as the **Magere Brug** (Narrow Bridge), which seems a more fitting symbol of Amsterdam's antique charm. An eccentric touch is added to the scene by the barge—constructed by the American artist Victor Bulgar—which sits below the Blauwbrug like a raft that has floated in from the South Seas. On the right are several splendid mansions, including a sober Doric house built by Adriaen Dortsman at Amstel 216. On the opposite bank is the Amstelhof, a 17thC senior citizens' home.

Overlooking a picturesque complex of sluices is the splendid **Theater Carré,** originally built as a circus in

The Magere Brug

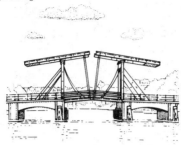

1887. Continuing beyond the Hogesluis—another of Springer's opulent bridges—you pass the legendary Amstel Hotel, built in 1867. Some of its splendor rubs off on Weesperzijde, as can be seen in the **De IJsbreker Cafe** (see "Amsterdam's Cafes" in **Dining**). Cross the **Nieuwe Amstelbrug**—built in 1902 by **Berlage**—to reach the fairy-tale 19thC house complete with giant gnomes on the roof, at Ceintuurbaan 251-255.

Continuing south takes you past the highly ornate neo-Renaissance **Gemeentearchief,** which often exhibits prints from the city's archives. A short detour to the right, down Tolstraat, is the **Technical Museum NINT,** while opposite is the brilliantly revitalized Cinétol library, which was built by J.A. Brinkman and L. C. van der Vlugt in 1926 as a Theosophical Hall and later used as a movie theater. The modern interior is particularly striking.

Farther down the Amstel, you will find 2 striking examples of modern Amsterdam architecture—the twin blocks of **Amsterdam School** housing on the right, facing a bridge, the **Berlagebrug,** which was one of Berlage's last projects. From here, continue down the Amstel, past scenes sketched by Rembrandt, to reach Amstelpark, or pick up a tram back to the center.

Amstelkring, Museum

Oude Zijds Voorburgwal 40. ☎ 20-6246604. Open Mon–Sat 10am–5pm; Sun, holidays 1–5pm. Admission: Adults Dfl. 5, children Dfl. 3.50. A short walk from Centraal Station.

Although this delightful museum is located on a shabby patch of canal in the red-light district, the visitor—once safely inside—is taken back to the Dutch golden age with its sober virtues and solid furniture. The private foundation responsible for restoring this building has gone to great lengths to create the appearance of an Old Master painting, and the neat arrangements of fruit and casually discarded clay pipes give the impression that the owner has just stepped out to supervise the arrival of spices from the East Indies. One of the house's most attractive rooms is the kitchen, which brings light into its darkest corners by means of ingenious windows and gleaming tiles.

The house is full of unexpected surprises: windows in strange places, labyrinths of creaking staircases, and a concealed priest's room in the belly of the building. But the biggest surprise is the bulky church constructed in the attic, which gives the house its memorable name: Onze Lieve Heer Op Zolder—Our Lord in the Attic.

The original owner was a Catholic merchant who built a clandestine church here after the Calvinist authorities outlawed Catholicism in 1581. The museum contains a map showing just how many of these ostensibly secret churches there were in Amsterdam in the 17th and 18th centuries. It also reveals the astonishing variety of religions practiced in the tolerant climate of Amsterdam. The present church, which extends over no fewer than 3 houses, was built in the 1730s. Its ingenious foldaway pulpit is a typical Amsterdam space-saving solution.

Looking from the upper windows toward the harbor, you can see the Baroque domes of **St. Nicolaaskerk,** which the congregation of Onze Lieve Heer Op Zolder erected in the 19thC when the ban on the Catholic church was finally lifted. Religious enthusiasm waned almost completely during the 20thC and, sadly, the church is now used only for occasional services.

Facing the museum is a magnificent neck gable in Vingboons style dating from 1656. Fabulous dolphins wreathed with strings of pearls decorate the claw pieces, although few people in this part of Amsterdam take much interest in such detail.

Amstelpark

Europaboulevard. Open dawn–dusk. Tram: 4 to Station RAI. On leaving the station turn right—the park entrance is just beyond the Novotel.

This restful park on the southern edge of the city near the RAI exhibition center contains an art gallery (**Het Glazen Huis**), a rosarium, Japanese garden, maze, and sauna, as well as animals such as seals and donkeys.

★ Amsterdams Historisch Museum (Amsterdam Historical Museum)

Kalverstraat 92. ☎ 20-5231822. Guidebooks in English, French, or German can be borrowed. Open Mon–Fri 10am–5pm; Sat–Sun

11am–5pm. Entrances at Kalverstraat 92, St. Luciensteeg 27,
Nieuwezijds Voorburgwal 357, Gedempte Begijnensloot and Begijnhof.
Admission: Adults Dfl. 7.50, children Dfl. 3.75. Tram: 1, 2, 5, 9, 16,
24, 25 to Spui.

How did a tiny fishing village on the Amstel develop
into one of the world's richest and most beautiful cities? What were Amsterdam's achievements and failings?
How did its citizens live? Amsterdam's historical museum attempts to answer questions such as these by
means of a fascinating collection of maps, portraits,
utensils, clothes, globes, models, books, sculpture, and
topographic views.

The vibrant, cosmopolitan spirit of Amsterdam is
best seen in the various views of the Dam in the 17thC
(room 6). The stillness of its great canals in the 18thC is
reflected in the attractive urban scenes of Jan de Beijer
and H. P. Schouten (rooms 9 and 10). The most remarkable map is Cornelis Anthoniszoon's 1544 wood-
cut showing the medieval city in minute detail (room
1). Amsterdam's finest moment is captured in H. C.
Vroom's *Return of the Second East Indies Expedition* (room
5), depicting the dramatic scene in 1599 when a flotilla
of small boats surrounded the 4 returning galleons.
The painful, slow decline of the city is symbolized
by the models of the unbuilt Nieuwe Kerk tower
(room 10), the paintings of the Napoleonic army entering Amsterdam (room 16), and the scenes of the 1930s
depression and war years (room 17).

An attic (room 10a) houses a working 17thC carillon from the Munttoren. Visitors are invited to play on
the wooden keyboard, which, with practice, will chime
the carillon bells. You can then listen to recordings of
music played on the 4 surviving 17thC carillons built
by the brothers François and Pierre Hemony (in
the Koninklijk Paleis, Oude Kerk, Zuiderkerk, and
Westerkerk).

The museum, which is housed in a 17thC municipal orphanage, is also the site of the **Regentenkamer,**
a beautiful 17thC classical room where governors met.
The small adjoining room commemorates one of the
orphans, Jan van Speyk, who heroically blew up his
ship during the 1830 Belgian revolt in order to prevent
its falling into enemy hands.

Other interesting details include the original orphanage entrance—dating from 1581—at Kalverstraat 92,
and a collection of facade stones displayed along
St. Luciensteeg (including a delightful scene of the
Montelbaanstoren, and a giant tooth).

★★ Amsterdamse Bos

Amstelveenseweg. Transportation: C and CN bus 170, 171, 172 from Amsterdam Centraal Station to Van Nijenrodeweg; for details of summer tram service, see Electrische Museum Tramlijn.

Amsterdam's largest park was built in the southwest suburbs in the 1930s as an employment creation scheme. Although inspired by the Bois de Boulogne in Paris, the Amsterdamse Bos has an unmistakably Dutch flavor, with carefully segregated routes for cars, bicycles, horses, and pedestrians. The park even includes an artificial hill. Notice also the distinctive wooden bridges, built in Amsterdam School style by P. L. Kramer between 1937 and 1957. Another feature is a rowing racecourse, the Bosbaan, which was built for the 1928 Amsterdam Olympics.

The Amsterdamse Bos can also be reached by bicycle. Follow the Amstel along Amsteldijk south to the Kleine Kalfje, a cafe on the outskirts of Amsterdam. At the Kleine Kalfje, turn right and follow the cycle path along Kalfjeslaan, which leads straight into the park. There is a small cycle rental shop at the Van Nijenrodeweg entrance to the park (Take A Bike, Amstelveenseweg 880-900, ☎ 20-6445473), and canoes and water bicycles can also be rented; follow signs to *kanoën waterfietsen verhuur* (see "Staying Active" for more information).

★★ Anne Frankhuis (Anne Frank's House)

Prinsengracht 263. ☎ 20-5567100. Open Sept–May: Mon–Sat 9am–5pm, Sun and holidays 10am–5pm; June–Aug: Mon–Fri 9am–7pm, Sun 10am–7pm. Closed on Yom Kippur. Admission: Adults Dfl. 8, children Dfl. 4.50. Tram: 13, 14, 17 to Westermarkt.

During the Nazi occupation of the Netherlands, 8 Jewish Amsterdammers hid for 25 months in the annex of this house near the Westerkerk to avoid deportation to concentration camps. Among them was the 14-year-old schoolgirl Anne Frank, who kept a diary recording her experiences in meticulous detail. Her observations ranged from complaints about the food to lyrical descriptions of the bells of the Westerkerk. Anne Frank and her family were eventually betrayed to the Germans and in 1945 she died in the Bergen-Belsen concentration camp. Her diary was published in 1947 under the title *Het Achterhuis*. (*Achterhuis* is the back part of a canal house that is used for everyday living.) Anne Frank and her family lived in the achterhuis of a house on the Prinsengracht canal.

The house has been kept in the same state as when the Franks were in hiding, and on the walls of the room occupied by Anne are photographs of Deanna Durbin and the British princesses, which she cut out of magazines, together with pencil marks indicating the growth of Anne and her sister.

Special exhibitions are organized by the Anne Frank Foundation to focus on contemporary manifestations of fascism, racism, and anti-Semitism. Anne was one of the more than 100,000 Dutch Jews to die during the Holocaust.

★ Artis (Zoo)

Plantage Kerklaan 38-40. ☎ 20-5233400. Open daily 9am–5pm. Admission: Adults: Dfl. 19, children Dfl. 13. Tram: 7, 9, 14 to Plantage Kerklaan.

Natura Artis Magistra (Nature is the Teacher of the Arts) is the official title of Amsterdam's zoo, although it has always been known simply as Artis. It was opened in 1838 in a garden on the unfashionable east side of the city and grew to become one of the world's largest zoos.

Its delights include the reptile house, which is landscaped like a steamy jungle, a nocturnal house, an aquarium, and a glass-walled seal pool. The owls peer out from a ruined city wall as in the paintings of Hieronymus Bosch. There is also a small farmyard, where children can wander freely and pet the domestic animals. Animals in Artis are given generous amounts of space, which does not leave a great deal for humans, and on weekends it can become somewhat crowded.

★ Aviodome

Schiphol. ☎ 20-6041521. Open Apr–Sept daily 10am–5pm; Oct–Mar Tues–Fri 10am–5pm, Sat–Sun noon–5pm. Admission: Adults Dfl. 8, children Dfl. 5. Transportation: Train to Schiphol, then 10-min. walk.

The Dutch national air museum is located near Schiphol airport in a futuristic dome that shudders each time a Jumbo jet takes off. Some 20 historic aircraft and spaceships are on display, ranging from the Wright Brothers' fragile 1903 *Flyer* to the *Spacelab*, along with models and memorabilia. The salvaged fragments from the bomber of Captain McVie, a World War II pilot, whose last words to his crew were "No panic, don't forget the pigeons," are particularly haunting.

★★ Begijnhof

Spui. ☎ 20-6249665. No set hours since people still live in this *hofje*. Catholic church open daily Oct–Apr 8:30am–5pm; May–Sept 8:30am–

Attractions in Central Amsterdam

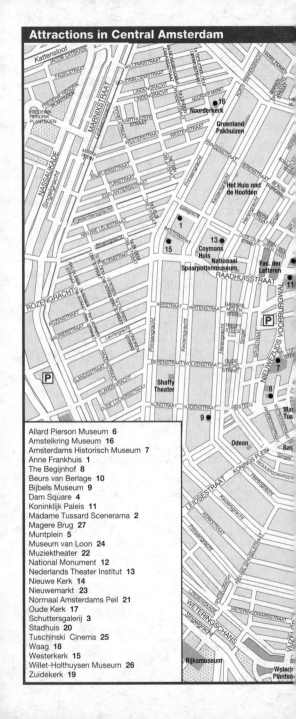

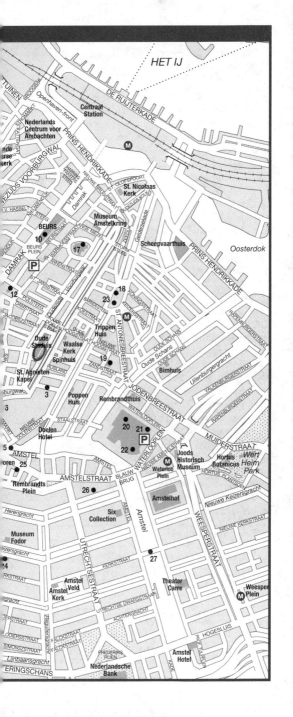

6pm; Engelse Kerk (English Church) open June–Aug Mon–Fri 2–4pm
and for daily church service at 11:30am. Concerts most Saturdays and
Sundays at 8:15pm. Admission free. Disabled people are advised to
use the side entrance on Gedempte Begijnensloot. Tram: 1, 2, 5 to
Spui.

The Begijnhof convent was founded by the Catholic
sisterhood of Beguinages in 1346 near the south limit
of the city, at a safe distance from the noise and confusion of the harbor. It is entered from the north side of
Spui through a modest doorway that leads unexpectedly into an enchanting courtyard filled with flower
gardens, grass, and birdsong—a secret garden in the
center of the busy city.

The sisters of this attractive religious order, popular
in Belgium and The Netherlands, took no vows but
otherwise lived as nuns. The Mother Superior occupied the tall house at no. 26, and services were held in
the charming Begijnenkerk, a church that dates from
1419.

In 1607, the church was offered to English Protestants fleeing England (many of whom later became
the Pilgrims who sailed for America in 1620) and
was renamed the English Church. (See "An Excursion
to Rotterdam" for more information on Pilgrims.)
Opposite, concealed behind a domestic facade, is the
clandestine chapel built in 1665 for the Catholic
Begijnhof residents, who had been allowed to retain
their property after the Reformation. Both churches
continue to coexist amicably.

Although most of the houses in the Begijnhof have
17th and 18thC facades, there is one splendid 15thC
survival at no. 34, with a tarred wooden front and a
simple spout gable. This is **Amsterdam's oldest house,**
built with stone side walls to prevent the spread of fire.
The small courtyard alongside contains several facade
stones illustrating religious themes.

★ Beurs Van Berlage

W. Damrak 279. ☎ 20-6265257. Office open 9am–5pm Mon–Fri.
Admission charged to view the building. Charges for concerts and
exhibitions vary. Tram: 4, 9, 16, 24, 25 to Dam.

H. P. Berlage's Koopmansbeurs (exchange) in Amsterdam is one of the key works of modern Dutch architecture. With its ornamental ironwork and tiled
mosaics, the building originally provided a spectacular
setting for the Amsterdam stock exchange. The
brokers have now gone elsewhere, and the Beurs van
Berlage is currently used for classical concerts and
exhibitions.

Bijbels Museum (Bible Museum)

Herengracht 366. ☎ 20-6247949. Open Tues–Sat 10am–5pm; Sun, holidays 1–5pm. Admission: Adults: Dfl. 3, children: Dfl. 2. Tram: 1, 2, 5 to Spui.

A somewhat evangelical collection of objects relating to the Old Testament is housed in 2 handsome canal houses built in 1662. The houses are worth a visit to look at the 18thC spiral staircase and the ceiling painted by Jacob De Witt with scenes from classical mythology.

Botanical Garden (see Hortus Botanicus)

★★ Curiosities

Amsterdam is dotted with curious details that reflect the quirky humor of the Amsterdammers. You will almost certainly come upon some of them by chance—a barge festooned with garden gnomes, perhaps, or a whimsically painted tram—but some bizarre sights are permanent fixtures of the city. For example, there is the 19thC apartment block with twin gnomes playing handball on the roof (Ceintuurbaan 251-5), the house with a church concealed in the attic (now the Museum Amstelkring), and the row of 7 19thC houses illustrating 7 different national styles of architecture (Roemer Visscherstraat 20-30). Almost every apartment block and bridge designed in the style of the Amsterdam School is eccentric, but the facade of the Scheepvaarthuis (Prins Hendrikkade 114) is particularly remarkable for its sea monsters, sailing ships, and protruding mariners' heads. These curiosities are best discovered during walks through Amsterdam's neighborhoods (see "Amsterdam Walks").

If you stand on Herengracht at the bridge over Beulingsloot, you will spy a white cat and mouse scrambling up the walls of opposite houses (Herengracht 395 and 397). The city is teeming with curious sculptural details such as this, including the extraordinary lampposts on the 19thC Blauwbrug that incorporate ships' prows and imperial crowns; the sea monsters on the bridges near the American Hotel (see "Accommodations"), and the figures of an architect and mason at work on the roof of the Rijksmuseum.

A puzzling sculpture of a turtle supporting a classical column on St. Antoniesbreestraat celebrates the reconstruction of the neighborhood in the 1980s. Another enigmatic column on Rokin is a relic from the medieval pilgrimage chapel built on the site of the Amsterdam Miracle. You might find a modest doorway labeled Manège (Vondelstraat 140), which leads into a vast neoclassical hall with an iron roof built by A. L. van Gendt in 1881. Modeled on the Spanish Riding School in Vienna, the Hollandse Manège still features occasional riding displays.

Classical scholars might be amused by a sophisticated jest carved on a neoclassical portal leading to the new casino (Kleine Gartmanplantsoen). The solemn Roman capitals spell out the words Homo Sapiens Non Urinat in Ventum (human beings do not piss in the wind).

Another kind of Amsterdam curiosity takes the form of surprising, sometimes hidden, passageways and courtyards. *Hofjes,* hidden courtyards surrounded by low-rent houses that were once almshouses or religious communities, can be found in many parts of the city, especially in the Jordaan (see "Walk 2: The Jordaan"). The entrance usually looks like any other door and is sometimes difficult to find. The Oudemanhuispoort, another hidden place that many visitors only chance upon, is a brick passageway lined with bookstalls and sellers of both antiquarian and academic books. The passage connects Kloveniersburgwal with O. Z. Achterburgwal and has a side door opening onto the courtyard of the University of Amsterdam.

★ Dam

Tram: 1, 2, 4, 5, 9, 13, 14, 16, 17, 24, 25 to Dam.

The main square in Amsterdam is named after the dam on the River Amstel built in about 1250 as a protection against floods. The Dam became the focus of the Dutch trading empire in the 17thC, with the old stock exchange (demolished) and the town hall (now the Koninklijk Paleis or Royal Palace) together controlling a sizable share of world commerce. The square has largely lost its former grandeur. The Gothic Nieuwe Kerk is no longer a church, and the former town hall lies empty for much of the year. Yet Dam continues to exude the vitality of Amsterdam, with a constant flow of trams, bicycles, taxis, and pedestrians. There is always something happening on Dam, whether it be street theater, fire-eating, low-key drug dealing, or a variety of street musicians playing everything from soulful saxophone to jovial Dutch barrel organ.

The **National Monument,** erected in 1956 as a memorial to those who died in the Second World War, has been a meeting place for young people for the last 30 years. In the 1960s, "Meet you at the Dam" was a common phrase among hippie travelers, who would use the Dam as a meeting ground to see old friends or find new travel companions. It is still a gathering place for young tourists and flocks of pigeons. The endless flux of life on Dam Square can best be watched from the cafe terrace at the Nieuwe Kerk.

Electrische Museum Tramlijn (Electric Tramline Museum)

Haarlemmermeerstation, Amstelveenseweg 264. ☎ 20-6737538. Open Apr–Oct: Sun, holidays only 10:30am–5:30pm; July–Aug Tues–Thurs, Sat 1–4pm; antique trams depart every 20 min., last ride 6pm. Admission (including round-trip ticket to Amstelveen): Adults Dfl. 5, children Dfl. 2.50. Tram: 6, 16 to Haarlemmermeerstation.

A group of tram enthusiasts has built up a collection of some 60 antique trams from Amsterdam, The Hague, Rotterdam, Groningen, Kassel, and Vienna, and on summer weekends operates service from the former Haarlemmermeer railway station to the **Amsterdamse Bos** and Amstelveen. The period detail is fastidiously maintained, to the extent that the conductor is required to descend at each crossing to control the traffic with a red flag.

★★ Grachtengordel

Tram 13, 14, 17 to Westermarkt (early 17thC area); tram 1, 2, 5 to Keizersgracht (mid-17thC); tram 16, 24, 25 to Keizersgracht (Golden Bend) or tram 4 to Keizersgracht (Amstel area).

Amsterdam's magnificent semicircle of canals and cross-streets (literally, the "canal girdle") was built under the ambitious "Plan of the Three Canals" drawn up by the city carpenter Hendrick Staets in the early 17thC. The 3 canals—**Herengracht, Keizersgracht,** and **Prinsengracht**—were built in 2 stages: initially from Brouwersgracht to Leidsegracht during the first half of the 17thC, and then from Leidsegracht to the Amstel after 1665. The different periods can be detected in the architecture: picturesque brick buildings such as the Renaissance **Bartolotti House** (see Nederlands Theater Instituut, below) in the older part, and sober sandstone palaces such as the **Museum Van Loon** in the final stretch. If you look carefully, you can see subtle differences between the aristocratic town-houses on Herengracht ("The Gentlemen's Canal"), the smaller middle-class dwellings on Keizersgracht ("The Emperors' Canal"), and the modest artisan homes and workshops on Prinsengracht ("The Princes' Canal").

The best introduction to the Grachtengordel is to take a boat tour along the canals, since this shows the buildings as they were meant to be seen: from the water. The tour also gives you an idea of the sights and areas that are worth exploring in greater detail. To obtain a glimpse of a typical canal house, visit the **Museum Willet-Holthuysen** or the **Nederlands Theater Instituut.** It is also fascinating to view the canal web from above, which is possible by climbing the **Westerkerk tower** (summer only).

After an overview, the very best way to experience the charm of Amsterdam's canals is by walking. Don't try to cover too much distance—Prinsengracht is 2.2 miles (3.5 kilometers) long, Keizersgracht 1.9 miles (3 kilometers), and Herengracht 1.6 miles (2.5 kilometers). Select a short stretch of canal and take time to stop and look at the wealth of detail in gables, doorways, staircases, and decorated facade stones.

Be sure also to explore the cross-streets, which still fulfill their original function as shopping streets and are full of exotic little stores. Between Brouwersgracht and Leidsestraat is the liveliest area of the Grachtengordel; the Weteringbuurt—between Spiegelgracht and Reguliersgracht—is the most peaceful.

Heineken Brouwerij

Stadhouderskade 78. ☎ 20-5239239. 2³/₄-hr. tour compulsory. Open: June 1–Sept 15, Mon–Fri, tours at 9:30am, 11am, 1pm, 2:30pm; Sept 16–June 31, Mon–Fri, tours at 9:30am, 11am. Closed holidays. Minimum age: 18. Admission: Dfl. 2. Tram: 16, 24, 25 to Stadhouderskade.

Heineken beer is no longer brewed in Amsterdam, but the company's giant brick brewery, built in the 1860s, has been preserved as a museum. The official guided tour takes in the granary, the brewhouse with its gleaming copper kettles, and the stables, which still accommodate the horses used to pull Heineken's ancient brewer's dray through the city. Tours end with free samples of Heineken brews.

★★ Herengracht

Tram 1, 2, 5 to Dam or Koningsplein, or tram 4 to Herengracht.

No visit to Amsterdam would be complete without at least a glimpse of Herengracht, the inner canal of the 17thC Grachtengordel ("canal girdle"). Although the older section of the canal—from Brouwersgracht to Leidsegracht—closely resembles parallel sections of Keizersgracht and Prinsengracht, the later stretch—from Leidsegracht to the Amstel—contains many of Amsterdam's most handsome 17th and 18thC houses. These were built during the second phase of the canal web developments, when Herengracht was envisaged as an exclusive residential area from which many industries were banned. Sugar refining (which was a notorious fire hazard), brewing (which produced unpleasant smells), and coopery (a noisy trade) were relegated to the Prinsengracht, the Brouwersgracht, and the Jordaan. The patrician families who moved here from the east side of the Amstel wanted to withdraw from the noise and smells of the trading city. Yet this absence of shops and warehouses produced a somewhat sterile atmosphere, not improved by the numerous banks and insurance companies that occupy these houses today. Consequently, my favorite stretch of the Herengracht is the more lively and residential but somewhat less grand section between Huidenstraat and Brouwersgracht.

Measuring about 1.6 miles (2.5 kilometers), Herengracht can be walked from end to end without too much difficulty; if you have only a short time to spare, concentrate on short stretches: from Brouwers-gracht to Huidenstraat, from Huidenstraat to Leidse-straat, or from Leidsestraat to Vijzelstraat (the Golden Bend).

From Brouwersgracht to Raadhuisstraat: The old end of Herengracht retains the flavor of the medieval city, especially on its east side, which was developed shortly after the construction of the 1585 city wall. Notice the curious sculleries attached to many of the corner houses, such as **Herengracht 1.** The most attractive relics from Herengracht's earliest period are the 2 warehouses **De Fortuyn** (Fortune) and **d'Arcke Noach** (Noah's Ark) at nos. 43–45, probably dating from around 1600.

A much grander style of architecture begins to appear on the first bend in Herengracht, particularly the **Bartolotti House** at nos. 170–72. This splendid Renaissance house, built by Hendrick de Keyser in 1617, is one of the finest facades in Amsterdam, and canal boats pause reverently on Singel to admire its jaunty red-and-white facade through the gap of Drie Koningenstraat. Its first owner was a brewer with the unremarkable name of Willem van den Heuvel, which he changed to Guillielmo Bartolotti to please his father-in-law. The building now accommodates the Nederlands Theater Instituut. Its rather more austere neighbor at **no. 168,** built in 1638 by **Philips Vingboons,** provides further accommodations for the museum. Notice the spectacular coat of arms in the neck gable, placed there by its first owner, Michiel Pauw, who in 1630 played a major role in the development of New York when he founded the colony of Pavonia,

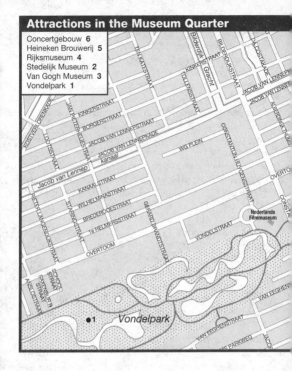

now Hoboken, New Jersey. Perhaps it was Pauw's self-important gable that prompted a later occupant of **no. 166** to adorn his cornice gable with the pious motto Solo Deo Gloria (Glory to God Alone).

From Raadhuisstraat to Huidenstraat (see "Walk 1: The Essential Amsterdam"): This section rambles along in a muddle of styles, with some fine 18thC gable tops to be seen on the west side, notably **De Witte Lelie** (The White Lily) at no. 274, with its ornate Louis XIV–style balustrade rising to a crested top.

From Huidenstraat to Leidsestraat: This beautiful stretch of Herengracht is best appreciated from the east side (where a few benches are provided). Philips Vingboons designed many of the houses on this bend, from the 4 dignified neck gables of the 1662 **Cromhouthuizen** at nos. 364–70, to the classical pilastered facade at **no. 386,** which, although built only 1 year later, represents a decisive break with traditional gables and provides a foretaste of the more formal styles that are to be seen in houses built in the 1660s and 1670s.

The ornate confectionery in French Renaissance style at **nos. 380–82,** seen by puritanical

Amster-dammers as the last word in bad taste, was built by A. Salm in 1889 for a rich client who wanted to emulate the chic mansions of New York's 5th Avenue. Twin houses seem to have been popular when this stretch of Herengracht was developed, and at **nos. 396–98** and **nos. 409–11** are 2 pairs of 17thC neck gables known respectively as the "twin brothers" and "twin sisters." Notice also the twin at **nos. 390–92,** built about 1665 with sculpture in the neck gable depicting a man and a woman mysteriously stretching a cord between them.

From Leidsestraat to Vijzelstraat: The legendary **Golden Bend,** which occupies this short stretch, comes as a slight disappointment. Although there are undoubtedly some magnificent houses—such as **no. 475,** built in the 1730s in a rich Louis XIV–style—most houses of the 1660s and 1670s present rather sober exteriors. Residences in this prime location include the **Andries de Graeff house** at no. 446, built for a prominent 17thC burgomaster; the **Huis van Deutz** at no. 450, designed by **Philips Vingboons** in 1663 for a banker; and the austere house by Adriaen Dortsman at **no. 462,** with its sculpture on the balustrade depicting the popular Dutch virtues of Welfare and Trade. **No. 476** was also built during the 1670s, but restyled in the 1740s to create one of Amsterdam's most elegant houses.

From Vijzelstraat to the Amstel: The final stretch of Herengracht is somewhat less solemn and includes the 4 splendid neck gables at **nos. 504–10**, whose claw pieces are decorated with dogs, mermaids, and dolphins. Numbers **571–81** date from 1664, when 4 wealthy citizens reached the unprecedented decision to build 4 identical houses. The agreement did not apply to ornament, however, which is why the owner of **no. 579** was able to add the oversized figure of the Archangel Michael slaying a dragon, together with various other frivolous touches. The **Museum Willet-Holthuysen** is at **no. 605.**

Hollandse Schouwburg

Plantage Middenlaan 24. ☎ 20-6269945. Open daily 11am–5pm. Admission: Free. Tram: 7, 9, 14 to Plantage Kerklaan.

The Dutch Theater (Hollandse Schouwburg), once a center of theatrical life, was taken over by the Germans during the occupation and used as a place where Amsterdam Jews were brought and confined before being sent to Westerbok, a Dutch concentration camp, and then on to the extermination camps. The roofless shell of the former theater now serves as a moving memorial to the Jewish victims of the war.

★ Hortus Botanicus (Botanical Garden)

Plantage Middenlaan 2. ☎ 20-6258411. Open Apr–Sept: Mon–Fri 9am–5pm, Sat–Sun, holidays 11am–5pm; Oct–Mar closes 1 hr. earlier. Transportation: Tram 7, 9 to Plantage Doklaan; sneltram 51 or metro to Waterlooplein.

This tiny botanical garden on the east side of the city, close to Waterlooplein, was established in 1682 for the cultivation of medicinal herbs. Many exotic species were shipped back from the Dutch East Indies, largely on the initiative of the East India Company director Joan Huydecoper. Highlights of this beautiful garden, now owned by the university, include the palm houses and the ornamental ponds. The colors are particularly vivid in August.

★★ Jewish Historical Museum (see Joods Historisch Museum)

★ Jodenbuurt

Transportation: Tram 9, 14 to Mr. Visserplein; sneltram 51 or metro to Waterlooplein.

Until World War II, Amsterdam's Jewish quarter was located on the islands to the east of Oude Zijde. First to settle were the Portuguese and Spanish Sephardic Jews, who fled religious persecution in the late 16thC. They were followed in the 17thC by Ashkenazi Jews, driven out of Poland and Germany. Drawn by Amsterdam's unique mixture of religious tolerance and economic opportunity, Jews played a profound role in the development of the city. Although they were originally excluded from many skilled crafts and barred from owning shops or joining trade guilds, the Dutch Jews filled the niches available to them—the new trades like diamond dealing and textiles. After Jews were granted civil equality in 1796, they were given more economic freedom but they tended to stay in the trades that had become familiar to them: the stock market, and the printing, diamond, and textile businesses. Jews also became an integral part of Amsterdam's theater and cabaret scene.

But this vibrant history of Jewish Amsterdam was brought to a terrible conclusion during the Nazi occupation, when more than 100,000 of Holland's 145,000 Jews were murdered. Approximately 25,000 Jews were hidden by the Dutch during the war; only 15,000 survived. Of the thousands of Jews who returned from exile or the camps after the war, only a small portion remained in Amsterdam. Some returned to find that their homes had been appropriated by their Dutch neighbors or used for firewood during the scarcity of the war years; for others, whose homes had been left untouched, the memory of the war was too much for them to remain. Consequently, many Dutch Jews emigrated to Israel or America. The entire Jodenbuurt fell into ruin after World War II and later became the scene of controversial developments such as the IJ tunnel access road, the metro, and the Stadhuis/Muziektheater complex, which together have destroyed much of the character of the old Jodenbuurt. Only recently has the area begun to show signs of revival, largely due to the highly imaginative municipal housing by the architects Aldo van Eyck and Theo Bosch. This area now contains some of the finest postwar Dutch architecture, alongside the tragic remains of its Jewish past.

The main Jewish buildings to have survived are the synagogues overlooking J. D. Meijerplein. This square also contains the *Dokwerker* statue by Mari Andriessen, which commemorates the February 1941 dockers' strike held in protest of the persecution of the Jews. The

north side of the square is dominated by the massive
Portuguese-Israelite Synagogue (☎ 20-6253509,
open Sun–Fri 10am–12:15pm, 1:30–4pm; closed Sat
and Yom Kippur), built by Elias Bouwman between
1671 and 1675.

On the south side of the square is the Synagogue
Complex, which is made up of 4 17th and 18thC
synagogues that have been linked by modern glass and
steel constructions to form The Joods Historisch
Museum (see listing below). The **Grote Sjoel** (Great
Synagogue) on the right was built in 1671 by Daniel
Stalpaert. A second synagogue, the Obbene Sjoel, was
built behind the Grote Sjoel in 1686. In 1700, the Dritt
Sjoel was added to the complex, and finally a fourth
synagogue—the ornate **Neie Shul** (New Synagogue)—
was built in 1752 in Louis XIV–style. Jodenbreestraat
and Sint Antoniesbreestraat, which connect Mr.
Visserplein with Nieuwmarkt, were devastated during
the construction of the metro. The only relics of the
old street are the twin neck gables at Sint Antoniesbreestraat 64-72 (which are suspended from the modern buildings on either side), the splendid classical
Pintohuis built in 1651 for Isaac de Pinto at Sint
Antoniesbreestraat 69, and the Rembrandthuis.

★★ Joods Historisch Museum (Jewish Historical Museum)

Jonas Daniel Meijerplein 2-4. ☎ 20-6269945; fax: 20-6241721.
Open daily 11am–5pm. Closed on Yom Kippur. Admission: Adults Dfl.
7, children Dfl. 3.50. Tram: 9, 14, sneltram 51, or metro to
Waterlooplein.

The Jewish Historical Museum provides insight into
the Jewish religious and cultural life in the Netherlands
and abroad. It does not dwell on the horrors of the
Holocaust. The museum's permanent collection includes
articles recovered from the 4 synagogues within which
the museum was built, as well as from the splendid Portuguese Synagogue across the street. A ritual bath com-
partment has been restored in one of the Ashkenazi
synagogues, and silver ceremonial objects recovered from
the once-wealthy Portuguese Synagogue are displayed
in another. Included with the treasures from the Portuguese Synagogue is a beautiful Art Nouveau prayer shawl
with an embroidered flower motif. A plaque tells you
that the man who once wore the shawl was killed in
Auschwitz on October 11, 1941—a disquieting reminder of the flourishing Jewish community that was
lost during the Holocaust.

The Holocaust exhibit itself is very small, but it is made powerful and real by the kind of mundane and bureaucratic remnants of the Holocaust that most Americans never see: shreds of legal notices and edicts concerning the closing and/or appropriation of Jewish homes and businesses, yellow-star cloth badges with their washing instructions, and a receipt for delivery to the Germans of 5 Jews (at Dfl. 7 per Jew). Another small exhibit tells a story, through both paintings and written text, of Charlotte Salomon, a young German art student who fled to southern France to escape the Nazis. Through her paintings and poems, she expresses her feelings about the war. (Although this exhibit, like the Anne Frank house, is popular with children, the museum staff advises that children under the age of 12 be accompanied by a guide or an informed adult.)

The museum also displays changing exhibits, such as a beautifully orchestrated multimedia exhibit on Jewish theater and cabaret (a lively and popular source of entertainment before World War II), or on the history of Jews in the Dutch textile and diamond businesses. A new exhibit will focus on Judaism, Christianity, and Islam.

The museum occupies an architecturally innovative complex of the 4 synagogues, which have been artfully converted using modern techniques. Overhead galleries offer unexpected views, and a street, formerly an alley with the Yiddish name Sjoelgass, passes through the museum. The museum cafe, situated in the smallest of the synagogues, offers kosher and Mediterranean delicacies, and the bookstore offers a fine selection of books, calendars, and cards.

★ Jordaan
Tram: 13, 14, 17 to Westermarkt.

This area was developed to the west of Prinsengracht at the same time as the Grachtengordel. Its role in the 1609 Plan was that of a humble industrial quarter; to cut costs, the majestic geometry of the great canals was abandoned in favor of a dense grid pattern with narrow canals cut east to west along the course of existing drainage ditches. This gives the Jordaan a logic quite different from the rest of the city, and even native Amsterdammers become lost when they venture west of Prinsengracht. It helps a little to know that the streets running north to south are usually called *dwarsstraten* (cross-streets) and numbered east to west as 1e, 2e, and 3e (sometimes written *Eerste, Tweede, Derde*), so that 1e

Laurierdwarsstraat is the most easterly street to cross Lauriergracht.

The Jordaan still houses many small businesses, but it is also a highly desirable, and increasingly expensive, residential area. Like New York's SoHo and Greenwich Village, the Brouwersgracht and Prinsengracht parts of the Jordaan are being renovated and gentrified with former warehouses being turned into art studios and large apartments. What attracts people, especially students and artists, to the Jordaan is its vitality and its mixture of innovative boutiques, galleries, restaurants, and cafes. Perhaps this creative energy is a legacy of the 17thC, when numerous Huguenot refugees settled here after Louis XIV's revocation of the Edict of Nantes. There is even a theory that the name Jordaan is a corruption of the French word *jardin* (garden), which seems plausible given canals in the area with names such as Rozengracht (Roses Canal) and Lauriergracht (Laurel Canal). However, another theory gives the name a less glamorous source (see "Walk 2: The Jordaan").

The Jordaan is cut through the middle by the busy Rozengracht, where Rembrandt spent his final years. However, it is the area north of Rozengracht that is most lively, with the best shops on the cross-streets such as 1e Leliedwarsstraat and 1e Egelantiersdwarsstraat. There are also good brown cafes, such as **'t Smalle** and **De Reiger** (see "Walk 2: The Jordaan" as well as "Amsterdam's Cafes" in "Dining"), on almost every corner.

Bloemgracht was once called the Herengracht of the Jordaan, and its historic atmosphere is maintained by colorful gable stones and hand-blown stained-glass windows. The splendid trio of step gables at **nos. 87–91** was built at the rather late date of 1642—long after the rest of Amsterdam had adopted classical styles. The curious **facade stones** depict a man of the city, a man of the land, and a man of the sea.

One of the special attractions of the Jordaan is its hidden **hofjes,** small almshouses founded by wealthy merchants in the 17thC. At Egelantiersgracht 105-141 is the intimate **St. Andrieshofje,** which dates from 1615; its courtyard is generally open to the public. The nearby **Anslo's Hofje** at Egelantiersstraat 36–50 is a picturesque jumble of houses around 3 courtyards, reached through a small doorway on 2e Egelantiersdwarsstraat. Also open for visits is the much larger **Huiszitten-Weduwenhof** in Karthuizersstraat, built by city architect Daniel Stalpaert in 1650 as a home for

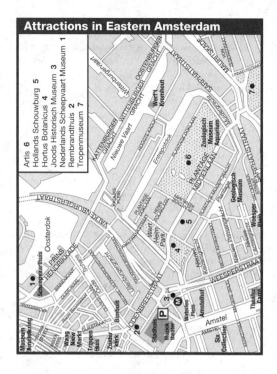

impoverished widows. Farther north at Lindengracht
149-163 is the **Suikerhofje,** established in 1670, with
an inner courtyard open to visitors. Look also for the
witty facade stones nearby at **Lindengracht 53** (the
Tangled Yarn) and **Lindengracht 55-57** (the Topsy-
Turvy World—which gives the date of construction
upside down and the street name backward). Two more
hofjes can be discovered in the quiet northwest corner
of the Jordaan at Palmgracht 20-26 and 28-38.

Keizersgracht

Tram 13, 14, 17 to Westermarkt; tram 1, 2, 4, 5, 16, 24, 25 to
Keizersgracht.

Keizersgracht is the central of the 3 great canals form-
ing the 17thC Grachtengordel. The early 17thC
section—from Brouwersgracht to Leidsegracht—
matches Herengracht in grandeur, but the later
section—from Leidsegracht to the Amstel—is much
more modest, as many 17thC Herengracht residents
bought up the adjoining lot on Keizersgracht to en-
large their gardens or build coach houses. The best
stretches of Keizersgracht to explore are Brouwersgracht
to Raadhuisstraat and Runstraat to Leidsestraat.

From Brouwersgracht to Raadhuisstraat: The area from Brouwersgracht to Herenstraat contains mainly early 17thC buildings, including the lovely **Groenland Pakhuizen** (Greenland warehouses), at nos. 40-44, where whale oil was stored in enormous 10,000-liter tanks. Between Herenstraat and Leliegracht, the 17thC architecture becomes rather more flamboyant. **Het Huis met de Hoofden** (The House with the Heads) at Keizersgracht 123 was built in 1622 by Hendrick de Keyser in a bustling Dutch Renaissance style, its 6 heads representing the classical deities Apollo, Ceres, Mars, Pallas Athene, Bacchus, and Diana (see "Walk 1: The Essential Amsterdam").

Overlooking Leliegracht is a lofty **Art Nouveau building** designed by G. van Arkel in 1905 for an insurance company. The tile tableau at the top of the tower invests the insurance business with a rather far-fetched religious symbolism. Between Leliegracht and Raadhuisstraat is the **Coymans Huis** (Keizersgracht 177), a sober building in Dutch classical style built a mere 2 years after the jaunty House with the Heads. Its reserved style found favor with the ruling elite, and the architect, Jacob van Campen, later won the competition to design the town hall (now the Koninklijk Paleis) on Dam.

From Raadhuisstraat to Leidsestraat: Between Raadhuisstraat and Reestraat, walk on the east side in order to admire the buildings opposite—especially **Keizersgracht 209,** with its statue of Hope holding a basket of fruit. From Reestraat to Berenstraat, don't overlook **Keizersgracht 244-246,** a matching pair of houses laden with lavish Louis XIV–style cornices. The stretch from Berenstraat to Leidsegracht is particularly rich in architectural interest. The **Felix Meritis building** at Keizersgracht 324 was erected in 1786 by a group of high-minded businessmen fired with the idea of spreading art and scientific knowledge. The society's name—Felix Meritis (Deservedly Happy)—says it all. The building has since had a varied history: It came into the hands of the Dutch Communist party in 1946 and in the 1960s became one of Amsterdam's first experimental theaters. It also has a lovely theater cafe (see "Amsterdam's Cafes" in "Dining").

Keizersgracht 319 has a dignified elevated neck gable built in 1639 by **Philips Vingboons,** whose brand of classicism kept alive the flamboyant tradition established by Hendrick de Keyser. The small portal at **Keizersgracht 384** was the entrance to the former

Stadsschouwburg (city theater), which a fire destroyed in 1772. **The Gilded Star** at no. 387 is another perfect example of the elevated neck-gable style, built almost at the end of the golden age in 1668. **Keizersgracht 446** is a splendidly ornate Louis XIV–style dwelling from the 1720s, which was at one stage occupied by the art collector Adriaan van der Hoop, whose treasures included Rembrandt's *The Jewish Bride.*

Overlooking Leidsestraat is a ponderous late 19thC building erected for the New York Life Insurance Company and later taken over by the furniture store Metz & Co. The **Rietveld penthouse** on the top floor provides a glimpse of the canal web from above.

Keizersgracht 508 is an appealing neo-Renaissance building with sculpture commemorating the 300th anniversary of the birth of the Dutch poet P. C. Hooft.

Between Leidsestraat and the Amstel: This stretch of Keizersgracht is essentially just a mews for the mansions on the "Golden Bend" of Herengracht. Examples of coach houses are at **Keizersgracht 481** and **485.** Any interesting buildings tend to be found on the west side, notably the splendid twins at **Keizersgracht 606-608** built in Louis XIV style in the 1730s. Also noteworthy are the twin houses by **Adriaen Dortsman** that form the **Museum Van Loon.** Almost directly opposite is the Fodor Museum, a center for contemporary art exhibitions.

★★ Koninklijk Paleis (Royal Palace)

W. Dam. ☎ 20-6248698. Open June–Aug daily 12:30–5pm; Sept–May Wed 2–4pm. Admission free. Tram: 1, 2, 4, 5, 9, 13, 14, 16, 17, 24, 25 to Dam.

The Town Hall of Amsterdam—now a royal palace—was built at the high point of the golden age, when the city was ablaze with civic pride. In 1648, some 13,659 wooden piles were driven into the ground to provide a stable foundation, and 17 years later the building (although still unfinished) was proudly opened. The tireless poet Vondel produced a 1,500-line ode to celebrate the occasion. The Town Hall, one of the glories of European Baroque architecture, so outstripped any other building in Holland that the Emperor Louis Napoleon fitted it out in 1808 as his palace, forcing the city dignitaries to shuffle off to the Prinsenhof on Oude Zijds Voorburgwal. The building is still occasionally used by the Royal Family, but most of the year it stands sadly dark and empty.

Exterior: Amsterdam's Town Hall was designed in a severe classical style by Jacob van Campen, whose use of sober yellow-gray Bentheim sandstone represents a decisive break with the red-brick and white-stone facades of the early 17thC. To offset the stern appearance of Van Campen's Baroque box, the Antwerp-born sculptor Artus Quellien (or Quellinus) was appointed to decorate the building, and for 14 years he labored with a small army of assistants to create some of the most inventive sculpture of the 17thC.

The moralistic carvings include the figure of Peace surveying Dam from the tip of the pediment. The motif of Peace recurs elsewhere as a reminder that the Town Hall was begun in the same hopeful year that the Treaty of Münster was signed, bringing to an end the horrors of the Eighty Years' War. The pediments are filled with magnificent Baroque sculpture depicting the Oceans (facing Dam) and the Continents (facing Raadhuisstraat) paying homage to the Maid of Amsterdam. Quellien's painstaking decoration can only properly be appreciated through binoculars, or by examining the preliminary models displayed in the Rijksmuseum and Amsterdams Historisch Museum.

"But where is the door?" visitors to the Town Hall often ask. The main entrance to this magnificent building is through a small, concealed doorway at the right-hand side of the arcaded avant corps.

Burgerzaal: This vast assembly hall rises through 4 floors to create the most spacious interior in Amsterdam. The Maid of Amsterdam sits primly at the east end of the Hall, flanked by the figures of Strength and Wisdom, while above the entrance to the Council Chamber (Schepenzaal) at the west end, the figure of Atlas overlooks a sculptural group in which Justice, seated between Death and Punishment, treads Avarice and

Koninklijk Palace

Envy underfoot. The Burgerzaal floor is inlaid with 3 maps—two depicting the hemispheres and the third the heavens—across which Amsterdam's ruling elite once proudly walked in their black robes, deliberating policies with global repercussions.

Galleries: The council offices were located in the Galleries to the north and south of the Burgerzaal, reached through arches decorated with figures depicting the 4 elements: Earth, Water, Air, and Fire. The different council offices are identified by some of Quellien's most imaginative work. Apollo, with his soothing lyre, guards the Chamber of Petty Affairs; Diana presides at the entrance to the Treasury; Venus (who appears more angry than inspired by love) indicates the room in which marriages were registered; festoons hung with ink pots, wax seals, and other symbols of bureaucracy flank the door into the City Secretary's Office; and a depiction of the Fall of Icarus once chastened debtors as they entered the Bankruptcy Court.

The paintings commissioned for the new Town Hall display a plodding moralizing tone, with none of the wit and imagination of Quellien's sculpture. Govert Flinck's *Solomon's Prayer for Wisdom* and Erasmus Quellien's *Amsterdam Glorified* in the Schepenzaal are heavily influenced by the Baroque of Rubens. The city magistrates' bias toward didactic bombast led to their rejection of Rembrandt's *Conspiracy of Claudius Civilis,* which they felt failed to exploit the full political potential of the revolt of the Batavians against the Romans.

As a souvenir of King Louis Napoleon's residence here in the early 19thC, the Royal Palace boasts an extensive collection of Empire-style furniture.

Vierschaar: The heavily fortified ground-floor rooms of the palace are occupied by prison cells, the city bank vaults, and the Vierschaar (Hall of Justice), where the death sentence was pronounced. This involved an elaborate baroque ceremony in which the condemned prisoner was brought before the city magistrates, who were seated on the long bench beneath the statues of 4 voluptuous Caryatids representing women in various states of remorse and anguish. The panels between the Caryatids are decorated with reliefs showing judicial incidents from the Bible and classical mythology, while the frieze above bears grisly reminders of death. After the prisoner had been led into this exquisite tomb, the bronze doors, decorated with thunderbolts, skulls, and a curling serpent, were closed and the death sentence solemnly pronounced.

★ Leidseplein
Tram: 1, 2, 5, 6, 7, 10 to Leidseplein.

Once the site of a gate at the southwest edge of the 17thC city, Leidseplein first began to assume a cultural role in the 18thC when the Stadsschouwburg (Municipal Theater) was rebuilt here. This was replaced in 1894 by an elaborate Renaissance confection by J. L. Springer. Leidseplein received a further boost with the completion in 1902 of the elegant Art Nouveau/Art Deco **American Hotel,** designed by W. Kromhout. A cafe society of writers and intellectuals began to develop in the grand **Café Américain.**

In the 1960s Leidseplein became the territory of the "Pleiners" (who modeled themselves on English "mods"), while the "Dijkers" (equivalent of the "rockers") hung out around the Nieuwendijk. It also became a mecca for hippies and the international youth culture who flocked to The **Melkweg** (Milky Way) and **Paradiso** for their rock concerts and psychedelic light shows. Leidseplein became a show in itself with an abundance of street performers from all over the globe.

Nowadays, Leidseplein is a hub of nighttime activity with movie theaters, a casino, jazz clubs, cafes, and several alternative centers for the arts including the still-intact Melkweg and Paradiso (see "Amsterdam After Dark"). There are also restaurants of every nationality, including an explosion of pizzerias. Leidseplein never sleeps: After the cafes have closed, there is still plenty of action in the discos and clubs.

Madame Tussaud Scenerama
Dam 20. ☎ 20-6229949. Open daily 10am–5:30pm. July–Aug 9:30am–7:30pm. Admission: Adults Dfl. 18, children Dfl. 13. Tram: 1, 2, 4, 5, 9, 13, 14, 16, 24, 25 to Dam.

The old Madame Tussaud's delighted visitors for some 20 years with its ghostly and grisly collection of lifelike wax models, including a wax attendant at the door (to which many a hapless visitor have presented a ticket). The British owners eventually decided that the time had come to revamp and rename the institution, and a team of 500 craftsmen toiled for 2 years to convert the top 3 floors of the Peek & Cloppenburg department store into the Madame Tussaud Scenerama. Many familiar faces from the original Tussaud's collection have been preserved, including Rembrandt in his atelier, Anne Frank penning her diary, and the Dutch Royal Family, but the wax attendant in the lobby has been replaced by a seductive Tina Turner. An elevator takes you up to the exhibition floors, where a 5-meter-high

American Hotel

animated figure representing Amsterdam Man descends amid puffs of liquid nitrogen smoke. You are led by a disembodied voice (speaking Dutch and American English) through an impressive reproduction of a 17thC Amsterdam street, complete with 1,000 genuine brick paving stones, and across a bridge spanning a sizable canal. The tour whisks you along at a brisk pace past a gruesome scene depicting the murder of the De Witt brothers in the Year of Disasters, and a handsome Vermeer-style interior with a woman playing a lute. The scenes are animated using the latest computer technology and special effects, including artificial smoke for a battle scene, cooking smells in a slum interior, and artificially chilled air to evoke a winter's day in the 17thC.

★★ Nederlands Scheepvaart Museum (Dutch Maritime Museum)

Kattenburgerplein 1, ☎ 20-5232222. Open June–Sept: Mon–Sat 10am–5pm, Sun and holidays noon–5pm. Admission: Adults Dfl. 12.50. Children Dfl.8 Bus: 22, 28 from Centraal Station to Kattenburgerplein.

The Dutch maritime museum is a must for anyone who loves ships, models of ships, figureheads, globes, maps, charts, sea battles, or portraits of admirals. If you finally tire of room after room of rigged ships and stormy seas, you can gaze through the arched warehouse doors to the busy harbor where gray warships slide slowly past brightly painted houseboats, and the spires of Amsterdam look like a 17thC painting.

In 1973 the museum moved to its present location in the former arsenal of the Amsterdam Admiralty. This stern classical block, designed by Daniel Stalpaert in 1656, stands in isolation on the edge of the Oosterdok. It was here that Amsterdam's warships were fitted with rigging and sails, and equipped with weapons, clothes and provisions for the long voyages to the East and West Indies. The gleaming brass pumps used to supply ships with drinking water can be seen in the courtyard, along with various war-damaged cannons.

The museum contains 30 rooms covering every aspect of navigation in the Netherlands—from Roman trade on the Rhine to surfboarding. For those who find their interest flagging after 14 rooms, an escape route to the restaurant is helpfully signposted. The museum also provides an informative illustrated booklet in English.

One of the most interesting exhibits is the beautiful bottle-green and gold trekschuit (room 5), a type of horse-drawn passenger boat used on the Dutch canal network from the 17thC to the 19thC. The trekschuit offered a reliable but—as almost every traveler complained—agonizingly slow method of transportation. Travelers from Rotterdam to Amsterdam, for example, would spend 11 hours in the cramped and smoky cabin watching the flat Dutch fields slowly glide by.

Also worth seeing are the curious Japanese paintings of the 17thC Dutch trading post in the Bay of Nagasaki (room 11), the tea clipper model (room 15) and, in the same room, the melodramatic mementos relating to the national hero Van Speyk (1802–31), who in the Belgian revolt of 1830 blew up his ship to avoid its capture. Attractions that might interest children include the submarine periscope (room 24), which gives a 360° view of the city.

The **_Koningssloep_** (royal sloop) on the ground floor is a magnificent barge built between 1816 and 1818 for the Dutch King, with a gilded figure of Neptune poised at the prow. There are several other restored ships

Maritime Museum

moored outside the museum including a herring drifter and a steam-powered icebreaker.

But the most remarkable vessel in the collection is the replica of the *Amsterdam,* an 18thC ship owned by the Dutch East India Company VOC, that sank off the south coast of England in 1749. The excavation of the wreck (which lay near Hastings) has provided much of the data for the replica, together with old plans and ship models. The fastidious reconstruction, carried out by a team of 300 volunteers from 1985 to 1991, is correct down to details such as furniture, hammocks, and the cannon.

The seldom-visited area around the Scheepvaart Museum is rich in maritime interest, with the imposing West India Company warehouses of 1642 overlooking Oude Schans at 's Gravenhekje, the early 17thC **East India Company warehouses** at Prins Hendrikkade 176, Admiral de Ruyter's house at Prins Hendrikkade 131, and a splendid row of 18thC warehouses lined up along the Entrepôtdok (reached through the monumental gate on Kadijksplein). It is also possible to walk along the Entrepôtdok to reach the Werf 't Kromhout (Hoogte Kadijk 147, ☎ 20-6276777), where you may visit a number of boats in various states of repair.

Nederlands Theater Instituut (Dutch Theater Museum)

Herengracht 168. ☎ 20-6235104. Open Tues–Sun 11am–5pm. Admission: Adults Dfl. 5, children Dfl. 3. Tram: 13, 14, 17 to Westermarkt.

Philips Vingboons's first neck-gable house, located at **Herengracht 168,** is one of five handsome canal houses that comprise the Dutch Theater Institute. Vingboons's 1638 house (see "Walk 1: The Essential Amsterdam"), built for the founder of the West India Company, Michiel Pauw, now contains a theater museum that organizes temporary exhibitions on theater, dance, mime, cabaret, film, and television in the Netherlands and draws on a fascinating collection of costumes, props, models, posters, recordings, and videos. Background information is generally provided in English.

The interior, refurbished in Louis XIV style in the 1730s, is well worth a glance. It includes lavish stucco decoration in the hall by the sculptor Jan van Logteren, a fine spiral staircase, and 2 rooms decorated with wall hangings by the landscape artist Isaac de Moucheron, depicting scenes from the life of Jephthah, an Israelite judge who sacrificed his daughter in fulfillment of a vow.

Nieuwe Kerk

Dam. ☎ 20-6268168. No set hours. Call for information on exhibits. Admission free. Tram: 1, 2, 4, 5, 9, 13, 14, 16, 17, 24, 25 to Dam.

The Nieuwe Kerk on Dam is one of the few churches in the Netherlands that is open to the public—not as a church but as a social and cultural center, which includes a brown cafe. At various times of the year, this huge whitewashed Protestant church is also used for exhibitions of paintings, photographs, and antiques.

When the Town Hall was converted to a royal palace in the 19thC, the Nieuwe Kerk was elevated to the National Church of the Netherlands. Since then Dutch monarchs have been crowned here, including the current monarch, Queen Beatrix, in 1980.

The oldest part of the church is the choir, built of rough stone around 1400, while the nave was added in the 1430s in a "streaky bacon" style of alternating rows of brick and stone. A number of small shops have been built onto the side of the church, while on Gravenstraat there is an imposing classical building of 1642, where poor relief was distributed.

The main feature of the interior is the magnificent organ, built in 1645. Jacob van Campen, the architect of the Town Hall, designed the casing to look almost like a classical neck-gable facade. Artus Quellien, who produced the Town Hall's sculpture, festooned the organ base with cherubs and musical instruments, while Jan Gerritsz. van Bronkhorst decorated the organ shutters with scenes from the life of David. The church also contains a remarkable pulpit built by Albert Jansz. Vinckenbrinck between 1645 and 1664 in a rich Mannerist style. The pulpit is illustrated with works of charity, while its large tester is adorned with a flamboyant tower.

★ Nieuwe Zijde (New Side)

Tram: 1, 2, 5, 13, 17 to Dam.

This area, the "New Side," which extends west from Damrak and Rokin to Singel, mirrors the canal pattern of Oude Zijde almost exactly. But its character is completely different due to the filling in of its canals in the 19thC, which lends a melancholy atmosphere. It is also very much more crowded, especially along Kalverstraat—Amsterdam's principal shopping street—which follows the course of the 13thC dyke along the west side of the Amstel. Less claustrophobic streets with interesting shops include St. Luciensteeg, just north of the Amsterdams Historisch Museum, and Gravenstraat, which bends around the back of the **Nieuwe Kerk.** There is a **stamp market** (see "Shopping") on Wednesday and Sunday on N. Z. Voorburgwal just south of Dam, and a cluster of **bookstores** between Spui and Dam, both of which add to the variety of Nieuwe Zijde.

North of Dam, notice the attractive group of houses at the **Blaeu Erf** (Blaeu's Yard) (N. Z. Voorburgwal 87–99), named after the printing works of the 17thC map-maker Jan Blaeu, which stood here. The picturesque 1633 Renaissance house at N. Z. Voorburgwal 75 is the **Makelaarsgildehuis** (real-estate agents' guild house), adorned with the righteous motto "Freedom is not for sale at any price." Farther north at N. Z. Kolk 28 is the 1620 **Korenmetershuisje** (corn exchange).

To the south of Dam, N. Z. Voorburgwal passes the Amsterdams Historisch Museum and leads to Spui, a small square where the 2 canals of Nieuwe Zijde once converged. The Begijnhof occupies the north side, while to the south is the 1787 **Maagdenhuis,** formerly a girls' orphanage. To the right is the 1633 **Old Lutheran Church.** The statue of an impish street urchin, **Het Amsterdamse Lieverdje,** was donated by a cigarette company and consequently provided a popular target for 1960s demonstrations against the tobacco industry. The Provos, provocative 1960s activists whose demonstrations often had a whimsical or humorous quality, made the statue a regular Saturday night meeting spot for their antitobacco campaign as well as some of their "happenings" that addressed everything from banning the atomic bomb to preserving the environment.

Voetboogstraat, which contains some unusual shops, leads south to the dramatic gateway of the **Rasphuis** at Heiligeweg 19, a model house of correction, set up in 1596, where men were put to work shaving a hard type of Brazilian wood used for dyeing. The portal, probably built by Hendrick de Keyser in 1603, shows the Maid of Amsterdam punishing 2 criminals above a rumination by Seneca: "It is virtuous to tame that which everyone fears."

Nieuwmarkt

Transportation: Sneltram 51 or metro to Nieuwmarkt.

The neighborhood surrounding Nieuwmarkt Square is particularly rich in sights associated with the Dutch painter Rembrandt van Rijn. To the south of Nieuwmarkt Square lies the university, and to the east a particularly beautiful area of silent, forgotten canals.

The fringes of the red-light district impinge slightly on the west and north sides of Nieuwmarkt, but the seediness can easily be avoided.

Standing in the middle of the square is the **Waag**, a former city gate. Another relic of the medieval city wall is the **Schreierstoren** (Tower of Tears) at the north end of Geldersekade, named for the grieving women who, legend has it, would climb this tower to watch their husbands' ships depart; some ships would never return.

Some of the former splendor of Kloveniersburgwal, a canal that runs south from Nieuwmarkt to the Amstel, can be seen in the **Trippenhuis** at Kloveniersburgwal 29. This splendid classical palace, modeled on the Town Hall on Dam, was built by Justus Vingboons between 1660 and 1664 for the brothers Louis and Hendrick Trip, who achieved unprecedented domestic grandeur by concealing their separated dwellings behind a single facade. The most remarkable feature of the house is its 2 chimneys, modeled on cannons. Other military emblems can be seen in the fresco—a reminder that the Trip family was one of Europe's largest and most unscrupulous arms manufacturers, with no qualms about supplying both the Roundheads and Cavaliers during the English Civil War. In 1815 the separate dwellings were joined to house the Rijksmuseum for a time.

Amsterdammers are fond of pointing out the exceptionally narrow house at Kloveniersburgwal 26, known as the **Kleine-Trippenhuis**, which was supposedly built in 1696 for a family servant, using stone left over from the Trippenhuis.

The west side of Kloveniersburgwal is dominated by drab 19thC university buildings, but there are one or two hidden delights to be found down the side streets, such as the 1633 wine merchants' guild house (**Wijnkopersgildehuis**) at Koestraat 10-12, and the former offices of the **Dutch East India Company** at Oude Hoogstraat 24. This almost forgotten relic of Amsterdam's trading past contains a courtyard worth entering to view the exceptionally ornate 1606 Mannerist scrolled gable, built some 4 years after the foundation of the East India Company.

Continuing south on Kloveniersburgwal, you come to no. 62, with its rich sea imagery, and the stately Poppenhuis at no. 95, built by Philips Vingboons in 1642. Directly opposite is the east gate of the **Oudemanhuis**, which was once a home for old men, with sculpture by Anthonie Ziesenis added in 1786.

One of my favorite hidden places is the **Oudeman-huispoort,** an arched brick passageway (built around 1600) between Oudezijds Achterburgwal and Kloveniersburgwal—with booksellers' stalls lining one wall. Some of the bookstands sell antiquarian books and drawings, but others sell contemporary textbooks on everything from art history to medicine. Amsterdam University owns the Oudemanhuis, whose doors open onto a lovely university courtyard.

The **Doelen Karena** hotel (see "Accommodations") overlooking the south end of Kloveniersburgwal is decorated with the 2 principal figures from Rembrandt's *The Night Watch,* a reminder that this was the site of the tower in which the company of civil guards met. Furthermore, the Syndics of the Cloth Guild, whom Rembrandt painted in 1662, met in the Lakenhal on the nearby Groenburgwal. A last relic of the once flourishing linen trade on this island is the Saaihal (serge hall), at Staalstraat 7, which was built by Pieter de Keyser in 1641. **Staalstraat,** a quiet little pedestrian street in an old neighborhood, is worth seeing, especially from the vantage point of one of its two comfortable brown cafe terraces that overlook the Kloveniersburgwal canal.

To reach the tranquil area east of Nieuwmarkt from here, continue north along the quiet Groenburgwal canal, turn right along Raamgracht, then left, following the Zwanenburgwal canal north to a picturesque lock, the **St. Antoniessluis.** Straight ahead is the Oude Schans, a canal that obtains a certain grandeur from the **Montelbaanstoren,** a defensive tower on the east edge of the 16thC city, which in 1606 was given an ornate spire by Hendrick de Keyser. On the corner of Oude

Montelbaanstoren

Schans and Prins Hendrikkade are the imposing warehouses built in 1642 for the Dutch West India Company, whose main trading interests were sugar and furs.

Head west along Binnenkant to reach the magnificent **Scheepvaarthuis,** built for 7 shipping companies in 1912 by the Amsterdam School architects Johan van der Mey, Michel de Klerk, and P. L. Kramer. Notice the fantastic maritime details decorating the outside of the building, such as whales, ships, navigators' heads, mermaids, ocean deities, and even rippling iron railings.

Walk around the outside of the Scheepvaarthuis and turn right down the seemingly rural Buiten Bantammerstraat. Now cross the medieval-looking Amsterdam School–style bridge and turn left to reach Lastageweg. This leads to the narrow canal Rechtboomsloot, where a right turn leads to Kromboomsloot, a dark, silent, and forgotten canal, where at no. 22 Amsterdam's Armenian community built a rococo church in 1714.

NINT Technisch Museum

Tolstraat 129. ☎ 20-5708111. Open Mon–Fri 10am–5pm; Sat–Sun, holidays noon–5pm. Admission: Adult Dfl. 10, children Dfl. 7. Tram: 4 to Lutmastraat.

Located in a former diamond-cutting factory in the 19thC district of Amsterdam Zuid, the NINT technology museum is particularly geared toward children. The aim is to make science fun, and there are countless push-button machines and models to demonstrate how things such as magnets, electricity, cars, and telephones work. The explanatory notes are in Dutch, but this need not be a deterrent since most children are quite content to dash from one working model to the next, leaving their parents to puzzle over the theory.

Normaal Amsterdams Peil

Stadhuis, Amstel 1. Transporation: Tram 9, 14 or metro to Waterlooplein.

Two Plexiglas (perspex) columns of water in the new **Stadhuis** (town hall) show the current North Sea tidal levels at IJmuiden and Vlissingen, perhaps to remind Amsterdammers that they spend much of their lives below sea level. For dramatic effect, water surges into a third Plexiglas column to indicate the water level during the disastrous Zeeland floods of 1953. A bronze button mounted on a concrete pile in the basement indicates level zero in the Netherlands (the Normal Amsterdam Level). A cross-section of the Netherlands on one wall indicates the perilously low situation of many parts of the Randstad, including Schiphol airport.

★★ Oude Kerk

Oudekerksplein 23. ☎ 20-6249183. Church open Easter–Sept: Mon–Sat 11am–5pm, Sun 1:30–5pm; Oct–Easter: Mon–Sun 1–3pm; tower open June to mid-Sept: Mon and Thurs 2–5pm, Tues and Wed 11am–2pm. Free admission. Tram: 4, 9, 16, 24, 25 to Dam, then 10-min. walk.

Begun around 1200, burned to the ground in 1274 by the troops of Count Floris V, rebuilt as a hall church, and then converted to a basilica around 1500, the Oude Kerk is Amsterdam's oldest and most fascinating church. Of particular interest to the visitor are the massive wooden vaulted roofs, the frescoed columns, the delightful misericords illustrating various traditional proverbs, the ornate gravestones of eminent Amsterdammers, and the 16thC stained-glass windows in one of the choirs, known as the Nieuwe Vrouwenkoor, depicting the life of the Virgin.

Dedicated to St. Nicholas, patron saint of sailors, the Oude Kerk echoes Amsterdam's seafaring past in features such as the Hamburgerkapel, which was built in the early 16thC by Hamburg merchants living in Amsterdam. Ships appear everywhere: on the vaulted roof, on the various monuments to Dutch admirals who died in battle, on the small organ, and even crudely carved on the back of the wooden choir screen. Rembrandt's wife Saskia, who died in 1642, is buried

Oude Kerk

in a grave numbered 29K, near the small choir organ. The Oude Kerk's famous large organ was built during 1738 to 1742 by Johannes Caspar Müller; the small choir organ was recently replaced, although the decorative casing dates from the 17thC.

The Oude Kerk also has a 17thC carillon built by bell-maker François Hemony, which is played every Saturday from 4 to 5pm. The late-Gothic spire, built by Joost Jansz. Bilhamer in 1565, can sometimes be climbed to obtain a view of the old city.

★ Oude Zijde (Old Side)
Tram: 4, 9, 14, 16, 24, 25 to Dam.

The "Old Side" runs east from Damrak and Rokin to Kloveniersburgwal, which marks the limit of the medieval city. This quarter consists of Warmoesstraat, formerly a dyke along the **Amstel,** and the 2 canals O. Z. Voorburgwal and O. Z. Achterburgwal, whose names literally mean before and behind the city wall.

As its name suggests, Oude Zijde is the oldest area of the city, and is packed with historic interest. Unfortunately, some of its finest buildings are buried in the red-light district, which lies to the north of the line formed by Damstraat, Oude Doelenstraat, and Oude Hoogstraat. But venture only a few steps south of this demarcation line to discover the most tranquil and beautiful area of the city, with numerous old **gateways** richly adorned with symbolic sculpture and verse.

To see Oude Zijde at its best, turn off Rokin down the narrow Langebrugsteeg to reach Grimburgwal. Now head left down O. Z. Voorburgwal and walk to Oude Hoogstraat, then turn right and right again to return by O. Z. Achterburgwal.

Grimburgwal is a particularly pleasing corner of the medieval city at the convergence of 3 canals. Many of the narrow streets in this part of town provide reminders of former convents and monasteries in names such as **Gebed Zonder End** (Prayer Without End), a narrow lane that once divided 2 convents. The view east of Grimburgwal is terminated by the **House on the Three Canals** at O. Z. Voorburgwal 249, an early 17thC step-gabled house built of rosy red brick trimmed with whitened sandstone. Turning left down O. Z. Voorburgwal you can see the former **St. Agnietenkapel** behind a jaunty 16thC Mannerist portal at O. Z. Voorburgwal 231. This 15thC chapel belonged to the convent of St. Agnes, which, like many in medieval Amsterdam, adopted the rather relaxed rules of the

Third Order of St. Francis of Assisi. The building now houses the historical collection of the **University of Amsterdam.**

The south end of O. Z. Voorburgwal was dubbed "the velvet canal" in the 18thC because of the numerous rich merchants who settled here, putting up ornate facades such as **O. Z. Voorburgwal nos. 237 and 217,** with their exceptionally fine Louis XIV tops. At no. 197 is a former **Stadhuis** (Town Hall) designed in Amsterdam School style during the 1920s and incorporating on the south side of the courtyard the classical **Admiraliteitsgebouw** (Admiralty Office), built in the 1660s. The city council moved here in 1808 when Louis Napoleon established his Royal Palace in the Stadhuis on Dam.

At O. Z. Voorburgwal 300 is the **Stadsbank van Lening,** the municipal bank, which was established here in a rugged warehouse built by Hendrick de Keyser in 1616. The famous Dutch poet Joost van den Vondel (1587–1679) worked in the bank as a bookkeeper until he was 81. Notice in the alley to the right of the building the doorway with a relief by Hendrick de Keyser depicting a woman pawning her property at the bank. The bank building to the left of the warehouses, which was added in 1669, has a lengthy edifying poem above the entrance explaining the virtues of pawn banks.

The curious Mannerist gate to the right of the alley Enge Lombardsteeg formerly led to an inn whose name De Brakke Grond (The Brackish Ground) tells something of the terrain on which Amsterdam was built. Other revealing names near here are Slijkstraat (Slime Street) and Rusland (Rushes Land).

Amsterdam's involvement in the slave trade is recalled by the sculpture decorating the 1663 facade at **O. Z. Voorburgwal 187,** which depicts exhausted black slaves and American Indians lying on tobacco bales.

To reach the Oude Kerk and the Museum Amstelkring, you must venture north of Oude Doelenstraat into the fringes of the red-light district. Above the door of O. Z. Voorburgwal 136 is a bust of Admiral Tromp and a scene from the Third Anglo-Dutch War of 1673.

Returning south by O. Z. Achterburgwal, you pass the attractive square, Walenplein, overlooked by the **Waalse Kerk** at O. Z. Achterburgwal 157. This chapel formerly belonged to a monastery and was given to the Walloon community in 1587. These French-speaking Protestants who had fled from the Spanish-occupied

Southern Netherlands added a Mannerist gateway on Oude Hoogstraat and in 1647 a classical entrance facing Walenplein.

At O. Z. Achterburgwal 185 is a dignified classical building built in 1645 as the **Spinhuis,** a house of correction where women were made to spin wool as a form of therapy. Notice the ornate Ionic portal in Spinhuissteeg, which bears a moralistic motto by the poet P. C. Hooft telling visitors not to be alarmed by the punishments because their motivation is love and not revenge. At the south end of O. Z. Achterburgwal are 2 more gateways, the **Oudemanhuispoort** (now lined with bookstalls) and the **Gasthuispoort.**

★★ Prinsengracht

Tram 13, 14, 17 to Westermarkt; or tram 1, 2, 4, 5, 16, 24, 25 to Prinsengracht.

"The Princes' Canal" is the outermost waterway of the 17thC Grachtengordel. Earmarked in the 1609 Plan for warehouses, workshops, churches, shops, and artisan dwellings, the canal lacks the architectural splendor of Herengracht and Keizersgracht, but offers instead a lively blend of brown cafes, boutiques, art galleries, and houseboats. It may be tiring to walk the entire 1.9 miles (3 kilometers) of Prinsengracht, so limit yourself to short stretches, such as that from Brouwersgracht to Rozengracht or from Reguliersgracht to the Amstel.

From Brouwersgracht to Nieuwe Spiegelstraat: The intersection of Prinsengracht and Brouwersgracht offers fine views in every direction, which can

Noorderkerk

be enjoyed from the traditional brown cafe **Papeneiland** or the newer, but just as brown, **'t Smackzeyl** (see "Walk 2: The Jordaan"). Proceeding south, one reaches **Noordermarkt,** a small square imbued with the village charm characteristic of the Jordaan and the site of a farmer's market on Saturdays (see "Shopping"). The unusual octagonal **Noorderkerk** was built as a Protestant church between 1620 and 1623 by Hendrick de Keyser (who did not finish the project). Some curious little shops and cafes have taken root around the church.

At Prinsengracht 85-113 is the **Starhofje,** built in a rather utilitarian early 19thC style. A much lovelier hofje is found between Noordermarkt and Westermarkt: **Zon's hofje** at Prinsengracht 159-71, built in 1765. The secluded courtyard is generally open to the public. Notice inside the impressive gateway with its facade stone showing Noah's Ark surrounded by a curious collection of animals. Beyond, the east side of the canal is dominated by 18thC warehouses, while the west side has numerous houses with 18thC shop fronts. Despite the factories, shops, and working-class homes, Prinsengracht is not architecturally mundane, and the frothy rococo sculpture decorating the top of Prinsengracht 126 is as lavish as anything on the more prestigious canals. Visit the brown cafe **De Prins** to enjoy the fine view down Leliegracht.

The **Anne Frankhuis** is located at Prinsengracht 263, while nearby is the Westerkerk. The French philosopher René Descartes spent the summer of 1634 living with a French schoolteacher at Westermarkt 6.

Between Westermarkt and Nieuwe Spiegelstraat, the modern-day Prinsengracht grows more upper-crust. The Pulitzer Hotel at Prinsengracht 315-331 (see "Accommodations") made a unique contribution to architectural conservation when it restored a block of 24 gable houses to create a 250-room hotel. **The Pulitzer Art Gallery** is located within the complex. Other art galleries and chic French restaurants have sprung up nearby, and **Café Van Puffelen** (see "Amsterdam's Cafes" in "Dining"), 1 block south, adds a touch of sophisticated but relaxed cafe society.

From Nieuwe Spiegelstraat to the Amstel: The stretch of Prinsengracht between Nieuwe Spiegelstraat and Reguliersgracht is more distinguished, and on the west side blends into the tranquil Weteringbuurt. At nos. 855–99 is the **Duetzenhof,** an almshouse established in 1695 by Agnes Deutz who, according to the inscription above the entrance, "exercised her love and faith as a comfort for the poor and an example to the rich" (closed to the public).

Overlooking Reguliersgracht is the wooden **Amstelkerk,** which looks out of place in its urban setting. Erected in 1670 as a temporary Protestant church, it was supposed to be replaced by a much larger building on the Amstelveld. The plan was abandoned, however, leaving the Amstelveld with a rather sad appearance, enlivened only by the plant market held here every Monday. Opposite is a rare 19thC neoclassical church, **De Duif.** The final stretch of Prinsengracht is postcard picturesque: houseboats and gable houses drenched in wisteria.

★ Het Rembrandthuis Museum (Rembrandt House)

Jodenbreestraat 4-6. ☎ 20-6384668. Open Mon–Sat 10am–5pm, Sun, holidays 1–5pm. Admission: Adults Dfl. 7.5, children Dfl. 5. Tram: 9, 14, sneltram 51 or metro to Mr. Visserplein.

Rembrandt was only 33 years old when he bought this distinguished red–shuttered classical house on the principal street of the Jodenbuurt. He lived here from 1639 to 1658, until financial difficulties forced him to move to a more modest house in the Jordaan. The main attraction of the museum is its extensive collection of some 250 etchings and drawings by Rembrandt. Many of these works illustrate biblical themes, while others show the gentle landscape of the river Amstel, which Rembrandt visited frequently after his wife Saskia's death. Perhaps the most delightful etchings, however, are those in the mezzanine room, showing Rembrandt's compassionate eye for beggars, street musicians, organ-grinders, rat-catchers, and other 17thC figures. Another feature of the museum is an informative exhibition on etching techniques.

★★ Rijksmuseum

Stadhouderskade 42. ☎ 20-6732121. Open daily Mon–Sun 10am–5pm. Admission: Adults Dfl. 10, children Dfl. 5. Tram 6, 7, 10 to Spiegelgracht, tram 2, 5 to Hobbemastraat, or tram 16 to Museumplein.

The national museum of the Netherlands houses a huge and diverse range of artworks, of which its unrivaled collection of 17thC Dutch paintings is by far the most important. Established by King Louis Napoleon in 1808 along the lines of the Louvre in Paris, the Rijksmuseum collection was initially housed in the Royal Palace on the Dam, but later moved to the Trippenhuis on Kloveniersburgwal. Eventually the collection of paintings and decorative art grew too large for this canal house, and P. J. H. Cuypers was commissioned to build

Rijksmuseum

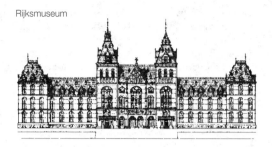

a new Rijksmuseum in the fashionable area of the 19thC ring near the Vondelpark.

The intention was to have a building in Dutch Renaissance style, but Cuypers—a fervent Catholic—could not suppress his Gothic tendencies, and the building, with its Burgundian roofs and exuberant decoration, has a medieval flavor. King William III was so upset at what he called "the monastery" that he refused to set foot in the building.

Planning a Visit: If you have only a short time to spare, concentrate on the works of Rembrandt, Vermeer, De Hoogh, and the other Dutch Masters. A useful introduction to the 17thC painting is the slide show (with English, French, and German commentary), shown every 20 minutes in the Film Theater. If time allows, set off to explore Medieval Painting, Sculpture and Applied Art, Dutch History, 18thC and 19thC Dutch Painting, and Asiatic Art for some delightful surprises.

The Rijksmuseum has 2 main entrances west and east of the tunnel. The west entrance is usually the more crowded, although either entrance gives access to the main collection of paintings. A quiet entrance at the rear of the building on Hobbemastraat takes you straight into the Drucker Extension, added in 1915 to house the growing collection of 18th- and 19th-C paintings and Asiatic art. If you are meeting someone, be sure to specify at which of the 3 entrances.

Exterior: The museum's architectural detail is best appreciated from the formal 18thC garden on Hobbemastraat, where you can admire a tile tableau depicting famous Dutch and Flemish artists, a relief showing Rembrandt at work on his Staalmeesters (above the tunnel entrance), and curious sculptures on the roof representing masons, apparently at work on the construction of the museum.

Seventeenth-Century Painting: The glory of the Rijksmuseum is its collection of 17thC Dutch paintings (rooms 208–36) and in particular its **Rembrandts** (rooms 221, 224, 229–30). Pride of place is given to *The Company of Frans Banning Cocq and Lieutenant van Rutenburch,* which hangs in a room, custom-built in 1906, at the end of the Gallery of Honor. This large painting was commissioned in 1642 by a company of the civil guards to hang in their meeting hall at the end of Kloveniersburgwal. Later it became so covered with grime that it was mistaken for a night scene, thus acquiring the totally unjustified name *The Night Watch.* Now that the painting has been thoroughly cleaned, it is possible to see the masterful way in which Rembrandt picks out details of expression and costume as the guards emerge dramatically from the building into a pool of sunlight.

The Rijksmuseum has a total of 18 Rembrandts spanning his working life, from an exquisite *Self Portrait* at the age of 22, before he moved from Leiden, to a troubled *Self Portrait* as the Apostle Paul, painted in 1661 after he had been forced to sell his house on Jodenbreestraat because of financial difficulties. His mastery of *chiaroscuro* (the Italian technique of combining light and shade) is seen in the tender *Holy Family,* in which Rembrandt sets the Nativity in the dark cellar of a Dutch house. Rembrandt produced some of his most tender work toward the end of his life, such as his portrait of *The Wardens of the Amsterdam Drapers' Guild* and the haunting *Portrait of a Couple* (better known as *The Jewish Bride*), painted when he was 61.

Another highlight of the Rijksmuseum is its collection of paintings by the **Delft School** (room 222). The Delft artist **Jan Vermeer** used strong light and bold colors to give an almost religious significance to quiet domestic scenes such as *The Kitchen Maid* and *Woman Reading a Letter.* He captured the warmth of Delft brick houses in *The Little Street,* which he painted from the window of his house looking across to the senior citizens' home opposite. Pieter de Hoogh also painted tranquil domestic interiors in Delft and Amsterdam such as *Maternal Duty,* which is bathed in a mellow golden light, and *Interior with Women beside a Linen Chest,* and was particularly fond of the *doorkijk*—a view through several rooms to the outside. The other paintings in the 17thC collection are arranged rather haphazardly. **Saenredam's** methodical studies of church interiors in Assendelft, Haarlem, and Utrecht possess a mystical stillness, while his view of the old town hall of Amsterdam conveys its shabby charm. The merry domestic scenes of **Jan Steen,** such as *The Feast of St. Nicholas* and the boisterous peasants of **Adriaen van Ostade's** *The Skaters,* might seem to belong to a more carefree world than Rembrandt, but the paintings had a deep moral purpose—for example, the eggshells casually strewn across the floor warn of the dangers of reckless indulgence.

Frans Hals was less inclined to turn a painting into a sermon, and his *Wedding Portrait of Isaac Abrahamsz Massa and Beatrix vander Laen* is full of good humor, while the almost Impressionistic *Merry Drinker* reflects the epicurean mood of Haarlem in the golden age. Amsterdam was a very serious and sober city by comparison, to judge from Werner van den Valckert's group portraits of the *Governors and Governesses of the Amsterdam Leper Asylum.* Even the figures in **Bartholomeus van der Helst's** *The Celebration of the Peace of Münster in the Headquarters of the St. George's Guard, Amsterdam* do not seem to be enjoying themselves. The feast is taking place in the guild's meeting hall on Singel, where the university library now stands.

The greatest landscape artist of the golden age was **Jacob van Ruisdael,** whose compellingly romantic *The Mill Near Wijk bij Duurstede* shows a heavily overcast sky threatening the small figures in the foreground. His uncle, **Salomon van Ruysdael,** favored a more placid landscape *(River Landscape with Cattle Ferry),* while **Jan van Goyen's** rural scenes were as shabby as Adriaen van Ostade's interiors.

Medieval Painting: The small medieval art collection (rooms 201–4) contains several fine works by 15thC Northern Netherlandish artists, notably **Geertgen tot Sint Jans** and the Master of the Virgo inter Virgines (named after his most famous work). The subject matter is invariably religious, although the artists do not hesitate to dress the figures in sumptuous 15thC garments and include views of blue-roofed Burgundian cities in the background. The most appealing work is the Master of Alkmaar's *Seven Works of Charity,* a painting that has had more than its share of misfortune: the monks' faces were vandalized during the Iconoclasm, and in later years dampness caused further damage.

The arrival of the Renaissance in the Netherlands is marked by **Jan van Scorel's** *Mary Magdalene* (room 205). His pupil **Maerten van Heemskerck's** *Erythraean Sibyl* is interesting for the hazy view of Delft in the background.

The excesses of Flemish Mannerism are illustrated by **Joachim Bueckelaar**'s irreverent *Jesus with Martha and Mary,* while **Joos de Momper**'s *River Landscape with Boar Hunt* conveys a breathtaking sense of space.

Sculpture and Applied Art: The Rijksmuseum's vast collection of sculpture and applied art is spread across the 3 floors of the west wing. The collection is arranged chronologically: medieval, Renaissance, and classical works on the first floor; 18thC works in Louis XIV and XV style on the ground floor; and finally Louis XVI, Empire, and Art Nouveau pieces in the basement. Among the medieval works (rooms 238–48), the most important are the exquisite late 15thC sculptures by **Adriaen van Wesel,** who is regarded as the greatest Dutch sculptor of the Middle Ages (rooms 241–42). The Flemish art of miniaturization is demonstrated by the incredible "devotional nut" (room 241) carved by Adam Dirksz, which was designed to be carried on pilgrimages in a copper case inside a velvet bag. The tormented Mannerism of the late 16thC is mainly represented by tapestries and furniture (room 250), and the solemn temper of mid-17thC Dutch classicism by the beautiful furnished room from a Dordrecht house (room 252), the room of sculptures by **Artus Quellien** (room 258), and the furniture designed by **Philips Vingboons** for the Huydecoper mansion on Singel (room 258a). The remarkable Chinese room from Leeuwarden illustrates the Dutch fascination with Oriental art in the 17thC (room 261). Descend to the ground floor for the highly popular **dollhouses** (rooms 162, 175), made in the 18thC with painstaking attention to detail.

The development of **Dutch interior design** from the early 18thC to the early 20thC can be followed in the furnished rooms: the Louis XIV style emerging under William III (rooms 164–65 and 167–69), the more delicate rococo or Louis XV style appearing in the mid-18thC (rooms 173–76, including the dollhouse in room 175), and the cool and formal Louis XVI style developing toward the end of the century (room 179 and basement rooms 25, 27, and 29). The gilded luxury of the Empire style was introduced during the French occupation (room 33), and a beautiful room in Art Nouveau style rewards those who manage to penetrate to the remotest corner of the museum (room 34).

Eighteenth- to Nineteenth-Century Painting: After the golden age, Dutch painting tumbled into whimsy. The pleasant little scenes of **Cornelis Troost** seem weak in comparison with the softly sensual pastels of the 18thC Swiss painter Jean-Etienne Liotard (room 139). Perhaps the most interesting Dutch work of the period is Jan Kels's *The Writer* (room 142), with its unmistakable hint of Vermeer.

Early 19thC painting (rooms 143–44) was highly Romantic in flavor, as in the landscapes of **Koekkoek** and **Nuijen** and the highly atmospheric view of Amsterdam's Raampoortje by **W. J. Troostwijk.** A new sensibility entered Dutch painting in the second half of the 19thC when the artists of the **Hague School,** inspired by the French Barbizon painters, turned their attention to the dune and sea landscape of the Dutch coast (rooms 145–48), producing placid scenes such as **Anton Mauve**'s *Morning Ride on the Beach.* The Amsterdam Impressionists preferred to capture action and excitement in their work, as expressed in **Breitner**'s thunderous *Horse Artillery.*

Asiatic Art: The peaceful department of Asiatic Art (rooms 11–23) contains some highly expressive examples of Indonesian art, such as the ferocious *Head of a Kala* and the exquisite *Head of Jatayu, King of the Birds.* Japanese art is represented by the miniature perfection of a birdcage, a smoking cabinet, and a casket in the shape of a crane.

The more monumental character of Chinese art is illustrated by the 12thC wooden statue of Avalokiteshvara, while the 12thC Indian bronze of Shiva is particularly impressive. Finally, look for the superb set of 12 Chinese cups from the Kangxi period, in which the months of the year are represented by different plants or flowers.

Dutch History: The medieval history section (room 101) unfortunately fails to come to terms with a potentially fascinating period, the most interesting exhibit being the set of panels of *The St. Elizabeth's Day Flood,* showing the aftermath of the disastrous flood of 1421, which created the vast inlet south of Dordrecht known as the Hollands Diep. At the exit of the room is the bookchest that Hugo Grotius purportedly hid in to escape from Loevestein Castle. The religious quarrels that led to Grotius' banishment are the subject of the nearby painting by A. van de Venne.

The center of attention is the spacious **17thC square,** which fills the former east courtyard of the building. The extent of Dutch trading interests is illustrated by the series of 6 paintings of East India

Company settlements, which originally hung in the company's Amsterdam head office on Oude Hoogstraat.

Of the rooms that follow, the most interesting is devoted to Dutch trading links with China and Japan, and includes an intriguing Japanese painting showing scenes from the Dutch settlement on Nagasaki. Foreigners were forbidden to enter the city, so that the Dutch were confined to a small fan-shaped island in the bay of Nagasaki. In 1996, renovations were completed on the South Wing of the museum. The wing now houses 18th and 19thC paintings, Asiatic art, and a costume collection.

Royal Palace (see Koninklijk Paleis)

Schuttersgalerij

Passage between Spui and St. Luciensteeg. Open 10am–5pm. Tram: 1, 2, 5 to Spui.

A passage between 2 wings of the Amsterdams Historisch Museum has been turned into a unique street gallery, the Schuttersgalerij (Guards' Gallery). The paved lane has doors at either end and a permanent guard, but you are free to use it as a public street. The brick walls are hung with large 17thC civic-guard group portraits, including a work by Rembrandt's pupil Govert Flinck.

Singel

Tram: To Centraal Station, Dam, Spui or Muntplein.

Measuring slightly more than 1 mile (1.6 kilometers), Singel is one of the most pleasant canals for walking and has a variety of architectural styles. This canal marks the transition from the compact medieval city with its narrow streets, to the spacious and elegant 17thC canal web. From 1487 to 1585 it formed a moat on the west side of the city—Singel means literally a girdle—and the buildings on the inside of the canal therefore tend to be older and somewhat lower in height than those opposite. Nothing now remains of the medieval wall on Singel except for the brick base of the Munttoren.

Northern End of Singel to Raadhuisstraat: This end of the canal has a breezy, maritime flavor, with seagulls swooping and screeching around the Haarlemmersluis, one of the locks used to pump out the canals each night.

Het Spaanse Huis (The Spanish House) at Singel 2 is a ruggedly utilitarian step gable from the 1600s that was used both as a warehouse and home by a merchant named Cruywagen; the facade stone showing a wheelbarrow (*kruiwagen*) is a play on his name—and a fine example of the Dutch love for puns.

The view south is beautifully accented by the circular **Lutheran Church,** a grand classical building designed in Doric style by Adriaen Dortsman in the 1670s on a somewhat cramped site. The church now serves as a splendid conference center for the Ramada Renaissance hotel (see "Accommodations"), and on Sunday mornings is used for concerts.

Several houses near the former harbor are adorned with sea imagery. The beautiful rococo top of **Vriesland** at Singel 24 shows an 18thC sailing ship, while **Zeevrucht** (Fruit of the Sea) at Singel 36 boasts a superb rococo centerpiece adorned with foamy waves. **The Poezenboot,** a refuge for stray cats, is located on a barge moored on this stretch of Singel.

Singel 7, which is no wider than a door, is featured in guided tours as the narrowest house in Amsterdam, although this is a myth. It is merely the back door of a perfectly normal house. Another curiosity is **Singel 64,** which retains a 17thC step-gabled top although the lower part was given a facelift in the 18thC, illustrating the casual way in which facades and parts of facades are regularly replaced.

Singel 116, between Blauwburgwal and Torensteeg, was affectionately dubbed "the house with the noses" after some friends of the 18thC owner offered to pay for the decoration of the claw pieces flanking the neck gable (provided that these included portraits of the owner and his 2 sons). The offer was taken up and these unflattering portraits were the result. The handsome **De Dolphijn** (The Dolphin) at Singel 140-42 was designed in a flamboyant Renaissance style by Hendrick de Keyser in the early 17thC. This jaunty house, with its double step gable, was later the home of Captain Frans Banning Cocq, the dashing character with the red sash who is seen leading the company of civil guards in Rembrandt's *The Night Watch.*

One of Amsterdam's more interesting modern buildings is Theo Bosch's **Faculteit der Letteren** (Literature Faculty), which fills almost an entire block, between Torensteeg and Raadhuisstraat. Those interested in architecture should enter the building to experience the structure's transparency.

From Raadhuisstraat to Muntplein: Singel, from Raadhuisstraat to Heisteeg, has a pleasing human scale, and the narrow alleys to the east are inviting places to explore (see "Walk 1: The Essential Amsterdam"). Here you find antiquarian booksellers, wizened stamp-dealers, and old-fashioned tobacconists in cramped interiors that retain a medieval character. The most splendidly rococo house on this stretch is **Singel 288.** The austere Art Deco **Bungehuis,** a 1930s office building now used by the university, provides a sharp contrast and adds to the variety of styles on the Singel.

The beautiful facade stone **In de Vergulde Haringbuys** (In the Gilded Herring Boat) adorns **Singel 358,** where Rembrandt's son Titus lived for a time with his family. Also worth a look is **Singel 390,** with reclining figures on the cornice and a highly ornate doorway. The Adam and Eve facade stone at **Singel 367** wittily (and in true Amsterdam fashion) recalls the apple market that formerly occupied this stretch of canal.

The stretch of Singel between Heisteeg and Muntplein features several bold buildings, such as the soaring church **De Krijtberg** at Singel 446, which was built during the neo-Gothic fever of the 19thC to replace a clandestine Jesuit church. The 1633 **Old Lutheran Church** opposite looks quite dainty by comparison. The row **Singel 421–425** now accommodates the university library. The middle building, known as the **Bushuis** (Arsenal), is a manic Mannerist invention of 1606, which originally housed the armory of the guild of crossbow archers. The new library building to the right stands on the site of the meeting hall of this guild, whose group portrait by Bartholomeus van der Helst hangs in the Rijksmuseum. The **Odeon** theater at Singel 460 occupies an attractive neck gable built by **Philips Vingboons.**

The final stretch of Singel is brightened on one side by the **Flower Market,** which is overlooked by the ornate spire of the **Munttoren,** erected on the brick stump of a medieval tower by Hendrick de Keyser.

★ Spui

Tram: 1, 2, 5 to Spui.

The little square called Spui is one of the most genial spots in the city. Situated near the old university, the square has been the scene of whimsical political demonstrations since the Provo happenings in the 1960s. Spui is more tame nowadays, and the Athenaeum Bookstore and Café Luxembourg are its main attractions.

Stadhuis (see Koninklijk Paleis)

★★ Stedelijk Museum

Paulus Potterstraat 13. ☎ 20-5732911. Open daily 11am–5pm. Admission: Adults Dfl. 7.50, children Dfl. 3.75. Tram 2, 3, 5, 12 to Van Baerlestraat, or tram 16 to Museumplein.

Amsterdam's municipal (*stedelijk*) museum of modern art looks old-fashioned from the outside, although the interior is ultramodern. It was built in 1895 in a neo-Renaissance style that was intended to counteract P. J. H. Cuyper's neo-Gothic Rijksmuseum at the opposite end of Museumplein. Under its energetic postwar director, Willem Sandberg, the interior was whitewashed, while his successor, Eddy de Wilde, was even more ruthless and disposed of the reputedly hideous collection of period furniture that was bequeathed to the museum by its founder, Sophia Augusta Lopez-Suasso. These sweeping measures, although somewhat unfair to Mrs. Lopez-Suasso, have turned this old building into one of the most striking modern-art galleries in Europe.

This dynamic approach means that nothing remains in the same place for very long in the Stedelijk. The best way therefore to approach the museum is to look first at the notice-board in the hall (room 1) to find out about temporary exhibitions and events. Then pick up the free plan and monthly bulletin from the information desk (room 15) to find out where the various collections are located. Photography is usually shown in room 13, applied art and graphic design in room 14, video art in the small sunken theater in room 14, prints on the mezzanine floor (room 114), and exhibitions of local art organizations in the new wing (rooms 30, 130). The permanent collection begins with a modest selection of late 19thC and early 20thC paintings, with works by **Cézanne, Monet, Chagall, Kandinsky,** and **Matisse** (including his large cut-paper work *La Perruche et la Sirène*). But the main strength of the Stedelijk is its coverage of more recent modern artists such as **Appel, Dubuffet, De Kooning,** and **Schoonhoven.** The Stedelijk's aim—to show the development of a particular artist's style—is most effective in the case of its large **Kasimir Malevitch** collection, since Malevitch himself selected this series of paintings to trace his development from Realism to Suprematism. His earliest paintings, dating from 1910, are splashed with bright colors in Impressionistic style; figures become more metallic in 1912 (*Taking in the Rye*); colorless abstraction appears in 1912 and 1913 (*Head of a Peasant Girl*); cubism in 1913 (*Desk and Room*); and finally, in 1915, Suprematism emerges triumphant.

Another important cluster of works covers the Dutch **De Stijl** group, who were clearly influenced by Malevitch. Both the painter Piet Mondrian and the architect Gerrit Rietveld strove to impose a framework of order on the free-floating forms of Suprematism.

The Stedelijk's postwar collection begins with the **Cobra group,** whose first exhibition was held in the Stedelijk in 1959. Willem Sandberg was so taken with Cobra that he commissioned Karel Appel to decorate the walls of the original museum coffee shop (room 15c).

Under Eddy de Wilde, the Stedelijk turned toward American trends of the 1960s such as Color Field Painting and Pop Art. The vandalized **Barnett Newman** painting *Who's Afraid of Red, Yellow, and Blue?* is now back in the museum after a costly and controversial restoration. A chilling note is struck by **Edward Kienholz**'s Beanery (room 12), modeled on a funky Los Angeles bar frequented by artists. You can enter the murky bar, squeezing past dusty waxwork dummies with clocks as faces. The restaurant, a popular meeting place for artists, overlooks an attractive sculpture.

Technology Museum (see NINT Technisch Museum)

Theater Institute (see Nederlands Theater Instituut)

Town Planning Information Center (see Informatiecentrum Ruimtelijke Ordening)

★ Tropenmuseum (Tropical Museum)

Linnaeusstraat 2. ☎ 20-5688215. Open Mon–Fri 10am–5pm; Sat–Sun, holidays noon–5pm. Admission: Adults Dfl. 10, children Dfl. 5. Tram: 9, 10, 14 to Mauritskade.

Devoted to the developing world and its problems, this museum is located on the east side of the 17thC moat, facing the grim Muiderpoort built between 1769 and 1771. The building was constructed between 1916 and 1926 to house the Dutch Colonial Institute. The lofty main hall with its cool arcades and colorful majolica friezes of plants brings a certain tropical allure to bland east Amsterdam, and the occasional Indonesian gamelan or Andean flute concert adds an exotic flavor to a rainy Sunday afternoon.

The bias of the former Colonial Institute is evident in the sculpture depicting episodes from Dutch colonial history, and in an attempt to produce a more balanced view of the Third World, the building was purged of all patronizing or derogatory exhibits in the 1970s and renamed the Tropenmuseum. The museum is divided by continent, with Asia and Oceania on the 1st floor, and Africa, Latin America, and the Middle East on the 2nd floor.

Although the labels are all in Dutch, the collection is worth a visit simply for the visual experience of
wandering through reconstructed streets from different
Third World countries and peering into the dark, dusty
interiors of shops and homes. Much of the audiovisual
material is also in Dutch, but the tape recordings of
musical instruments are worth listening to.

The museum is constantly buzzing with exhibitions
and activities, many of which are aimed at children.
The **Kindermuseum** (☎ 20-5688300) is a place where
children 6 to 12 are introduced to a hands-on approach
to tropical plants, herbs, and musical instruments (see
"Amsterdam with Kids" below).

★ Tuschinski Cinema

Reguliersbreestraat 26. ☎ 20-6262633. Open 2–10pm. Guided tours
July–Aug, Sun and Mon at 10:30am. Tram: 4, 9, 14, 16, 24, 25 to
Muntplein.

This lavish 1921 Art Deco movie theater was the dream
of Abram Tuschinski, a Jewish emigré from Poland who
later died in a concentration camp. The Cannon Group
now own the 6-screen complex and have carefully preserved the original style. Although the main lobby is
accessible to the general public, only holders of tickets
for a performance will be admitted to the rest of the
building. When visiting Tuschinski, it is worth paying
the extra money for a balcony seat to enjoy the full
impact of the glamorous setting. (Check theater and
music listings for occasional concerts on the cinema
organ.)

★★ Van Gogh Museum

Paulus Potterstraat 7. ☎ 20-5705200. Open daily 10am–5pm.
Admission: Adults Dfl. 12.50, children Dfl. 5. Tram 2, 3, 5, 12 to Van
Baerlestraat, or tram 16 to Museumplein.

The museum was opened in 1973 to house the superb
collection of some 200 paintings and 500 drawings bequeathed by van Gogh's brother Theo to his son Vincent.
The building, a modern design by the Dutch **De Stijl**
architect **Gerrit Rietveld,** is set in the small park between the Rijksmuseum and the Stedelijk. The spacious interior is particularly impressive.

The ground floor covers the years 1880 to 1887.
This includes the bleak paintings from the 2 years van
Gogh spent in the small Brabant town of Nuenen,
culminating in his painting *The Potato Eaters.* There are
also a few Impressionist works from his Paris period.
The 1st floor covers the final 3 years of his life, from
1887 to 1890—a period of astonishing creativity. The

paintings are arranged chronologically, following the dramatic changes that occurred after his move to Arles in Provence in early 1888. The spring blossom was one of the first things to catch van Gogh's eye, then the beach at Les Saintes-Maries in the summer, and the harvest at La Crau in the month of June, 1888. But many of his finest works were painted after his admission to a sanatorium near St.-Rémy (following the well-known episode in which he cut off his ear): *Branch of Almond Tree in Blossom* and *Still Life: Vase with Irises.* Finally, there are the tormented landscapes painted during the last 3 months of his life while staying at Auvers-sur-Oise, including the ominous *Crows over the Wheatfield.*

The 2nd floor of the museum is devoted to van Gogh's collection of 19thC Japanese prints, mainly of actors and courtesans with tormented expressions. The 3rd floor contains further works by van Gogh as well as a small collection of paintings by contemporaries of the artist, such as Emile Bernard and Toulouse-Lautrec.

★ Van Loon, Museum

Keizersgracht 672. ☎ 20-6245255. Open Sun 1–5pm, Mon 10am–5pm; ring bell to enter. Admission: Adults Dfl. 5, children Dfl. 4. Tram: 16, 24, 25 to Keizersgracht.

The museum provides a rare opportunity to venture behind the facade of a stately canal and into its well-loved interior. The building and its twin at Keizersgracht 674 were built by Adriaen Dortsman shortly after the completion of this section of the **Grachtengordel** and illustrate the dry classical style of the 1670s. The only touches of decoration are the 4 classical deities on the balustrade, representing Minerva, Mars, Vulcan, and Ceres.

One of the earliest occupants of no. 672 was Rembrandt's pupil Ferdinand Bol, who lived here until 1680. In 1884 the house was bought by the Van Loon family, who still own it. For those who enjoy piecing together family trees, the museum owns some 50 portraits of family members, ranging from 17thC oil paintings of heroic Dutch rebels to sepia photographs from the 1920s, by which time the Van Loons had become solid pillars of respectability.

Previous generations have left their mark in other ways too, such as the initials of Abraham van Hagen and Catharina Trip that are worked into the staircase balustrade, and the monogram of Hendrik Sander in the master bedroom. The dilapidated rococo moldings and chairs too frail to sit upon add to the mood of faded grandeur.

The most splendid feature of the house is its formal garden, leading to a coach house disguised as a neoclassical temple. Notice the adjoining coach house, with its reclining statues and pretty clock tower buried behind the foliage.

★★ Views

The flat landscape of the Randstad sometimes creates a yearning to see above roof-level. You can climb the classical tower of the **Westerkerk** to look down on the narrow streets of the Jordaan, or ascend the winding stair in the **Zuiderkerk tower** to survey the new architecture in the former Jewish quarter. The **Oude Kerk tower** gives you a glimpse of the red-light district from a neutral vantage point.

Twenty-three floors up, the Ciel Bleu restaurant and bar of the **Okura Hotel** (see "Accommodations") offers a sweeping view of the city's southern quarter and terrific sunsets.

One of the best canal views in the city is from the **bridge** at the intersection of Reguliersgracht and Keizersgracht, where you can count 7 separate bridges receding into the distance, illuminated with strings of lights on summer nights.

★★ Vondelpark

Stadhouderskade. Tram: 1, 2, 5, 6, 7, 10 to Leidseplein.

Named after the prolific 17thC Amsterdam poet Joost van den Vondel, Vondelpark is an extensive area of woods and lakes in the 19thC ring between Leidseplein and the Rijksmuseum. The park was designed in 1865 by the Dutch landscape architects J. D. and L. P. Zocher, who abandoned the formal French-garden style popular in 18thC Holland in favor of the more Romantic and irregular English style.

In the 1960s and 1970s the Vondelpark became a famous hippie campground. Although such spontaneity is now discouraged, the Vondelpark still attracts street musicians, fire-eaters, jugglers, and a flood of young tourists. It also hosts whimsical art exhibits, such as a series of wax Buddhas, floating in one of the small lakes, on whom local artists had painted colorful—but totally incongruous—ties.

Vondelpark has something for everyone: playgrounds for children, benches for seniors (who use them to sit and watch the lake, after a Sunday morning bike ride).

In the summer, regular performances of music, theater, and poetry are given in the open-air theater in the middle of the park. The summer sunbathers, bicyclists, joggers, rollerbladers, and picnickers make Vondelpark a lot like New York's Central Park—a place to socialize.

The cafe terrace of the **Filmmuseum,** good for meeting people or people-watching, overlooks the scene. On a hot sunny day, its shady terrace may be one of the coolest and balmiest spots in Amsterdam.

★ Waag

Nieuwmarkt. Metro: To Nieuwmarkt.

The dominant feature of Nieuwmarkt is the dusky medieval Waag, formerly a turreted city gate on the east edge of the city. When the city expanded outward in the 17thC, the moat around the gate was filled in and the building converted to a weigh house. Various local guilds met in the upstairs rooms, which were reached by separate staircases in the different towers.

The highly ornate 17thC entrances still survive: the guild of artists used the door decorated with the figure of St. Luke, while the masons' entrance is distinguished by a mason's head and tools. Notice also the tower with its curious trial windows, which were painstakingly built by apprentices in order that they might qualify as master masons. The guild of surgeons, which used the door inscribed Theatrum Anatomicum, commissioned Rembrandt's famous early work, *The Anatomy Lesson of Dr. Tulp,* now hanging in the Mauritshuis in The Hague.

Waterways: Amsterdam is built around a web of intersecting waterways, of which the most important are the Amstel River and the Singel, Herengracht, Keizersgracht, and Prinsengracht. Oil tankers, cruise ships, and Rhine barges sail down the IJ River, which can best be seen from the ferries, which are free. The canals are increasingly used by tour boats, pedal boats, canal buses, and pleasure craft. Some waterways, such

Waag

as Prinsengracht and Binnenkant, are lined with old Rhine barges that have been converted into houseboats, and one barge opposite the Koepelzaal on Singel is now a home for stray cats.

Several important buildings in the city stand on islands, including Centraal Station and the Nederlands Scheepvaart Museum, while others float on the water, such as the flower market on Singel (see "Shopping") and the Chinese restaurant in the harbor.

The sluices are closed every night by turning a wooden wheel (between 7 and 8pm) to allow the canals to be pumped out. You can watch the operation being carried out at the sluice on the Amstel opposite Theater Carré or the Haarlemmersluis at the north end of Singel. One of the most memorable events on the canals is the annual Prinsengracht classical music concert (see "Calendar of Events" in "The Basics"), when an orchestra performs on a flotilla of barges and thousands of music-loving Amsterdammers fill the streets alongside the Prinsengracht canal.

★★ Westerkerk

Prinsengracht 281. ☎ 20-6247766. Church's stated opening hours and months are subject to change, so call first to check. Apr–mid-Sept: Mon–Sat 10am–4pm; tower open June to mid-Sept: Tues, Wed, Fri, Sat 2–5pm. Tram: 13, 14, 17 to Westermarkt.

The architect Hendrick de Keyser was commissioned in 1620 to build a new Protestant church on the west side of the Grachtengorde. The Westerkerk (named, like most of Amsterdam's Protestant churches, after its geographical position—West church—rather than after a saint) and its tower, the Westoren, became dominant landmarks in the surrounding Jordaan and Prinsengracht neighborhoods. De Keyser's aesthetic was

Westerkerk

in keeping with Protestantism in so far as he chose simplicity over more decorative styles. However, the nave is Gothic, and de Keyser's overall style retains some Mannerist elements.

Although Amsterdam had broken with its Habsburg past by the time the church and tower were constructed, the city chose to top the tower with the imperial crown granted to the city by Maximilian I in 1489. The tower features in several sketches by Rembrandt, who spent the last years of his life in a house on the Rozengracht, and is buried in the churchyard.

For a terrific view of the canals, climb the tower— still the tallest in Amsterdam. The carillonneur climbs the tower to play the bells on Tuesdays from noon to 1pm.

Willet-Holthuysen, Museum

Herengracht 605. ☎ 20-5231870. Open daily 11am–5pm. Admission: Adults Dfl. 5. Tram: 4, 9, 14 to Rembrandtsplein.

This museum offers a rare opportunity to enter a handsome 18thC **Herengracht** residence once owned by various wealthy Amsterdam families—via the tradesmen's entrance. Consequently, the first room entered is an 18thC kitchen, aglow with bright copper utensils and gleaming tiles decorated with exotic caged birds. The house is a monument to Dutch interiors and the decorative objects that were once typical of patrician households. The floor plan is typical 18thC; in the basement are a kitchen, larder, and cellar with upper stories containing a living room, dining room, office, and bedroom.

In the back of the house, you can see an impressive 18thC French garden complete with a sundial and an assortment of mythological characters—statues of Mercury, Flora, and Pomona (representing trade, flowers, and gardens respectively).

Zoo (see Artis)

Zuiderkerk

Zuiderkerkhof 72. Church open year-round Mon–Fri noon–5pm, Thurs noon–10pm. Tower open July–Sept: Wed–Sat 2–4pm. Transportation: Tram 9, 14 to Waterlooplein; sneltram 51 or metro to Nieuwmarkt.

Completed in 1611 by Hendrick de Keyser, this was the Netherlands' first Protestant church. Although laden with Renaissance ornament, the design is still largely Gothic, as is seen in the octagonal tower with its pearshaped top. No longer used for services, the church now houses the Informatiecentrum Ruimtelijke Ordening. The church tower can be climbed in the summer for a panoramic view of the renovated Nieuwmarkt. Siena's famous main square inspired the layout of the Zuiderkerkplein, which provides a pleasant spot to listen to the carillon concerts on Thursdays from noon to 1pm.

Amsterdam with Kids

Amsterdam has few parks or open spaces where children can romp. But there are places—you just need to look carefully for them. Vondelpark, located close to museums and Leidseplein, has several children's playgrounds as well as lakes, grazing cows, bicycle paths, grassy lawns for Frisbee or picnics, a pancake house, and several ice-cream stands. The park is also a good place for walks with baby strollers. Some cycle lanes, especially in the parks and on the outskirts of the city, make bicycling quite safe. Canal bikes (pedal boats) are another safe and scenic way for children to see the city.

Parents with small children may have trouble finding places to change diapers. A few progressive Dutch museums, including the **Amsterdams Historisch Museum** and the **Boymans–Van Beuningen Museum** in Rotterdam, now provide a table with a changing mat (sometimes signed *babyverzorging*). Elsewhere, department stores are usually adequate. The **Stedelijk Museum** provides rucksacks for carrying small babies.

For baby-sitting services, call **Babysit Centr** (☎ 20-6972320), **De Peu Terette** (☎ 20-6796793), or **Kriterion** (☎ 20-6245848).

Following are a number of experiences particularly recommended for children and their families. See "Amsterdam's Sights A to Z" above for specific information on the establishments mentioned below.

Feeding the Ducks

An integral part of the Amsterdam canals are the ducks, geese, and swans that live near them. Most are friendly, hungry, and fun to feed—and bread crumbs are readily available. Be aware, however, that while ducks are gentle, geese and swans may be more aggressive.

Parks & Zoos

Probably the top spot for children in Amsterdam is **Artis,** a well-designed zoo with numerous indoor attractions, such as an aquarium and nocturnal-animal house, to keep children amused on rainy days. Artis also has a petting zoo and 3 playgrounds with jungle gyms and slides shaped in the forms of giraffes and other zoo animals.

The best parks for children are **Amstelpark,** with its miniature train, pony rides, farmyard, maze, miniature golf, seals, and pancake house; and the **Amsterdamse Bos,** with boat rides, horseback riding, and rollerblading. Amsterdamse Bos can be reached on summer weekends by the **Electrische Museum Tramlijn** (☎ 20-67337538) from Haarlemmer-meerstation. **Beatrixpark,** with its lovely lawns and gardens, is nice if you happen to be in Amsterdam South.

Although most Dutch parks have excellent biking trails, only a few rent bikes. Vondelpark does not rent bikes, and you may have to venture to Leidseplein or Dam Square in order to rent one. Occasionally hotels have rental bikes available—ask the concierge.

Children might also enjoy a visit to one of the children's farmyards (*kinderboerderijen*) in Amsterdam. These unusual city farms are found at Artis and Amstelpark.

Museums & Workshops

The most interesting museums for children are **Madame Tussaud Scenerama** (waxwork figures); **Aviodome Aeroplane Museum** (the Schiphol airplane museum); the **Nederlands Scheepvaart Museum** (ship models, head phones, and a beautiful old boat); **NINT Technisch Museum** (fun, hands-on science activities); **Zoological Museum** (the natural history museum at the zoo); and the **Tropenmuseum** (reconstructed Third World villages). The Tropen-museum also has a separate children's department, the **Kindermuseum TM Junior** (☎ 20-5688200) where children can sniff tropical herbs and play instruments made in the tropics, among other things. The museum considers the needs of small children: It is very hands-on and is tolerant of children running about. Dutch children also seem to enjoy the modern art (and par-ticularly the video shows) in the **Stedelijk Museum.**

The **Anne Frankhuis** with its compelling story of an adolescent girl in hiding during the Nazi occupa-tion of Holland draws in children of all ages, although it may be best suited for children over the age of 10. The **Joods Historisch Museum** has exhibits featuring the artwork and war stories of children; these tend to be more inspiring than depressing, although best suited for older children and teenagers.

Theaters, Movies & Circuses

Children usually enjoy the spectacle of **street theater,** which flourishes in the summer months around

Leidseplein and in front of the **Koninklijk Paleis** on the Dam.

Uitkrant, a publication of Amsterdams Uit Buro, has a special section, "Jeugdagenda," devoted to children's events in Amsterdam. Dutch-speaking children may also dial the **Jeugdtheaterlijn** (☎ 20-6222999) for a chatty recorded message informing them of coming events.

The **Amsterdams Marionettentheater** (☎ 20-6208027) puts on occasional shows featuring traditional marionettes. Guided tours backstage let you into the secrets of the art. Occasional shows are also put on by **Elleboog** (☎ 20-6269370), the children's circus. This is actually a circus school where children learn circus tricks, such as juggling and walking on large balls, so they can put on their own performances.

The main venue for children's theater is **De Krakeling** (☎ 20-6245123). Most shows will be in Dutch, but occasionally there is mime or music.

Movies for children are shown at the **Rialto** movie theater (see "The Arts"). The weekly film listings include details of children's matinees (*kindermatinees*). Most of these are dubbed into Dutch (indicated by the words: *Nederlands gesproken*).

Boat Trips & Tram Rides

Canal-boat trips are always fun, and most operators have reduced rates for children. A more energetic way to explore the canals is by canal bicycle (see "Staying Active"). The less adventurous can also get to know the city by tram. On summer weekends, old-fashioned trams run regularly to the Amsterdamse Bos (call **Electrische Museum Tramlijn,** ☎ 20-6737538; also listed above in "Amsterdam's Sights A to Z"). A tourist tram also departs from Dam (mid-Apr–Sept from 10:30am–6pm, every 45 min.) on a 70-minute tour of the city.

Ice-Skating & Rollerblading

These sports are popular with both adults and children; consequently there are numerous paths suitable for rollerblading that wind through Dutch towns and the countryside. There are also rollerblading rinks where children can take lessons and practice the sport. In the winter, if the canals and lakes freeze, there are many outdoor skating areas and Dutch skating clubs organize skating tours of the countryside (tours are publicized in newspapers and on TV). In many cases, summertime rollerblading centers become indoor and outdoor ice rinks between October and March. In Amsterdam, try

Jaap Edenbaan (Radioweg 64, ☎ 20-6949894) for either rollerblading or ice-skating.

Swimming

Amsterdam has several swimming pools, of which the **Mirandabad,** with its slides and artificial waves, has the most to offer energetic kids (see "Swimming" in "Staying Active"). And, for listings of toy stores, see "Shopping."

Cafes & Restaurants

In Holland, children are welcome in some but not all cafes, where they enjoy *chocomel* (chocolate-flavored milk) and *warme chocolade* (hot chocolate). Among the cafes that might appeal to children is **De IJsbreker** for delicious hot chocolate and a grassy riverbank good for romping or feeding the ducks (see "Amsterdam's Cafes" in "Dining"). The outdoor terrace at **Café Américain,** with its roomy terrace and playful—and enormous—ice-cream desserts, is also a nice place for kids, as is the 2-story Pancake Bakery with its fruit pancakes, fanciful ice-cream desserts, and child-friendly design.

Some restaurants offer an inexpensive *kindermenu* (children's menu), which usually involves dishes designed to appeal to children, although they may horrify diet-conscious parents with their emphasis on french fries, ice cream, and soda. **Bolhoed,** a vegetarian restaurant, is healthier—and promises to "love your child" (see **Dining** for more information).

Amsterdam also boasts a children's restaurant, **Het Kinder Kookcafé** (Oude Zijds Achterburgwal 193, ☎ 20-6253257), where meals are prepared under adult supervision by children aged 6 to 12. Although most of the diners are children, parents may, if they wish, accompany their offspring.

AMSTERDAM WALKS

A MSTERDAM IS A CITY MADE FOR WALKING. IT IS SMALL in scale, rich in architecture, and full of social and architectural subtleties that can best be seen on foot. Only when walking can you gaze long enough to appreciate the window art, the puns on the gable stones, and the hidden courtyards. And only on foot can you experience the changes in pace and atmosphere as you dodge trams on Leidseplein, stroll peacefully along a canal, shop with the glitterati on P. C. Hoofstraat, cafehop on the Spui, or wander through the red-light district of the old city. Although the city may at first seem large and complex, most of these experiences are an easy (and safe) 10- or 15-minute walk from the center of town.

The walks in this chapter take you inside Amsterdam. Walk 1 takes you into the Prinsengracht/Herengracht/ Keizersgracht canal neighborhood where the 17thC patrician canal houses, serene canals, and side streets lined with exotic goods from around the world may take you back to the golden age—until you spy the wacky window art, designer fashions, colorful houseboats, hopping cafe scene, and fine French restaurants. The walk also takes you to the Begijnhof hofje, the Spui, the Nederlands Theater Institute, the Bijbels Museum, and the Westerkerk. The Royal Palace and the Amsterdam Historical Museum are a 5-minute walk away.

In Walk 2 you stroll the Jordaan, taking in the modest but colorful 17th and 18thC architecture, charming village streets, hidden hofjes, and ubiquitous window art. Here you'll experience 2 distinctly different Amsterdam subcultures: the working class Jordaaners who sing the Old Amsterdam music, and the younger artists, musicians, and yuppies who have turned the Jordaan into a Dutch version of New York's SoHo.

The brown cafes, groceries, and shops still cater to both groups, although the younger generation seems to be taking over. Other sights on the walk are Westerkerk, Nooderkerk, and the Anne Frank House.

When you walk in Amsterdam, take an umbrella. Showers are intense—and unforeseeable. If you get caught in a downpour, head for the nearest cafe. It will probably be crowded and cozy, since other people have also just dashed in from the street and are looking for coffee and conversation.

A word of caution: Don't wander in front of trams or bicycles when you are looking up at gables and cornices. Keep to the sidewalks, not the streets.

Note: Most of the sights, shops, restaurants, and cafes in the walking tours are described at greater length in the chapters "Sights & Attractions," "Shopping," and "Dining."

Walk 1: The Essential Amsterdam

Begin at Westerkerk.

Transportation: Tram 13, 14, or 17 will take you directly to Westermarkt, the square around Westerkerk, which is situated between the Prinsengracht and Keizersgracht canals. You can also take the **Canal Bus** directly to Westerkerk (on the Prinsengracht side) or to Keizersgracht (on the Keizersgracht side of the church and adjacent to the Homomonument).

Best Time for Walk: It is best between 1 and 4pm— the late afternoon is a good time to browse in the small shops, take in the street life, sip coffee at a cafe, or bask in the sun on a canalside terrace. If you prefer window shopping, the walk is most interesting at dusk or after dark when the shops and canal-house windows are lit up, and you can see the beautiful interiors. An evening walk also takes you past some of Amsterdam's best French restaurants at dinnertime.

Time: About 2 hours, more if you visit the museums. (*Note:* Since Westerkerk is the starting and ending point for both Walk 1 and Walk 2, it is possible to combine the walks if you have the energy and time.)

When I'm in Amsterdam, I avoid the neon Leidseplein, the hectic shopping streets, and slip off to the neighborhoods to live like an Amsterdammer, not a tourist. I usually head straight for the canals, to the Prinsengracht neighborhood. It's a special place—rich in brown cafes, cozy restaurants, golden-age architecture, and whimsical "window art." Prinsengracht is a

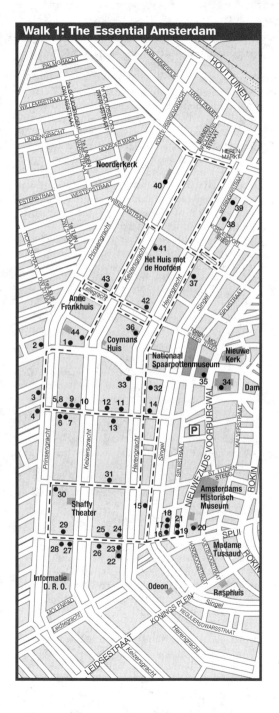

Walk 1: The Essential Amsterdam

HOUTTUINEN

PALMGRACHT

WILLEMSSTRAAT

LINDENGRACHT

ESTERSTRAAT   WESTERSTRAAT

NOORDERMARKT

Noorderkerk

40

39

38

41

Het Huis met
de Hoofden

37

43

Anne
Frankhuis

42

36

Coymans
Huis

44

1

2

33

Nationaal
Spaarpottenmuseum

32

Nieuwe
Kerk

35

34

Dam

5,8 9 10

12 11

14

6 7

13

31

30

Shaffy
Theater

15

Amsterdams
Historisch
Museum

18

29

17 21

25 24

16 19 20

SPUI

28 27

26 23

Madame
Tussaud

22

ROKIN

Informatie
D. R. O.

Odeon

Rasphuis

MOLENPAD

KONINGS PLEIN

LEIDSESTRAAT

fine place to sample life on the canals and to begin an aesthetic, culinary, historical, and cultural tour of Amsterdam.

In the golden age, Amsterdam merchants living in grand houses on the canals brought goods from all over the world to sell in the snug little shops on the nearby side streets. Many shops still occupy these 17thC storefronts, and the merchants, like their predecessors, are world traders with a taste for the unusual and exotic. But even more exceptional than the variety of goods are the window displays—an art form that represents an aesthetic and a sense of humor unique to Amsterdam, which in itself is worth a trip to the canals.

Residential windows also reflect this whimsical humor. If you look closely at other windows and window sills as you walk along, you will see everything from beautiful sculptures to comical objets d'art looking back at you. You are expected to appreciate the display, but not to linger or stare inside.

Begin your tour at ①　**Westerkerk,** the 17thC church built by Hendrick de Keyser (and the church where both Rembrandt and his son are buried—though no one knows quite where). The 280-foot church spire bears the imperial crown that Emperor Maximilian granted to the city coat of arms. Westerkerk presides over both the Jordaan and the Prinsengracht neighborhoods and is an important landmark for these areas.

The church's interior is surprisingly simple except for the monumental organ that was made by the 17thC craftsman Johannes Duyschot and decorated by Gerard Lairesse, a painter known for his decorative frescoes and whose work was much in demand among the residents of the Herengracht mansions (see "Sights & Attractions"). Listen for the tolling of Westerkerk's bell, to which local clocks have been set for centuries. If you climb the tower you will be rewarded by one of the best views in Amsterdam.

At **Westermarkt,** for an authentic taste of Old Amsterdam, try the pickled herring or smoked fish at the fish stand on the square. The smoked *paling* (eel) broodje is particularly good; it tastes like white fish. The stand also sells cold drinks and lemon flavored Spa to rinse away fish and brine.

Now, turn your back to Westerkerk, face the Prinsengracht canal, with Rozengracht Street on your left, and take the bridge to the other side. (If you find yourself at the Keizersgracht, you have gone the wrong way.) After you cross the bridge, turn right for a visit to an aromatic old coffee-and-tea shop at **no. 180 Prinsengracht** named ② **Keyser Thee.** In 1817, the store was a father-and-son establishment. The shop sells a wide variety of coffees and teas as well as state-of-the-art coffee makers, teapots, and esoteric coffee paraphernalia.

Retrace your steps. As you leave the shop, turn right on Prinsengracht toward Raadhuisstraat, a busy street with tram lines. Cross Raadhuisstraat and proceed up the Prinsengracht canal. Notice the houseboats with bicycles on the decks and gardens on the rooftops. Many of the 2,400 houseboats in Amsterdam are moored on the Prinsengracht or Brouwersgracht canals. After you pass Rozengracht on your right, you will see ③ **'t Winkelje,** a "little store" at **no. 228 Prinsengracht** that is very Amsterdam. Notice the painted heads above the 1st-story windows staring out across the Prinsengracht. 't Winkelje sells everything from tasteful glassware and picture frames to goofy plastic toys and porcelain shepherds.

On your right as you continue up the canal, you will pass ④ **Klamboe,** a small mosquito-netting store at **no. 232** with surprisingly romantic window displays. Its young owner traveled the globe—and brought a business back from the tropics just like Dutch traders centuries before.

At this point, take the bridge across the Prinsengracht. As you cross, notice the variety of bell gables, neck gables, and hoisting posts from **nos. 301–307.** This wedge of the Prinsengracht was once the site of factories. A group of factories—across the street at **nos. 315–331**—was renovated in the late 1960s with the financial help of one of the Pulitzers (descended from the family that founded the Pulitzer prize). Now these buildings are part of the ⑤ **Pulitzer Hotel** of which 315–331 is the entrance.

The bridge street becomes **Reestraat.** Proceed down Reestraat, and if you are thirsty or hungry stop in at ⑥ **Hoek's Koffiehuis** on the corner to your right. It may look inconsequential, but Hoek's is a popular neighborhood hangout where Amsterdam politicians and artists stop in for coffee and conversation.

Reestraat, a street bringing together refined and worldly tastes with offbeat, "alternative" ones, is typical of the neighborhood. At **no. 21,** you'll find ⑦ **Terra** with its displays of delicate hand-painted old and new pottery from Southern Spain; ⑧ **Kramer Kaarsen Olie,** at **no. 20,** is both delightful and odd.

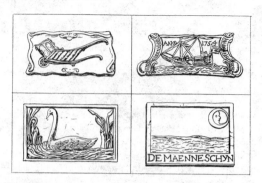

Before buildings were given street numbers, they were identified by engraved cartouches (gable stones), which used symbols to reflect the professions or identities of the inhabitants.

Every inch of wall space is packed with colorful candles. The window displays appeal to a surprising spectrum of tastes and religious persuasions: there are plump Buddha candles and serene Madonnas as well as Wicca candles, Krishna candles, and a menorah or two. ⑨ **Pappen en Berendokter** (the Doll Doctor), next door at **no. 18,** is owned by Mr. Kramer from the candle store who sells beautiful old dolls as well as some new ones. Mostly, he repairs dolls, and his tiny shop has the necessary though ghoulish merchandise: doll heads and cupboards full of eyes.

The block ends with another popular import— French food at ⑩ **De Goudsbloem,** a romantic restaurant situated in a former 17thC pharmacy that is now part of the **Pulitzer Hotel.** The hotel, comprised of 24 canal houses from the 17th and 18th centuries, is worth a look—as is the exhibit of contemporary art shown in the lobby. (If you pass by around 4pm, you might try tea in the enclosed Pulitzer gardens.)

This brings you to the **Keizersgracht canal.** Cross it and proceed to **Hartenstraat,** the narrow street on the other side. Hartenstraat is packed with charming little shops selling everything from secondhand clothing to Asian silks. This street offers some good examples of Dutch "window art" as well as some subtle architectural touches that you can see only if you look carefully at the decorative gargoyles, gable stones, and doorways.

The aroma of freshly baked breads and sweets wafting out of ⑪ **Mensink de Warme Bakker** (no. 12) might draw you in for a snack. For dinner (if you have reservations), you could step into ⑫ **Van Harte** *(no. 24),* a cozy French restaurant with a great wine list and one of the most enticing sidewalk terraces in the neighborhood (see **Dining**). Notice the **lion-head gargoyles** guarding the 2nd story windows of Van Harte. And don't miss another lovely touch of Old Holland—the antique amber, green, and blue **Delft tiles** lining the doorway at ⑬ **no. 17 Hartenstraat.**

At the end of Hartenstraat, you come to the **Herengracht canal**—the gentlemen's canal—where the wealthiest Dutch merchants once lived and conducted business. Homes here are larger and grander than those on the Prinsengracht. Don't forget to look up at the ornate gables, gable stones, and cornices. Since 17thC houses bore no street numbers, gable stones once functioned as addresses by identifying pictorially the profession—or the name—of those who lived inside. Some gable stones are puns on the name of the owner or business; some are decorative, with biblical scenes or popular designs. As you cross the bridge over the Herengracht, notice the bunches of fruit, a popular 18thC motif, decorating the house at **no. 249.**

The bridge street becomes **Gasthuismolensteeg,** a short narrow street with fanciful shops. ⑭ **Vliegertuig,** at **no. 8,** takes kites seriously as the object of art and sport, displaying vividly colored racing kites designed with inventive, aerodynamic geometry and elaborate gizmos.

Turn right on the **Singel canal**—one of the older canals that, from 1487 to 1585, formed a moat on the west side of the city. Singel means "girdle," and the buildings on the inside of the canal tend to be a bit older than those on the outside. The buildings here are also smaller than those on the Herengracht, and some shops retain a cramped medieval character. Notice the beautiful facade stone *In de Vergulde Haring-buys* (In the Gilded Herring Boat) adorning ⑮ **Singel 358:** it depicts herring fishing—with a large fishing boat in the foreground and 2 small boats in the background. Also notice the cherubs over the doorway at **Singel 390.**

As you see **Wijde Heisteeg** on your right, turn left instead. Take the bridge over the Singel canal. As you cross the Singel, notice the various gable styles and the facades from the 1600s: **no. 410** on the corner dates from 1647. Then go straight on **Hei Steeg** (which looks like a medieval alley) toward **the Spui.** Here you will enter a small square—a hub of activity where architectural styles and cultural trends from several centuries converge.

At this point, I suggest you head for a cafe. You have several popular places to choose from lined up to your left. There is the ⑯ **Luxembourg** with its comfy reading table and its terrace packed with the beautiful and well-heeled. Just beyond, there is ⑰ **Hoppe**—a famous, crowded, traditional brown cafe, dedicated to preserving the rituals of Amsterdam beer culture. For a more bohemian crowd, mosey across the alley to ⑱ **De Zwart.** If you are ready for lunch, try one of the many restaurants on Spuistraat (see Luden, Lucius, Haesje Claes, Kantijl en de Tijger in "Dining").

The Spui is trendy and historically important. Both the Luxembourg and Hoppe are at the hub of Amsterdam's fashionable cafe scene. The square they face was once the scene of 1960s Provos happenings and political protests that took place at the foot of ⑲ *Het Lieverdje* ("The Little Darling"), a statue of a mischievous waif who was given to the city by a tobacco company. Within yards of this site of sixties' irreverence is the ⑳ **Begijnhof,** a *hofje* built in the 15thC as a cloistered community for the Beguines, a lay order of nuns. *Hofjes* are houses for the poor, old, or disenfranchised built around protected courtyards. They are typically Dutch and still in use in Amsterdam. At this time, the Begijnhof is inhabited by elderly or widowed women. Other *hofjes,* in the Jordaan for instance, are devoted to students or people with low incomes.

After your break: To find the Begijnhof, cross the Spui, walking past *The Little Darling,* the ㉑ **Athenaeum Boekhandel,** and the piano store (on your left). You will then find a row of white stone houses. Continue walking until you find a red-brick facade with an arched doorway protected by St. Ursula (or so says the engraving above it). Enter an arched passageway lined with tiles, and emerge in the peaceful courtyard of the Begijnhof, enclosed on all sides by sturdy 17thC houses and thus insulated from the noisy traffic of the Spui. Each house has a tiny front yard tended by the elderly women who live in the complex. The houses are brick, and nearly identical, except **no. 34**—one of the two medieval wooden houses remaining in Amsterdam and the only house in the Begijnhof to survive the massive fires of 1421 and 1452.

In the center of this courtyard is a medieval Gothic church built in the 1400s. It stood empty during the Reformation, was later used as a warehouse, and then, in the 17thC, was given to Protestant dissenters who had left England in search of religious freedom. The church became known as the English Church, and it is said that some of its members sailed to America as Pilgrims in 1620. If you look carefully, you may find another smaller church—a once-clandestine Roman Catholic church (see "Sights & Attractions").

To leave the hofje, follow the church to your right and exit at no. 1. Turn right at the Spui, and retrace your steps across the square to resume the walk on the canals. Go back on **Hei Steeg** and cross the bridge over the Singel canal.

Proceed on **Widje Heisteeg,** and notice on your left the plaque (under the 2nd-story window of no. 5) illustrating a bakery scene and thus identifying the shop of **Paul Kaiser, Warme Bakker.**

Pause before crossing the **Herengracht.** You are just yards away from several of the canal's most architecturally interesting buildings and may want to walk over for a closer look. After you cross over the Herengracht, turn left to **nos. 364–370,** known as the **Cromhouthuizen**—a group of 4 natural stone facades and 4 neck gables that form 2 pairs of buildings designed by **Philips Vingboons** between 1660 and 1662. The buildings are classical with the typical festoons, pilasters, and oeil-de-boeuf windows. On the gable stone at **no. 366** you can see a reference to the owner's name: an illustration of curved or vaulted wood, since Jacob Cromhout's surname means "vaulted frame."

The Cromhouthuizen also houses the ㉒ **Bijbels Museum,** which displays the Delft Bible printed in 1477 as well as other biblical texts reflecting both Jewish and Christian faiths. Adding to the grandeur of the architecture, the building has a ceiling painted by 18thC artist Jacob De Witt.

After this dip into the wealthy past, walk back down the Herengracht to **Huidenstraat** for more window art, new furniture, old upholstery, heavenly chocolate, and a phenomenal array of lamps. On your left is ㉓ **Binnenhuis** *(no. 5)* with ever-so-contemporary furniture and other homey items by the best young Dutch designers. You'll see figure-eight bookshelves, high-tech toasters, elegant goblets—and natural cotton bathrobes. At ㉔ **no. 10,** the golden age returns in the form of traditional Dutch drapery and upholstery, with strong colors and rich brocades.

And then there is chocolate. At ㉕ **no. 12,** you'll find **Patisserie Pompadour**—with the finest of home-made chocolates laced with whiskey, Grand Marnier, tea, strawberry puree, and 41 other combinations. The chocolates can be packed in neat little boxes for gifts or in small bags with handles that you can dip into as you continue the walk. You can also sit in the adjacent tea-room and eat in style.

A place to slip in for a cold drink or coffee is ㉖ **De Pels,** a brown cafe at **no. 25** where Provos and 1960s artists and romantics once gathered to plan happenings at the Spui and to change the face of Amsterdam. Some of the old crowd still drop in from time to time.

Almost half of the shops on Huidenstraat are devoted to lamps. If you like the Art Deco and Art Nouveau fixtures in the brown cafes, this is the place to find them. It is also the place to find almost any kind of vintage or contemporary lamp.

Cross the Keizersgracht (the Emperor's canal) to **Runstraat,** one of the best streets for quirky Amsterdam window art. ㉗ **Haruro,** at **no. 3,** displays an odd but intriguing assortment of colorful bow ties, bow-tie earrings, and plastic ears (in primary colors). ㉘ **De Witte Tanden Winkel** (the **White Teeth Store**), at **no. 5,** is an Amsterdam fixture. The fancifully painted toothbrushes whirling around on the Ferris wheel in the window has been a source of awe for children who squeal, "They look just like people!" Some adults have been known to visit the display on return visits to Amsterdam—just to make sure it's still there.

If you turn with your back to the Ferris wheel and look up at the 2nd-story window of ㉙ **no. 10 Runstraat,** you will see another window-art institution: a 3-foot doll in a short dress waving at you from a window that is strung with tiny electric candle-lights. She's been there for years.

At the **Prinsengracht canal,** turn right. The atmosphere on this canal is more casual than that of the Herengracht and Keizersgracht, making the canal a popular mooring spot for houseboats. (Some of the best specimens are located to your right. If you get into a houseboat viewing mood, turn right on the Prinsengracht and then left on the Brouwersgracht.)

To continue on the walk and see buttons-as-art-form or a special edition Donald Duck, turn right on **Berenstraat.** At the ㉚ **Animation Art Gallery** *(no. 39 Berenstraat),* you'll find Dumbo and Mickey Mouse special edition cartoons framed and beautifully displayed. To see the buttons, take the bridge over the Keizersgracht and go straight on Wolvenstraat until you get to the ㉛ **Knopen Winkel (Button Store)** at

no. 14 where you will find mother-of-pearl buttons from Sri Lanka and hand-painted wooden buttons from Indonesia. Buttons made from less exotic materials are arranged according to color in rich mahogany shelves.

At this point you are leaving behind the eccentricities of the little streets and heading for the grand golden-age houses and peaceful canals. When you get to the **Herengracht,** cross the bridge and then turn left on the other side of the canal, heading back toward Westerkerk. Since the Herengracht was, and is, the wealthiest of the canals, it has the most elaborate gables, crests, and carved wooden doors.

You will pass �32 **Out of Africa, no. 215** on your right, a shop with African artifacts and jewelry and an impressive stock of fertility goddesses who, the proprietor tells me, are good at what they do.

At the corner of Herengracht and **Raadhuisstraat,** several centuries of architectural styles converge. To your left is the �33 **Art Nouveau shopping arcade,** with graceful arches and fierce gargoyles, designed in 1894 by A. L. van Gendt. Further to your left is Hendrick de Keyser's **Westerkerk,** previously described. The church was built in 1620 but the 280-foot tower was added in 1638. To your right, several blocks away, is the �34 **Royal Palace,** built by Joseph van Campen in classical style—rich in ornament—and meant to symbolize Amsterdam's prosperity. In the Palace, Campen moves away from the red-brick and white-stone facades of the early 17thC, using sober Bentheim sandstone instead. The foundation stone was laid in 1648, but the building was not occupied as the town hall until 1655. The building was given to King William I after the Revolution of 1813 and has been owned by the royalty since that time. What was once the massive post office across the street from the Royal Palace, now �35 **Magna Plaza,** was built in 1899 by C. H. Peters with lots of brick and ornamentation and several towers. (Its neo-Gothic turreted skyline was once ridiculed in a 19thC cartoon as "the pear mountain—an experiment in fruit architecture.")

You are standing on the oldest stretch of the **Herengracht canal.** This part of the canal was dug between 1585 and 1609 and was designed to attract rich merchants by permitting them to buy large plots of land. Artisans with noisy or smelly trades were not allowed to work here, and were sent to the Jordaan. Take some time to observe the wealth of detail in gables, doorways, and decorated gable stones and plaques. You'll see a grand style of architecture and one of the finest facades in Amsterdam in the ㊱ **Bartolotti House and Theater Museum** at **no. 170-172 Herengracht.** Hendrick de Keyser built this splendid Renaissance house in 1617. His houses tended to have step-gabled facades with whitened sandstone set off against rosy-red brick. Notice the step gables and the Calvinist motto in the gable stone of the Bartolotti House: *Ingenio et assiduo labore* (Through ability and hard work). The owner of this house originally bore a typical Dutch name—Van den Heuval—but it is said that he took the Italian name Bartolotti to please his Bolognese father-in-law.

The house next door, **no. 168,** provides more space for the Theater Museum. This house, known as the **"White House"** because of its sandstone facade, was built by architect Philips Vingboons in 1638 and commissioned by Michiel Pauw, a founder of the Dutch West India Company. Vingboons invented the neck gable, and this was his first neck-gable house. Neck gables remained popular in both the 17th and 18th centuries.

If you go inside the White House, look for ceilings painted in later years by Jacob De Witt. De Witt was also at work next door at 170–172, painting doors and ceilings with goddesses and gods. During the Nazi occupation, the Germans took a liking to this Dutch grandeur and used the garden of nos. 170–172 as a command post.

The Theater Museum presents changing exhibits on theater, mime, dance, and cabaret.

Continue down the Herengracht until you reach **no. 115.** Behind its stone Berlage facade, this building houses ㊲ **Sauna Deco,** a sauna artfully constructed from original Deco pieces. Among its treasures are a balustrade of wrought iron lilies by Edgar Brandt and a magnificent scalloped lamp by Rene Lalique. Other than the French Deco, the sauna is typically Amsterdam, complete with a *gezellig* sauna policy—no intrusive behavior or loud conversation, and no bathing suits please—only towels.

As you approach the corner of Herengracht and Blauwburgwal, note the gable stone depicting a merchant scene to your right at **no. 105 Herengracht.** Turn right on **Blauwburgwal** for some picturesque gables and crests. Notice how some of the houses lean toward the canal or from side to side. A forward lean can be functional since it makes hoisting furniture through the upper windows a smoother and easier task. Come full circle around Blauwburgwal, and take the bridge over the Herengracht. You can stop to rest at the sidewalk cafe on the corner, or, if you are in the mood for designer shops, turn off on **Herenstraat** and **Prinsenstraat.** Otherwise, continue down the Herengracht. On your right at **no. 71,** you'll find an old warehouse, with the typical red shutters, called ㊳ **"De Kriekeboom,"** and at ㊴ **nos. 55–63** you'll see a series of beautiful gables.

You are now approaching the scenic **Brouwersgracht canal**—the most photographed canal in the city. Here you'll find swooping birds, magnificent houseboats, and massive, red-shuttered brick warehouses turned into some of the most desirable lofts and apartments in Amsterdam. This is one of my favorite places to walk and bicycle, especially if I'm feeling closed in by the city. The Brouwersgracht seems more expansive to me than the other canals, with more water and sky.

The Brouwersgracht, or Brewers' Canal, was named for its many breweries. It was an industrial area with factories, warehouses, and all the accompanying smells and polluting by-products. Whale oil, coffee, sugar, and spices were stored in warehouses that can be identified by their brightly painted wooden shutters.

If this canal charms you, keep walking. But for a quick taste of the Brouwersgracht, simply take Herengracht to Brouwersgracht, turn left on Brouwersgracht, and then turn left at **Keizersgracht.** (For the best views of architectural detail, walk both sides of the canal.)

At **nos. 40–44** Keizersgracht is the ㊵ **Groenland Pakhuizen** (Greenland Warehouse) where 10,000 liters of whale oil were once stored in massive tanks. Whalebones, which would later be made into knives, were stored on the upper stories. Walk to **De Rode Hoed** (the red hat) at **no. 102,** which refers to the hatter's gable stone at **no. 104.** The Rode Hoed is now a concert hall and an unusual place to stop for lunch: Its cafe has "opera lunches" (opera performed at lunch). At Keizersgracht **no. 123,** you will find ㊶ **Het Huis met de Hoofden** (The House with the Heads), built in 1622 by Hendrick de Keyser in Dutch Renaissance style with 6 decorative heads representing classical gods and goddesses such as Apollo, Ceres, Mars, Athene, Bacchus, and Diana.

Soon you will approach the **Leliegracht canal,** a transverse canal stretching between Herengracht and Prinsengracht. This spot is surprisingly rich in bookstores, many of them secondhand English language paperbacks. The Leliegracht also has 2 very good French restaurants— ㊷ **De Luwte,** a romantic little place at **no. 26** Leliegracht, and ㊸ **Christophé,** one of Amsterdam's best, at **no. 46** Leliegracht. (Make reservations in advance if you plan to have dinner.) If you are interested in viewing the **Anne Frank House** at **no. 263 Prinsengracht,** you are only 1 block away. Take Leliegracht to Prinsengracht and turn left.

To complete the walk, take the west side of the Keizersgracht back to **Westermarkt,** stopping at the pink triangle at the water's edge. This is one of the three triangles making up the ㊹ **Homomonument** commemorating gays who were persecuted by the Nazis during World War II, and, more recently, those who died from AIDS. The triangle was the sign that homosexuals were forced to wear during the German occupation. The other 2 triangles lie behind, on Westermarkt.

When you are ready to go, you can take tram 13, 14, or 17. Before 5pm, you can also take the Canal Bus to several convenient locations.

If you are not yet ready to leave, find yourself a table at a Prinsengracht brown cafe like **De Prins** *(Prinsengracht 124),* **Van Puffelen** *(Prinsengracht 377),* or **Twee Prinsen** *(Prinsenstraat 27).* For a more regal canal-house cafe, try the theater cafe in the **Felix Meritis** building *(Keizersgracht 324).* You are within a few blocks of several good restaurants—**Koh-I-Nor, Christophé, De Luwte, Goudsbloem,** and **Van Harte** as well as several brown eetcafés—**Van Puffelen, De Prins,** and **De Reiger** (see "Dining").

Walk 2: The Jordaan—A Village Within the City

Begin at Westerkerk.

Transportation: Tram 13, 14, or 17 will take you directly to Westermarkt, the square around Westerkerk, which is situated between the Prinsengracht and Keizersgracht canals. You can also take the **Canal Bus** directly to Westerkerk (on the Prinsengracht side) or to Keizersgracht (on the Keizersgracht side of the church and adjacent to the Homomonument).

Best Time for Walk: If you want to browse at the open-air food markets, take the walk on Saturday between 9 and 11am. Another pleasant time is in late afternoon, around 4pm, when the streets are peaceful, the shops are open, and cafe terraces have seats for rest stops.

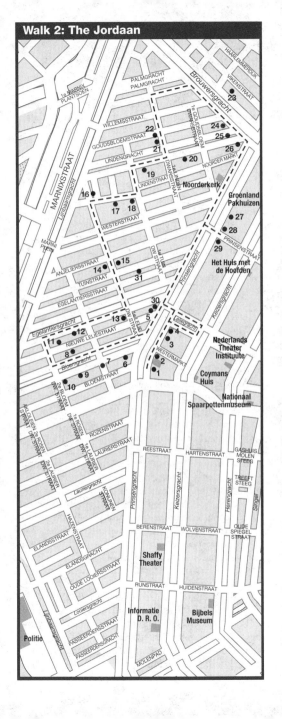

Walk 2: The Jordaan

HAARLEMMERDIJK

VIKENSTRAAT

Brouwersgracht

23

PALMGRACHT
PALMGRACHT

1e MARNIX
PLANTSOEN

WILLEMSSTRAAT

22

24

1e GOUDSBLOEM
PRINSENSTRAAT

GOUDSBLOEMSTRAAT

25

21

26

LINDENGRACHT

20

NOORDER MARKT

MARNIXSTRAAT

19

LINDENDWARSSTRAAT

Noorderkerk

Lijnbaansgracht

16

LINDENSTRAAT

Groenland
Pakhuizen

17 18

27

WESTERSTRAAT

DW. STRAAT

28

MARNI
PLEIN

PRINSENSTRAAT

ANJELIERSSTRAAT

15

29

14

TUINSTRAAT

DW. STRAAT

Het Huis met
de Hoofden

EGELANTIERSSTRAAT

31

Prinsengracht

30

Keizersgracht

Egelantiersgracht

13

DW. STRAAT

5

12

Leliegracht

4

Nederlands
Theater
Instituute

11

NIEUWE LELIESTRAAT

3

Lijnbaansgracht

8

WESTERMARKT

2

7

Bloemgracht

6

Coymans
Huis

9

1

BLOEMSTRAAT

10

2e BLOEM
DW. ST STRAAT

Nationaal
Spaarpottenmuseum

ANJELIER 2e ROZEN
DW. ST STRAAT

ROZENSTRAAT

REESTRAAT

HARTENSTRAAT

GASHUIS
MOLEN
STEEG

LAURIERSTRAAT

1e LAURIER
DW. ST STRAAT

TREEFT
STEEG

2e LAURIER
DW. ST STRAAT

Prinsengracht

Keizersgracht

Herengracht

Singel

Lauriergracht

KONINEN
STRAAT

BERENSTRAAT

WOLVENSTRAAT

OUDE
SPIEGEL
STRAAT

HAZENSTRAAT

ELANDSSTRAAT

ELANDSGRACHT

Shaffy
Theater

OUDE LOOIERSSTRAAT

RUNSTRAAT

HUIDENSTRAAT

Looiersgracht

Informatie
D. R. O.

Bijbels
Museum

Lijnbaansgracht

PASSEERDERSSTRAAT

PASSEERDERSGRACHT

Politie

MOLENPAD

Time: Allow 2 hours.

The Jordaan is a village in the midst of Amsterdam. With its inviting narrow streets, little houses, and quiet canals, the Jordaan is small in scale and one of the friendliest, safest places in Amsterdam. Neighbors chat on front stoops and greet each other in the many cafes, shops, and restaurants. This centuries-old working-class community has maintained a relaxed, sociable feeling despite the recent influx of artists, musicians, and young professionals who have designated the Jordaan a hip address. The newcomers have turned old workshops into studios and designer boutiques and added a trendy, bohemian dimension to a neighborhood grounded in jovial sing-a-longs, kitsch, and gezelligheid.

Jordaan comes from the French word *jardin* (garden), or the biblical Jordan River, or possibly from the Jordanne, a river in the Auvergne region of France—historians are not quite sure. But the Jordaan was never literally a garden; it was designed as a 17thC working-class area to which the noisier, more polluting trades were relegated. Nevertheless, the streets were named after flowers (such as *Angelier* for carnation and *Goudsbloem* for marigold), and the Jordaan evolved its own convivial, spirited culture despite poverty and overcrowding.

As you walk through this neighborhood, you will find 2 Jordaans. There is the traditional Jordaan with its lace curtains, spy mirrors (placed outside 2nd- or 3rd-story windows so nosy residents can "spy" on people in the street), porcelain tchotchkes, sentimental songs, and liqueurs with names like "lift up your shirts."

And there is the new Jordaan, still playful, but ironic and avant-garde. Food, wine, and gezelligheid are taken seriously by this new generation of Jordaaners, and you will see some of the best restaurants (**Bordewijk, Christophé, Toscanini**) and most gezellig brown cafes (**'t Smalle, De Prins, Papeneiland**) in Amsterdam.

Architecturally, the Jordaan is not as grand as the Herengracht, but it is rich in gable stones that portray artisans at work or make whimsical pictorial puns, and some of its homes and cafes still have the original 17thC stained-glass windows. The neighborhood also has an abundance of **hofjes**—almshouses with quiet courtyards and gardens, often completely hidden from the street. The first hofjes dated from the 1700s; many of them still provide inexpensive housing for the poor, the widowed, or, in the spirit of the new Jordaan—for music students.

Officially, the Jordaan is the area bordered by the Prinsengracht, Brouwersgracht, Lijnbaansgracht, and Looiersgracht. This walk will take you to the northern part of the neighborhood and will include the Westerkerk side of the Prinsengracht (which is "unofficially" Jordaan).

If you like open-air markets, take the walk on Saturday (9am–4pm) during the Lindengracht and Boerenmarkt markets (see "Shopping" for more details). Go early, between 9 and 11am, to avoid the crowds and find a piece of warm apple cake at **Café Thijssen** (at Lindengracht and Brouwersgracht).

I go to the Jordaan in late afternoon, around 4pm, when the streets are peaceful, the light is good enough for architectural detail, the shops are open, and my favorite cafe terraces have available chairs.

Note: The Jordaan is a pleasant place to bicycle since its streets are free from trams and busy traffic. Taking this route by bicycle is good for a quick tour of the Jordaan (taking about 45 min.), but you will miss much of the architectural detail. To rent a bike, arrive at **Bike City** *(Bloemgracht 70,* ☎ *20-6263721)* early to get one of the better bicycles and check the brakes. If you rent a bike, double-lock it every time you leave it to enter a hofje or cafe.

Begin the walk at ① **Westerkerk,** the symbol of the Jordaan. Listen for the ringing of the bells that Jordaaners have been setting their clocks to for centuries. The church bells, which have recently been restored, are made of 42 separate parts. For a spectacular view of the Jordaan, climb the church tower.

Notice the plaque on the tower of Westerkerk commemorating a famous Jordaan singer and local hero, Willy Alberti (1926–85), who sang the Amsterdam music that you can hear today at **De Twee Zwaantjes** *(Prinsengracht 114)* and **Café Nol** *(Westerstraat 109).* Music, both organ and sentimental accordion tunes (a Dutch equivalent of mariachi music), has played an important role in the Jordaan. The barrel organs in the streets have been replaced by Jordaan-style karaoke, although sometimes at the more earthy bars, someone will unexpectedly break into song.

Facing the Prinsengracht canal, turn right. As you leave the church, you will pass ② **Rum Runners** *(no. 277)* which was once a yard where stone masons worked on gravestones for the church cemetery. At **no. 263,** you come to the ③ **Anne Frank House,** the hiding place of the Frank and van Daan families during the Nazi occupation of Holland. It was here that Anne wrote her diaries before the 2 families were sent to German concentration camps. On the walls of her attic refuge, you can see the pictures of her childhood heroines that she clipped from magazines and tacked to the walls—just as she left them.

On the corner of Prinsengracht and Leliegracht, the 2 canals come together. To your right, is the ④ **Greenpeace** store, with books and T-shirts addressing issues of world ecology. (Ironically, Greenpeace is only 2 blocks away from the former Greenland warehouse which once stored 10,000 liters of whale oil.) Turn right to explore the secondhand and antiquarian bookstores and shops on both sides of the **Leliegracht,** and then take the bridge to the other side of the Prinsengracht. Notice the variety of gable styles: ⑤ **nos. 120–126 Prinsengracht** provide some particularly good examples of both simple and rococo gable styles.

You are approaching 2 brown cafes that are both, in completely different ways, quintessential Jordaan. To the right of the bridge, at **no. 114,** is **De Twee Zwaantjes** with its working-class clientele that sings the sentimental "Amsterdam music." **De Prins** *(no. 124)* at the foot of the bridge, is one of the original "P" cafes (see "Amsterdam's Cafes" in "Dining"), attracting a 20- to 40-something, educated, bohemian crowd. It is a relaxed place to stop for lunch; dinner fare is also good, but the cafe is uncomfortably packed by 7:30pm.

Gable-watcher's guide

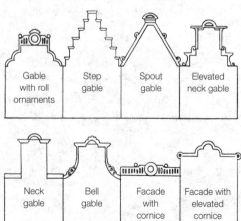

| Gable with roll ornaments | Step gable | Spout gable | Elevated neck gable |

| Neck gable | Bell gable | Facade with cornice | Facade with elevated cornice |

Turn left on Prinsengracht. One of the first shops you will pass is a tchotchke store typical of the Jordaan: a hodgepodge of high-tech clocks, sleek candelabras, fuzzy bears, and a porcelain hen with a chick or two. The latter are the kind of objects you will see placed comically—or seriously—on window sills throughout the neighborhood. These are the kinds of things that verge on the *tegezellig*—"too gezellig," or "too cute and cozy" (depending, of course, on your individual tastes—and whether you belong to the new or the old Jordaan).

Cross Nieuwe Leliestraat, and look behind you at **Café Westertoren,** an old brown bar on the corner that has the original stained-glass and lead windows above the door.

Turn right on ⑥ **Bloemgracht** (Flower Canal), a residential and peaceful canal with many of its buildings well-preserved historic monuments. The gable stones on the first 3 blocks of Bloemgracht colorfully illustrate artisans at work, depict symbolic animals, or assert religious themes. Notice the pelican at **no. 19** and the lion at **no. 23.** The gable stone at **no. 29,** called **"De Enhoorn,"** is more abstract, showing a unicorn with a golden sun shining behind him. At **no. 21,** the gable stone shows a bricklayer and architect at work; **no. 77,** in the next block, depicts a man ("De Saayer") sowing seeds.

At ⑦ **nos. 49–51,** you'll see a convergence of the old architecture and the new art. At no. 51 is an art gallery, a modern building displaying contemporary art both inside and out. Look up at the 5th story where you will see the torso of a naked woman done in bronze. Across the street from her, on Eerste Bloomstraat, on top of an old dilapidated corner building, a postmodern metallic triangle juts up from the roof.

Across the Bloemgracht from ⑧ **Hotel Van Onna** *(no. 104),* there is a series of well preserved plaques and step gables at ⑨ **nos. 83–85** dating from 1739. ⑩ **Nos. 89–91** Bloemgracht are renovated buildings with step-gable facades dating from 1642. The traditional red-shuttered windows contain small, green-tinged panes of glass. These houses, known as **"De Drie Hendricken"** (the Three Hendricks) belonged to Vereniging Hendrick de Keyser and now belong to the Hendrick de Keyser Association, which is dedicated to the preservation of historic buildings.

At this point the street names might get confusing. It helps to remember that streets running from north to south are often called *dwarsstraat* (cross-streets) and numbered east to west as 1e, 2e, and 3e (*Eerste, Tweede, Derde*), so that Derde Leliedwarsstraat is the most westerly street to cross Leliestraat. Turn right on **Derde Leliedwarsstraat.** Cross over Nieuwe Leliestraat. To your right, at **no. 142,** you will see ⑪ **Speciaal,** a place to note if you're interested in excellent Indonesian rijstaffel (see "Dining"). Continue on what was Derde Leliedwarsstraat—even if the street names change—until you get to **Egelantiersgracht.** Then turn right. At ⑫ **nos. 107–145,** you'll come to an innocuous green door that looks just like the other doors on Egelantiersgracht except that it says **Sint-Andries Hof.**

Open the door, walk down a hallway lined with Delft tiles hand-painted in 1614, and step into a quiet little garden with a lone tree, a bird feeder, a fountain, and an antique water spout (for which you need a key). The sign over the door says "Peace be with You"—and it is hard to imagine otherwise in an enchanted place like this so hidden from sight and insulated from street sounds.

Go back through the Delft passageway and reenter Egelantiersgracht. Turn right. Notice the tiled doorways at **nos. 83–85** and the stylishly renovated basement apartments. At the corner of Eerste Leliedwarsstraat, you can take a break and head for coffee or a cold drink at ⑬ **Café De Reiger** *(to your right at Nieuwe Leliestraat no. 134; see "Amsterdam's Cafes" in* **Dining***),* you can browse in the gallery on the corner (no. 1), or you can turn left at the corner, take the bridge over the Egelantiersgracht, which becomes Tweede Egelan-tiersdwarsstraat, which then becomes one of the main streets of the quirky, bohemian Jordaan. It's packed with shops, restaurants, and cafes.

The easiest method for finding your way is to think: turn left at Egelantiersgracht—and make no turns until you reach Karthuizersstraat. Then turn right.

But you are still at the corner on Egelantiersgracht. So turn left and cross the canal, noticing the houseboats to your left and right and the variety of gables and hoists as you look straight ahead down **Tweede Egelantiersdwarsstraat.** Continue straight to pass a row of ethnic restaurants, offering foods from Greece, Italy, and the Middle East. On warm summer nights, the sidewalks on several consecutive blocks are lined with tables and chairs brought outside from cafes, restaurants, and private homes. The tables are lit with candles and the streets festooned with lights.

You will find clothing shops (vintage or eccentric), a comic-book store, eetcafés, brown cafes, and an array of undefinable shops selling the strange little objects people place in their windows. If you are hungry, try ⑭ **Burger's Patio,** a pleasant Italian restaurant at 2e Tuindwarsstraat **no. 12.** For ice cream (or cigarettes—a combo not so strange in Amsterdam where most everyone blithely smokes and eats sweets) stop at ⑮ **Snack Bar Henk** at **no. 9.**

The next block or two erupt in wacky window art and gable stones and plaques restored—or reinvented—in bright or gaudy colors. Continue until Karthuziersstraat. If you are interested in the height of Jordaan designer fashion proceed across the street to ⑯ **Boutique 1992: Timeless Fashion.** At least check out the fanciful window displays.

Turn right on Karthuziersstraat to ⑰ **Huys Zitten Weduwen-Hofe,** built for widows in 1650 by city architect Daniel Stalpaert on the site of a Carthusian monastery. To find the hofje, go past no. 170 and look to your right for a long symmetrical building with dark-green shutters. The hofje's entrance is an open hallway with Huys Zitten Weduwen-Hofe written above the door. You enter a tiled passageway and find a shady courtyard from another century, 2 tidy gardens surrounded by short white fences, and 2 antique wells with exotic roofs looking like something from *Arabian Nights.*

At the corner of **Boomdwarsstraat,** note on your right the hair salon—and mirror-sculpture—of ⑱ **Rob De Wilde** at 2e Boomdwarsstraat **no. 2** (see **Shopping**), and on your left a playground. Turn left onto **2e Lindendwarsstrat.** Then turn right on **Lindengracht,** a wide, busy street for the Jordaan and a seemingly unlikely spot for 2 hofjes. If you're interested in hofjes, the one at ⑲ **nos. 149–163 Lindengracht,** the **Suyckerhofje,** has an unusually wild garden and the atmosphere of an overgrown churchyard. This hofje was established in 1667. The **Linden Hofje,** at **nos. 94–112 Lindengracht,** established in 1616, is one of the oldest in Amsterdam.

On Lindengracht you'll also find some of the Jordaan's best restaurants and my favorite Italian restaurant, ⑳ **Toscanini** *(no. 75 Lindengracht),* that serves the best veal lasagna in town (see "Dining"). You'll also find some lively cafe terraces. Cross Lindengracht and stop at ㉑ **de Kat in de Wijngaert** *(Lindengracht 160),* a friendly neighborhood brown cafe with a wooden plaque of a cat peering from behind barrels in a wine cellar.

To complete the walk, take **Tweede (2e) Goudsbloemdwarsstraat** past **de Kat.** On your left, at **no. 20,** you'll see a gable stone with a plump pink pig marking the address ㉒ **"The Fat Pig,"** which was a butcher shop in 1624 and has been one ever since.

Continue straight ahead until you reach **Palmgracht** (not Palmstraat). Turn right on Palmgracht until you reach the **Brouwersgracht** canal, one of the most picturesque canals in Amsterdam and the northernmost border of the Jordaan. The Brouwersgracht, or "Brewer's canal," was once, as its name suggests, the home of breweries as well as large warehouses and factories. Grain, sugar, and coffee were stored in these warehouses—still identified by their brightly painted wooden shutters. Now the massive 17thC warehouses, or *Pakhuizen,* are converted into some of the most desirable lofts and apartments in Amsterdam.

The Brouwersgracht—an expansive canal with an impressive skyline—is a fine place to unwind. You'll find a peaceful rhythm, magnificent houseboats (barges turned into spacious, inventively designed homes), tiny old brown cafes—and more of Amsterdam's architectural eccentricities. When you get to ㉓ **nos. 204–212,** look up at the rooftops. Yes, those are deer. Three of them: stags—complete with antlers—placed there to identify 3 buildings when they were warehouses storing grain. The warehouses were named *hert*—a Dutch word meaning stag, so, of course, the roofs must have stags. The first building on the left side is called "Met grote groene hert"—the big green deer—and the third one is called "Met kleine groene hert"—the small green deer.

When you come to **Lindengracht,** turn right. You will find ㉔ **Café Thijssen** (*Brouwersgracht 107–109*) to your right and to your left, ㉕ a small square with a statue of Theo Thijssen, socialist writer and schoolteacher who wrote about his childhood in the Jordaan in his novel *Kees de Jongen.* The **Lindengracht Market,** selling everything from fish to tomatoes, is held here every Saturday from 9am to 4pm (but it is best to arrive 9–11am before the crowds and before Café Thijssen runs out of apple cake). Thijssen was once a market cafe, attracting a wide range of clientele. On Saturdays it still draws in the old guard, but at night the former regulars feel out of place when the cafe fills up with a boisterous 20-something crowd.

Just 1 block further is **Noorderkerk** (see "Sights & Attractions") and **Noordermarkt,** where the Saturday **Boerenmarkt,** a friendly and "very Jordaan" organic produce market, is held. Facing Noordermarkt is **Bordewijk** *(Noordermarkt 7),* one of Amsterdam's best French restaurants.

The intersection of the ㉖ **Prinsengracht** and Brouwersgracht canals offers a fine view in every direction that can also be enjoyed from inside the traditional brown cafe **Papeneiland** *(no. 2 Prinsengracht).*

Turn right on the Prinsengracht. On this stretch of the canal there were once breweries, sugar refineries, and possibly a stable since the facade with 3 gable stones at ㉗ **no. 175** across the street (dated 1661) portrays 3 animals: *out schaep* (a sheep), *de bonte os* (the "colorful" bull), and *iong lam* (a young lamb).

The Prinsengracht or "Prince's Canal" was designed in 1609 for workshops, warehouses, churches, shops, and housing, and has less architectural splendor but more social activity than the Herengracht or Keizersgracht. The Jordaan slice of the Prinsengracht lends itself to lively brown cafes and cafe terraces which, on a warm summer's evening, are buzzing with conversation from 7pm to midnight. Brown cafes are integral to the Jordaan lifestyle. There is probably more conviviality per square inch in Jordaan brown cafes than in any other part of Amsterdam. If you're hankering for the essential Jordaan and want to hear the old "Amsterdam music," the places to go are **De Twee Zwaantjes,** a relaxed, down-home bar, and **Café Nol,** which is more boisterous and gaudy (see "Amsterdam's Cafes" in "Dining").

Papeneiland cafe

You could also end your walk in one of two cafes on the lively corner across the canal: ㉘ **De Vergulde Gaper** or ㉙ **De Twee Prinsen** *(Prinsenstraat 27)*. Both draw crowds on warm evenings. You could go further up the Prinsengracht to ㉚ **De Prins** *(Prinsengracht 124)*, which is brown, laid-back, but noisy after 10pm. I go to **'t Smalle** *(Egelantiersgracht 12)*, a tiny brown cafe, because its sidewalk terrace overlooks the Egelantiersgracht, and its stained-glass windows (dating from 1780) and neighborly atmosphere are so gezellig. In the 18thC, 't Smalle was a "tasting bar," or *proeflokaal,* for Hoppe Jenever (gin). However, on cold days, when the outdoor terrace is unusable, it's almost impossible to find a seat inside.

If you're interested in Dutch food with contemporary flair, try ㉛ **Claes Claesz;** turn right on Egelantierstraat (the 4th street past Noorderkerk) and go to **no. 24-26.** Next door to the restaurant, at **no. 18-20,** you will find the **Claes Claeszhofje** or **Anslohofje** which, in the spirit of the new Jordaan, houses music students.

The Jordaan has a wide variety of restaurants—and some of Amsterdam's best. Other places to eat after (or during) your walk are **Bordewijk** *(Noordermarkt 7),* **Bolhoed** *(Prinsengracht 60-62),* **Christophé** *(Leliegracht 46),* **De Luwte** *(Leliegracht 26-28),* **At Mango Bay** *(Westerstraat 91),* **The Pancake Bakery** *(Prinsengracht 191),* **Speciaal** *(Nieuwe Leliestraat 142),* and **Toscanini** *(Lindengracht 75).* These restaurants are popular, and reservations are always a good idea (see "Dining"). For less expensive eetcafés, try **De Prins** or **De Reiger.**

When you are ready to return home, proceed south on Prinsengracht toward Westerkerk to pick up tram 13, 14, or 17 at Westermarkt. You can also leave by Canal Bus from Westerkerk or Keizersgracht, but the last boat leaves between 5 and 6pm.

If you are leaving the neighborhood before 5pm, you'll have time to stop at Westermarkt for some fresh-cut flowers and a taste of *nieuwe haring* (herring) or *paling* (cooked eel) at the friendly fish stand, which is one of the best in Amsterdam.

Staying Active

Amsterdam's flat and watery countryside provides the ideal setting for cycling, sailing, windsurfing, and rollerblading. If the canals and lakes freeze, skating is also possible. The main recreation areas for jogging, rollerblading, cycling, and Frisbee in Amsterdam are **Vondelpark, Sloterpark,** and **Rembrandtspark.** The spacious **Amsterdamse Bos** to the southwest is the place for long-distance running, boating, cycling, and horseback riding; in the Gaasperplas to the southeast, visitors can go boating, windsurfing, and fishing (metro to Gaasperplas). Het Twiske to the north is suitable for cycling, windsurfing, rowing, canoeing, horseback riding, walking, and bird-watching.

Bicycling

Cycling through the bustling streets of Amsterdam can be a stressful experience, but to the north and south of the city are a number of quiet roads that are ideal for short excursions on two wheels. A short trip to **Oude Kerk** is scenic and relatively easy. The brochure *Cycling in Holland,* available from the Netherlands Board of Tourism (see "Before You Go" in "The Basics" for address), contains practical advice for the cyclist, with information on recommended long-distance routes and details of special vacation packages.

Yellow Bike (Nieuwe Zijds Voorburgwal 66, ☎ 20-6206940) organizes an 18.6-mile (30-kilometer) guided bicycle tour from Amsterdam to Marken and the villages of Waterland. If you are not yet ready for long trips, bicycling in Vondelpark or along the Amstel River (see "Jogging" below) might give you a taste for bicycling in Holland. Biking along the Prinsengracht or Brouwersgracht canals past houseboats,

17thC houses, and cafes is a way to ease into biking in Amsterdam—and one of the most scenic canalside routes in the city.

Boating

Canoes can be rented at the **Amsterdamse Bos** and **Het Twiske.** For general information on canoeing on Dutch inland waters, contact the **Netherlands Canoe Association** (☎ 294-418331). Good maps can be obtained from Jacob van Wijngaarden (see "Shopping").

Canal bikes (*grachtenfietsen*), pedal boats for 2 to 4 people, can be rented at 4 locations on the main canals: **Leidsekade** at the American Hotel; **Prinsengracht** at Westermarkt; **Singelgracht** at the Rijksmuseum; and **Keizersgracht** at Leidsestraat. (Call 20-6265574 for canal bike rentals.) The Canal Bike company also offers an organized 2½-hour "Mystery Tour" that crisscrosses the 17thC ring of canals. Tours are available in English and can accommodate up to 350 people. Rowboats can also be rented at the **Amsterdamse Bos** and **Het Twiske.** To rent sailboats, travel south of Amsterdam to the Vecht River and the Loosdrecht lakes.

Fishing

Visitors can fish in the canals or in Amsterdamse Bos (call 20-6264988 for more information). If larger lakes appeal to you, you can drive to Loosdrecht or Friesland for the day. Check with the VVV (☎ 06-34034066) regarding fishing licenses.

Advance information on fishing can be obtained from the Netherlands Board of Tourism before your departure (see "The Basics").

Golf

There are several public golf courses in and around Amsterdam. **Golf en Conference Center Amstelborgh** (Borchlandweg 6, ☎ 20-6975000) is a 9-hole, par 3 golf course with driving ranges and putting greens that also offers a restaurant/bar and 3 conference rooms. The **Sloten** golf course (Sloterweg, ☎ 20-6142402) near Schiphol Airport has a difficult 9-hole, par 65 course with numerous water hazards. The **Waterland Golfbaan** (☎ 20-6361010), 10 minutes north of Amsterdam, offers 18 holes on a watery—and difficult—course.

Health Clubs

In general, Amsterdam health clubs tend to be small, with just a few carefully selected machines and free-weights. However, there is a trend toward large clubs and, just recently, toward large pools at the health facilities (since most gym pools are frustratingly small).

The Victoria Active Club (in the Victoria Hotel, Damrak 1-6, ☎ 20-6200522) is a quiet health club with state-of-the-art weight-training equipment, rowing machines, stationary bicycles, a sauna, a personal trainer, a professional physiotherapist, a dietitian, and a very small pool. You can buy a pass for 1 day or longer. Hotel guests receive a 50% discount in the health club. For nonguests the fee is a pricey Dfl. 37.50 per hour.

Bronzed Amsterdammers maintain the body beautiful at the Splash Fitness Club (Kattengat 1, ☎ 20-6271044), which offers modern weight machines, aerobics and step classes, Turkish bath, and a whirlpool—but no swimming pool. One-day passes can be bought at the desk for Dfl. 25 and 1-week passes for Dfl. 65.

The Barbizon Centre (Stadhouderskade, ☎ 20-6851351) has a good gym that is available for a price—even for hotel guests. The Barbizon Palace (Prins Hendrikkade 59-72, ☎ 20-5564899) has a gym, Stair-Master, steam room, and sauna along with aerobics, free-weights, Technogym machines, and deep massage for Dfl. 25 per day. And Hotel Okura is currently opening a fully equipped gym and pool meant to rival all others. The pool is a large one—for Amsterdam.

Fitness Aerobic Center Jansen (Rokin 109, ☎ 20-6269366) is another gym where you can work out.

Horseback Riding

Riding is generally expensive within the city. Try Amsterdamse Manege (☎ 20-643342) or Hollandse Manege (☎ 20-6180942) in Vondelpark. Longer, more relaxed rides may be arranged in Amsterdamse Bos or in the countryside. Contact the VVV for information regarding riding in the provinces.

Jogging

Vondelpark, a 10-minute walk from both Leidseplein and the Museum Quarter, is the most convenient place to run. The running path is primarily asphalt and shared with bicycles, baby carriages and, on summer afternoons, throngs of international youth. But the setting is pretty and very Amsterdam—lakes with lilies and floating Buddhas, a pasture with grazing cows, playgrounds, green lawns, Frisbee players, and ice-cream stands. Sunday and weekday mornings are the best times to run in Vondelpark. Summer afternoons, especially weekends, are the worst. To have the best of several worlds, run in the morning and relax at Café Vertigo, a cafe on a shady edge of Vondelpark, in the afternoon. Never run, walk, or bike in Vondelpark alone at night.

Mudwalking

It is also possible to walk across the Wadden Sea from the mainland of the Netherlands to some of the Frisian islands—Schiermonnikoog, Ameland, and Engelsmanploat. This tromping across the low-flats of the Wadden Sea is called **"Wadlopen."** It is a muddy, strenuous trek at low tide—but as close as you'll ever get to walking on water. The trek requires expert guides, so don't try to do it yourself. For more information call: **Wadloopcentrum,** Pieterburen, Post Box 1, 9968 ZG Pieterburen, ☎ 595-528300.

Rollerblading

Some of the newer, more evenly paved bicycle paths also provide excellent rollerblading through parks, urban areas, and Dutch countryside. **Vondelpark, Rembrandtspark, Sloterpark,** and some routes near the Amstel River toward Oude Kerk are particularly scenic—and smooth. Few places rent rollerblades—so bring your own or buy a fine new pair in Amsterdam since most sporting goods stores stock *skeelers* (the Dutch name for in-line skates). For lessons, limited rentals, and suggested skating routes, call the sport shop at **Jaap Edenbaan** (☎ 20-6949894). If you are interested in racing, this is also the place to call.

Sailing

Sailing is a passion in Holland, and sailing opportunities abound on lakes, canals, rivers, and sea. Traditional sailing boats with crew can be rented in Amsterdam: contact Stichting Het Varend Museumschip (☎ 20-6270001); or in Enkhuizen contact Zeilvaart Enkhuizen (☎ 228-312424). For sailing with the company of crusty Frisian captains, try Heeg (**Hotel De Watersport**, De Skattig 44, ☎ 515-442229) or Hindeloopen (contact the VVV Office in Hindeloopen, ☎ 514-521278) in the northern province of Friesland. You can also hire historic boats—flat-bottomed *botters* (fishing boats), schooners, clippers, and barges—from M. Hendricksen, ☎ 20-6715375. Charters on traditional boats are available in **Muiden** (near a castle and the entrance to the IJsselmeer) or **Monnickendam** (an old fishing village on the IJsselmeer), through **Holland Zeil Charters,** ☎ 299-652351, or **Zeilvoot Muiden,** ☎ 294-263927 or 294-263929. Charts and almanacs can be bought from L. J. Harri (see "Shopping").

Before you depart for Amsterdam, you can request a copy of the brochure *Holland Water-Sports Paradise* from the Netherlands Board of Tourism (see "The Basics"). It contains practical information and recommended itineraries.

Sauna

To take a Dutch sauna is a hedonistic experience. Two that are aesthetically pleasing, as well, are **Sauna Deco** (Herengracht 115, ☎ 20-6238215), a beautiful sauna designed with French Art Deco lamps, wrought-iron banisters, and frosted-glass doors; and **Sauna Oibibio** (Prins Hendrikkade 20, ☎ 20-5539311), a contemporary New Age sauna with a roof-top view of the city. Both are friendly, but not too friendly, low-key, and coed (the Deco even has a coed dressing room). A visit involves the usual sauna ritual of steam bath, sauna, cool pool, and rest. These saunas also observe typical Amsterdam sauna decorum—no bathing suits, only towels. Massage is available by the half-hour or hour.

Skating

Skating was once a national winter pastime, but in recent years the canals and lakes freeze only occasionally. When the canals do freeze, everybody skates and stores quickly run out of skates (which in Holland are long-bladed speed and distance skates called *noren,* though some stores sell hockey and figure skates). If you plan to be in Holland between December and March, bring your own skates—unless you are willing to dash off at a moment's notice to buy Dutch skates.

It is possible to skate through towns (although not always under bridges where the ice is soft) or through the countryside on 6.2- to 124.3-mile (10- to 200-kilometer) organized tours. Watch for tour announcements in newspapers and on TV.

A note of caution: Every skating season some over-zealous Dutch skaters take to the ice too early, fall through, and drown. Do not skate until the ice has been tested and approved for safety. Always avoid yellow or deeply fractured ice.

If the canals do not freeze, **Jaap Edenbaan** (Radioweg 64, ☎ 20-6949894) has a large outdoor and a small indoor skating rink that are open from October to March. The skating shop offers everything from speed skates to rollerblades. Lessons for adults and children are given by well-trained, seasoned skaters.

Swimming

Amsterdam's most modern pool, located in the affluent Amsterdam South suburb, is the well-equipped **De Mirandabad** (De Mirandalaan 9, ☎ 20-6428080), which has artificial waves, slides, diving boards, indoor and outdoor pools, and palm trees. The pools are full of children, but if you arrive during the "peaceful hours" (7–9am or 8–10pm) you may be able to swim. **Marnixbad** (Marnixplein 9, ☎ 20-6254843), conveniently located in the Jordaan, offers a plain, modern indoor pool that caters to adult lap-swimmers. **Zuiderbad** (Hobbemastraat 26, ☎ 20-6792217), an older and prettier pool near the Rijksmuseum, is another good place for serious lap-swimmers. **Sloterparkbad** (Sloterpark, ☎ 20-6133700) is far from Amsterdam's center, but a beautiful place in the summer. The 3 outdoor pools—a small pool, a baby pool, and a large pool complete with several diving boards and a high dive—tend to attract a lot of loud, exuberant children, but adults can find peaceful lap-swimming in the large pool between 6:15 and 7:15pm on Wednesday and Friday evenings. Sloterpark also has a small lake, and adults can take refuge on an island set aside for nude swimming.

Table Tennis, Pool & Snooker

Homesick Americans are thrilled to discover real pool tables at the **Table Tennis and Pool Center** (Keizersgracht 209, ☎ 20-6245780). Their British counterparts are to be found bent over the snooker tables at the **Snookercenter Rokin** (Rokin 28, ☎ 20-6204974).

Tennis & Squash

For court time, try the following: **Frans Otten Stadion** (Stadiumstraat 10, ☎ 20-6628767) with 5 indoor tennis and 20 squash courts, **Gold Star Tennis Park** (K. Lotsylaan 20, ☎ 20-6445483) with 10 indoor tennis courts, and **Squash City** (Ketelmakerstraat 6, ☎ 20-6267883), which also has a sauna.

Water Sports for People with Disabilities

The Association for Water Sports for the Handicapped (SWG) offers many opportunities for people with disabilities to practice water sports. They organize sailing camps for children and sailing trips for adults. For instance, on one trip they take the 2-masted clipper *Lutgerdina* out on the IJsselmeer and the Wadden Sea (Dutch inland waters). The ship accommodates several instructors, 13 disabled people, and 7 volunteers. Trips of several days to 1 week can be arranged. Contact: Association for Water Sports for the Handicapped (SWG), Postbus 157, 1600 AD Enkhuizen, ☎ 228-312828).

Windsurfing

Holland's inland waters are ideal for windsurfing. The most popular areas close to Amsterdam are Het Twiske; Gaasperplas (southeast Amsterdam); the **Amsterdamse Bos;** the Gouwzee (off Monnickendam); the Kinselmeer (northeast of Durgerdam); Zaandvoort, on the North Sea; and the Hoornse Hop (off Hoorn). Contact the **Royal Netherlands Water-Sports Foundation:** Koninklijk Nederlands Watersport Verbond, (Postbus 53034, 1007 RA Amsterdam, ☎ 20-6642611). In Zaandvoort, boards and equipment can be rented at **Klijn Watersport** (Noordstrand tent 23A, ☎ 2507-17600).

SHOPPING

IN THE GOLDEN AGE, AMSTERDAM MERCHANTS BROUGHT in fabrics, ceramics, and spices from all over the world and displayed these goods in snug little shops on the narrow streets between the canals. Many shops still occupy these same 17thC storefronts, and here you can still find the fruits of Amsterdam's world trade: silks from China, art from Africa, terra-cotta from Spain, mosquito netting from Indonesia, hammocks from Mexico, and flutes from Peru. But today's shop owners bring contemporary style, imagination, and a penchant for playful surprise to these 300-year-old storefronts. The result is sometimes stunning, sometimes odd, occasionally funny—and almost always worth a look.

Best Buys

The Dutch are famous for Delftware (blue-and-white hand-painted pottery made in Delft that is the Dutch version of Chinese porcelain) and Makkumware (multicolored hand-painted porcelain made in Makkum), pewter, crystal, old clocks, antiques, wooden shoes, ice skates, and lovely old maps. Although these are relatively expensive items, you can find higher quality and better bargains in the Netherlands than in most other countries.

For the best buys in Delftware and diamonds, go directly to the factories where you can see pottery being hand-painted or diamonds being cut. The factories tend to offer the highest quality, the lowest prices, and the best selection. For **Delftware,** the best factory is **De Porceleyne Fles** (Rotterdamseweg 196, ☎ 15-2560234) of Delft, about 30 minutes south of Amsterdam. For **Makkumware,** the best factory is **Tichelaars Makkumware** (☎ 515-231341), in Mak-kum, Friesland, which is an hour's drive to the northwest. Delftware is also available in Amsterdam shops along P. C. Hooftstraat and the canals (see listings for Delftware), but for the best values, you may need to do some price comparisons. For quality, you always can go to **Folke & Meltzer** (P. C. Hooftstraat 65-67).

The **diamond** factories are more easily accessible; Coster and Gasson are located within walking distance of the Museum Quarter. Fine diamonds at good prices can be found in both jewelry stores and factories, although the factories tend to be less expensive. See "Diamonds," below, for more information.

Pewter and **crystal** can be found on P. C. Hooftstraat, but for better prices and a wider selection, you can go right to the source: to Leerdam and Maastricht for crystal and to Tiel for pewter. (*Note:* Although lead is now banned from the newest pewter, the older pieces may still contain lead and be unsafe for use with food.) **Antiques** and decorative old clocks from Zaandam (*Zaanseklok*) or Friesland (*Friese Stoelklok*) can be found in shops on Nieuwe Spiegelstraat for a handsome sum or in the numerous antique markets (see listings) for a bargain. Many tourists are unaware of the fine **antique maps** available at the antiquarian bookstores scattered throughout Amsterdam or the antique wood and steel **skates** from Friesland (*Friese doorlopers*), sold at flea markets, that are still used as beginner skates for Dutch children. More high-tech, but no less a Dutch specialty, are Dutch speed skates and rollerblades made by Zaanstra and available in great variety and at reasonable prices. **Wooden shoes,** currently used in the Netherlands for gardening and farming, are far more practical than you might think—and are available at specialty stores and markets in the city. You also can have wooden shoes custom-made at a factory in Zaanse Schans, about a 20-minute drive from Amsterdam.

The less expensive Dutch products like **cheese** are available at cheese shops and grocery stores as well as in cheese centers like Gouda and Edam. **Chocolate,** especially Droste and Van Houten, can be purchased at most small grocery stores or souvenir shops. More expensive and exotic chocolates are sold in small shops throughout the city. But an inexpensive—and most convenient—place to buy cheese or chocolate is at Schiphol airport in the duty-free shops as you are leaving Amsterdam.

For bargains on everything from fabrics to produce, try the **markets** at Albert Cuypstraat, Waterlooplein, Lindengracht, Noordermarkt, and Westerstraat.

Shopping Districts & Streets

Amsterdam's shopping districts are easy to find, easy to navigate, and designed for every taste and price range. Although the **P. C. Hooftstraat/Van Baerlestraat** district is reputed to be a pricey Dutch Beverly Hills, you can find some reasonably priced Dutch or Italian shoes as well as down-to-earth sportswear in rich fabrics and affordable prices. In August and September, even the most expensive sportswear goes on sale as the new winter lines come in, and you can find terrific bargains. Some shops, however, live up to the district's exclusive reputation as the place to go for designer clothing and shoes, Persian rugs, fine porcelain and crystal, Lalique glass, and the very best perfume.

Two small shopping areas lie at either end of the Van Baerlestraat district. By continuing down Van Baerlestraat toward Amsterdam South, you will come upon fashionable but more moderately priced clusters of shops on **Beethovenstraat**—a tree-lined street between Vondelpark and the Amsterdam Hilton where the young and upwardly mobile do their shopping. The **Spiegelkwartier,** the center of Amsterdam's antique stores and galleries, consists of quiet Spiegelgracht and Nieuwe Spiegelstraat. Both are about a 10-minute walk from P. C. Hooftstraat and a 5-minute walk from the Rijksmuseum.

Mainstream and inexpensive shopping for all ages, but particularly for a younger crowd, can be found on **Kalverstraat,** the "shopping street" where a hundred years ago cattle were led to market. Now herds of tourists and Amsterdammers wander shoulder to shoulder past endless displays of boots, sportswear, suits, chintzy slippers, fast food, pajamas, and an array of sneakers and hiking boots. The street is noisy, ugly, and crammed with people, but, if you look carefully, you will find some very good shoe stores, book shops, and boutiques. Two department stores—Vroom & Dreesmann and Maison de Bonneterie (which is more conservative and expensive) have their entrances on Kalverstraat. Maison's other entrance on **Rokin** is part of a more upscale row of boutiques and jewelry stores facing the fashionable Amstel neighborhood and the Hotel de l'Europe.

Leidsestraat and **Koningsplein** (which Leidsestraat becomes as it approaches the Singel canal) are shopping streets similar to Kalverstraat but less herdlike and slightly more fashionable.

The **Jordaan,** a 17thC working class neighborhood with narrow streets and its own lively traditions, harbors a hodgepodge of boutiques, artists' studios, and curious shops. Several up-and-coming clothing designers have moved to the Jordaan to set up trendy boutiques. Secondhand clothing stores are also popular here as are small novelty shops where you can buy anything from brandy snifters to bow ties. The window art of the Jordaan reflects 2 unique and very different cultures: the tidy white lace curtains and porcelain kitties that are "typical Jordaan," and the outlandish dolls, comical piggies, and surprising objets d'art of the ironic young newcomers. Go to the Jordaan to look, if not to shop.

Shopping in **the canal district,** especially in the narrow old streets between the Spui and Westerkerk, introduces you to an aesthetic and a kind of humor unique to Amsterdam. It is here that the art of Amsterdam window displays reaches its zenith, and the extent of Amsterdammers' love of the unusual and exotic becomes most apparent. The specialty stores for which this area is famous display everything from Mediterranean ceramics to racing kites. You can get just about anything here: authentic Delftware or not-so-cheap copies, hip designer clothes or outrageous vintage ones, sleek modern jewelry or African beads, contemporary furniture or traditional upholstery. You can also find the best chocolate, the prettiest buttons, the cutest toothbrushes, and the widest selection of Art Deco and Nouveau lamps. For shopping breaks, almost every street has a French restaurant or a brown cafe. *Note:* In this neighborhood there is an abundance of well-loved dogs. Since this is relaxed Amsterdam, there are no curb laws—so watch your step.

Amsterdam has well-appointed department stores on **Dam Square. Bijenkorf,** popular and convenient, is an institution: if you can't find it elsewhere, go to Bijenkorf. The nearby **Magna Plaza,** a new shopping center in an architectural masterpiece (once the post office), was designed a century ago by Cornelius Hendrick Peters. It's gaining a good reputation for its variety of interesting shops—everything from music boxes to riding clothes—and its long hours (it's also one of the few places in Amsterdam where you can shop on Sunday afternoon). A few blocks away on the Spui, **Esprit** is dressing the young, slender, and affluent.

When you are planning to shop in **the canal district,** you have many options, but the highest concentration of specialty stores is near the Spui (tram 1, 2, or 5) or Westerkerk (tram 13, 14, 17 to Westermarkt, Canal Bus to Westerkerk or Keizersgracht).

Tram lines run around the **Jordaan** but not through it. For transportation to the Jordaan, take tram 13, 14, or 17 to Westermarkt, the Canal Bus to Westerkerk, or tram 3 to Haarlemmerplein.

Markets

Amsterdam's markets are particularly fascinating since they attract a cross-section of the city's population to the tents, stalls, and corner squares where antiques, new and used clothes, shoes, ice skates, birds, fish, books, art, stamps, and fresh produce can be found at bargain prices. It is also interesting to visit one of the many food markets, if only to witness the size of Dutch vegetables (many vegetables are hot-house grown). Go early, if you can, to avoid the crowds. And keep an eye out for pickpockets.

The **Albert Cuypstraat** market (Albert Cuypstraat) is the best and biggest general market in Amsterdam with 350 specialized stalls selling everything from potatoes to champagne. This crowded, cosmopolitan street market is held Monday to Saturday 9am to 4:30pm on a 19thC street. People of many nationalities flock here to buy olives, fresh herbs, Indonesian spices, Dutch *nieuwe haring,* cheese, dates, and fresh fish. The restaurants along Albert Cuypstraat are the best family-run international restaurants in town. To avoid the crowds, go in the morning on weekdays.

You can find a similarly cosmopolitan fruit and vegetable market in the **Ten Katemarkt** (Ten Katestraat, Mon–Sat 9am–4pm), a daily market where you can sample Italian, Surinamese, or Turkish food. **Waterlooplein** (Waterlooplein, 9am–5pm daily), a large general market covered with tents, is a good place to hunt for African fabrics, secondhand clothes, old books, and other curiosities. Before World War II, this was a vibrant market in a flourishing Jewish neighborhood. Then you could find quality antiques here, but Amsterdammers will tell you regretfully that its heyday is long past. However, you can unearth some nice treasures in the Sunday antique and book market, and the neighborhood scene—with the market, the Muziektheater, the war memorial, the Joods Historisch Museum, and what remains of the old Jewish neighborhood—is worth the trip in itself.

There are also some smaller neighborhood markets that are less overwhelming and more personal than the Waterlooplein and Albert Cuyp markets. Several farmers' markets in the Jordaan create a small-town atmosphere. The **Lindengracht** (Noordermarkt and Lindengracht, Sat 9am–4pm) and the **Boerenmarkt** (Noordermarkt, Sat 9am–4pm), just around the corner, are the friendliest and the most varied markets in the neighborhood. The Boerenmarkt specializes in organic produce while the Lindengracht sells chickens, cheeses, yogurt, and fish. Across the street, the Thijssen cafe terrace, a "market" brown cafe recently turned trendy, fills the air with its fragrant, homemade apple cake. Show up early (from 9–11am)—before the crowds, and before Thijssen runs out of apple cake. Another Jordaan market, the **Lapjesmarkt** or **Noordermarkt** (Noordermarkt, Mon 9am–1pm), which spills over into Westerstraat, specializes in textiles. These markets are all located near two of the most scenic Amsterdam canals, the Brouwersgracht and Prinsengracht, making a trek to these markets a pleasure.

Amsterdam also has unusual markets selling flowers, stamps, art, books, and antiques—both the authentic and the yard-sale variety. The most famous and the most typically Dutch are the flower markets. Amsterdam's spectacular **Floating Flower Market** or **Bloemenmarkt** (Singel between Koningsplein and Muntplein, Mon–Sat 9am–5pm) is a lovely sight: a row of permanently parked barges selling fresh-cut flowers, bulbs, and potted plants. The quality is high and the prices fair. Since the flower market is a popular tourist attraction, there are stalls selling maps, wooden shoes, souvenirs, and postcards. Somehow, despite its popularity, this is a soothing place where Amsterdammers stop to pick up flowers on their way home from work. At the **Plantenmarkt** (Amstelveld—Kerkstraat at Reguliersgracht, Mon 9am–3pm), the plants and fresh-cut flowers are high quality but less expensive than those of the Bloemenmarkt. The best time to experience this colorful flower, plant, and seed market is early on Monday mornings between May and October.

Also typical of Amsterdam, are the book markets. A special one that is not to be missed is the **Boeken-markt** (Oudemanhuispoort, Fri, Mon–Sat 10am–4pm), an unusual passageway containing 18 tiny shops dating from the 18thC, most of which are occupied by antiquarian booksellers who keep irregular hours and sell old prints and used books—novels in a variety of languages, art books, and texts in academic subjects like psychology, sociology, and medicine. This is one of Amsterdam's most intriguing hidden places, lying unannounced behind stately archways next to the court-yard of the University of Amsterdam. Another inter-esting, but less atmospheric, used-book market takes place on the Spui on Fridays from 10am to 6pm. If you don't find a used book, you can always wander into the Athenaeum Bookstore, one of the best—and most gezellig—bookstores in Amsterdam for those with intellectual tendencies.

The **Stamp Market** or **Postzegelmarkt** (Nieuwe Zijds Voorburgwal, Wed and Sat 1–4pm), a quirky, make-shift coin-and-stamp market near numerous philately stores, is a place for stamp-lovers and -fanatics. Grizzled men stand in small, plastic-ceilinged stalls, exhibiting their stamps on tiny tables.

At Amsterdam antique markets, you will find both genuine antiques and yard-sale items, depending on your luck and your point of view. **Antiekmarkt De Looier** (Elandsgracht 109; ☎ 20-6249038; open Sat–Wed 11am–5pm, Thurs 11am–9pm, closed Fri) and the **Rommelmarkt** (Looiersgracht 38, Sat–Thurs 11am–5pm) are connected and comprise a sprawling indoor market in a huge building between 2 canals where you can find everything from used toys to antique jewelry. The overall quality is closer to high-quality yard sale than valuable antique. Prices are moderate. Fortunately, the **Art Markets** are a bit more promising, especially the one on the **Spui** (open some Sundays Apr–Dec 10am–6pm) where you tend to find a better quality of art than in the **Thorbeckeplein Market** (Sun, Mar–Dec 10:30am–6pm). The Spui tends to draw more serious artists.

Museum Shops

Amsterdam museum shops are a safe bet for quality and selection. The shop at the **Stedelijk Museum** sells books, reproductions, posters, and postcards of art after 1900; the **Rijksmuseum** has a similar repertoire—but of art before 1900. You will find a staggering collec-tion of posters and cards at the **Van Gogh Museum,** and a nice selection of cards and etchings at the **Rembrandthuis.** And the **Joods Historisch Museum** has an impressive collection of books (in several languages), cards, and calendars as well as a deli serving blintzes, bagels, and Middle Eastern desserts. (See "Sights & Attractions" for more information on all of these museums.)

Shopping A to Z
Antiques

Rokin and the **Spiegelkwartier** are the centers for antique dealers. The coziest shops are on the Spiegelgracht and Nieuwe Spiegelstraat, which run from the Rijksmuseum to the Golden Bend on Herengracht. It is worth shopping around and obtaining a signed certificate of authenticity from a dealer before making a major purchase.

Amsterdam Antiques Gallery
Nieuwe Spiegelstraat 34. ☎ 20-6253371.

Twelve antique dealers gathered under one roof, offering icons, dolls, 19thC paintings, and pieces of 16thC Spanish armor.

Couzijn Simons
Prinsengracht 578. ☎ 20-6232654.

Antique dolls, dollhouses, and tin toys are sold in this beautiful 18thC shop. Expect Queen Anne dolls and other fine European dolls valued by collectors.

Degenaar en Bijleveld
Nieuwe Spiegelstraat 45–60. ☎ 20-6277774.

Antique Dutch nautical clocks, sextants, and chronometers—some developed during the Dutch golden age—are the specialties here. Expect craftsmanship and precision in both the marine instruments and the interesting collection of model steamboats and trains.

Italiaander Galleries
Prinsengracht 526. ☎ 20-6250942.

Primitive African art, antique Indonesian shawls and ritual garments, and collector fragments of pre-Columbian textiles create the atmosphere of a museum—not a shop. Italiaander is one of the largest Amsterdam dealers in African art and is known for its fine collection of traditional statues, fetishes, and masks.

E. Kramer
Nieuwe Spiegelstraat 64. ☎ 20-6230832.

The Dutch tiles, old clocks, and fine crystal represent the special heirlooms of Old Holland. The Delft tiles, dating from 1580 to the present, bear traditional Dutch patterns: sailing ships, animals, farmers, hunters, and

Fast Facts

Tax Refunds: Non-EU (European Union) residents buying goods in the Netherlands may be entitled to a tax refund of the 14.9% sales tax (b.t.w. in Dutch) levied on most goods. This can be refunded, minus commission, provided that the total expense per day in one shop is Dfl. 300 and the goods leave the European Union within 30 days of the purchase date.

When you leave the Netherlands, have the goods—**with their tags and the invoice or Europe Tax-Free Shopping Cheque (ETS)**—ready to show to customs officials. The ETS will be given to you at stores when you make purchases. Do not wear the items you purchased, since they are to be "unused" at the time of departure. If you remember these details, you can proceed directly to get your refund at one of the banks in the airport that accepts them. Ask the customs official to direct you to the closest bank. You may also get your refund by mail, bearing in mind the possible complications that may arise with the mails and bureaucracies. Simply send the stamped Tax-Free Shopping Cheque to ETS (Europe Tax-Free Shopping, Leidsevaartweg 99, 2106 AS Heemstede; ☎ 20-5241909, fax 20-5246164); the refund will be remitted to your credit card or to you in the appropriate currency.

Information and Guides: The **VVV Amsterdam Tourist office** provides brochures on shopping for art and antiques and for shopping in the little shops between the canals. A new brochure on the Beethovenstraat/P. C. Hooftstraat area is also available. For more information on shopping, contact the VVV Amsterdam or try tour guide agencies (Guidor, ☎ 011-31-703202500) or walking tour agencies such as Artifex Travel, ☎ 20-6208112.

---

playing children. The clocks are Dutch or French antiques from 1880 to 1940.

Leidelmeijer

Nieuwe Spiegelstraat 58. ☎ 20-6254627.

You can find lovely Art Nouveau and Art Deco objects here, including the distinctive Amsterdam School lamps that are a feature of so many of the city's brown cafes. Although the furniture and lamps are functional, the Leerdam glass is primarily decorative.

Premsela & Hamburger

Rokin 120. ☎ 20-6249688.

In this shop you enter the opulent world of antique silver and leave the informal and less expensive little shops of the Spiegelkwartier behind. Both modern and antique silver jewelry and objets d'art are available for sale or admiration.

Art Galleries

There are more than 150 small commercial art galleries in Amsterdam, featuring a broad range of Dutch and international art. Many galleries are located close to the Rijksmuseum, along the streets and canals running from Leidsestraat to Vijzelstraat. Others are clustered around hotels such as the Pulitzer, which has its own gallery, and the Ramada Renaissance, which owns a fine collection of modern painting and sculpture. Events worth watching out for include **Kunst RAI** in June, when many Dutch and European galleries mount exhibitions at the RAI center; and the **spring art fair** in the Nieuwe Kerk, where several hundred major Dutch galleries exhibit works.

The Uitkrant (available free of charge from the Uit Buro at Leidseplein 26) provides a monthly galleries listing. Gallery owners lead unpredictable lives, and it is worth phoning to check if a gallery is open before visiting. Generally, major galleries open from Tuesday to Saturday noon to 6pm. A few galleries are also open on Sunday.

Animation Art

Berenstraat 39. ☎ 20-6277600. Open Tues–Fri 11am–6pm; Sat 10am–5pm. Tram 13, 17 to Westerkerk.

If you like Disney, you can find Disney characters taste-fully framed and beautifully lit in gallery style. The shop displays include limited editions, original hand-painted celluloid stills, and souvenir cups featuring Disney as well as other famous cartoons. Joining the impressive line-up of framed cartoons are a huge cardboard Betty Boop and a bunch of Tweety Bird cups.

Collection d'Art

Keizersgracht 516. ☎ 20-6221511. Open Wed–Sat 1–5pm. Tram 1, 2, 5 to Keizersgracht.

This is a major, but somewhat conventional, gallery exhibiting paintings, watercolors, drawings, and sculptures. Look for works by COBRA artists such as Constant and Brands, and Abstract Expressionists such as Armando and Esterek.

Barbara Farber

Keizersgracht 265. ☎ 20-6276343. Open Tues–Sat 1–6pm. Tram 13, 14, 17 to Westermarkt.

Barbara Farber travels to the far corners of Europe and America to discover exciting new talents. Her Amsterdam canal-house gallery, with its incongruous Old World Baroque ceiling, is often the first European gallery to show work by members of New York's avant-garde. The gallery is said to have helped international contemporary painters and sculptors establish their reputations.

Pulitzer Art Gallery

Prinsengracht 315–331. ☎ 20-5235235. Open daily—in hotel lobby and hallways. Tram 13, 14, 17 to Westermarkt.

At the Pulitzer Hotel, the work of both up-and-coming and accomplished artists is exhibited in a beautiful sunlit gallery that zigzags through a leafy garden, from the hotel entrance on Prinsengracht to the bar on Keizersgracht. These exhibits change frequently—and are some of the most interesting in Amsterdam.

SWART

Van Breestraat 23. ☎ 20-6764736. Open Wed–Sat 3–6pm. Tram 2 to Jacob Obrechtstraat.

This dynamic gallery shows contemporary European art—paintings, sculptures, and video. Every year SWART exhibits the work of up-and-coming young artists from Italy, Germany, and Holland. The gallery also shows work by established European artists.

Auction Houses

Watch out for *kijkdagen* (viewing days) advertised at the various auction houses in Amsterdam. **Christie's** (Cornelis Schuytstraat 57, ☎ 20-6642011) and **Sotheby's** (Rokin 102, ☎ 20-6275656) both have branches in Amsterdam. **Van Gendt** (Keizersgracht 96–98, ☎ 20-6234107) specializes in books, prints, and maps.

Books & Newspapers

Amsterdammers are polyglots with cosmopolitan reading interests, and they have no hesitation in picking up books in English, French, or German. Their tastes are so eclectic that you can find almost any book, new or secondhand, in Amsterdam. Most stores have some books in English and there are several English and American bookstores that carry only, or mostly, English books. Amsterdam also has a rich selection of antiquarian bookstores and specialty bookstores devoted to nature, travel, cookbooks, or the arts. Book-hunting is made particularly pleasurable by the wealth of attractive bookstores, mainly on the canal ring formed by Singel and Kloveniersburgwal.

English-Language Bookstores

American Discount Book Center
Kalverstraat 185. ☎ 20-6255537.

This large and complete bookstore, owned by an American expatriate, is one of the best English-language bookstores in Amsterdam. You'll find plenty of imported US novels, magazines, and unusual subjects catering to almost every taste: Japanese classics, gay fiction, New Age philosophy, bodybuilding, how-tos, and sci-fi.

W. H. Smith
Kalverstraat 152. ☎ 20-6383821.

This helpful branch of the British bookstore chain occupies 4 floors with its vast stock of titles, from Beowulf to BBC books.

General Bookstores

Allert De Lange
Damrak 62. ☎ 20-6246744.

A serious literary bookstore with a wide range of Dutch, English, French, and German novels, together with excellent travel and art sections. The French selection is especially good.

Athenaeum Boekhandel & Nieuwscentrum
Spui 14–16. ☎ 20-6233933.

This beautiful 1904 Art Nouveau shop, with a labyrinthine interior designed in the 1960s, is a pleasure to browse in. And it is one of the best stores in town for anyone with an intellectual bent since Athenaeum carries all the finest—and latest—novels, plays, poetry, literary theory, and biographies in Dutch, English, French, or Spanish. There is also a small section devoted to Dutch literature in translation. The adjoining newspaper store (☎ 20-6242972) is stocked with newspapers and magazines flown in from every corner of the world.

The Book Exchange
Kloveniersburgwal 58. ☎ 20-6266266.

This is a good, university-style secondhand bookstore with a wide selection of English-language detective and science fiction novels as well as headier books on philosophy, sociology, and music.

Scheltema, Holkema, Vermeulen
Koningsplein 20. ☎ 20-6267212.

Amsterdam's main university bookstore has a wide range of novels, art books, and textbooks in English, Dutch, French, and German.

Special-Interest Bookstores

Architectura & Natura
Leliegracht 44. ☎ 20-6236186.

Every day that goes by, the piles of unsorted books seem to increase in this bookstore devoted to the owner's 2 consuming passions, architecture and the natural world. A must for all lovers of Frank Lloyd Wright or Amsterdam bookstore ambiance.

International Theater Bookshop
Leidseplein 26. ☎ 20-6226489.

This unique bookstore is typical of polyglot, cosmopolitan Amsterdam: Books and periodicals are available in 7 languages on theater, ballet, opera, cabaret, circus, and magic.

Intertaal
Van Baerlestraat 76. ☎ 20-6715353.

The Dutch hunger for foreign languages is evident in this beautiful bookstore that stocks textbooks, dictionaries, cassettes, videos, and computer programs in about 120 languages, with titles ranging from *English for Bank Cashiers* to *Basic Tagalog for Foreigners and Non-Tagalogs*.

De Kookboekhandel
Runstraat 26. ☎ 20-6224768.

His devotion to the joys of eating and drinking has earned Kookboekhandel owner Johannes van Dam the nickname "the pudding professor." Chefs and gourmets flock from all over the world to his well-stocked international cookbook store.

Robert Premsela
Van Baerlestraat 78. ☎ 20-6624266.

This art bookstore opposite the Stedelijk specializes in art, architecture, graphic design, photography, ballet, and fashion. When it comes to art books, its selection is better than the museum shops.

Antiquarian Books

De Slegte
Kalverstraat 48–52. ☎ 20-6225933.

Remaindered books are kept on the ground floor, and a vast treasure trove of rare antiquarian books is displayed upstairs.

Kok
Oude Hoogstraat 14–18. ☎ 20-6231191.
Kok is the place to go for beautiful, frameable antiquarian maps of the Netherlands, Europe, and the colonies as well as for a wide selection of old line-drawings
and secondhand books.

Travel Books

Evenaar
Singel 348. ☎ 20-6246289.
The books you'll find here are for those with the Dutch
travel fever (which includes travel books to Indonesia,
Africa, Thailand, and Turkey).

Het Griekse Island
Westerstraat 96. ☎ 20-6268509.
If you like modern Greek literature or music, or if you
are planning a trip to Greece, this shop can offer hours
of good browsing and reading with its shelves of travel
books, maps, and books on Greek music. The owner
also leads bicycle tours of Crete, Corfu, and the Greek
mainland during the spring and summer.

Children's Books

Kinderboekwinkel
Eerste Bloemdwarsstraat 23. ☎ 20-6224761. (Also at Nieuwe Zijds
Voorburgwal 344, ☎ 20-6227741.)
Dutch children's books are sometimes accessible pictorially to English-speaking children. If the children are
getting fussy as you walk through the Jordaan, duck in
here: Young readers (and their parents) are welcome to
browse and look at the picture books.

Crafts
Although the Netherlands is not renowned for crafts,
(except for hand-painted wooden furniture and kitchen
utensils from Hindeloopen and some of the fishing villages on the IJselmeeer), you can find small workshops
in Amsterdam producing tasteful pottery or handmade
gifts.

Jeroen Bechtold
Korte Leidsedwarsstraat 159. ☎ 20-6249871.
Jeroen Bechtold displays his own work along with the
work of both well-known and up-and-coming ceramic
artists. The ceramic pieces are "hardly ever functional—
but related to function," says Bechtold of the bowls and
other objets d'art. Expect contemporary designs that
are unique and decorative.

De Voetboog
Voetboogstraat 16. ☎ 20-6260169.

This small arts-and-crafts center exhibits tasteful silver and gold jewelry, ceramics, watercolors, and paintings. The jewelry is sleek, contemporary—and without diamonds. Although the ceramic objects include functional teapots and cups, most are objets d'art.

Porcelain, Glass & China
High-quality, hand-painted Delftware porcelain is still produced by **De Porceleyne Fles** in Delft, and Makkumware porcelain is still made by **Tichelaars** in Makkum. Delftware is blue-and-white, and it was developed as a Dutch version of expensive Chinese porcelain. Designs tend to portray windmills, Dutch country scenes, or ships at sea, although the Delft tiles are more varied and show men, women, or children in traditional Dutch costumes engaged in traditional Dutch activities, such as skating and trading. Makkum tiles portray similar figures but in various colors. Makkum pottery is also colorful and includes floral and Asian-influenced designs as well as typical Dutch scenes. Although this fine porcelain is sold in shops throughout Amsterdam, for the best buys, the widest selection, and interesting tours, go to the sources in Delft and Makkum.

Focke & Meltzer
P. C. Hooftstraat 65–67. ☎ 20-6642311.

One of the best stores for authentic Delftware and Makkumware as well as fine crystal, glass, porcelain, China, and silver, Focke & Meltzer has a wide selection and an excellent reputation.

De Munt
Muntplein 12. ☎ 20-6232271.

Situated in a dusky neo-Renaissance building next to the Munttoren, this shop stocks a good selection of royal Delftware and Makkumware, tiles, Dutch arts and crafts, and dolls in traditional Dutch costumes.

Heinen
Prinsengracht 440. ☎ 20-6278299.

If you want to take home Delftware but find the original De Porceleyne Fles prohibitively expensive, you can find hand-painted blue-and-white as well as multicolored porcelain at this father-and-son shop on the Prinsengracht canal. The quality is good and the designs are traditional (windmills, villages, sailing shops) or else reflect Asian influences.

Rosenthal Studio-Haus
Heiligeweg 49–51. ☎ 20-6245865.

The committee of German experts that selects the items sold in Rosenthal shops is clearly biased in favor of clean-cut modern Scandinavian design, but they also carry other styles of glass, crystal, china, and cutlery.

Galleria d'Arte
Prinsengracht 170. ☎ 20-6233431.

This personal little shop across the canal from Westerkerk is packed with a wide variety of old and new hand-painted Delftware—everything from plates and platters to ashtrays and teacups. Although most of the designs are typical Dutch, you can also find some unique and unexpected designs, such as the artist-signed Passover candelabras.

Department Stores

Amsterdam has only a few large department stores, which are located mainly along Rokin or near Dam Square or the Spui.

De Bijenkorf
Dam 1. ☎ 20-6218080.

The Bijenkorf (beehive) is Amsterdam's most fashion-able—and most dependable—department store. When in doubt, go to Bijenkorf. The 1st floor has been redesigned as a series of boutiques devoted to Mondi, Mexx, Esprit, and other labels. You can also find conservative business suits, warm coats, and a nice selection of perfumes, chocolates, international newspapers, and stationery.

Hema
Nieuwendijk 174. ☎ 20-6234176. (Also at Reguliersbreestraat 10, ☎ 20-6246506.)

The Hema chain is a subsidiary of De Bijenkorf (see above) and stocks inexpensive clothes, brightly colored kitchen utensils, and a wide variety of items. Consider it Amsterdam's K-Mart.

Maison De Bonneterie
Rokin 142. ☎ 20-6262162.

With its glittering chandeliers and spacious interior, Maison de Bonneterie maintains an old-fashioned elegance. Its fashions are conservative for Amsterdam, especially in the men's department where they carry Ralph Lauren and similar stylish but traditional designers. However, the women's department carries classics for older and younger women and has recently introduced more colorful and relaxed clothes alongside the traditional corduroy, tweeds, tartans, and cashmeres. There is a small golf shop upstairs.

Metz & Co.
Keizersgracht 455. ☎ 20-6248810.

Metz & Co., founded in 1740 by a French draper from Metz, occupies a striking corner building laden with caryatids looking down balefully on the throngs of Leidsestraat. In the early 20thC, Metz encouraged furniture and fabric designers such as Bart van der Leck and Sonia Delaunay, and in 1933 the architect Gerrit Rietveld was commissioned to design the rooftop exhibition cupola (*koepel*), which he offered as an example of "the space which we need to preserve in our structures." The other floors of Metz are devoted to the finest in modern furniture, fabrics, kitchen utensils, and gifts.

Vroom & Dreesmann
Kalverstraat 201. ☎ 20-6220171.

This is the Amsterdam branch of the Netherlands' main mid-range department store chain that is more upscale than Herma but less expensive than De Bijenkorf or Maison de Bonneterie. It is a good place to buy a reasonably attractive but affordable sweater or raincoat for abrupt changes in the weather.

Diamonds

The diamond trade was introduced to Amsterdam by refugee Jews in the 16thC, and in 1908 the world's largest diamond, the "Cullinan," was cut in Amsterdam by the Asscher Company. Today Amsterdam is one of the world's most important diamond centers. Demonstrations of diamond polishing can be seen in most factories and diamond stores, and visitors are under no obligation to buy. If you are interested in diamond rings, most factories and well-established stores tend to have an ample supply. However, with the exception of a few classical settings, rings tend to be heavy on the gold and the filigree. If you prefer simple, contemporary settings, buy the stone in Amsterdam and the settings in the states. Another option is to have a setting designed for you in Amsterdam—if you can find a goldsmith who can design to your taste.

The Amsterdam Diamond Center
Rokin 1–5. ☎ 20-6245787.

Here you will find an impressive selection of diamond jewelry by a variety of designers with diamonds cut in

Amsterdam. Some designs are classic and conservative, but the tendency is toward lots of gold and lots of diamonds.

Bonnebaker Diamonds

Rokin 88–90. ☎ 20-6232295 or -94.

Bonnebaker is known as one of the finest jewelry stores in Amsterdam. Expect beautifully cut stones in expensive settings.

Coster Diamonds

Paulus Potterstraat 2–6. ☎ 20-6762222.

This is where, in 1852, the Kohinoor (Mountain of Light) diamond was cut for the British Crown Jewels. Coster, located near the Rijksmuseum, is a diamond factory where it is possible to see diamond cutters at work as well as to see a display of stones and jewelry in the showrooms. It is smaller and more personal than the Gasson factory.

Gasson Diamonds

Nieuwe Uilenburgerstraat 173–175. ☎ 20-6225333.

Samuel Gasson was a diamond cutter before World War II, and in 1945, after the war, he founded Gasson's Diamonds, which was located in the Diamond Exchange. Now run by Benno Lesser, Gasson's grandson, the factory occupies a massive, formerly steam-driven, diamond-cutting factory. The factory is an impressive place where it is possible to watch diamond cutters and goldsmiths at work, to view stones and jewelry in private or group showrooms, or to sip coffee in the cafe. Stones are of the highest quality. However, the tourist volume is high, and the place can be a bit impersonal.

Hans Appenzeller

Grimburgwal 1–5. ☎ 20-6268218.

This is elegant, expensive jewelry with diamonds or other gemstones in settings more subtle and personal than those shown in most other Amsterdam shops.

Lyppens

P. C. Hooftstraat 30. ☎ 20-6758986. (Also at Amstel Hotel Prof. Tulpplein, ☎ 20-6389792.)

The name Lyppens comes up when diamonds are mentioned. It is an old, established, and reliable jewelry store. You can count on beautifully cut stones, but the jewelry tends to be heavy on the gold and could be considered ostentatious.

Fabrics

Bold, brightly colored traditional materials imported from Latin America, Africa, and Asia are popular in Amsterdam and can be found in the tiny streets between the canals, in the P. C. Hooftstraat district, as well as in the markets at Waterlooplein, Albert Cuypstraat, and Westerstraat (see "Markets" above).

Capsium
Oude Hoogstraat 1. ☎ 20-6231016.

This is a wonderful little store stocked with exotic fabrics from India, China, Japan, Africa, Thailand, and Portugal, mostly handwoven from natural fibers. The bedspreads and quilts are especially nice.

McLennans Pure Silk
Hartenstraat 22. ☎ 20-6227693.

At this small specialty shop in the canal district, you'll find resplendent rolls of pure silk from China, Thailand, and India in a myriad of intense colors—red, magenta, gold, and blue.

Fashions

The fashionable Amsterdammer's wardrobe leans heavily toward casual, comfortably fitting clothes. The coats are long, loose, and beautifully cut. The jeans, worn almost everywhere, are "European cut," which means tailored in a relaxed-but-stylish kind of way. Apart from Italian and French lines, clothes are designed for tall Dutch women (the Dutch claim to be the 3rd tallest people in the world). But most stores also include sizes for women of medium height.

Successful Dutch designers often make their home on P. C. Hooftstraat, while younger designers may have a boutique in the Jordaan, in the small streets between the canals, or in the increasingly fashionable area of Nieuwe Hoogstraat and Sint Antoniesbreestraat. The most affordable fashions can be found on Leidsestraat, Kalverstraat, or, during the August and September sales, in the P. C. Hooftstraat/Van Baerlestraat district.

Women's Clothing

La Culotte
P. C. Hooftstraat 111. ☎ 20-6715910.

Classy, lacy, exceptionally pretty lingerie is the specialty here. The garments are far more unusual and subtle than anything at Victoria's Secret.

In Wear
Leidsestraat 1. ☎ 20-6380851.

Classic, contemporary styles that *stay* in fashion distinguish this Danish boutique from all the other trendy shops on Leidsestraat and Kalverstraat. In Wear offers a selection of sweaters, skirts, dresses, coats, and shoes appealing to women of all ages.

Lesser
P. C. Hooftstraat 117. ☎ 20-6795020.

Lesser is the classiest clothing store on P. C. Hooftstraat. It is also very expensive. Lesser's clothes are of the finest fabrics and the sleekest lines; her coats are never too heavy, her suits never too stiff. Even the leather coats are soft and regal. And the cashmere dresses and suits have a classic but original style that make them a rare find. The colors are subtle, interesting, and appropriate for a woman any age—with a slender figure.

Raymond Linhard
Van Baerlestraat 50. ☎ 20-6790755. (Discount branch: Van Baerlestraat 40.)

The 2-story boutique offers an appealing and reasonably priced selection of skirts, pants, sweaters, leggings, and coats in subtle colors, interesting textures, and recent styles. In August and September, the store also has some fabulous sales. A few doors away, the discount branch offers an attractive, affordable, but limited selection of casual wear and coats. However, the fabrics aren't the best and may not wear too well.

Mexx
P. C. Hooftstraat 118. ☎ 20-6750171.

A popular shop for trendy young women (or the young at heart) who like short skirts, saucy jackets, and rich colors.

Margriet Nannings
Prinsengracht 24. ☎ 20-6203413.

One of the interesting designers to set up shop in the Prinsengracht/Jordaan neighborhood, Nannings has a neighborhood following but also draws customers from all over Amsterdam. She designs colorful clothes for women with adventurous tastes. Expect imaginative high fashion.

Oilily
P. C. Hooftstraat 131–133. ☎ 20-6723361.

Oilily specializes in playful combinations of color and whimsical, cheerful, youthful fashions (although they are not only for the young). These are casual clothes with a country feel—lots of denim and floral patterns based on traditional Mediterranean and Eastern European designs. The attached children's store carries a variety of bright, wacky overhauls, dresses, boots, socks, and shoes. Prices are higher than you might expect.

Pauw

Heiligeweg 10. ☎ 20-6244780. (Also at Leidsestraat 16, ☎ 20-6265698; Van Baerlestraat 72, ☎ 20-6717322; and Beethovenstraat 82, ☎ 20-6713299.)

This successful Amsterdam chain of fashion boutiques stocks well-made, stylish but casual clothes in the latest colors and fabrics. Colors tend toward the subtle and styles toward the hip-yet-classic or the mainstream. No two shops are the same, and there are also branches for men and children.

Elizabeth Royaards

Herengracht 70. ☎ 20-6265026.

This designer makes original, haute couture clothes for a loyal, well-heeled following. You will find elegant evening dresses, bridal dresses, and business suits. Styles are wearable but unconventional. When it comes to fabrics, everything goes: silk, wool, linen, cotton, leather—even plastic.

Sissy Boy

Van Baerlestraat 15. ☎ 20-6715174. (Also at Kalverstraat 210, ☎ 20-6260088; and Leidsestraat 15, ☎ 20-6238988.)

A snappy and stylish boutique with everything from bright colors to herringbone, Sissy Boy appeals to women who wear short, smart skirts and bold, tailored jackets. The Kalverstraat and Leidsestraat stores may be directed at young customers, but the clothes are expensive.

Timeless Collection

Prinsenstraat 26. ☎ 20-6381760.

Timeless is the best designer boutique in the Jordaan/ Prinsengracht area that appeals to a variety of tastes, ages, and figures. The style is simple, with beautiful materials and contemporary designs that can be either casual or dressy. Prices are high, but sale prices are quite reasonable.

Edgar Vos

P. C. Hooftstraat 134. ☎ 20-6626336.

This popular Dutch designer, one of the best known in Holland, creates exclusive suits and dresses at affordable prices for women of all ages.

Vintage or Secondhand Clothes

Laura Dols

Wolvenstraat 7. ☎ 20-6249066.

A vintage-clothing store with imaginative window displays and flamboyant clothes from the 1920s through the 1950s, Laura Dols appeals to an offbeat aesthetic.

Window displays feature orange leather coats, multi-colored and multilayered petticoats, and straw hats with enormous flowers.

Lady Day
Hartenstraat 9. ☎ 20-6235820.
This wood-paneled shop in the canal district sells reasonably priced secondhand clothing. The clothes are high-quality, but not terribly exciting at first glance: It takes patience and some poking around to find something out of the ordinary.

Zipper
Huidenstraat 7. ☎ 20-6237302.
Zipper, a popular secondhand clothing store in the canal district, carries stylish and high-quality clothes from the 1950s on. Zipper's clothes have more zing than those at Lady Day and are more wearable than the flamboyant styles of Laura Dols.

Men's Fashions

Barbas
P. C. Hooftstraat 140. ☎ 20-6713537.
This shop carries casual and formal, trendy and conservative clothes for men of all ages. Expect fashions by designers like Hugo Boss.

The Last Detail
Huidenstraat 6.
The selection of sample suits, sports coats, and ties from designer collections makes The Last Detail an affordable find. The Italian suits are hip, beautifully made, and appropriate for men of all ages.

Oger
P. C. Hooftstraat 79–81. ☎ 20-6768695.
Beautiful fabrics, sophisticated style, and continental flair set the suits and coats at Oger apart from those at other stores on the exclusive P. C. Hooftstraat.

Pauw
Van Baerlestraat 88. ☎ 20-6646653.
Situated on Van Baerlestraat near the Museum Quarter, Pauw sells chic, though rather conventional, fashions for young men and carries smart blazers and bankers' overcoats.

Sissy Boy
Kalverstraat 199. ☎ 20-6260088. (Also at Van Baerlestraat 12 and Leidsestraat 15.)

This shop sells casual, loose-fitting clothes for young men (and women) who like trendy but comfortable outfits in a wide variety of colors and fabrics.

Children's Clothes

Kickeboe
35 Hartenstraat. ☎ 20-6265586.
This is a cozy children's clothing shop near the canals carrying hip, subtly colored, comfortable, and mostly striped clothes "made somewhere in Holland."

Oilily
P. C. Hooftstraat 131–133. ☎ 20-6723361.
Oilily carries the most cheerful children's clothes. The shop specializes in exuberant color schemes and comfortable, practical styles. Clothes for children include overhauls, dresses, sweaters, shoes, socks, and caps at high prices.

Food & Drink

Holland produces tangy cheeses that travel well, exemplary chocolates, unique licorice (known as *drop*), pickled herring (*nieuwe haring*), smoked eel (*paling*), subtle liqueurs, and gin (*jeneever*). Quality teas, coffee, cigars, French wines, and a staggering variety of Belgian bottled beers are other notable items.

Chocolates

Leonidas
Damstraat 11. ☎ 20-6253497.
Leonidas sells sumptuous and exclusive Belgian chocolates made with fresh cream.

Patisserie Pompadour
Huidenstraat 12. ☎ 20-6239554.
A portrait of Madame de Pompadour looks down with smiling approval on Arnold Reijers's 45 varieties of handmade chocolates, which can be sampled individually in the Louis XVI–style tearoom. This chocolate shop is world famous—and with good reason. Expect smooth, not-too-sweet chocolates laced with tea, strawberry puree, Grand Marnier, and 42 other luscious combinations of chocolate with something surprising and delightful.

Food

Eichholtz
Leidsestraat 48. ☎ 20-6220305.

You can find an eclectic range of typical Dutch foods to take home to friends, including Van Houten cocoa, dark chocolates, aged Gouda cheese, and crisp honey waffles. If you're homesick, you can also buy classic American packaged foods such as breakfast cereals, macaroni and cheese, and brownie mix.

De Natuurwinkel
le Constatijn Huygensstraat 49–55.
☎ 20-6851536. (Also at Weteringsschans 133, ☎ 20-6384083; and Haarlemmerdijk 174, ☎ 20-6266310.)
If a steady diet of french fries, mayonnaise, and other high-fat Dutch fare sends you out foraging for health food, this is where to find it.

Wout Arxhoek
Damstraat 23. ☎ 20-6229118.
This small shop has a good selection of Dutch cheeses for export, not just Edam and Gouda, but delicacies such as the unusual *Friese nagelkaas* (Frisian clove cheese).

Herbal Remedies

Jacob Hooy & Co.
Kloveniersburgwal 12. ☎ 20-6243041.
The heady aroma of spices and herbs wafts across Nieuwmarkt from Jacob Hooy, which has been curing Amsterdammers' aches and pains since 1743. This doggedly old-fashioned shop stocks some 600 spices and herbs in a magnificent array of 19thC wooden drawers and earthenware jars labeled in Latin. Jacob Hooy also sells 38 types of drop, a Dutch licorice delicacy which can be salty, bitter, or sweet.

Drink

Geels & Co.
Warmoesstraat 67. ☎ 20-6240683.
Here, on the edge of the red-light district, you will discover an old-fashioned coffee and tea store with a tiny private museum upstairs (open Tues, Fri, Sat 2–4:30pm) crammed with antique coffee-brewing equipment.

Hart's Wijnhandel
Vijzelgracht 27. ☎ 20-6238350.
Even if you aren't interested in buying wine or beer, this shop is worth a look: Its stunning Art Nouveau interior stocks a carefully chosen selection of French

wines, some tempting beers, and an interesting collection of Dutch liqueurs.

Keijzer
Prinsengracht 180. ☎ 20-6240823.

This old-fashioned tea-and-coffee store, furnished in Old Dutch style, has sold tea and coffee for many generations. It now offers a selection of contemporary tea-and-coffee paraphernalia along with a wide selection of coffees and teas.

D'Oude Gekroonde
Oude Spiegelstraat. ☎ 20-6237711.

To dip into the Dutch beer subculture, visit this specialized beer store with some 500 types of bottled beer and a wide range of matching glasses.

H. P. De Vreng En Zonen
Nieuwendijk 75. ☎ 20-6244581.

In this distillery, you'll find a vestige of Old Holland— a traditional family distillery where they still prepare 35 Dutch liqueurs and 12 *jenevers* (gins) according to old recipes, without any artificial additives. Buy a basic *Oud Amsterdam jenever,* or experiment with a specialized liqueur such as the ruby-tinted *Roosje Zonder Doornen* ("rose without thorns"). The amber-colored *Kus me snel* ("kiss me quick") and the bright green *Pruimpje prik in* are alleged aphrodisiacs. *Maagbitter* is said to cure indigestion, while the *Heksen Elixir* ("witches' elixir"), flavored with honey and herbs, is an old wives' remedy for just about everything.

Waterwinkel
Roelof Hartstraat 10. ☎ 20-6755932.

This specialized shop sells bottled waters from more than 100 sources in locations from Sweden to China.

Hair Salons

De Schoonheidsstudio
Van Baerlestraat 148. ☎ 20-6645084.

This hair salon in Amsterdam's exclusive shopping area offers both conservative and contemporary cuts.

Rob De Wilde
2e Boomdwarsstraat 2. ☎ 20-6235520.

De Wilde, one of the best hairstylists in Amsterdam, offers a range of classic to contemporary cuts and the versatility to fit the cut to the face. He's done hair for album covers, billboards, and magazines, and has worked in Los Angeles and Berlin, but he keeps a down-to-earth, *gezellig* atmosphere in his Jordaan shop. Prices are reasonable.

Jewelry

Traditional jewelers tend to be found along **Kalverstraat, Rokin,** and **P. C. Hooftstraat,** while avant-garde boutiques, specializing in brightly colored and highly imaginative designs, occupy tiny shops in narrow streets such as **Grimburgwal** and the streets between **the canals.** For shops selling diamond jewelry, see the section "Diamonds," above.

Hans Appenzeller
Grimburgwal 1-5. ☎ 20-6268218.
This shop is more subtle and personal than most of the Amsterdam jewelry stores. It sells expensive modern jewelry by one of Holland's leading designers.

André Coppenhagen
Rozengracht 54. ☎ 20-6243681.
If you like beads, you will find a huge selection here in different colors and sizes for crafting inexpensive home-made jewelry.

Grimm
Grimburgwal 9. ☎ 20-6220501.
This small boutique specializes in low-cost, avant-garde jewelry by young Dutch designers: light, colorful, and delicately constructed objects showing traces of De Stijl and the 1950s.

Maps

The great 17thC Dutch explorers appear to have given their descendants an inexhaustible taste for travel. Specialized maps and guides can usually be found in Amsterdam at both map stores and antiquarian book-stores (see "Antiquarian Books" above).

A La Carte
Utrechtsestraat 110–112. ☎ 20-6250679.
An international selection of travel books and guides, as well as a range of maps covering everywhere from New York's East Village to the planet Mars.

L. J. Harri
Schreierstoren, Prins Hendrikkade 94–5. ☎ 20-6248052.
Sailing books, sea charts, and nautical instruments are featured in this 16thC tower that is covered with bronze plaques commemorating historic sea voyages.

Pied À Terre
Singel 393. ☎ 20-6274455.

In this cozy shop on the Singel canal, crammed with detailed maps and guidebooks, you can map out a cycling trip, walking vacation, or an armchair traveler's dream.

Jacob van Wijngaarden
Overtoom 76. ☎ 20-6121901.

Amsterdammers seized with wanderlust instinctively head for this shop, whose specialized map and travel book collections cover virtually the whole world.

Postcards

Specialized postcard stores stock a wide range of imaginative, witty, and bizarre cards as an alternative to the ubiquitous tulips and windmills.

Art Unlimited
Keizersgracht 510. ☎ 20-6248419.

Art Unlimited publishes a huge range of postcards to suit every whim, including reproductions of Dutch paintings, Amsterdam bicycles, misty polder landscapes, and eccentric Italian furniture. Look out for the series of postcards based on Theo van den Boogaard cartoons, including an ironic Götterdämmerung (named after Wagner's opera) showing the traffic chaos in front of the Muziektheater. Many of Art Unlimited's best works are available upstairs in poster format.

Shoes & Leather Goods

When Amsterdammers want to size you up, they look down—at your shoes. Shoes, apparently, tell them all they need to know, for first impressions at least. What results is an abundance of shoe stores and a fine selection of beautifully made, predominantly Italian, Dutch, or French shoes. Shoe fashions fluctuate wildly in Amsterdam. The Dutch are particularly good at designing smart, comfortable boots. They are even better at importing Italian boots made with style but with room in the toe. Italian shoes are frequently less expensive in Amsterdam than in the US, so it's a good place to shop for them.

Antonia
Gasthuismolensteeg 12. ☎ 20-6272433.

A small, trendy shoe store on a narrow 17thC street, Antonia features fancy but solid Dutch shoes or high fashion Italian shoes designed specifically for tall, active Dutch women.

Bassotto
Van Baerlestraat 19, ☎ 20-6710741; Kalverstraat 14,
☎ 20-6245910.

At Bassotto you can find stylish Italian shoes for women who like high fashion and fine leather. These shoes are also especially comfortable and roomy. Although Bassotto also has a New York store, the prices in New York may be twice as high. For great bargains, look out for August and September sales.

Dr. Adam's
P. C. Hooftstraat 90. ☎ 20-6623835.

Dr. Adam's, one of the most popular shoe stores in Amsterdam, sells stylish but tough shoes made to survive Amsterdam's notorious sidewalks. The exclusive designer styles are made of fine but durable leather. The shoes are comfortable, well-made, and a good buy.

Freelance Shoes
Rokin 86. ☎ 20-4203205.

This shop sells shoes designed by 2 French brothers who started in France but have branched out to New York and many European cities. Their original designs set trends every season. The shop offers a wide selection of expensive shoes in high-quality leather. Expect prices from Dfl. 250 to Dfl. 650.

Hester Van Eeghen
Hartenstraat 1. ☎ 20-6269212.

On a quiet street in the canal district, this shop carries chic, unusual purses, wallets, gloves and briefcases in a rainbow of colors that are designed by a Dutch woman in a small atelier below the shop.

Hopman
P. C. Hooftstraat 76. ☎ 20-6625584.

These are sensible shoes for a variety of tastes: classic pumps, adventurous heels, trendy boots, stylish but sturdy walking shoes. Prices range from reasonable to expensive. Expect Italian designer shoes such as Pollini, Pancaldi, Guazzo, and Lara Manni.

Stephanie Kelian
P. C. Hooftstraat 99. ☎ 20-6734022.

This chic shoe store sells very expensive, trendy, and colorful pointy-toed French and Italian shoes.

Pisa
Muntplein 4. ☎ 20-6710741. (Also at Kalverstraat 14,
☎ 20-6245910.)

Pisa is a find, with smart Italian styles that are comfortable and roomy. There's a range of prices—most shoes are affordable. The Muntplein shop tends to carry casual styles while the Kalverstraat store has a more sophisticated stock. August and September sales bring such good prices that you could leave the shop with more than 1 pair.

Sacha Shoes
P. C. Hooftstraat 96.

These high fashion shoes are feminine, slender, and, curiously enough, extremely popular—and expensive—in China. They are somewhat less pricey in Amsterdam.

Specialty Stores

Condomerie Het Gulden Vlies
Warmoesstraat 141. ☎ 20-6274174.

This oddly wholesome little store displays an array of condoms in bright colors and whimsical shapes. Some are hand-painted to resemble kitties, puppies, and other fanciful critters which, displayed "face" up, look like children's decals or night lights. There are also racier condoms, similar to those of the sex shops down the street.

Droomdoos
Oude Leliestraat 1. ☎ 20-6201075.

One of the unusual specialty stores on the canals, Droomdoos has beautifully decorated handmade covered boxes for jewelry, love letters, or gifts.

50s and 60s: Before and After
Huidenstraat 13. ☎ 20-6232653.

Here you can browse for hours discovering collectibles from several eras: lamps, toasters, gadgets, and various objets d'art.

De Knopen Winkel
(Button Shop), Wolvenstraat 14. ☎ 20-6240479.

In this cozy store, buttons from Indonesia, South America, and Africa are displayed like beautiful paintings. On one small shelf alone, you may find 80 buttons—and almost as many shades of mauve.

Kramer Kaasten Olie
Reestraat 20. ☎ 20-6265274.

This candle and incense shop displays exotic candelabras and candles for every taste and religious persuasion.

There are Buddha candles, Wicca candles, a Madonna candle, and a menorah or two. Colorful candles line the walls of the interior.

Norman Automatics
Prinsengracht 292. ☎ 20-6380500.

This store is "typical Amsterdam" in its surprising collection of Americana such as jukeboxes and neon signs.

Out of Africa
Herengracht 215. ☎ 20-6234677.

One of the more appealing African art and jewelry stores, this canalside shop has a helpful, intelligent owner and a broad selection of jewelry, sculpture, and artifacts.

De Poppendokter
Reestraat 18. ☎ 20-6265274.

The Doll Doctor carries old dolls, new dolls—and cupboards full of eyes. In the shop next door is an entirely different scene: a candle store.

Terra
Reestraat 21. ☎ 20-6385913.

Terra brings earthy, beautifully designed terra-cotta pottery from Spain and the Mediterranean to a neighborhood where 17thC Dutch world traders sold their goods.

Vliegertuig
8 Gasthuismolensteeg. ☎ 20-6233450.

Vliegertuig takes kites seriously as art form and sport, displaying large, brightly colored racing kites as well as small kites for children (and parents) on a windy afternoon. The kites come in a myriad of sizes and shapes. If you wish, the owner will make you a kite according to your specifications (and his helpful suggestions).

De Witte Tanden Winkel
(The White Teeth Shop), Runstraat 5. ☎ 20-6233443.

This is one display window I want to stay unchanged—as do many Amsterdammers and children. Toothbrushes, sitting like people in tiny chairs, whirl round and round on a miniature Ferris wheel. Of course these are not ordinary toothbrushes. Some have sparkles or leopard stripes or red hearts. Others bear resemblances to puppies or giraffes. The store does not stop with toothbrushes and claims to have "everything for the teeth." They aren't kidding.

Tobacconist

P. G. C. Hajenius
Rokin 92–6. ☎ 20-6237494.

This famous tobacconist has the air of an English gentlemen's club, with its dark mahogany cabinets and gleaming marble walls. Although you can buy a simple pack of cigarettes here, the assistants are happiest when explaining the merits of pipes or the temperament of different cigars, including Hajenius's famous Grande Finale.

Toys, Games & Models

Amsterdam has several well-stocked toy stores that appeal to adults and children alike. Dutch children grow up playing with the same toys as their peers elsewhere: Lego, Playmobil, and Fisher-Price are sold in most shops, but Amsterdam is also an excellent hunting-ground for beautifully crafted models.

Authentic Models Holland
Nederlands Scheepvaart Museum, Kattenburgerplein 1. ☎ 20-6246601.

Modeling enthusiasts will find a wide range of finely detailed wooden ships, including IJsselmeer fishing boats, in the basement of the maritime museum shop.

Beestenwinkel
Staalstraat 11. ☎ 20-6231805.

This is one of the best toy stores in Amsterdam, featuring beautifully made "beasties" for tots and children. Toy critters of various sizes and textures are packed into every nook. Some of them are soft stuffed lambs and bears. Some are wooden pull-toys: alligators, dinosaurs, turtles. The toys are expensive, but durable.

Speelgoedzaak Intertoys Holland
Heiligeweg 26028. ☎ 20-6221122.

Amsterdam's biggest toy store offers everything from dolls to Danish lollipops. The model railway department on the 1st floor has a vast stock of trains, including the bright yellow Dutch models, plus accessories ranging from Old Berlin streetlamps to flocks of sheep.

Wooden Shoes

Wooden clogs were once common footwear in the boggy regions of the Netherlands and are still used as gardening or fishing shoes. They are also used as plant holders.

De Klompenboer
Nieuwe Zijds Voorburgwal 20. ☎ 20-6230632.
This cluttered downtown clog workshop sells authentic wooden clogs (klompen)—and kitschy souvenirs.

't Klompenhuisje
Nieuwe Hoogstraat 9. ☎ 20-6228100.
Here you can find an assortment of Dutch wooden shoes, ranging from sturdy clogs to gaudy souvenirs as well as some conventional footwear like slippers, thick socks, and sandals.

THE ARTS

AMSTERDAM REMAINS VIBRANT 24 HOURS A DAY. FROM concert halls to blues clubs, the city offers an impressive cultural variety—if not always the quantity or quality—to equal anything in Europe. Classical music at the Concertgebouw (internationally known for its excellent acoustics and orchestra) is world-class and popular with both Amsterdammers and tourists. Amsterdam's cinemas cater to film buffs by offering a wide selection of foreign films in a variety of settings—modern theaters, Art Deco monuments, and outdoor terraces. Other attractions for visitors are opera and dance at the **Muziektheater,** pop concerts at the Paradiso, and jazz at small concert halls and cafes. Amsterdam is a city that consumes music—everything from traditional opera to experimental modern music to American blues. Surprisingly, much of this music is offered free—or very affordably—in churches, parks, clubs, and cafes. The city also boasts a very active alternative arts scene that offers an array of dance, theater, and multimedia events to anyone who seeks them out.

Amsterdam continues to welcome, as it did in the 1960s and 1970s, a thriving community of street mimes and musicians from all over the world who perform on the Dam or Leidseplein before crowds of Amsterdammers and tourists. It is possible, even likely, to hear some reasonably good jazz or blues on an Amsterdam street corner.

Ballet & Dance

The Muziektheater's dance company, the **Het National Ballet** (Dutch National Ballet) (information available at the Uit Buro, ☎ 20-6268811, or the Muziektheater's box office, Waterlooplein 22, ☎ 20-6255455), is less popular than the modern dance companies, but the

Box-Office Tips

To attend any musical, theatrical, or dance events, buy your tickets early. You can get tickets by calling box offices, the **Amsterdam Uit Buro** (☎ 20-6211211), or the **VVV Tourist Office** (☎ 66-34034066 and from the US 31-6-34034066). The Uit Buro will book tickets 1 month in advance as a special courtesy to travelers. A knowledgeable hotel concierge can also help with tickets and reservations.

Tickets to the Nederlands Opera and the Concertgebouworkest, the city orchestra, often sell out. For last-minute tickets, call the box office to get on a waiting list, and show up an hour or two before the performance.

Discounted tickets are available for students under 25 (with an international student card) and senior citizens over 65.

For information and advice regarding tickets, visit the **Amsterdam Uit Buro** at Leidseplein 26, across from Hotel American (Mon–Wed and Fri–Sat 10am–6pm, Thurs 10am–9pm, ☎ 20-6268811). The office is friendly, centrally located, and full of brochures for current and upcoming arts events.

For mainstream, radical, and fringe events, consult the monthly English-language magazine *What's On In Amsterdam.*

Most concert, theater, dance, and music performances begin at 8:15pm. Jazz concerts usually begin at 9 or 10pm, although special concerts may start earlier or later.

dancers are accomplished and the company has recently expanded its repertoire. **The Nederlands Dans Theater** (Netherlands Dance Theater, ☎ 70-360993 or 20-5518911), which performs both ballet and modern dance, is on the ascendant, and some of Amsterdam's small modern-dance companies are becoming well-known in Europe as well as in Montreal and New York for their contemporary vision and the technical excellence of their dancers.

The modern dance company of **Krisztina de Chatel** draws crowds to see de Chatel's minimalist (but increasingly more dramatic) dances that portray abstract—and somewhat tortured—states of mind.

The dances relate to what is happening in the world without being heavy-handedly, or even concretely, political. **Itzik Galili,** an Israeli dancer and choreographer, brings more directly political themes such as war and peace to the Amsterdam stage. He is a self-styled dancer, influenced by classical modern-ballet, who produces for some of the larger Dutch companies as well as for his own small one.

Christopher Steel and Suzi Blok create acrobatic, playful, and teasing dances to pop music. **Pieter Ruiter,** on the other hand, uses his modern-ballet background to work with dance movement and vocabulary. His company is very small (3–6 dancers), and his themes tend toward the abstract and heavy. **Harigono Roebana** is even more abstract and aesthetic. His dances tend toward pure form with no clear content. Like Ruiter, his company is small and project-based (which means that his company performs only intermittently).

Other Amsterdam dancers to look for are **Andrea Leine** and **Paul Selwyn Norton,** although Norton's visceral themes, relating to dying, breathing, and digesting, are not for everyone.

The annual Amsterdam dance festival held in July is a particularly good time to see Amsterdam's dancers perform. Performances are also held from September to June at theaters such as **Felix Meritis** (Keizersgracht 324, ☎ 20-6231311), **Frascati** (Nes 63, ☎ 20-6235723), **Muziektheater** (Amstel 3, ☎ 20-6255455), **Bellevue** (Leidsekade 90, ☎ 20-6247248), and the **Stadsschouwburg** (Leidseplein 26, ☎ 20-6242311).

For general information on dance performances, call Amsterdam Uit Buro (☎ 20-6211211). Professional dancers, choreographers, and dance teachers may contact Mr. Stockfis, the Dance Officer at the Nederlands Theater Institute (☎ 20-6235104, fax: 20-6200051).

Carillon Concerts

Amsterdam's 17thC carillon bells provide delightful background music as one wanders through the streets. The bells normally chime automatically every 15 minutes, but weekly recitals are given by professional players whose repertoire ranges from national anthems to nursery rhymes. Plan your day to be in the neighborhood of a church during a recital. Performances take place at the Westerkerk (Tues noon–1pm), the Zuiderkerk (Thurs noon–1pm), the Munttoren (Fri noon–1pm), and the Oude Kerk (Sat 4–5pm).

Cinema

Amsterdam is a good city for cinemas and film. Dozens of movie theaters, which range in style from stunning Art Deco buildings to modern multiple-screen complexes, show a variety of American, Dutch, and foreign commercial and art films in the original languages. Some of the less commercial cinemas such as **Desmet** and **Kritereon** organize film festivals and theme programs. Most foreign language films are shown with Dutch or English subtitles (except for children's matinees and movies marked *Nederlands gesproken*—Dutch spoken).

Movies change on Thursdays and most cafes display the current listings. For other listings check Amsterdam newspapers. The most extensive listings are published on Thursdays. Cinema listings are also available at the Uit Buro office. Prices range from Dfl. 10 to Dfl. 13, although tickets at the art houses tend to be less expensive. For insomniacs there are Nachtvoorstellingen (night screenings), beginning around midnight.

Film cafes, attached to some of the smaller cinemas, provide cozy gathering spots for film buffs of all ages. Some cafes serve dinner (see "Amsterdam's Cafes" in **Dining**)—which you can bring with you into a small, intimate, and sometimes beautiful movie theater. The **Film Museum**, which overlooks a lake in Vondelpark, shows open-air movies on summer evenings, and the adjacent Café Vertigo serves drinks and light snacks.

Most of Amsterdam's cinemas are located near Leidseplein (**Alfa, Bellevue, Cinecenter**), Rembrandtsplein (the Art Deco **Tuschinski**), or Waterlooplein (**Desmet, Kriterion**).

Leidseplein is the best place to find the newest and most popular American, English, and foreign films. **ALFA** (Hirschgebouw, Leidseplein ☎ 20-6278806) consists of 4 comfortable theaters showing the latest English and American films. The nearby **Bellevue Cinerama** (Marnixstraat 400, ☎ 20-6234876) shows popular American films on giant screens with Dolby stereo—and has the best sound in town. **City** (Kleine Gartmanplantsoen, 13–25, ☎ 20-6234579), a 7-screen complex, also shows American movies. **Cinecenter** (Lijnbaansgracht 236, ☎ 20-6236615), a 4-theater complex across from Melkweg, shows independent and commercial films. **Melkweg** (Lijnbaansgracht 234a, ☎ 20-6241777), the alternative multimedia center once famous for its 1960s acid rock and pot brownies, now

Tuschinski Cinema

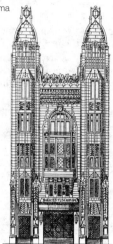

shows offbeat, late-night (sometimes all-night) theme or cult films like *Road Warrior,* horror movies, or "scare 'em straight"-type movies from 1950s American high-school drivers ed. Its cafe still serves the infamous brownies.

Near **Rembrandtsplein,** you will find the Art Deco **Tuschinski Cinema** (Reguliersbreestraat 26, ☎ 20-6262633), which is opulent, top-of-the-line Deco and a work of art in itself. Its 6 screens show popular international movies. At the nearby inexpensive and considerably less elegant **Riksbioscoop** (Reguliersbreestraat 31, ☎ 20-6243639) you can see last year's best films for Dfl. 2.50.

For a real treat if you like classics, foreign films, or quality commercial movies, try one of the cinemas with a "film cafe"—Desmet, Kriterion, or The Movies. **Desmet** (Plantage Middenlaan 4a, ☎ 20-6273434) is a small Art Deco movie theater near Waterlooplein with a program of avant-garde films, premiere movies, and old black-and-white favorites. On Saturday nights and Sunday afternoons, Desmet shows gay films and on Sunday afternoons special documentary programs or theme movies. Call between 10am and 6pm to buy tickets. The theater includes a cozy brown cafe good for late-night coffee and conversation.

Kriterion (Roetersstraat 170, ☎ 20-6231708), within an easy walk of Desmet, is a 2-theater complex with a stirring history. After World War II, student members of the Dutch Resistance movement took over what had been a Nazi theater and turned it into a cinema. Before the Nazi occupation, the Art Deco–Amsterdam School building had been a Jewish diamond factory. The cinema and attached cafe, still owned and operated by students, shows "the best commercial movies" as well as politically progressive films or foreign films hot from the Berlin or Venice film festivals. The students offer special inexpensive screenings for the elderly. They also bring in internationally known directors and critics to speak at Kriterion's film festivals.

The Movies (Haarlemmerdijk 161, ☎ 20-6245790) is an attractive 3-theater complex in Egyptian Art-Deco style. The program offers a good selection of international movies and classics. The attached cafe offers a dinner/movie special where you can take dinner with you to the cinema.

For open-air movies on summer evenings, as well as a fine selection of classic and foreign films the rest of the year, the **Filmmuseum** (Vondelpark 3, ☎ 20-5891400) is a comfortable and sophisticated place to be—as is Café Vertigo next door. The Filmmuseum is located in a grand pavilion that was built as a fashionable cafe in the 1880s. Movies shown here vary from vintage German Expressionism to W. C. Fields comedies.

Further away from the city center is the **Rialto** (Ceintuurbaan 338, ☎ 20-6623488), a 2-screen theater showing foreign films with political themes such as *The Conformist* and *The Damned*—with Dutch or English subtitles. It also has some children's programs.

Classical & Modern Music

Of the conventional (and more expensive) places to hear classical music, the **Concertgebouw** (Concertgebouwplein 2-6, ☎ 20-6718345) is the best because of its exceptional acoustics, excellent orchestra, and opulent decor. The elegant concert hall is home to Holland's foremost orchestra, the **Concertgebouworkest,** directed by Riccardo Chailly. Recently restored at enormous cost, the concert hall, built in 1888 by A. L. van Gendt, boasts flawless acoustics. Watch out for special events such as the free lunchtime concerts (Sept–May) in the Kleine Zaal, a small hall used for chamber music. Formal dress is not obligatory. The cafe across the street, Bodega Keyser, is an integral part of the concert experience since it is a hangout for classical musicians and their fans.

Concertgebouw

Het Muziektheater (Amstel 3, ☎ 20-6255455) is less impressive in terms of acoustics; its opera and dance productions are popular, but less internationally acclaimed than the classical music of the Concertgebouw. Amsterdam's Muziektheater, which opened in 1986, was built on the site of a former Jewish orphanage that was raided during the Nazi occupation of Holland. Home to the national ballet (Het Nationale Ballet) and the Dutch opera company (De Nederlandse Opera), the Muziektheater also features performances by major foreign companies on tour. Free concerts of chamber music are held on Tuesdays at lunchtime, and the adjacent Grand Café Dantzig, with a terrace on the Amstel River, is a pleasant spot to spend the afternoon.

For more modern, minimalist music and one of the most beautiful cafes in Amsterdam, proceed up the Amstel to **De IJsbreker** (Weesperzijde 23, ☎ 20-6681805), a small concert hall specializing in contemporary music by the finest Dutch and international composers.

Given the quirkiness of Amsterdam, classical music is sometimes performed in unconventional settings. One of these is **Bethanienklooster** (Barndesteeg 6b, ☎ 20-6250078), where free concerts of classical and modern chamber music are held in a former nuns' dormitory in a restored 15thC convent on the edge of the red-light district. Opera lunches are held in an offbeat cafe, **De Rode Hoed** (Keizersgracht 102, ☎ 20-6257368), housed in a converted church. At **Cristofori** (Prinsengracht 583, ☎ 20-6268485), piano recitals and chamber concerts are held twice a month in a salon above a piano shop. And **Beurs Van Berlage** (243 Damrak, ☎ 20-6270466), the former 1903 stock-exchange building designed by Berlage, sometimes holds classical concerts.

Muziektheater

Churches are a popular spot for free concerts, and one of the most interesting of these is in the **Engelse Kerk** (Begijnhof 48 [entrance on Spui], ☎ 20-6249665) in the center of Amsterdam's most famous hofje, the Begijnhof. Here evening concerts are held in a peaceful, cloistered little church where the Pilgrim Fathers once worshipped. In the medieval part of the city, occasional organ concerts are held from May through September in **Oude Kerk** (Oudehartsplein 23, ☎ 20-6258284), Amsterdam's oldest (and coldest) church. Sunday concerts by small ensembles are given in **Koepelzaal** (Kattengat 1, ☎ 20-6239896), an unusual 17thC, round, classical church. **Waalse Kerk** (Oude Zijds Achterburgwal 157, ☎ 20-6232074) also holds occasional chamber music concerts.

In the Museum Quarter, the **Stedelijk Museum** (Paulus Potterstraat 13, ☎ 20-5732911) offers contemporary music concerts on Saturdays at 3pm, from September to June, and **Sweelinck Conservatorium** (Van Baerlestraat 27, ☎ 20-6647641) holds free classical concerts by accomplished young music students.

Cultural Institutes

As a major international city, Amsterdam has its fair share of cultural institutes, all of which act as a showcase for the cultures of various countries. **The British Council** (Keizersgracht 343, ☎ 20-6223644) shows British films, and the **Maison Descartes** boasts a bistro offering French cuisine (Vijzelgracht 2, ☎ 20-6224936). German movies are screened at the **Goethe Instituut** (Herengracht 470, ☎ 20-6230421). Occasional Italian cultural events are held at the **Istituto Italiano di Cultura** (Keizersgracht 564, ☎ 20-6265314), while the Flemish region of Belgium promotes Dutch-language theater and contemporary art at **De Brakke Grond** (Nes 45, ☎ 20-6266866).

Café De Balie (☎ 20-624382), a cultural and political institute for politically progressive or left-of-center intellectuals and artists, holds lectures, discussion groups, literary presentations, interviews with Dutch authors, musical programs, and various offbeat happenings. (See "Amsterdam's Cafes" in "Dining.")

Jazz

Amsterdammers have embraced American jazz and blues more fully than most Americans: The music has taken firm hold in Amsterdam cafes, clubs, and summer music festivals. The 3-day **North Sea Jazz Festival,** which brings leading jazz artists to Holland, is held each year in The Hague (P.O. Box 87840, 2508 DE, The Hague, ☎ 70-3501604). Jazz is popular enough in Holland to have its own special **Jazz-line** (☎ 20-6267764) that gives recorded information (in Dutch) on forthcoming concerts.

Although fine jazz players like John Schofield do perform in Amsterdam, the jazz scene by no means rivals those of New York, Paris, or Copenhagen. What is appealing about jazz in Amsterdam is that it is relaxed, inexpensive or free, and easily accessible in the small clubs around Leidseplein.

African and Latin music has also been adopted by these former world traders who, for hundreds of years, have brought the best of other cultures back home to Amsterdam. In this case, fine musicians from other cultures have immigrated to Holland.

A friendly jazz cafe with an older crowd, seasoned jazz musicians, and free jazz nightly is **Café Alto** (Korte Leidsedwarsstraat 115, ☎ 20-6263249), an intimate, cosmopolitan cafe that offers a welcome escape from the commercial Leidseplein. Although the Alto gets crowded, it is well ventilated and seldom smoky. The outdoor tables are pleasant—and full—on warm evenings. The **Bamboo Bar** (Lange Leidsedwarsstraat 64, ☎ 20-6243993) is not solely a jazz cafe—it offers fusion and rhythm-and-blues bands as well as jazz. It is often less crowded than the Alto and draws music lovers of all ages. **Bourban Street** (Leidsekruisstraat 6, ☎ 20-6233440) offers a selection of live jazz and blues nightly to energetic audiences.

Bimhuis (Oude Schans 73-77, ☎ 20-6231361) offers serious jazz for a 20- to 50-something crowd in a setting more formal than the Alto and the Bamboo Bar. It also charges admission (a reasonable fee). The Bimhuis is located on a canal on the east side of town, not far from the **Rembrandthuis,** but the address will change in the near future. Bimhuis was set up in the 1970s, by the Professional Jazz Musicians' Union, in a former warehouse.

De Engelbewaarder (Kloveniersburgwal 59, ☎ 20-6253772), a "literary" brown cafe on a quiet canal, draws students, weathered intellectuals, and writers to its jazz sessions every Sunday afternoon from 4 to 7pm. (See "Amsterdam's Cafes" in "Dining.")

Other clubs offer a wide variety of jazz—everything from Dixieland to jazz-influenced piano bar. **Joseph Lam Jazzclub** (Van Diemenstraat 242, ☎ 20-6228086), an atmospheric Dixieland jazz club, requires real motivation on the part of its clientele since it is located in a remote part of the old harbor, best reached by cab.

De Koningshut (Spuistraat 269, ☎ 20-6264276), conveniently located on the Spui near cafes, restaurants, and the Amsterdam Historical Museum, offers jazzy piano music in a cozy club with a jovial Brueghelian interior and antique beer tankards, jawbones, and other curious paraphernalia dangling from the roof beams.

Pianobar le Maxim (Leidsekruisstraat 35, ☎ 20-6241920) caters to a 30-something mainstream crowd around Leidseplein while **De Kroeg** (Lijnbaansgracht 163, ☎ 20-4200232) draws a more alternative crowd with its reggae, rock, and jazz concerts. The atmosphere is friendly and relaxed.

Rum Runners (Prinsengracht 277, ☎ 20-6274079), a canalside Caribbean restaurant near the Jordaan catering to a mainstream, cocktail-drinking crowd, plays Latin music—and occasionally Latin jazz. For more soulful Latin music, try the **Canecao Brazilian Bar** (Lange Leidsedwarsstraat 68–70, ☎ 20-6261500).

Multipurpose/Alternative Centers

The days of offbeat sixties' sensibilities live on, in a sense: Amsterdam's multimedia centers offer live music (salsa, reggae, funk, and music in its newest incarnations), experimental dance performances, and programs involving poetry and politics.

The most well-known of these centers are **Melkweg** (Milky Way) and **Paradiso,** with programs appealing to 20- to 50-somethings of various nationalities. **Melkweg**

(Lijnbaansgracht 234a, ☎ 20-6241777), occupying a large converted dairy off Leidseplein, is a surprisingly topical and up-to-date "relic" of the 1970s, where you can watch movies, listen to live bands, or buy marijuana from a shop that resembles an old-fashioned grocery store. Dance groups frequently perform innovative works in the Fonteinzaal, while solemn European theater is staged in the Nieuwe Vleugel.

The Melkweg cafe (decorated like a 1950s milk bar) stays open during the day and serves everything from orange juice to space cakes (pot brownies). At night the complex is only accessible by means of an iron drawbridge, which is to be found behind the Stadsschouwburg. Visitors must buy a membership ticket at the door, valid for 1 month.

The **Paradiso** (Weteringschans 6-8, ☎ 20-6264521), famous since the sixties, is housed in a 19thC church, and is still, 20 years later, Amsterdam's best club for pop, rock, folk, blues, and reggae. Expect greats like Los Lobos and the Stones as well as up-and-coming young bands. Paradiso occasionally collaborates with **Café De Balie,** a political and cultural institute down the street, in offbeat and politically progressive art and cultural events. (See "Amsterdam's Cafes" in "Dining.")

De Meervaart (Osdorpplein 205, ☎ 20-6107393) is a modern cultural center that is further afield in an attractive garden city on the west edge of Amsterdam— but worth the tram ride for its special jazz, blues and pop music, and poetry events.

Some of Amsterdam's cultural or multimedia events are held outdoors in **Vondelpark** (open-air theater, ☎ 20-5237790) "Muziektent" (☎ 20-6731499 for general information, June–Aug call 20-6731499). In the summer months, concerts, poetry readings, and plays are held in the Vondelpark, in the open-air theater close to the round, blue teahouse—a pleasant place to come on fine evenings.

Opera

Opera is very popular in Amsterdam, with seats in much demand for classical and modern performances by **The Nederlandse Opera.** Even though aficionados say these performances can't compete with first-rate Italian opera, the performances are lively, professional, and well received. Tickets are hard to come by: Some people buy tickets a month in advance. For last minute tickets, call the Muziektheater box office

(☎ 20-6255455) and show up an hour or two before the performance to put your name on the waiting list.

Theater

The notorious "tomato protest" of 1968, when the cast in a production of Shakespeare's *The Tempest* at the Stadsschouwburg was bombarded with tomatoes, signaled the end of conventional theater in Amsterdam. What resulted was a new, exciting period of Dutch experimental theater for which Amsterdam became internationally known. But theater, like dance, ossified somewhat in the late eighties, losing some of its former originality and verve. This is not to say that theater isn't interesting and sophisticated in Amsterdam; it is just not as exciting as it was 20 years ago. However, theater is still an important part of Amsterdam culture. Check the files at **Uit Buro** (Leidseplein, across from Hotel American, ☎ 20-6268811) for reviews and to see what is being offered. Bear in mind that plays are performed in Dutch, English, French, or German. Traditional theater has not totally died, despite the tomatoes. Everything from Shakespeare to Strindberg is performed in both large and small theaters.

Amsterdammers tend to be fluent in English. **Studio Theater** (Lijnbaansgracht 238, ☎ 20-6255454), located behind the Stadsschouwburg, occasionally has English-language productions as does the **University Theater** (Nieuwe Doelenstraat 16, ☎ 20-6230127). The **Fijnhout Theater** (Jacob van Lennepkade 334, ☎ 20-6184768) presents popular, mainstream theater performed in English by touring companies. Both mainstream and offbeat Dutch theaters sometimes put on productions in English. For listings, call the Uit Buro (☎ 20-6268822).

Of the Dutch-speaking theaters, **Stadsschouwburg** and the **Koninlijk Theater Carré** are the most mainstream. **Stadsschouwburg** (Leidseplein 26, ☎ 20-6242311), Amsterdam's ornate neo-Renaissance municipal theater on Leidseplein, has recovered from the 1968 tomato protest and now offers an indecisive mixture of traditional and contemporary theater (occasionally in English) and is expanding its program to include performances by European touring companies. **Theater Carré** (Amstel 115-125, ☎ 20-6225225), located on the bank of the Amstel river and originally built for a circus, still houses a circus over the Christmas holiday but usually presents popular musicals and dance productions. And **The Kleine Komedie** (Amstel 56, ☎ 20-6240534), also on the Amstel and one of Amsterdam's oldest theaters, offers Dutch theater, cabaret, and opera.

Of the alternative theaters, **Boom Chicago** (Lijnbaansgracht 238, ☎ 20-6392707) is the only one that performs regularly in English since the entire company is American. The company performs politically savvy and provocative improvisational comedy in the spirit of Chicago's Second City comedy troop (whose members once filled the ranks of Saturday Night Live). Dutch and American audiences fill the house— so buy tickets in advance. Boom Chicago also offers its own quirky tour by "Boom Boat" of the red-light district.

Felix Meritis (Keizersgracht 324, ☎ 20-6231311), a lively center of experimental drama, music, film, and dance, provides more serious avant-garde productions in the splendid 18thC neoclassical canal house of the Felix Meritis society. Brahms, Schumann, and Grieg were among the 19thC Romantics who once performed in this building. **Frascati** (Nes 63, ☎ 20-6235723) is another one of the more lively, energetic alternative theaters where you can find avant-garde as well as more conventional plays. Some of the more interesting and accomplished new dance companies also perform here.

Bellevue (Leidsekade 90, ☎ 20-6247248), attached to the theater cafe De Smoeshaan, presents less-than-conventional plays to audiences of 200. Other theaters include **Balie** (Kleine Gartmanplantsoen 10, ☎ 20-6232904), a political and cultural center, **Brakke Grond** (Nes 45, ☎ 20-6266866), the Flemish cultural center, **Nieuwe de la Mar** (Marnixstraat 404, ☎ 20-6233462), and **Soeterijn** (Linnaeusstraat 2, ☎ 20-5688500), an unusual theater attached to the **Tropenmuseum** that features exotic programs of non-Western dance, music, theater, and film. Plays are sometimes performed in English.

AMSTERDAM
AFTER DARK

A MSTERDAM IS A LIVELY CITY AT NIGHT, BUT IN ITS
own relaxed and quirky way. In the 1960s, Amsterdam gained a reputation for its permissiveness regarding sex and drugs, and permissiveness still influences the city's nightlife. The **Melkweg** still sells "space cakes" (pot brownies) and provides a venue for up-and-coming bands. The **Bulldog** and other "smoking coffee shops" still offer a staggering selection of exotic marijuana and hashish (although the Netherlands is considering further regulating soft drugs and limiting the number of coffee shops). And the **red-light district** still advertises sex and prostitution in its nonchalant, well-regulated, and very Amsterdam way. Along with gritty sex shows, dark rooms, and sex shops with the latest in S&M fashions, you'll find **The Bananenbar** (featuring an offbeat "banana show" as well as male and female strippers) and the **Condomerie Het Gulden Vlies,** specializing in cute designer condoms.

Dance clubs throb with reggae, hip-hop, salsa, blues, and house music until 4 or 5am and, with the exception of a few ultra-in spots like the Roxy, foster a relaxed atmosphere with little hype and no dress codes. The gay clubs on **Reguliersdwarsstraat** and **Amstelstraat** play some of the best dance music in town and provide an atmosphere comfortable for both gays and straights. Even the more flamboyant gay clubs like **iT** designate a special night for straights or draw a mixed crowd much of the week.

But Amsterdam has more to offer than sex, drugs, and rock and roll. Amsterdammers like to go out at night, and the city offers some of the most interesting, varied, and inexpensive nightlife in Europe. Cafes are central to Amsterdam nightlife. They begin to fill up at 6pm and remain open and buzzing until at least midnight on weekdays and 1 or 2am on weekends. Unique to Amsterdam are the special-interest cafes—jazz cafes, theater cafes, film cafes, journalist cafes—to help you find your cultural niche in the city. (See "Amsterdam's Cafes" the "Dining" chapter.)

The focus of entertainment of all kinds is **Leidseplein,** where many of Amsterdam's theaters, cinemas, clubs, and cafes are located. The **Paradiso** and **Melkweg,** two of Amsterdam's best—and most historic—live music venues lie on either side of Leidseplein. **Rembrandtsplein** and the nearby late-night party streets, **Reguliersdwarsstraat** and **Amstelstraat,** form a second, somewhat less frenetic hub of activity, with lively bars and nightclubs like **iT, Soul Kitchen, Escape,** and **Havana Club** that keep the streets bright and filled with people until the wee hours.

The notorious **red-light district** is also brightly lit, awake, and safe in a seedy kind of way, all night long. Its most popular street, **Oude Zijds Voorburgwal,** has a bawdy red-glow and a very mixed crowd. Girls sporting bikinis or alluring lingerie sit in canal-house windows lit with red neon. The streets are alive with tourists, groups of carousing and curious men, occasional drug dealers and junkies, and a bouncer or two to keep things in line. Entertainment ranges from the gritty to the humorous.

For a more genteel late-night scene at bars and discos in quiet neighborhoods, try the upscale hotels, although this is not the nightlife for which Amsterdam is known. The Renaissance Hotel has a stylish disco with a 50- or 60-something crowd. Of the hotel bars, the most comfortable and typically Dutch are at the Pulitzer and Victoria hotels. The most elegant continental bars are those at Hotel de l'Europe, the Amstel, and the Okura.

A Word About Safety   You will be relatively safe in all the neighborhoods mentioned here if you avoid the dark, narrow side streets (especially around the Dam, Centraal Station, and the red-light district), and keep to the lights and the crowds. But watch out for pickpockets. If you feel threatened by anyone, head for the nearest cafe and enlist the bartender to assist you or call a cab.

Bars

Although bars may lack the bohemian charm of brown cafes, they can be quiet and comfortable places for cocktails and conversation.

The **Amstel Hotel Bar** (Prof. Tulpplein 1, ☎ 20-6226060) is a beautiful, romantic place for a riverside drink with live piano music in an opulent setting. **Ciel Bleu** (Okura Hotel, Ferdinand Bolstraat 333, ☎ 20-6787111), the Okura Hotel's 23rd-floor bar, is especially nice in the early evening when the house pianist plays to a splendid sunset panorama of the whole city. For a cozy bar in a 17thC canal house overlooking the Keizersgracht, try the **Pulitzer Bar** (Keizersgracht 234, ☎ 20-5235235), which is decorated with 17thC maps and prints and serves up Dutch history and gezel-ligheid. The turn-of-the-century **Victoria Hotel** bar is also comfortable, and traditionally Dutch in decor and atmosphere.

Pastorie (SAS Royal Hotel, Rusland 17, ☎ 20-6231231), the bar of the SAS Royal Hotel located in a former parsonage, is furnished in handsome Old Dutch style with wooden cabinets, gilt-framed mirrors, and chandeliers. This is nicest in winter when you can sit by the fireplace where the pastor once toasted his toes, and listen to the house pianist playing old favorites (6–10:30pm).

Casinos

Casinos are viewed with some suspicion by the Dutch, and the country's gamblers are confined to the 8 official establishments run by Holland Casinos. But it seems the Dutch are becoming less squeamish about casinos: The new **Amsterdam Lido** (Max Euweplein 62, ☎ 20-6201006) claims to be the largest in Europe. Behind the gleaming marble facade on the Singelgracht, there are roulette tables, a bingo hall, and ranks of gaming machines. The Lido has a smart restaurant and a reasonably priced waterfront brasserie that is a pleasant place to sit on summer afternoons and evenings, but more commercial and crowded than the waterfront terraces at De Jaren and Hotel de l'Europe.

Dance Clubs

Clubs in the Leidseplein and Rembrandtsplein area tend to be crammed to capacity with an under-30 crowd—with the notable exception of **Paradiso** (where The Rolling Stones, Los Lobos, and The Fabulous Thunderbirds still play to 40- and 50-something audiences), **The Soul Kitchen,** and **Odeon.** Some of Amsterdam's discos are, strictly speaking, private clubs and will only admit you, if at all, after you have purchased a temporary membership, although sometimes this is negotiable. Most clubs don't really rock until after 10pm, and they pick up more momentum around 1am—after the cafes have closed. Many clubs stay open until 4 or 5am.

Odeon (Singel 460, ☎ 20-6249711) brings music lovers from 20 to 50 together in the 3 floors of a beautiful, renovated canal house, although the club is mostly popular with students from the nearby university. There's jazz in the basement, sixties and seventies music on the 3rd floor, and top-40 on the floor in between. In 1782 John Adams negotiated the first U.S. loan to the Netherlands in this elegant 17thC neck-gable house designed by Philips Vingboons. The stately *voorkamer* (front room), with its painted Baroque ceiling, is now a late-night bar.

Soul Kitchen (Amstelstraat 32a, ☎ 20-6202333), the most popular soul club in town, has an older, more relaxed and funkier crowd than most of the clubs in the Amstelstraat neighborhood. Almost everyone is over 25. **36 Op De Schaal Van Richter** (Reguliersdwarsstraat 36, ☎ 20-6261573) is a small club with good soul and disco music and an older, hard-living, more weathered crowd than some of the other trendy clubs in the neighborhood. Richter's decor of shattered mirrors and brick rubble is intended to suggest the aftermath of an earthquake measuring a theoretically impossible 36 on the Richter scale. Jazz is featured on Sunday. **Paradiso** (Weteringschans 6-8, ☎ 20-6237348), once a progressive Protestant church, and known in the 1960s for excellent bands and psychedelic light shows, is still one of the best music venues in Amsterdam, attracting such accomplished musicians as Los Lobos and The Rolling Stones as well as up-and-coming young bands. Audiences range in age from their 20s to 60s. Despite its popularity, the steps are steep and rickety and the chairs small and hard. The **Melkweg** (Lijnbaansgracht 234a, ☎ 20-6241777), famous in the sixties for hippies and pot brownies, is now a multimedia center that offers mixed dance music—from reggae to house—after midnight on weekends. Melkweg mostly functions as a live-music venue, playing a variety of music and bringing in folks ranging in age from 18 to 50.

Roxy (Singel 465, ☎ 20-6200354) is one of the few clubs in Amsterdam where your entrance may be refused based on your clothes, your looks, or the whims of the person at the door. Sometimes only members are admitted to this popular and hipper-than-hip disco that plays a variety of music and has one of the best sound systems of the Amsterdam clubs. Expect people 25 to 40. Put on your dancing shoes and your party clothes in order to get through the door. Another trendy bar for a somewhat older (25–35) set with soul, hip-hop, and rock music is **Seymour Likely 2** (NZ Voorburgwal 161, ☎ 20-4205062). **Thijm** (NZ Voorburgwal 163–165, ☎ 20-6224541) also caters to a 25-plus audience and plays jazz, soul, and hip-hop.

Amsterdam has a progressive and lively music scene when it comes to the latest forms of hip-hop, house, and techno music; reggae is also popular and widely played, especially for the coffee shop set. **Akhanatan** (Nieuwezijds Kolk 25, ☎ 20-6243396) has a young, alternative scene where neohippies dance to salsa as well as new music. **Dansen Bij Jansen** (Handboogstraat 11, ☎ 20-6201779) is a student disco founded by and for students and playing the latest dance music. Bring your student ID card.

Escape (Rembrandtsplein 11, ☎ 20-6221111) is Amsterdam's largest dance club with a great sound system, a mixed crowd, and mediocre music. The best nights are Thursday through Sunday. At **Herenhuis** (Herengracht 114, ☎ 20-6227685), on the peaceful Herengracht canal, a 30-something crowd once danced to soul, jazz, and rock, but now Herenhuis is playing house music in an attempt to draw a younger crowd. **Korsakoff** (Lijnbaansgracht 161, ☎ 20-6257854), an alternative grunge club, plays a variety of sounds for the young and disheveled. **Mazzo** (Rozengracht 114, ☎ 20-4200626) was rather self-consciously set up as a hip club for the trendy and avant-garde who like to make the scene. Mazzo's wall-to-wall audiovisual entertainment makes it popular with Amsterdam's avant-garde artists, musicians, and fashion designers, but the techno-trance music loses an older audience. Expect techno, house, and ambient music.

At the other end of the age spectrum is the **Boston Club** (Kattengat 1, ☎ 20-6245561), an exclusive disco for mature swingers in the basement of the Ramada Renaissance Hotel.

Jazz & Blues

Amsterdam has a lively jazz and blues scene, and good-quality (sometimes world-class) music can be heard in a surprising number of venues throughout the city.

The local scene is characterized by its relaxed atmosphere and very low, or nonexistent, cover charges. The city supports a jazz hotline (☎ 20-6267764) with recorded information on forthcoming concerts but, unfortunately, it is only in Dutch. A better bet might be to get a copy of the English-language *What's On In Amsterdam* or *Uitkrant* (a free Dutch monthly that lists cultural events) to find out what's going on during your stay.

Many of the clubs listed under "Dance Clubs," above, feature jazz or blues nights on a regular basis, and some cafes (see the "Dining" chapter) also feature jazz evenings, afternoons, or Sunday brunches. For a list of clubs and other venues that specialize in jazz see the "Jazz" section of "The Arts" chapter.

Gay Nightlife

Amsterdam has an open, relaxed gay scene with gay bars, cafes, restaurants, and discos catering to a wide spectrum of ages and tastes. A high concentration of these clubs and cafes may be found near Rembrandtsplein by simply walking down **Amstelstraat** or **Reguliersdwarsstraat.** Some of these discos, like **The Havana Club** (Reguliersdwarsstraat 17-19, ☎ 20-6206788) cater to a mixed gay-straight crowd. This club, one of the more popular ones, draws in gays, yuppies, and artists—and closes early. **Homolulu** (Kerkstraat 23, ☎ 20-6246387) is a pleasant gay and lesbian disco with a restaurant and a women's night on Sundays. **COC Disco** (Rozenstraat 14, ☎ 20-6263087) caters to young lesbians and has a women's night every Saturday.

The **iT** (Amstelstraat 24, ☎ 20-6250111) is a large, extravagant, and internationally known gay disco—the largest venue and the biggest, most festive gay club in the city. Saturday night is exclusively gay but Thursday and Sunday nights draw a mixed crowd. Expect flamboyant transvestite garb as well as down-to-earth T-shirts and jeans. The owner, who recently died of AIDS, threw himself a large, flamboyant funeral and asked everyone to wear pink. They did. At **Saarein** (Elandsstraat 119, ☎ 20-6234901), a relaxed, women-only brown cafe with a billiards table, expect a cozy atmosphere; at the **Women Of Colour Cafe** (see COC at ☎ 20-6263087), a new cafe run by a group of women who refer to themselves as "dykes to watch out for," expect a feistier scene.

The Red-Light District

Amsterdam has been famous since the 17thC for its red-light district, known as *De Walletjes* (little walls) and located between 2 canals, Oude Zijds Voorburgwal and Oude Zijds Achterburgwal. This is Amsterdam's "old side" (see "Sights & Attractions"), located near the port and Centraal Station.

By the late 15thC, Amsterdam's port area had a thriving prostitution business. Even then, Dutch authorities tried to regulate prostitution by requiring prostitutes to live under supervision on either Pilsteeg or Halsteeg. Although some Protestants tried to ban prostitution in the 16thC, the punishment for prostitutes was mild compared to the punishment of their adulterous clients. Tolerance became the rule in the 17thC—and has been the pervading Amsterdam attitude ever since.

The early Dutch prostitutes were either poor, unmarried women with few other options, or entrepreneurs who chose "the oldest profession" as their career. Although contemporary Amsterdam prostitutes have frequently been portrayed as independent businesswomen, some are still poor young women, often from Third World countries, who came to Amsterdam to seek their fortune. Others have been lured into the trade under false pretenses and against their will and are unable to leave the red-light district due to intimidation, drug addiction, or language barriers.

However, some Amsterdam prostitutes are independent, strong-willed—and organized. The *Rode Draad* (Red Thread), a prostitute's union, was formed to protect their rights (and health) in 1985. Another organization, the Pink Thread, was later created as a support group for prostitutes.

Despite the progressive Dutch attitudes, Amsterdam prostitution is decriminalized—but not legalized. Women in brothels are still under the thumb of madams and pimps. Although prostitution itself is not illegal, running a brothel is, but Amsterdammers choose to "look the other way" and permit brothels unless they create a nuisance or break another law (for example, by employing minors). Brothel owners can apply for a local license, which allows them to operate.

One hundred years ago Dutch prostitutes advertised by tacking portraits of themselves to doors and storefronts. Now, with a frankness that is unique to Amsterdam, scantily dressed women sit in the front windows of 17thC gable houses, reading, knitting, flirting, and doing their nails. This eccentric form of exhibitionism has turned Amsterdam's red-light district into a major tourist attraction.

Night clubs featuring old-fashioned strip shows are mainly found on **Thorbeckeplein** (the statue of Thorbecke, who drafted the 19thC constitution of the Netherlands, discreetly faces away from the inviting neon signs). Grittier strip shows and sex shows can be found in the heart of the red-light district along **Warmoesstraat, Oude Zijds Voorburgwal,** and the nearby side streets. A less conventional and lighter-hearted strip show may be found in **The Bananenbar** (Oudezijds Achterburgwal 37, ☎ 20-6224670), which features male and female strippers as well as a "banana show." A must-see in the district is the whimsical—and almost wholesome—**Condomerie Het Gulden Vlies** (Warmoesstraat 141, ☎ 20-6274174), with unusually flavored and festively colored condoms, or hand-painted ones in the form of kitties, giraffes, and other fanciful creatures.

Because of its popularity, the red-light district is fairly safe at night, but women venturing here alone, especially on weekend evenings, can expect some uncomfortable (although not necessarily dangerous) encounters. Pickpockets are drawn to this area, so hold onto your purses and pockets and avoid looking nervously at street maps (which signals a naive tourist—and makes you an easy mark).

For a witty and safely detached tour of the district, try the **"Boom Boat"**—a small tour boat run by the **Boom Chicago** improvisational comedy theater. The Boom Boat leaves from a canal near Leidseplein. Call 20-6392707 for more information, or check with the theater box office at Lijnbaansgracht 238. Departure times vary.

Only in Amsterdam: Smoking Coffee Shops

Unique to cafe-crazy Amsterdam is the "other" kind of coffee shop, the "smoking" coffee shop that serves orange juice, fruit shakes—and exotic kinds of hashish and marijuana. These establishments are made obvious by Rastafarian colors or pictures of marijuana leaves displayed on the doors or windows. Sometimes you will see potted marijuana plants carefully tended and snipped, or you will hear reggae or acid rock blaring from inside. Most coffee shops serve healthy food (make sure you know what you're ordering, however, as hash is baked into a number of the goods sold) and orange juice. They cater to tourists, since Amsterdammers rarely frequent these places. For Amsterdammers, the coffee shops are old hat and somewhat unhip—neither forbidden nor romantic.

The drug laws in Holland reflect typical Dutch tolerance and practicality. However, do not assume that soft drugs are totally legal. They aren't. You may smoke pot and hash in designated places (like smoking coffee shops) and may possess them in limited amounts. Although the Dutch government once permitted the possession of up to 30 grams (1.1 oz.) of pot or hash, it is now considering changing the allowed amount to only 5 grams (.2 oz). This policy change is motivated by a desire to curtail the growing problem of "drug tourism" and to discourage those attempting to take drugs out of the country.

The most touristy and popular of the coffee shops are the chains: **The Bulldog** (Leidseplein 15 and Oude Zijds Voorburgwal 90) and **The Grasshopper** (Oude Brugsteeg 16, Utrechtsestraat 21, and Nieuwezijds Voorburgwal 59). However, these are by no means the most sophisticated, atmospheric, or pleasant of Amsterdam's smoking places. The Bulldog is big, loud, and commercial, whereas the Grasshopper is a little less hectic. **Siberie** (Brouwersgracht 11) and **Rusland** (Rusland 16) are more relaxed and friendly, and Rusland offers 43 kinds of tea as well as the usual orange juice and fruit shakes. Some coffee shops, like **So Fine** (Prinsengracht 30), have pool tables; others, like **Dreadlock** (Oude Zijds Voorburgwal), show big-screen cartoons; and some, like **De Tweede Kamer** (Heisteeg 6), look—and feel—like brown cafes.

An Excursion
to Rotterdam

Rotterdam, located 45 miles (72.4 kilometers) southwest of Amsterdam (just 50 minutes by car or train), is Europe's busiest port. A stream of ships from every continent brings vitality to its sprawling waterfront. Bulky container vessels ease into the giant docks downstream of the city, while long convoys of barges sail up the broad River Maas and the Rhine, bound for the heart of Europe. The visitor to Rotterdam can't ignore the port, whose activities extend to every corner of the city. You will see aged gravel barges crammed into the Leuvehaven and Oude Haven, rusting East European cargo ships moored alongside the city park, and sleek German cruise liners gliding past the geodesic dome of the Tropicana swimming pool.

Even in the center of the city, you can feel the presence of the port through the proliferation of shipping firms, maritime insurers, and churches for foreign seamen. One of the first sights you will see on leaving the main rail station is an oil-tanker superstructure planted in the middle of Kruisplein. Even the postwar architecture in Rotterdam, with its promenade decks and portholes, looks as if it was designed by a naval architect. Unless, of course, it looks like a flying saucer, or an inside-out pyramid which is the whimsical, futuristic side of Rotterdam's imagination and a reason in itself to visit the city.

Rotterdam was founded on the right bank of the Maas River in the 13thC and grew into one of the great ports of the Dutch maritime empire. However, most traces of the old city have been erased, first by the course of 19th and 20thC progress, and then more brutally by the German bombings of 1940.

But Dutch ingenuity, engineering, and architectural imagination prevailed. The bombed city has been restored so seamlessly that you are barely aware of the massive scale of the destruction that occurred here. Rotterdam invested huge sums to build a new port to the west of the old town. Now Europe's principal harbor, it sprawls for some 23 miles (37 kilometers) along the Nieuwe Maas waterfront. Giant tankers pump crude oil into the huge storage tanks at the Europoort, while container ships unload vast tonnages of fruit, tea, and tobacco at the Waalhaven docks.

In the triple alliance of Randstad cities (Amsterdam, The Hague, and Rotterdam), Rotterdam has traditionally played the part of the working partner, while The Hague housed the government and Amsterdam was home to the arts. But that blue-collar stereotype no longer holds true. Rotterdam has opened several innovative new museums devoted to shipping, architecture, and ethnography, while the imaginative new architecture at Blaakse Bos and Leuvehaven has given Rotterdam one of the most exciting urban waterfronts in Europe.

Getting There

By Train   Trains leave Amsterdam's Centraal Station every 15 minutes for Rotterdam and the whole trip takes about 50 minutes (if you take the express train, not the local train). A round-trip second-class ticket costs Dfl. 37. The train station is *not* within walking distance of the harbor and museums, but taxis and trams located just outside the station can take you to the harbor or museums in about 10 minutes.

By Car   To reach Rotterdam from Amsterdam, take the A4 to The Hague and then the A13 from The Hague to Rotterdam. The whole trip takes about 50 minutes, and parking is available in municipal parking lots (at Dfl. 3 per hour) once you arrive.

Driving can be time efficient but more aggravating than the train since the freeway is a busy one, and Dutch highway roundabouts can be confusing.

Getting Around

By Metro, Tram or Bus   Rotterdam's extensive network of **metro, trams, and buses** has a system of tickets that is the same as Amsterdam. The city has a modern and efficient metro system, which penetrates deep into the outlying suburbs. The 2 lines of the network run roughly east to west and north to south, and intersect at Churchillplein/Beurs. To buy tickets, and to pick up free maps of the metro network, go to the RET office on Stationsplein (facing Centraal Station). Tram fare from the station to the port is Dfl. 3.

By Taxi   Taxis can be ordered by telephone (☎ 10-4626060), in which case they arrive almost immediately, or you can get one at one of the taxi stands at rail stations, major hotels, squares, and near important sights. It costs Dfl. 15 to go from Centraal Station to the water taxi dock in Veerhaven. Taxi fare from the train station to the port is also Dfl. 15.

By Bicycle   Rotterdammers are somewhat reluctant cyclists—and there's a good reason for this. Although the city does have extensive cycle lanes, the traffic on many routes is heavy, which is distracting and somewhat risky. Unless you are really dedicated to biking, stick to trams and the metro in Rotterdam.

Tourist Office   For information about transportation, parking, and tours of the city, call the **Rotterdam VVV** (Coolsingel 67, 3012 AC Rotterdam, ☎ 10-4023200 or 10-4130124).

Organized Tours

Bus Tour of Rotterdam   The VVV Tourist Office offers afternoon 90-minute bus tours of the city between April and September. The tour is recommended if you wish to orient yourself before starting a more in-depth exploration of the city.

Harbor Tours   If you find beauty in industrial shipping—tugs, dredges, tankers, and barges—you'll like ★ **Spido Havenrondvaart's** (Willemsplein, ☎ 10-4135400) 75-minute boat tours of the harbor. The commentary is well informed and the boat is large, stable, comfortable, not too crowded, and attracts an amiable international bunch of visitors. If your time in Rotterdam is limited, see the sights first and take the boat trip last. Tours are offered daily April to September every 30 to 45 minutes from 9:30am to 5pm; daily from March to October at 10am, 11:30am, 1pm, and 2:30pm; and daily November to February at 11am and 2pm. Cost is Dfl. 12 for adults, Dfl. 6 for children under 13. To reach the office take Tram 5 to Willemsplein or the metro to Leuvehaven. Spido also offers Music Dinner Cruises and tours of the Delta.

Other harbor tours include **Rederij Rondvaart Waterstad Delftshaven** (Voorhaven, ☎ 10-2134151), an unusual tour of the waterfront conducted in a bright-orange lifeboat; and **Radar Stoomboot de Nederlander (Party Boat)** (Velkstraat 62, ☎ 10-4146744), which gives 45-minute tours of the river on an old steam tug.

Festivals

Rotterdam stages a few major summer events that are themselves enough reason to plan a visit to the city. Contact the VVV tourist office (see "Getting Around" above) for information on these and other special events in the city.

June's ★★ **Poetry in the Park** (Park at the Euromast), designed to help cultivate a climate of tolerance, is a popular multicultural event. Poets from all over the world (as far away as China) read poetry in their native languages as translators give Dutch or English versions. International foods and arts and crafts are available at the many booths, and bands from such countries as Turkey and Tunisia play on stages set up for the occasion.

Also in June, the **Historic Maritime Pilgrim Week** in Delftshaven is a festival celebrating the successful crossing of the Pilgrims. Delftshaven's atmospheric harbor and charming restaurants and cafes are reason enough to drop in for Pilgrim Week.

In August, ★★ **Day of the Romantic Music** (Park at the Euromast) draws crowds of all ages for a festival that offers romantic music of all kinds (classical piano solos, exotic gypsy bands, big bands, and a folk singer or two). Some like to dress up in romantic clothing—straw hats, white linen suits, summery white dresses—and feast on wine, cheese, and Dutch mussels.

★ **Heineken Jazz and Blues Festival** takes over Rotterdam's waterfront and harbor in August. The music is international, but with few, if any, big names. The biggest draw: reasonably good music, lots of beer, and pleasant restaurants in a waterfront setting.

Exploring the Harbor: A Walking Tour

Many of Rotterdam's museums, interesting architecture, cafes, restaurants, and jazz clubs are near the port. It's pretty easy to explore Rotterdam's harbor on foot in 1 day. Although this is primarily a walking tour, it includes a water-taxi ride to Hotel New York (located on an island in the harbor) and then a ride back to the harbor via the Maritime Museum.

This walk will take you to the harbor to experience its vibrancy, its futuristic architecture, and its international flavor. If you like to breeze through museums, and can take in more than two in 1 day, you will have many choices along the harbor and Witte de Withstraat. But only a few museums really capture the essence of Rotterdam. The most significant for this harbor tour are the **Museum of Ethnology,** the **Maritime Outdoor Museum,** the **"Prins Hendrik" Maritime Museum,** and the **Dutch Architectural Institute.**

Take a morning train from Amsterdam to Rotterdam. It is best to go before or after the commuter crush—before 7:30am or after 9am. When you arrive at Centraal Station, take a cab or tram 5 to Westplein, which brings you to ★★ **Veerhaven** (harbor of the Ponce) and the ① ★ **Museum voor Volkenkunde** or **Museum of Ethnology** (Willemskade 25, ☎ 10-4111055, or 10-4112201). The museum is open Tuesday through Saturday 10am to 5pm; Sunday and holidays 11am to 5pm. Admission is Dfl. 6 for adults and Dfl. 3 for children.

Rotterdam's museum of geography and ethnology occupies a distinguished neoclassical building that was originally the clubhouse of the Royal Netherlands Yacht Club. The museum displays art, artifacts, music, and films from Indonesia, Africa, Asia, America, and the Islamic world and devotes considerable space to temporary exhibits on festivals and rituals. Its goal is to foster intracultural appreciation and tolerance.

After leaving the museum, turn right for a walk around Rotterdam's genteel harbor, the **Veerhaven,** with its tidy gardens, stately old merchant's houses, and the exclusive yacht club, ② **The Row and Sail Society (Roei-Zeil Ver. De Maas)** at no. 1 Veerdam. Walk along the harbor to admire the beautiful boats—schooners, sailing vessels, and old freighters ingeniously rebuilt for recreational purposes.

For a quiet boat ride across the harbor and a terrific view, take the **Water Taxi** (Mon—Fri 8am—10pm, Sat–Sun 9am—midnight; Dfl. 3.5 one-way from Veerhaven to Hotel New York, and Dfl. 4.5 one-way from Hotel New York to Leuvehaven) to ③ **Hotel New York.** This architecturally and interesting historic hotel is located in the former Holland-Amerika Line building on an island in the River Maas. To take the water taxi, go down to the dock beneath The Row and

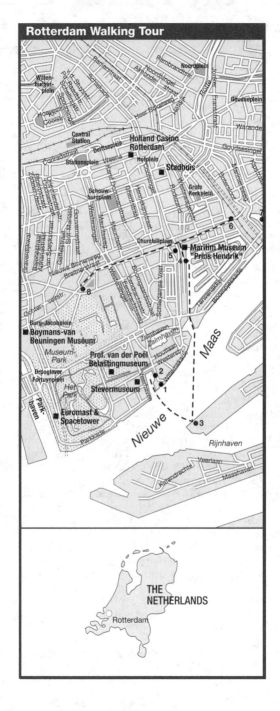

Rotterdam Walking Tour

Walenburgerplein

Noordplein
Rembrandtstraat
Noordsingel
Alfrondo
straat
Banierstraat
Route
Johnke
Schiekade
KD
Coolsf.
Hoogst
Goudseplein
Heer Bokelweg
Kortek.
Warande
Central
Station
Conradstraat
Stationsplein Weena
Delftseplein
Holland Casino
Rotterdam
Hofplein
Goudsesingel
Stadhuis
Schouw-
burgplein
Pompenburg
Heer Bokelstraat
Schowburgplein
Heer Doormanstraat
Mauritsweg
Hennekijnstraat
Grote
Kerkplein
Westersingel
Mariniersweg
Westerstr.
Churchillplein
Nieuwe Binnenweg
Breitnerstr.
5
4
Maritim Museum
"Prins Hendrik"
6
7
Gravendijkwal
8
Gaffelstr.
Witte de Withstraat
Wijnhaven
's-Gravendijkwal
Schiedamsedijk
Terwenakker
Boompjeskade
Burg-Jacobplein
Boymans-van
Beuningen Museum
Museum
Park
Zalmhaven
Zalmhaven
Houttuin
Westerstr.
Maas
Prof. van der Poël
Belastingmuseum
2
Droogleever
Fortuynplein
Het
Park
Stevermuseum
1
Park-
haven
Euromast &
Spacetower
Parkkade
Nieuwe
3
Rijnhaven
Veerlaan
Katendrechtse
Maashaven

THE
NETHERLANDS

Rotterdam

Sail Society. If no water taxis are present, you can call one by phoning the **Hotel New York** (☎ 10-4390500).

The water taxi is a cozy, covered boat with polished wood and comfortable cushions that allows you to see the harbor, avoid the tourist crowds, and travel in style (all for only Dfl. 3.5). The water taxi goes to and from Hotel New York and 2 harbors—Veerhaven and Leuvehaven. Begin at Veerhaven, visit Hotel New York, and then return to **Leuvehaven,** where you will find 2 maritime museums.

As you cross, take in the terrific view of the south bank of the harbor and its major project of urban renewal and gentrification: the new luxury housing, office buildings, and cafes, which will make Rotterdam even more modern in style and atmosphere.

★★ **Hotel New York** (Koninginnenhoofd 1, ☎ 10-4390500, fax 10-4842701) is a curious combination of grand hotel, turn-of-the-century office building, and functionalist design experiment that provides a magnificent view of the waterfront, the Rotterdam skyline, and, in early evening, beautiful sunsets. From the taxi, you'll step off onto a pier lined with freight containers and see the impressive 19thC former head-office of the Holland-Amerika Line looming before you. The cafe and 2 restaurants here all have exhilarating views. They are also unique is design and atmosphere: There is an outdoor restaurant with an open grill and a bar made of old freight container boxes, and an airy indoor cafe-restaurant. The interior of the hotel is itself an architectural museum. The metal work on the central staircase is over a century old. The decor is both 19thC and contemporary functional—amidst the grandeur you can see exposed pipes and insulation.

The history of Hotel New York is as moving as the bombing of the harbor. Between 1873 and the 1930s, many European immigrants left for America from Rotterdam to escape religious persecution and poverty. In 1873, the **NV Nederlandsch Amerikaanse Stoomvaart Maatschapping** (NASM) was established as a steamship line whose primary destination was New York City. The company became known as the **Holland-Amerika Lijn** in 1896, and reached its peak in transporting European immigrants from Rotterdam to New York between 1901 and 1914 and became a symbol of escape to freedom.

A boarding house for immigrants, named Hotel New York after the destination of which they dreamed, was established not far from where the ships departed from the Rotterdam harbor. The current—and far more luxurious—Hotel New York took over this name. The hotel takes good care of its contemporary patrons; each of the 72 rooms has a panoramic view and exotic, finely woven cotton sheets (that can be purchased for Dfl. 80 in the gift shop downstairs). Hotel New York is a fine place to have coffee or lunch; the menu is varied and you can order full dinners or à la carte.

After a rest and exploration of the hotel, take the water taxi to Leuvehaven. You will pass underneath the new **Erasmus Bridge** that's currently being built to connect central Rotterdam with the modernized southern bank. The taxi docks conveniently at the ④ ★★ **Maritiem Buitenmuseum Leuvehaven** (Leuvehaven 50-72, ☎ 070-4048072; open Mon–Sat 10am–12:30pm and 1–4pm, Sun 12am–4pm; metro Blaak, tram 3, 6, 7 to Churchillplein/Beurs, or water taxi from Hotel New York; admission free). The Leuvehaven quay has become an open-air maritime museum, with berths for historic commercial vessels and with cranes and repair yards sprawling along the waterfront. Occasional exhibitions are organized in the bright-red lighthouse, **Het Lage Licht.** You can watch the 1917 sailing ship *Ooster Schelde* being repaired along iron catwalks inside the repair sheds (enter at street level).

The open-air museum is adjacent to the ⑤ ★★ **"Prins Hendrik" Maritiem Museum** (Leuvehaven 1, ☎ 10-4132680; open Tues–Sat 10am–5pm, Sun and holidays 11am–5pm; metro or tram 1, 3, 4, 6, 7 to Churchillplein/Beurs, or water taxi from Hotel New York; admission: adults Dfl. 6, children Dfl. 3). Holland's oldest maritime museum, founded by the seafaring Prins Hendrik in 1852, occupies a striking modern building overlooking animated Leuvehaven. The museum shows a series of dioramas illustrating the evolution of the harbor from the 15thC to the present, with various special effects including medieval street noises. There is a special exhibition for children 4 to 14 entitled "Professor Plons." As well as displaying a fascinating assortment of maps, globes, paintings, and ship models, the museum has a small fleet of 19th and 20thC barges and steam tugs moored in the harbor (see **Buiten-museum** below). The **Museumcafé** is in a glass-walled wedge of the building that looks like the bow of a ship.

When you leave the museum, go right and follow the street in front of the museum to Blaak, where you will turn right for a short walk to the architecturally innovative cubical apartment complex of ⑥ ★★ **Het**

Blaakse Bos (Overblaak 70, ☎ 10-4142285; Dec–Feb: Fri–Sun 11am–5pm. Mar–Oct daily 11am–5pm; admission: adults: Dfl. 3.50, children Dfl. 2.50). The cubes, otherwise known as *Kijk-Kubus,* come together at bizarre, dizzying angles and are built on a bridge straddling a main road. Model apartments are open to the public, so you can have the direct experience of what life is like inside the sloping walls and slanted windows.

As you emerge from this world askew, the market Grotenmarkt will be on your left and the river and ⑦ ★ **Oude Haven,** the old harbor, on your right. You are only a few minute's walk from Oude Haven, which is packed with old industrial vessels and harbor equipment. Devastated by a Nazi air raid in 1940, Rotterdam's old harbor area now contains some of the most extraordinary modern architecture in the Netherlands. Along with the cubical cluster of apartments that you just left, Oude Haven includes the pyramidal **Gemeentebibliotheek** (public library) designed by Van den Broek and Bakema Bureau, which has as its hallmark a tangle of yellow ventilation ducts on its exterior.

Oude Haven has old boats, outdoor terraces—and lots of tourists. But the cafes and harbor vistas are usually worth tolerating the crowds. If you become claustrophobic and want a more peaceful version of Rotterdam's harbor, you can either return to Veerhaven or escape to the ★★ **Delftshaven,** from which the **Pilgrim Fathers** departed for America in 1620 (see "Other Sights And Attractions" below).

For a visit to **The Netherlands Architectural Institute (NAI),** backtrack to Blaakse Bos and make your way toward the futuristic model of a flying saucer hovering just above the ground: It is the top of the subway station. You will need to buy a Dfl. 3 ticket to go 2 stops to **Eendrachtsplein** (in the direction of Marconiplein). At Eendrachtsplein, go upstairs and follow signs to the architectural museum. You will emerge on a square that intersects with West Blaak. Go east (with the Park Hotel on your left and fashionable shops on your right) about 109 yards (100m) toward the museum—a curved concrete wall standing on concrete pillars behind which you will see a glass building, the ⑧ ★★ **Nederlands Architectuur Institute** (Museumpark, ☎ 10-4366975; Tues–Sat 10am–5pm, Sun 11am–5pm; tram 5 to Witte de Withstraat; admission: adults Dfl. 7.50, children

Kijk-Kubus

Dfl. 4). The institute is featuring an urban-planning exhibit entitled "Rotterdam 2045," which is a bit dry but still interesting. More compelling are the exhibitions on recent and ancient Dutch architecture and engineering, showing how the Dutch have ingeniously created land from mud and altered the landscape by the use of windmills and dikes. The sophistication of Dutch engineering and architecture, even as early as the 1600s, is a marvel. Beautiful old maps show how one-third of the country was once submerged. Windmills, locks, and hoists are also displayed. Other exhibitions show the new Dutch design, and the building itself, designed by Jo Coenen, is a good example of innovative, contemporary architecture.

Leave the NAI through the front entrance and you will find yourself facing **Museumpark,** an ultramodern park with shells instead of grass, and many choices for dinner in the area (see "Dining" below).

Other Sights & Attractions

★★ Boymans-van Beuningen Museum
Museumpark 18-20. ☎ 10-4419400. Open Tues–Sat 10am–5pm, Sun 11am–5pm. Admission: Adults Dfl. 7.50, children Dfl. 4.
This museum has a fine collection of art from the 14thC to the present including such artists as Brueghel, Bosch, Rembrandt, Cézanne, Picasso, Dalí, and Magritte.

Euromast
Parkhaven 20. ☎ 10-4364811. Open July–Aug: Tues–Sat 10am–10:30pm, Mon–Sun 10am–7pm (Space Tower 10am–6pm); Apr–June and Sept 10am–7pm; Oct–Mar 10am–5pm. Admission: Adults Dfl. 14.50, children Dfl. 9.

The 560-foot Euromast offers terrific views of the harbor—and vertigo if you fear heights. (I prefer to view the harbor from the Hotel New York myself.) The lower part of this tall, thin "mast" has a crow's nest with 2 restaurants—one self-service and one more elaborate. The Space Tower includes a slowly revolving drum that ascends to the top of the mast, offering a magnificent panorama. The inexpensive self-service restaurant offers sandwiches and drinks from 10am to 7pm. The more elaborate French restaurant is open Tuesday to Saturday from 6 to 10pm; a 3-course dinner (including wine and coffee) costs Dfl. 110.

★★ Delftshaven

Transportation: Metro to Delftshaven or tram 4, 6 to Spanjaardstraat.

Delftshaven is charming, compact, and one of the few parts of Rotterdam to escape the 1940 bombing. The peaceful waterways and relaxed cafe scene feels a lot like Amsterdam. I find its friendly restaurants and sidewalk cafes a welcome haven after a day at the busy, industrial harbor or an afternoon of tourist crowds at Oude Haven.

The tiny port of Delftshaven was founded by the city of Delft in 1389 and remained within its jurisdiction until 1825, when it was granted independent status, only to lose it 61 years later to Rotterdam. Two decorated gable stones mounted on the wall of the 17thC **Zakkendragershuisje** (House of the Guild of Grain Porters) recall that Delftshaven was once an important whaling and fishing port. Its main claim to fame was that it was here that the **Pilgrim Fathers** departed for America in 1620. Their ship, the *Speedwell,* proved unseaworthy, however, and they put into Plymouth a few days later. From Plymouth they set sail again on the *Mayflower.*

Situated in a handsome 19thC warehouse, the historical museum **De Dubbele Palmboom** (Voorhaven 12, ☎ 10-4761533; open Tues–Sat 10am–5pm, Sun 1–5pm) contains relics relating to local trades such as peat-cutting, shipbuilding, and *jenever* (gin) distilling. Excellent information sheets are available in English.

Dining

Within a few blocks of the **Museumpark** are 2 excellent, but expensive, restaurants, **De Engel** (Eendrachtsweg 16, ☎ 10-41338256), a French restaurant in a luxurious old merchant house, and **De Harmonie** (Westersingel 95, ☎ 10-4363610), a Mediterranean/French restaurant with a large garden terrace. You can find some inexpensive Middle Eastern restaurants of varying quality nearby on Witte de Withstraat, or you can venture further afield to explore the inexpensive ethnic restaurants on Nieuwe Binnenweg. The more reliable, middle-priced restaurants (Dfl. 55–65) are a 10- to 15-minute walk—but well worth the effort. Near Veerhaven, you'll find **Zinc** (Calandstraat 12, ☎ 10-4366579), a French restaurant with African and Asian influences, and **Café Loos** (Westplein 1, ☎ 10-4117723), a French restaurant with German and Italian influences.

Another option is to eat near **Het Park** and the **Euromast,** which are about a 15-minute walk from the museums. **Heerenhuys de Heuvel** (Baden Powell-laan 12, ☎ 10-4364249) is a cozy, midpriced restaurant in the park with a French/Mediterranean kitchen and a lovely outdoor terrace. Further north, approaching the ethnic and interesting Nieuwe Binnenweg, are the moderately priced eetcafés **Lux** ('s Gravendijkwal 133, ☎ 10-4762206), serving Italian food, and **Hoezo** ('s Gravendijkwal 140b, ☎ 10-4366700), serving French-international cuisine. Both of these restaurants are close to one of Rotterdam's best jazz cafes, **Dizzy** ('s Gravendijkwal 127a). Although Nieuwe Binnenweg beckons with its cafes and inexpensive ethnic restaurants, do not go west from 's Gravendijkwal on this street, since it rapidly turns scruffy—and dangerous.

THE BASICS

Before You Go
Tourist Offices

You can obtain maps, brochures, and other information from the **Netherlands Board of Tourism** (**NBT**)
before you leave for Holland. This can be helpful in
planning parts of your trip in advance and can alert you
to special exhibits, concerts, bicycle trips, train passes,
or festivals and events that you may not otherwise hear
about. In the United States, the main information
office of the NBT is at 225 North Michigan Avenue,
Suite 326, Chicago, IL 60601, ☎ 312-819-0300 or
800-953-8824, fax 312-819-1740. Other NBT Offices
that provide helpful information (but not brochures)
are: NBT New York, 355 Lexington Avenue, 21st floor,
New York, NY 10017, ☎ 212-370-7369, and NBT
Los Angeles, 9841 Airport Boulevard., Suite 103, Los
Angeles, CA 90045, ☎ 310-348-9339, fax 310-348-9344.

Documents

For citizens of the United States, Canada, Australia,
New Zealand, and European Community countries, a
valid passport is the only document required for visits
not exceeding 3 months. For some other nationals a
visa must be obtained in advance from a Dutch consulate in the country of departure. American citizens
wishing to stay longer than 3 months need a residence
permit (*verblijfsvergunning*). This should be obtained in
advance since you will not be able to apply for a permit
once in the Netherlands; contact the **Dutch Embassy**
in Washington, DC (4200 Linnean Ave., NW, Washington, DC 20008-3896, ☎ 202-244-5300, fax 202-
362-3430), or a **Dutch Consulate** in a major city
near you.

European Community citizens who have found a job
in the Netherlands may apply for residence permits at

the Alien's Police (*Vreemdelingenpolitie*) in Amsterdam (Waterlooplein 9, 1002 CS Amsterdam, ☎ 20-6919100).

Visitors arriving by private boat should report to the nearest customs office on entering and leaving the Netherlands.

Money
Currency
The unit of currency in the Netherlands is the **guilder**—written as *f, Hfl,* and *Dfl* (a holdover from the days when the florin was the coin of the realm), or internationally indicated by NLG. The guilder is divided into 100 **cents** (ct), although 1-cent coins are no longer in use. There are coins for 5ct (known as *stuivers*), 10ct (*dubbeltjes*), 25ct (*kwartjes*), Dfl. 1 (*guilders*), Dfl. 2.5 (*rijksdaalders*), and Dfl. 5 (*vijf guilders*). Brightly colored banknotes, with embossed markings for the blind, are issued in denominations of Dfl. 5, Dfl. 10, Dfl. 25, Dfl. 50, Dfl. 100, Dfl. 250, and Dfl. 1,000. It is always a good idea to bring some Dutch money (preferably 100–250 guilders) with you into the country to cover immediate expenses and to save you from long lines at airport banks. There are no restrictions on the amount of currency that may be imported or exported.

The safest way to handle money in Amsterdam is to use traveler's checks, credit cards, or ATM cards. Don't carry large amounts of cash since pickpockets can be a problem. The best exchange rates are usually found at ATM machines (see below). Using an ATM card with either traveler's checks or a credit card makes dealing with currency and financial transactions much easier and more efficient.

ATM Machines
At one time banks offered the best exchange rates, but times have changed and **automated teller machines** (**ATMs**) now secure you the most favorable rate of exchange. ATMs can be found at airports, railway stations, some post offices, and at many other central locations throughout Amsterdam. Approximately 250,000 Automated Teller Machines (ATMs) in 100 countries are tied to international networks like Cirrus and Plus. By using your bank card to withdraw money you will debit the amount from your account. When using an ATM abroad, the money will be in local currency. Note that international withdrawal fees will be higher than domestic—ask your bank for specifics. To use your bank card at an ATM you will need a Personal Identification Number (PIN). Contact your bank to

program your PIN for the area you will be visiting. Most ATMs outside the United States require a 4-digit PIN.

To receive a directory for Cirrus ATM's exact locations call 800-424-7787; for Plus locations call 800-336-8472. You can also access the Visa/PLUS International ATM Locator Guide through Internet: http://www.visa.com/visa.

Exchanging Money

Though ATMs give the best exchange rates, banks will give you better rates than shops, hotels, and bureaux de change. Currency may be changed, and traveler's checks and Eurocheques cashed, at all banks and at the **Grenswisselkantoren** (**GWK** bureaux de change) found in many rail stations. Branches of the GWK have the advantage of being open longer hours than ordinary banks and they allow you to use major credit cards to obtain cash. The one at Centraal Station and the one at the Schiphol Airport Railway Station (downstairs from the airport) are open 24 hours. Other exchange bureaus include **Change Express,** with branches at Damrak 26 (☎ 20-6246682), Kalverstraat 150 (☎ 20-6278087), and Leidseplein 1 (☎ 20-6221425), and **Thomas Cook,** with branches at Dam 23-25 (☎ 20-6250922), Leidseplein 31a (☎ 20-6267000), and Damrak 1-5 (☎ 20-6203236). Thomas Cook also offers exchange rate information and locations of offices; call 800-CURRENCY. Post offices, some tourist offices, long-distance trains, and major department stores will also handle foreign exchange. You may have to show your passport when changing money.

Traveler's Checks

Traveler's checks issued by all major companies, including **American Express** and **Visa** (☎ 800-227-6811), are widely recognized. Make sure you read the instructions included with your traveler's checks and note separately the serial numbers of your checks and the telephone number to call in case of loss. Specialist traveler's check companies such as **American Express** (main Amsterdam office ☎ 20-5401999, branch offices ☎ 20-5207777 and 20-6714141) provide extensive local refund facilities through their own offices or agents. American Express also provides traveler's checks that can be signed by either of 2 people.

Credit Cards

The major credit cards such as American Express, Diners Club, MasterCard, and Visa are widely, although not universally, accepted in shops, hotels, and restaurants in Amsterdam. Most large establishments take credit cards, but recently more and more small shops, restaurants, and hotels are also accepting the major credit cards. **Eurocheques,** written in guilders, are the most common method of payment for larger sums. American citizens who also bank in Europe can make use of the Eurocheque Encashment process whereby they can cash personal checks with a Eurocheque Encashment Card.

Getting Money from Home

Located in more than 70 countries, agents at **American Express MoneyGram** (☎ 800-543-4080 in the US) can wire money around the world. Senders must go to an agent in person. Up to $1,000 can be charged on a credit card (only Discover, MasterCard, or Visa—you can't use American Express). Amounts over $1,000 must be paid in cash; the maximum amount for a single transaction is $10,000. Recipients must present a reference number (phoned in from sender) and identification to pick up the cash. The main American Express Office in Amsterdam is at Amsteldijk 166, 1078 AX Amsterdam (☎ 20-5401999, open 9am–5pm, Mon–Fri). Branch offices are located at Damrak 66 (☎ 20-520777, open 9am–5pm, Mon–Fri), and Van Baerlestraat 38 (☎ 20-6714141, open 9am–5pm Mon–Fri and 9am–noon Sat).

Western Union works in a similar fashion, except that they also allow customers to wire money over the phone by using their credit cards (MasterCard and Visa only). Call 800-325-6000 for its worldwide locations. In Amsterdam, Telecenter PTT Telecom, Raadhuisstraat 48, fax 20-6263871, has telephone, telex, and telegram services.

Fees for both MoneyGram and Western Union range from 5% to 10%, depending on the amount sent and method of payment.

Customs & Duties

You are allowed to bring in 1 liter of hard liquor, 1 carton of cigarettes, and as much foreign currency as you like. To protect yourself from unnecessary duty charges when you are leaving the country, keep the receipts for any new valuables you brought with you into the country so they are not mistaken by customs as items you purchased while in the Netherlands.

Prohibited or restricted goods include drugs, weapons, meat, fruit, plants, flowers, and protected animals.

Dogs and cats brought into the Netherlands from countries other than Belgium and Luxembourg must have a certificate of vaccination from the official veterinary service of the country of departure.

Travel & Medical Insurance

It is advisable to take out an insurance policy covering loss of deposits paid to airlines, hotels, tour operators, etc., and emergency costs, such as special tickets home, as well as a medical insurance policy. But before taking out any additional insurance, check to make sure that you are not already covered for travel by medical, automobile, home-owners, auto club, credit card, or travel club policies.

Medicare will cover Americans only if they are traveling in Mexico or Canada, so if you rely mainly on Medicare, you may need some temporary coverage during your stay in Europe.

If you find that you do need insurance, a short term policy covering both lost luggage and broken bones is the most cautious way to go. Three companies providing this kind of coverage are: **Access American International** at ☎ 800-284-8300 and 212-949-5960, **Travel Guard** at ☎ 715-345-0505 or 800-826-1300, and **Mutual of Omaha** at ☎ 402-345-2400 or 800-228-9792.

Those Americans with medical insurance are entitled, by law, to medical insurance coverage in Holland. For more information, contact **ANOZ Verzekerkingen** (Health Service–Foreign Affairs Department), P.O. Box 85315, 3508 AN Utrecht, ☎ 30-565300, fax 30-565489.

Medical Precautions

You might want to prepare for possible medical problems by packing prescription and nonprescription drugs you might need (Holland is stricter about some over-the-counter remedies). It's also a good idea to bring refills or prescriptions of generic versions of any drugs you might require. If you suffer from a chronic illness, wear a **Medic Alert Identification Tag** to make things easier for medical personnel who may not speak English and to give foreign doctors access to the Medic Alert hotline in order to obtain your medical history. For further information, call the **Medic Alert Foundation** at ☎ 800-432-5378.

If you do become ill in the Netherlands, the VVV Tourist Office, the **Central Medical Service** (☎ 06-35032042), or your hotel concierge can help you find a doctor. For medical emergencies, you can always dial 06-11 for an ambulance. (Bear in mind that Amsterdam streets are narrow and sometimes blocked and that ambulance response times are not ideal. If you have a serious health problem, stay in a hotel with easy street-access that is relatively close to medical facilities.)

When packing , consider things that you might need and could not easily replace during your stay in Holland: extra glasses, over-the-counter medications (which are sometimes difficult to buy without a prescription in Holland). Include a list of your medications by their generic name to make them easier for Dutch doctors and pharmacists to identify them should you need refills. You might consider refilling some of your prescriptions to have a standby supply while you are traveling. Bring a bee-sting kit if you have an allergy. And take it with you on walks or bicycle trips, or even at cafe terraces.

When to Go
Climate
If you like tulips, sailing, or sightseeing on foot or by bicycle, the best time to visit Holland is between April and September. After late September the weather can get gray, wet, and cold. Holland has a maritime climate with relatively mild but windy winters and unpredictable summers that are sometimes cool and sometimes hot. To an American Midwesterner, Dutch winters (Nov–mid-March) are almost balmy, with temperatures staying between 30° and 45°F. However, even if the temperature rarely falls below freezing, the wintry combination of rain and wind can get dreary and chilling. Even late August can become cold and blustery enough (45–50°F) for jackets and scarves. During the coldest months, January and February, the temperatures occasionally fall below freezing for days at a time, resulting in the canals and lakes freezing solid enough for ice-skating.

March usually marks the end of winter, and spring finally appears in April, although the temperatures can hover unpredictably between 45° and 50°F. Tulip season begins in late April or early May and usually lasts through late May. The colder the winter, the later tulip season begins.

Although the Dutch may apologize for (and complain about) the wet, unreliable weather, it does create exceptionally dramatic, partly cloudy skies known, by some Nederlanders, as "the Dutch sky."

The summer months still have cool, rainy days and plenty of "Dutch sky," but there are also warm, sunny days where temperatures reach into the 80s. During summer, you can experience several climates in 1 day with temperatures ranging from 65°F and rainy to 75°F and clear.

Travelers who want the latest weather updates for locations around the world can call 1-900-WEATHER (95¢ a minute).

The least expensive time to visit Amsterdam is from mid-January through March. During these months airlines often announce special-sale fares (sometimes at the last minute), and hotels and car rentals are much less expensive than they are in spring and summer. In April and May—tulip season—prices go up again for hotels, car rentals, and most airlines. However, **Martinair,** a Dutch charter company, offers inexpensive air fares from April through October.

The least comfortable time to visit Amsterdam is in August when the hotels are jammed with tourists and conventioneers.

Calendar of Events

January/February
Late January–early February: *Film Festival Rotterdam.* International film festival of noncommercial films, Rotterdam. ☎ 10-4118080, fax 10-4135132.

February 25: *Commemoration of the February dockworkers strike* against Nazi occupation in 1941 at J. D. Meijerplein, at the *Dokwerker* statue, Amsterdam.

March
March 15–March 16: *Blues Festival Amsterdam* at the Meevart. MV Olderen Bluespromotion, ☎ 20-6961111, fax 20-6961111. Program features first-rate American blues and R&B bands.

April
3rd weekend in April: *National Museumweek.* A weekend when 400 museums in the Netherlands offer free or greatly reduced admission. Amsterdam and several cities. ☎ 71-133265, fax 71-140441.

April 30: *The Queens Birthday, Koninginnedag.* The Queen descends on rural Dutch communities while anarchy reigns in Amsterdam. Amsterdam declares a "free market" where anyone can sell anything. The streets become jammed with thousands of makeshift stalls where enterprising locals sell used clothing, old books, 1950s furniture, and ethnic food. Amsterdammers party—especially in the Jordaan.

May

May 4: *Remembrance Day.* Ceremonies are held to honor the dead of World War II at the National Monument on the Dam in Amsterdam.

May 5: *Liberation Day.* Commemorates the day the Netherlands was liberated from Nazi occupation during World War II.

2nd weekend in May: *National Windmill Day.* The Dutch take to their bikes and visit working windmills in the countryside and towns. Sarphatistraat 634, 1018 AV Amsterdam, ☎ 20-6238703.

End of May: *Opening of the herring season* in ports such as Schevenningen. Dutch gourmets crowd around the fish stalls to sample the new batch of cured young herring. The very first batch, however, is presented to the Queen in The Hague.

June

June–August: *The Royal Palace,* Dam Square, Amsterdam, ☎ 20-6248698, opens to the public.

June: *Holland Festival* brings cultural events including opera, concerts, dance, theater, and film to Amsterdam. ☎ 20-62765566, fax 20-6203459.

June: *KUNST RAI modern contemporary art fair* with 100 galleries represented. RAI, Europaplein 8, Amsterdam, ☎ 20-5491212, fax 20-6464469.

Late June–August: *Cheese and craft market* takes place on Thursday mornings from 10am to noon in Gouda. Gouda is located 29km southwest of Amsterdam—a 50-minute train ride from Amsterdam's Centraal Station. The market is held at the Waag on the market square—about a 15-minute walk from the station. Contact St. Gouda Hart van Holland, Markt 27, 2801 JJ Gouda, ☎ 01820-11300.

July

July: *North Sea Jazz Festival.* Over a thousand accomplished jazz musicians perform on more than 13 stages in Den Haag. ☎ 70-3548000, or 70-3512851.

July–August: *Open-air concerts and theater in Vondelpark,* Amsterdam. For general information June–Aug, call ☎ 20-6731499; for open-air theater, call ☎ 20-5237790; for Muziektent, call ☎ 20-6731499. (See "Amsterdam After Dark" for more details.)

August

See also "June" above.

August: *Sneekweek.* A major sailing festival on the 'Sneeker' lake in the northern province of Friesland, home of crusty sailors and fishermen. Includes a naval review, fair, and fireworks. VVV SNEEK, ☎ 51-5414096, fax 51-5423703.

End of August on Friday evening: *The Pulitzer Concert.* The Pulitzer Hotel puts on a free, open-air classical concert on a barge on the Prinsengracht canal (in front of the hotel). Admission free. Prinsengracht 315-331, Amsterdam, ☎ 20-5235235.

Last weekend in August: *Uitmarkt* in Amsterdam. Theatrical groups, opera companies, and dance troupes present forthcoming cultural attractions throughout the city at special stages set up in squares or parks. Admission free. AUB Uitboro, Leidseplein 26, Amsterdam, ☎ 20-6211211, or 20-6268811.

September

Early September: *Open monuments day.* Nearly 3,000 public buildings throughout The Netherlands are open to the public free of charge. Look for special flags that mark the buildings, many of which are private homes and office buildings of historical significance. Open Monumenten dag Stichting, ☎ 20-4205557.

September: *Parade/Procession Bloemencorso Aalsmeer.* A parade of flower-covered floats begins in Aalsmeer and passes through Amsterdam. ☎ 297-334567.

Mid September: *The Jordaan Festival,* 2 lively festivals in 2 different parts of the Jordaan. One is centered on Westerstraat and resembles a street fair with booths, games, beer, and plenty of Amsterdammer music traditional to the Jordaan. Egelantiersgracht hosts a similar party, with beer, games, and more Amsterdammer music.

November

Mid November: *Arrival of St. Nicholas.* The Dutch Santa Claus, a friend to children, arrives by boat at Centraal Station and parades through Amsterdam on a white horse, distributing candy to children. Call the VVV Tourist Office for dates and times, ☎ 20-6266444 or 20-6211211.

December

December 5: The Dutch gather in their homes to celebrate *Pakjesavond* (Parcel Evening), otherwise known as *Sinterklassavond* (St. Nicholas's Eve), by exchanging gifts and reading rhymes they have written to go along with the presents.

December 31: *Oudejaarsavond* (*New Year's Eve*) is celebrated with parties and fireworks. Some bars stay open all night.

What to Pack

In the spring and summer, packing for Amsterdam is a challenge since it means planning for warm summer days as well as for cool, rainy, or windy weather. Consequently, it is difficult to travel light. For travel during June through September, pack a sweater or two and a jacket to break the wind or, better yet, a raincoat to fend off both wind and rain. Either bring a fold-up umbrella, or be prepared to buy one when you arrive. For warm days, bring summer clothes. You might want to bring a bathing suit for a quick side-trip to the beach or shorts for biking in Vondelpark. For fall, winter, and spring, bring a warm coat, a warm sweater, and a hat.

Bring shoes that you can walk in—and that can resist rain and cobblestones. This, too, can be a challenge if you wish to remain fashionable. Thin-soled shoes don't wear well on rough Dutch roads and spiked heels are treacherous. For walking, your best bets are shoes with thick soles and good tread.

Aside from a penchant for good Italian shoes, Amsterdammers are casual dressers. Blue jeans are acceptable in all but the most chic restaurants. But then, what is chic depends on point of view and neighborhood. In the Jordaan, this could mean well-cut blue jeans, a sweater, and stylish shoes. If your plans include exclusive restaurants or an evening at the theater, the casino, or the Concertgebouw, pack to dress up. (For men, this means a suit and sometimes a tie. Dress is a little more flexible for women.)

If you plan to travel by train, you will have to carry your own luggage, so you may want to avoid heavy, cumbersome suitcases. Streamlined suitcases on wheels are suitable, as are fabric shoulder bags. A well-balanced, adequately padded backpack is always a practical choice.

Tours
Special Interest Tours

Passages Unlimited, Inc. (10 Liberty Square, Boston MA 02109, ☎ 800-232-2939, fax 617-482-1422) offers horticulture tours as well as art and architecture tours. **Expo Garden Tours** (145 4th Avenue, Suite

4A, New York, NY 10003, ☎ 800-448-2685, fax 212-260-6913) runs garden and horticultural sightseeing programs.

More luxurious tours are available from **Travcoa** (☎ 800-992-2004), which provides specialty tours on art and culture; **Abercrombie & Kent** (☎ 800-323-7308, fax 708-954-3324) offers barge cruises of the canals and rivers; **AESU** (☎ 410-323-4416, fax 410-323-4498) offers specialty tours for the 18- to 35-year-old market; and **Avanti Destination** (☎ 503-295-1100, or 800-422-5053, fax 503-295-2723) offers reasonable city packages.

Backroads Bicycle Touring (☎ 510-527-1555, or 800-245-3874) and **Euro-Bike Tours, Inc.** (☎ 815-758-8851, or 800-321-6060) offer specialty bicycle tours. You can also find Dutch bicycling tours originating in Friesland or in the lake region around the Vecht River (for more information, call the **Netherlands Board of Tourism,** 312-819-1636).

Tours that specialize in art and architecture are available through **Academic Travel Abroad** (32100 Grace Street NW, Washington, DC 20007, ☎ 800-556-67896) and **Art Horizons International** (369 Lexington Avenue, 11th floor, New York, NY 10017, ☎ 212-682-9419).

You can arrange jazz tours to the North Sea Jazz Festival or the Heineken Jazz festival through **Ciao! Travel** (☎ 619-297-8112, fax 619-297-8114).

General Tours

The following tour companies operate international tours: Deluxe tours can be booked at **Tauck Tours,** 11 Wilton Road, Westport, CT 06881 (☎ 203-226-6911 or 800-468-2825) and **Maupintour,** Box 807, Lawrence, KS 66044 (☎ 913-843-1211 or 800-255-4266). In the first class category, tour operators include **Collette Tours,** 162 Middle Street, Pawtucket, RI 02860 (☎ 401-728-3805 or 800-717-9191), **Domenico Tours,** Domenico Building, 751 Broadway, Bayonne, NJ 07002 (☎ 800-554-8687), and **Globus,** 5301 South Federal Circle, Littleton, CO 80125 (☎ 303-797-2800, or 800-221-0090). Globus also operates a budget tour company called **Cosmos,** which is reachable at the same address and phone number.

Independent Packages

Many airlines and tour operators offer packages that can be less expensive than making individual book-ings. Airlines usually offer a package of airfare and accommodations with or without car rental. Check **American Airlines FlyAAway Vacations** (☎ 800-321-2121) and **United Airlines Vacation Planning Center** (☎ 800-328-6877). Before you make your choice, find out if any airlines are offering a special sale on fares (you might save more money by booking a discounted flight and arranging your own lodging). If you plan on renting a car at your destination, check whether an airline has a tie-in package with a car-rental agency that will give you a money-saving rate.

In all package deals, find out what is or is not included in the price, such as airport transfers and taxes.

Reservations for Special Events

To secure tickets for exhibits, plays, or concerts before you leave the United States, contact the **Amsterdam Uit Bureau,** Leidseplein 26 (Ticket Office), 1017 PT Amsterdam. You can call them at ☎ 20-6211211 for information and bookings. Ticket offices that arrange bookings by phone are **Kaartenhuis** (☎ 1-5136050) and the **Netherlands Reservations Center** (☎ 70-3175454, open Mon–Fri 8am–8pm), which makes definite reservations only for hotels and cultural events in Amsterdam. The **Amsterdam VVV Tourist Office** (Stationsplein 10) can book tickets for you at their office, but only in person—not by phone. For other information on bookings call AUB Uit Buro (☎ 20-6211211) or stop by the Uit buro office on Leidseplein and pick up a copy of *What's On in Amsterdam* (the VVV magazine) or *Uitkrant,* a free monthly in Dutch that provides a good list of cultural events. Cinema listings are available in English at the Uit Buro office.

For Travelers with Disabilities

The Netherlands Board of Tourism publishes a useful booklet entitled *The Handicapped,* which lists hotels, restaurants, and sights accessible to people with disabilities. Contact the NBT in Chicago at ☎ 312-819-0300 or 800-953-8824. Special tours and water-sports camps are available to handicapped adults and children. Other agencies to contact for more information include: **Mobility International Nederland** (Postbus 165, 6560 AD Groesbeek, ☎ 8891-71744) and **Association for Water Sports for the Handicapped** (SWG) (Postbus 157, 1600 AD Enkhuizen, ☎ 2280-12828).

In Amsterdam there are numerous obstacles to mobility, such as steep, narrow staircases in old buildings, and uneven, narrow sidewalks often blocked with cars. Although some restaurants and hotels are at ground-level and are thus accessible to wheelchairs, their bathrooms are frequently too small to allow wheelchair access. Sometimes bathrooms are up or down a narrow flight of stairs. Many of the major hotels have wheelchair-accessible restaurants and bathrooms, but only 1 or 2 hotel rooms that can accommodate disabled people.

To move around Amsterdam, a person in a wheelchair either needs an assistant to help negotiate curbs or an adapted car.

Netherlands Railways (NS) will provide information and assistance for disabled people on request. You can reach them at ☎ 30-2355555, Monday through Friday from 8am to 4pm. (For travel on weekends and Mondays, call before 2pm Friday.) You can request special help at some stations, but not all provide this service. Phone 1 day in advance. Special services for the handicapped include: a train timetable in braille, special telephones and bathrooms, and a footbridge. For assistance at **Schiphol Airport**, call 20-6480093.

Resources in the United States

Organizations that dispenses advice and assistance to the disabled (for free or a small donation) are: **MossRehab,** 1200 West Tabor Road, Philadelphia, PA 19141, phone inquiries only (☎ 215-456-9603, TDD 215-456-9602); **The Society for the Advancement of Travel for the Handicapped,** SATH, 347 5th Avenue, Suite 610, New York, NY 10016 (☎ 212-447-7284, fax 212-725-8253); and **Information Center for Individuals with Disabilities,** Fort Point Plaza, 27-43 Wormwood Street, Boston, MA 02210 (☎ 617-727-5540 or 800-462-5015, TDD 617-345-9743).

The *Directory of Travel Agencies for the Disabled* (published by Twin Peaks Press, Box 129, Vancouver, WA 98666, ☎ 206-694-2462 or 800-637-2256; $19.95 plus $2 for shipping) lists close to 400 agencies worldwide. One such agency that specializes in cruises, tours, and independent travel for the disabled is **Flying Wheels Travel,** 143 West Bridge Street, Box 382, Owatonna, MN 55060 (☎ 507-451-5005 or 800-535-6790).

Car Rentals & Driving

Transportation from the airport to Amsterdam is excellent by train, bus, and taxi. For side trips to the

Dutch countryside, cars are a more direct and time-efficient way to travel. But if you are planning to visit only Amsterdam, a car is more of a burden than a convenience.

Most major international car-rental firms such as Avis, Hertz, Budget, EuropCar, and EuroDollar have branches in Amsterdam and at Schiphol Airport. Payment by credit card is generally required. A current driver's license is required, and the minimum age is usually 18.

Although it may be easier to book in advance through a familiar American rental company, this is not always the least expensive way to go. Some European rental agencies are less expensive; it's best to call around and compare prices, since prices vary widely from week to week and from season to season. Prices run from about Dfl. 50 per day to Dfl. 170 per day. Some hotel concierges can also be helpful.

Some American companies, such as Avis, offer special prepaid advance rates if you pay for the rental car from 1 to 2 weeks in advance. Hertz has a special early booking rate for rentals booked before March 31—even if you are traveling in June. But such deals are also subject to change.

For U.S. rental companies that can book reservations overseas, contact:

Avis Rent a Car (☎ 20-6836061; 800-331-1034 in the U.S.)

Hertz Rent a Car (☎ 20-6122441, 20-6236123, or 20-6015421 at the airport; 800-654-3001 in the U.S.)

Budget Rental (☎ 20-6126066; 800-545-8208 in the U.S.)

Thrifty Car Rental (☎ 800-367-2277 in the U.S.)

Dutch car rental companies include **AmCar** (☎ 20-6624214), **Diks** (☎ 20-662-3366), and **EuropCar** (☎ 20-6832123).

Arriving by Plane

Amsterdam's **Schiphol Airport,** 8 miles southwest of the city (☎ 063-5034050 for flight and general information), is a major international airport with direct flights from all over the world, including many cities in the United States. It is regularly voted the world's most popular airport. It is definitely well organized and a tranquil place in which to arrive (especially compared to Amsterdam's Centraal Station).

The Airlines

From the United States, **KLM** (☎ 800-777-5553), the "royal" Dutch airline, offers the most nonstop flights to Holland's Schiphol Airport. KLM flies direct to Amsterdam from Atlanta, Baltimore, Boston, Chicago, Detroit, Houston, Washington DC, Los Angeles, Minneapolis, Montreal, New York, Orlando, and San Francisco. KLM's advance purchase (APEX) fares are similar to those of other airlines. But if you are flying off-season (particularly in Feb or Mar), KLM may well offer the best package deals, since some low fares require little or no advance notice and packages include some of the better Amsterdam hotels. However, during high season (Christmas, New Year's, and mid-Apr–Sept) KLM can be expensive.

Martinair (☎ 800-366-4655), a charter company that playfully calls itself "the other" Dutch airline, offers comprehensive but seasonal service to Schiphol. If you plan your trip well in advance and fly between late spring and early fall, you may benefit from an inexpensive charter flight through Martinair. The airline flies nonstop from Ft. Lauderdale, Los Angeles, Miami, Newark, Oakland/San Francisco, Seattle, Tampa, and Denver.

Other airlines flying directly from the United States to Amsterdam are **Delta** (Atlanta, New York), **Pakistan International** (New York), **Royal Jordanian Airlines** (New York, Chicago), **Singapore Airlines** (New York), and **United Airlines** (Washington).

Many flights from America arrive at Schiphol in the morning—which often means you have missed a night's sleep. Some theories hold that in order to prevent major jet-lag and to reset your biological clock, you should try to adjust by staying awake during daylight hours (with the exception of a catnap or two) and by eating regularly on the "new schedule" of breakfast, lunch, and dinner.

If you arrive at Schiphol late at night or in the wee hours of the morning, you might consider spending your first night at one of the clean and comfortable hotels near the airport (see "Accommodations").

Arriving by Train

The rail station at Schiphol Airport lies on the main line from Amsterdam to Leiden, The Hague, and Rotterdam. The night train service links the main cities of Holland, namely Utrecht, Amsterdam, Leiden, The Hague, and Rotterdam. For train information call 06-9292 **(Dutch services)** or 06-9296 **(international services),** Monday to Friday 9am to midnight, Saturday and Sunday 7am to midnight. Although Amsterdam has several suburban train stations, all major domestic and international trains go through **Amsterdam Centraal Station** which, as its name indicates, is located in Amsterdam's historic center within a few yards of bus, tram, train, and boat lines, as well as taxis and rental bicycles. Centraal Station also provides regular train connections to all parts of the country.

Staying in Amsterdam
Getting Around

Filled with side streets and tree-lined canals, Amsterdam is a compact city ideal for **pedestrians.** Walking enables you to observe the city's interesting but subtle touches, like stained-glass windows, carved wooden doors, gargoyles and such. You can see the houseboats with their odd rooftop gardens, wander into a *hofje* or a curious passageway, or impulsively peek into shops that strike your fancy.

Cycling is also an excellent mode of transport, and a great way to tap into the city's rhythm since so many citizens rely on their bikes. Most places you'll want to visit are within easy walking and cycling distance (especially if your destination falls within the "canal ring" that forms concentric circles around the city's historic center). You may benefit by taking a short tour to orient yourself (see orientation tours) before deciding on your mode of transportation.

Trams provide a quick and inexpensive way to travel. They go almost everywhere and they're great if you're in a hurry. But although trams are convenient, they tend to remove you from the Amsterdam street life and the peaceful canals that are such vital parts of the city. Trams, like other crowded places, can also attract pickpockets, so hold onto your money.

You are more likely to take **buses** for trips to the suburbs or the country, or at night when the trams and trains stop running, but they are efficient and inexpensive.

Taxis are quick and easy, but very expensive—even for short distances. **Cars** are an asset in the Dutch countryside, but a liability in the city since parking is nearly impossible, meters are barely identifiable, and parking penalties are harsh. However, in the Museum Quarter and Amsterdam South, parking is relatively easy to find.

Although some Amsterdammers use **trains** to commute to or from the suburbs or from the city center to RAI, most people do not use trains to travel within the city of Amsterdam.

Between the Airport & the City

When you arrive at Schiphol Airport, you can easily get to Amsterdam by taxi, KLM Shuttle, bus, train, or private rental car. The least painful way, especially if you are tired and burdened with heavy luggage, is by taxi or KLM Shuttle. A **taxi** (which can be found lined up in front of the airport) is very expensive: One will take you from the airport to your Amsterdam hotel in 20 minutes or half an hour for Dfl. 60. For Dfl. 17.50, the comfortable **KLM Shuttle** will take you to one of 10 hotels (depending on whether you choose the orange or the yellow line). You can take the shuttle whether or not you flew KLM or are actually staying in any of these hotels. Since each bus only makes about 5 or 6 stops, the ride can take anywhere from 20 to 45 minutes, depending on where you are on the route. The shuttle is one of the most comfortable and efficient ways to travel into Amsterdam provided that your destination is reasonably close to Hotel Pulitzer, Hotel Krasnapolsky, Holiday Inn Sonesta, the Victoria Hotels, or the Barbizon Palace (all on the "orange line"); or Hotel Ibis, the Hilton Hotel, the Barbizon Centre, Parkhotel, or the Apollo Hotel (all on the "yellow line"). If you are carrying very heavy luggage, it may pay to take the KLM Shuttle to the hotel on the route that is closest to yours and then take a cab from the shuttle stop to your hotel.

The **train** is an efficient and inexpensive way to get into the city. It only takes 20 minutes. A one-way ticket costs Dfl.6 in second class and Dfl. 9 in first class. Roundtrip tickets are Dfl. 10.25 in second class and Dfl. 15.50 in first class. Trains leave for Amsterdam every 20 minutes, departing from the station underneath the airport. It's easy—pick up your luggage at the baggage claim, plop it on one of the many available carts if you have a lot, proceed down the escalator or ramp, and follow the signs to the train. If you are traveling light, your journey will be simple. You'll simply arrive at Amsterdam's Centraal Station, walk out the front door, and take a tram or boat to your hotel. You may even be close enough to walk. Another way to get to your hotel from Centraal Station, if you don't have a lot of heavy luggage, is by the **Canal Bus** (located on the canal in front of the station). But be warned that it's slow—it takes at least 40 minutes to reach the last stop.

A word of caution: Centraal Station attracts some rather artful pickpockets, so hold onto your luggage and cameras.

To drive a **car** from Schiphol Airport to Amsterdam (about 16km/10 miles), you must take highway A9 toward Aalsmeer, 4A toward Sloten, turn off at A10 toward Osdorp, and at junction no. 5105 proceed on A10 into Amsterdam. If you are planning to drive to Amsterdam, have a good road map in hand; the Dutch method of marking roads can take some getting used to.

Group sightseeing tours seeking transfers to Amsterdam or other parts of the Netherlands should contact **KLM Roadtransport Schiphol,** ☎ 20-6495631 or fax 20-480470.

Public Transportation

In trams and buses, as in trains, you can always buy tickets from the driver, but it is much cheaper to buy a multistrip ticket, known as a *strippenkaart,* in advance. You can purchase these at post offices, rail stations, public transportation offices, VVV tourist offices, and at news agents and tobacconists displaying the strippenkaart symbol. A 1-hour ticket costs Dfl. 4.50, a "2-strip" ticket costs Dfl. 3, a 3-strip ticket costs Dfl. 4.50, and the 8-strip ticket is Dfl. 12.

The country is divided into zones and the strippenkaart has to be folded and stamped according to the number of zones traveled, plus a flat rate of 1 strip per journey. Therefore if you are traveling within a single zone (e.g., from Dam to Spui in Amsterdam), you should stamp the ticket on strip 2, and if you travel through 2 zones, the ticket should be stamped on strip 3. It is possible for 1 ticket to be used by more than 1 person— just stamp the required number of strips for each person. The machine for stamping tickets is usually located at the back of the tram.

If you need to begin a new card, simply stamp the last strip of the old card and then the remaining strips required on the new card. As well as stamping the zone in which you begin your journey, the machine records a time on the ticket. Your ticket will then be valid for connections on any tram, bus, or metro for 1 or 2 hours after the time stamped depending on the zone you are traveling through. Sound complicated? Don't worry, if you're baffled just state your destination to the driver, who will then stamp your ticket.

A route map is usually displayed above the doors on trams, while the name of the stop is given on a signpost, together with the zone number, timetable, and map of zones. Stops are requested by pressing a red button. But if you are confused by all of this, simply ask the driver to alert you when you approach your desired stop.

Trams and metros usually run until midnight, while night buses (*nachtbussen*) run throughout the night on certain routes.

For information about transportation in and around Amsterdam (as well as tickets) contact the public transportation office outside Centraal Station (Mon–Fri 7am–7pm, Sat and Sun 8am–7pm, ☎ 06-9292).

Getting Around by Car

Driving in Amsterdam, especially near the canals or the Historic Center, is far more crazed and anarchic than you might imagine. Amsterdammers drive fast on narrow streets that are sometimes obstructed. Cars, bicycles, and trolleys quickly converge at tiny intersections, making driving stressful, if not hazardous. If you can avoid driving in the city, do so. Driving in the Museum Quarter, Amsterdam South, or the suburbs, however, is not such a problem, but not a necessity.

Driving in the Dutch countryside is another matter. The roads are wide, flat, and smooth, and the rich, green *polderland* (lowland) dotted with windmills, farming cottages, black Frisian horses, and cows is a pleasure to behold. Both the Utrecht lake country and the beach at Zandvoort are only a half-hour drive from Amsterdam.

Driving rules: The speed limit in towns and populated areas is generally 50kph (31 m.p.h.), but in some suburban areas and in special residential districts known as *woonerven* (newly built family neighborhoods in the suburbs indicated by a blue sign showing a white house) it is 30kph (19 m.p.h.). Two-lane highways have a limit of 80kph (50 m.p.h.), main roads outside cities have a limit of 100kph (62 m.p.h.), and superhighways (motorways) have a limit of 120kph (74 m.p.h.).

Traffic coming from the right has priority unless otherwise indicated. Drivers should take particular care when turning right, as cars must yield to cyclists on their inside that are proceeding straight ahead. Trams have priority, and pedestrians at a crosswalk must be given right of way. Seat belts are compulsory.

Parking: The most annoying aspect of having a car in Amsterdam is parking. Dutch parking meters do not bear any resemblance to the American variety. It is easy for Americans to simply not notice a meter—and end up with "the yellow boot" (or Denver boot) clamped to the wheel of their car. This metal boot locks the wheel and immobilizes the car. Ask your hotel concierge, an Amsterdammer, or a policeperson (if you can find one) to show you what a Dutch parking meter looks like and how to put money in it (since this may all be somewhat hard to describe). Then, park your car only at authorized places—and feed the meter. If you don't, the fine can be Dfl. 120 plus service costs. You have 24 hours to pay the fine before it becomes Dfl. 250. If your car is **towed away,** you can collect it at 25 Cruquiuskade, ☎ 20-5559800.

The best solution is to park in a lot or buy a 3-day parking pass, which you can buy at Dienst Parkeerbeheer (Weesperstraat 105a, ☎ 20-5530300, or 20-5530333 for general information). Some possible places to park are **Parking Byzantium** (1g Tesselschadestraat, ☎ 20-61666416) or **Parking Plus** (P+), (Amsterdam Centraal, 20a Prins Hendrikkade, ☎ 20-6854061). Many hotels either have parking or can arrange nearby parking, so ask your concierge for suggestions.

Getting Around by Bicycle

Holland is the land of the bicycle. There are 11 million bicycles in the country and 6,200 miles (9,900 kilometers) of cycle lanes. People of all ages use their bicycles in all weather to commute to work (briefcases and all), to go shopping, to transport their children, and to exercise their dogs. Sturdy, black, 1-speed bicycles with pedal-operated brakes can be rented at more than 100 rail stations in the Netherlands. Special attachable seats for small children are also available. There are hourly, daily, and weekly rates. Bicycle **rental** costs from Dfl. 7.5 to Dfl. 10 per day with special weekly rates of around Dfl. 50. Bicycle rental usually requires a passport or other identification and a deposit of Dfl. 200 in cash or by credit card, but most bicycle rental places do not accept the final payment by credit card.

Some hotels either arrange for bicycle rentals or recommend rental shops. The most popular rental shops include: **Bike City** (Bloemgracht 70, ☎ 20-6263721), **Damstraat Rent-a-Bike** (Dwarsstraat 11,

☎ 20-6255029), **Holland Rent-a-Bike** (Damrak 247, ☎ 20-6223207), **MacBike** (Marnixstraat 220, ☎ 20-6266964), and **Koenders take a bike** (Stationsplein 33, ☎ 20-6248391). It is best to rent a bike early in the day before the best ones are already taken.

Before you set off, it is advisable to check that the brakes, lights, and bell are in working order. Be sure also to take a few minutes to get used to the bicycle—and in particular the brakes.

Proceed cautiously until you are accustomed to the rules of the road. Riding in cycle lanes, designated by a blue sign with a white bicycle, or marked *fietspad* or *rijwielpad,* is compulsory. Routes particularly suitable for bicycles are indicated by signposts with a red bicycle. There are often separate traffic lights for bicycles, and you are permitted to cycle the wrong way down one-way streets if the no-entry sign declares "*m.u.v. fietsen*" (bicycles excepted). Finally, you should keep in mind that cars usually have priority when entering a road from the right.

If you leave your bicycle outside, you should use at least **two strong locks**—one to lock the wheels and another to attach the bike to something solid. Also remove all detachable parts, such as lamps and pump. Never turn your back on an unlocked bike; bike thieves are fast and wily. Most rail stations provide manned bicycle sheds where, for a small charge, you can keep your bicycle locked up overnight or for longer periods. You can take your bicycle with you by train, but you will have to pay rather a lot to do so. Bicycles can also be taken on the Amsterdam metro; the fare is the same as for children.

The most useful **maps** for the cyclist are the ANWB 1:100,000 scale series. The Amsterdam region is covered by Map 5. (See "Shopping" for map suppliers.) An informative booklet, *Cycling in Holland,* can be obtained from the Netherlands Board of Tourism.

Getting Around by Boat

Amsterdam was designed for boat travel, but few tourists make use of the boats that are available for transportation. The **Canal Bus** is a relaxing and educational way to get around Amsterdam. It makes its rounds from 9am until around 6pm, stopping every 20 minutes along its scheduled route. There are 2 lines—the red and the green—and between the two of them the Canal Bus offers adequate transportation within the canal ring, stopping at Leidseplein, the Rijksmuseum, City Hall/Waterlooplein, Centraal Station, Westerkerk (near the

Anne Frank House and the Jordaan), and Keizersgracht (also near the Anne Frank House). For a day-ticket at Dfl. 16.50 you can take the boat as often as you wish. Children under 5 are admitted free. Although the whole route can take 40 minutes to an hour, going from point to point, say the Rijksmuseum to Waterlooplein, is an efficient and restful way to get around the city. During the summer months, the Canal Bus offers discount and 2-day passes. You may purchase tickets for both the canal bus and the museum boat at canalside kiosks located near Centraal Station, the Rijksmuseum, and at the major boat stops throughout the city.

The **Museum Boat** is a good idea for a day of museum hopping; the charge includes free or discounted admission to several museums, and the boat stops within walking distance of 20 museums. A day-ticket for an adult is Dfl. 20, and for children aged 4 to 13, Dfl. 17.50.

More expensive ways to get around by boat are by **water taxi** (☎ 20-6222191). City tours on beautiful vintage boats are available through private companies, such as **Aquadam** (☎ 06-52854796 or 23-5165165), as well as hotels like the Pulitzer, the Hilton, Hotel de l'Europe, and the Amstel. Some boats will even take you, by water, from Amsterdam to the lakes and villages of the surrounding countryside.

Holland's dense web of rivers, canals, and lakes makes it possible to reach most points by boat. The IJsselmeer, which can be reached from Amsterdam via the river IJ, is ideally suited to dinghies, and its coastline is dotted with historic towns offering mooring facilities. The **Loosdrechtse plassen** (an area of lakes between Amsterdam and Utrecht) offers more sheltered sailing conditions. One of the most attractive routes for cruising is from Amsterdam to Utrecht via the Amstel, Holendrecht, Angstel, and Vecht rivers. The NBT publishes an excellent guide to sailing in the Netherlands, *Holland Watersports Paradise,* available from Netherlands Board of Tourism offices.

Getting Out of Town by Train

Travel by rail throughout the Netherlands is quick, efficient and reasonably priced. The trains run on time—which means they also *leave* on time. Some important words of caution to train travelers: *Don't be late.* If you are even 1 minute late you could easily find yourself missing the train. Time between trains can be short, which is good news if you are in a hurry. Carefully check the destination sign on the train—and on the car you sit in: Some trains have 2 sections which, at some point, will split and go to 2 separate locations. Make sure you are sitting in the correct section. Do not expect the conductor to announce all the stops. Dutch train conductors, even a few years ago, could be depended upon to clearly and loudly announce each stop. For some reason, this is no longer the case—which means you must pay careful attention and ask other passengers about stops or you may find yourself on an unintended side-trip. Buy your tickets at the ticket counter. Although it is possible to buy tickets on board from the conductor, it is much more expensive. Inquire about special discount fares that include travel for several days to several weeks.

Traveling by train is both comfortable and quick. NS (Netherlands Railways, Centraal Station Information Desk, ☎ 06-9292) operates frequent services between all the main towns, as well as night trains between Utrecht, Amsterdam, Schiphol, Leiden, The Hague, and Rotterdam. An **intercity** is a fast train linking main cities, while a **stoptrein** calls at intermediate stations as well. A full timetable (*spoorboekje*), with explanatory notes in English, can be purchased at rail stations.

One-way tickets (*enkele reis*) and return tickets (*dagretours*) are valid in the Netherlands on the day of issue only. There are various special tickets such as day tickets (*dagkaarten*, for unlimited travel throughout the Netherlands for 1 day); 3-day and 7-day Rovers (Holland Rail Passes) entitling the holder to unlimited train travel for a specified length of time (for an extra charge, these can be used on other forms of public transportation); weekly tickets (*weeknetkaarten*); and group tickets (*meermanskaart*), for unlimited travel on 1 day for 2 to 6 people traveling together. Children under 4 travel free, while those aged 4 to 9 pay a nominal fare. The NS also offers a number of bargain trips (*dagtochten*) to popular sights, museums, exhibitions, and parks, which include the round-trip rail fare, any bus or boat fares necessary, entrance charges, and perhaps a refreshment. These make excursions easy and economical, while leaving you free to decide when to travel and how long to stay. Information on train services can be obtained from Netherlands Board of Tourism offices.

The **Netherlands Board of Tourism** in the United States offers special 3-' and 5-day passes for unlimited train travel in Holland within a 10-day period. Tickets are issued year-round. The 3-day pass costs $68 for second class and $88 for first class. The 5-day pass costs $104 for second class and $140 for first class.

For summer travel, rail passes purchased in Holland are less expensive. A **Summer Tour Pass** gives you 3 days of unlimited train travel anywhere in Holland over a 10-day period during the months of June, July, and August. A second class ticket costs Dfl. 85 for one person and Dfl. 115 for two people. First class tickets run Dfl. 105 for one person and Dfl. 155 for two people. Another summer special, the **Summer Tour Plus,** includes bus, tram, or metro tickets in addition to the train ticket for an additional Dfl. 17 for one person or Dfl. 25 for two people.

Laws & Regulations

The Dutch Criminal Code certainly does not read like a manifesto for license, yet many visitors assume it must, given the permissive attitude in Amsterdam and other large cities toward soft drugs, prostitution, and pornography, which are to a large extent decriminalized. But decriminalized does not mean legal, and there are limits to Dutch tolerance. Drugs are a case in point. You are legally entitled to possess 30 grams of marijuana for your personal use—and the police are legally entitled to confiscate it (although they do not). But you are not permitted to take drugs out of the country. Under such circumstances, Dutch lenience no longer applies.

Electric Current

The Netherlands runs on 220 volts of electricity instead of the 110 volts used in the United States. Consequently, it is important to buy a converter before you leave for Holland to prevent having to comb Amsterdam for an appliance store when you arrive. (If you forget or lose your converter, try **Aurora** near Muntplein.)

Local & Foreign Publications

For information on what's going on around town, try *Time Out* and *What's On in Amsterdam* (a VVV publication available at tourist offices).

Between the **American Book Center** at Kalverstraat 185, **W. H. Smith** at Kalverstraat 152, or the **Athenaeum Nieuwscentrum** on the Spui, you will find an impressive selection of English-language magazines and books. A good selection of international publications are also available at Athenaeum, as well at several cafes (see Walem, De Jaren, and Luxembourg in

Dining). The better **Dutch newspapers** (if you read Dutch) are *NRC Handlesblad, De Volksrant,* and *Het Parool.*

Mail

Post offices (*postkantoren*) in Holland are marked **PTT.** Amsterdam's **main post office,** located at Singel 250-256 (on the corner of Raadhuisstraat, several blocks from Dam Square, ☎ 20-5563311), is open Monday to Wednesday and Friday from 9am to 6pm; Thursday until 8:30pm; and Saturday until 3pm. The post office at Oosterdokskade 5 is open Monday to Friday from 8:30am to 9pm and Saturday from 9am to noon. In large cities elsewhere in the Netherlands, the main post office is normally open Monday to Friday from 8:30am to 5:30pm, and on Saturday morning.

Stamps can be obtained in post offices, from coin-operated machines, and from many newsstands selling postcards. Letter boxes are red and marked PTT; the slot marked *streekpost* is for local mail only. Allow 7 to 10 days for letters between the Netherlands and the United States; 4 days between the Netherlands and the United Kingdom. There is also an express mail service (expresspost) for urgent mail. At press time, **air-mail rates** to North America are Dfl 1.60 for a standard-sized letter and Dfl 1 for postcards.

Mail and MoneyGrams can be received at the **American Express** offices: Damrak 66, open Monday to Friday from 9am to 5pm, Saturday from 9am to noon, ☎ 20-5207777; Van Baerlestraat 38, open Monday to Friday from 9am to 5pm, Saturday from 9am to noon, ☎ 20-6714141; Head Office: Amsteldijk 166, 1078 AX Amsterdam, open Monday to Friday, from 9am to 5pm, ☎ 20-5401999, fax 20-6428514.

Opening & Closing Hours

Banks in the Netherlands are normally open Monday to Friday 9am to 4pm and sometimes later on *koopavond* (late-night shopping, see below) days. Branches of the **Grenswisselkantoor** (GWK), located at major rail stations, airports, and superhighway crossings, are open additionally in the evenings and on weekends. The GWK branches at Amsterdam Centraal Station and Schiphol Airport stay open 24 hours.

Most **museums** are closed on Sunday morning, all day Monday, and on certain public holidays. Opening times for museums vary and are subject to change. Most museums open between 9 and 11am and close between 5 and 6pm.

Shop hours are strictly regulated in the Netherlands. Normally, shops are open Monday 1 to 6pm, Tuesday to Friday 9am to 6pm, and Saturday 9am to 5pm. Shops in city centers may also remain open late 1 evening a week (*koopavond*): This is Thursday in Amsterdam, The Hague, and Utrecht, and Friday in Rotterdam and Delft.

Public Holidays

The following holidays are celebrated in Amsterdam: New Year's Day, January 1; Easter Monday; Queen's Birthday, April 30; Ascension Day, 6th Thursday after Easter; Whit Monday, 2nd Monday after Ascension; Christmas, December 25; and December 26. All banks and most shops are closed on these days, although museums are sometimes open. Good Friday is also a bank holiday, but most shops open for at least part of the day. Some government offices close on Liberation Day (May 5).

Rest Rooms

There are very few public rest rooms in Amsterdam. You will find clean facilities in rail stations, museums, art galleries, cafes, and major department stores such as the Bijenkorf and Vroom en Dreesmann. Expect to pay about 25ct in rail stations and department stores. However, while there are few public rest rooms, there are many cafes with rest rooms. To be polite, you might order something as a token "thank you" for the use of their toilet.

Note: If you ask to use the bathroom, some Dutch won't understand you, since, for them, the bath is frequently in a room separate from the toilet (the consequence of narrow houses and old plumbing).

Safety

Amsterdammers feel safe in their city, and men and women of all ages walk or bicycle down the streets until 1 or 2am, ambling home from the cafes or a late movie. At midnight, you will often hear the rhythmic hum of bicycle wheels and people talking on their way home from the bars. Amsterdam is one of the safest cities in Europe, safer than Rome, Barcelona, or Paris. The kind of crime you are most likely to find in Amsterdam is petty crime: pickpockets and thieves, especially bicycle thieves.

To protect yourself from pickpockets, wear a money belt or keep money and purses where you can see them—and hang onto them. Pockets and backpacks are not the safest place to store valuables. Be especially careful in crowded places like Centraal Station, markets, and trams. To discourage street thieves, do not leave valuables visible in your car—and lock your bicycle at least twice with heavy bike locks. Use hotel safes to store valuables whenever possible.

Most Amsterdam neighborhoods are peaceful, safe, and well-trafficked; it is unlikely that you will be mugged or otherwise harassed on an Amsterdam street. But such things are possible—especially in certain neighborhoods. The area behind Dam Square attracts some scruffy characters late at night, and it is best to avoid the Dam, the Nes, and the side streets nearby after dark, and most definitely after 10 or 11pm. The Nes, with its theater cafes and street lights, may be safer than it was a few years ago. But it is still better to venture there in threes or fours after dark.

Centraal Station and the surrounding neighborhood attracts pickpockets who are artful enough to lift your wallet or snatch your camera before you even notice. Although Damrak is well-lit and visited by throngs of tourists at all hours, the side streets behind Damrak and off Kalverstraat are another matter: Avoid them after dark.

The red-light district is well-trafficked and watched over by some large and formidable bouncers, but at night it attracts some unsavory characters, including the occasional junky or dealer. Since the district also attracts throngs of tourists, the streets are relatively safe (though popular with pickpockets), but women alone or in twos might feel uncomfortable here at night. If you feel threatened, go to the nearest cafe; enlist the bartender's help—or call a cab. And again, avoid the dark side streets.

Nieuwemarkt, Amsterdam's Chinatown—an area near the red-light district that has been undergoing some gentrification—has nice cafes, good restaurants, and a population of junkies. The neighborhood is not overtly dangerous—just a bit scruffy. Most of the junkies are peacefully waiting for the methadone van.

As in any city, avoid such desolated places as the parks and the harbor area after dark.

Smoking

The Dutch are social smokers. The walls of their cozy cafes are stained brown with years of cigarette smoke, and few cafes have nonsmoking rooms, although dining rooms tend to be less smoky than the bar areas.

Many hotels have nonsmoking rooms or floors, most trains have nonsmoking cars, but few restaurants have nonsmoking sections. See "Customs, Etiquette & Some Aspects of Dutch Culture" in "Amsterdam ... A Cosmopolitan Village" for more on smoking and the Dutch.

Taxes

Tourists can shop tax-free at some shops in Holland, and these shops will give you the necessary papers to recover the VAT (value added tax) when you leave the country. Look for a tax-free shopping sign in the shop window or ask about VAT before you make purchases.

Telephones

Public telephones are green and marked **PTT Telecom.** They are found in post offices, cafes, museums, large department stores, and occasionally in the street. Dialing instructions are given in numerous languages. Most telephones take 25ct, Dfl. 1, and Dfl. 2.5 coins. Coins must be inserted before dialing. However, the easiest way to use Dutch telephones is by **phone card** (*telefoonkaart*), a laminated card that fits into the telephone. Certain telephones can only be operated with these cards, which are sold at post offices and train stations. You can buy Dfl. 5, Dfl. 10, and Dfl. 25 telefoonkaarts. If you plan to make a few calls, buy the Dfl. 25 card since it is good for about 115 units of telephone time, and it is less likely to expire in the middle of a call.

Telephone numbers beginning with the digits 06 are free. The dialing code for Amsterdam and Schiphol is 20, but don't dial this within the city. Phone numbers and codes for many other parts of the country changed in October of 1995 to accommodate the increasing demand for phone lines. Now all phone numbers (except those with the access code 06) have 9 digits. Now each number will consist of a 2-digit area code and a 7-digit subscriber number or a 3-digit area code and a 6-digit subscriber number. From the United States, you dial 011-31-20 and the number you are calling.

The ringing signal is a long, low intermittent tone, the busy signal a higher and more rapid tone. A 3-tone sound indicates the number is not available.

For lengthy calls or long distance calls, your least expensive option is to call from a PTT phone center (see below) where you will be charged approximately Dfl. 2.80 per minute during business hours and Dfl. 2.50 on nights and weekends for calls to the United

States (although these rates are subject to change). Calling through a hotel switchboard or dialing direct from your hotel room can be alarmingly expensive, although more physically comfortable than a PTT phone booth. Before you opt for the comfort, ask the hotel desk about charges for calls.

There is a **Telecenter PTT Telecom** (with services for telephone, telefax, telex, telegrams) at Raadhuisstraat 48-50, ☎ 20-4843654 (open from 8am until 2am). The rates are low, and you can monitor the length and cost of your call by watching the meter inside your booth. The least expensive time to make calls is between 8pm and 8am. Most other commercial phone centers also have meters and rates less expensive than those of the hotels. You can also find telephone services at: **Telecompany** (Magna Plaza, 182 NZ Voorburgwal, ☎ 20-4222333) and **Teletalk Center** (Leidsestraat 101, open 10am–midnight). There are also some commercial telephone centers on Damrak.

Whether you are in your hotel room or in a public booth, you can use the direct dialing method to call home. AT&T, MCI, and Sprint all have easy direct-dialing numbers that connect you directly with a US operator. To reach the **AT&T** operator, dial 06-0229111 and then your number; for **Sprint Express,** call 06-0229119, for **MCI,** call 06-0229122; and for **Phone USA,** call 06-0220224.

Television

Amsterdam receives numerous television channels by cable, including three Dutch stations, three German, two French, BBC 1 and 2 (from England), Belgian Flemish, and Belgian French. International news coverage is excellent. Movies on Dutch stations and Belgian Flemish are broadcast in the original language; foreign movies on French and German channels are dubbed in French and German respectively. Dutch television also receives American movies and television series.

Time Zones

The Netherlands is 6 hours ahead of Eastern Standard Time and from 7 to 9 hours ahead of the other time zones in the United States. It is 1 hour ahead of Greenwich Mean Time (GMT) in winter and 2 hours ahead in summer.

Tipping

In restaurants and cafes in the Netherlands, service charges and sales tax are almost invariably included in the price (*inclusief BTW en bediening*). You need not leave a tip unless you want to show your appreciation for the service, but tipping by both Amsterdammers and visitors is becoming more common. Some merely round up to the nearest guilder, or to the nearest 5 or 10 guilders for an expensive meal. Some leave a flat 5% to 10% tip, especially if they have ordered a large meal or occupied a table for an hour or two. Taxi fares also include service and taxes, but drivers still expect an additional tip (approximately 10%) if they have assisted you with luggage. Small tips of Dfl. 2.50 to Dfl. 5 are also given to hotel porters and Dfl. 5 and up to helpful concierges.

Useful Telephone Numbers & Addresses

American Express Travel Services   Offices in Amsterdam are: Head Office, ☎ 20-5048504; Damrak 66, ☎ 20-5207777; and Van Baerlestraat 39, ☎ 20-6414141. To report lost or stolen cards call ☎ 20-6424488.

Banks   ABN Bank, ☎ 20-6299111; Rabobank, ☎ 20-6268731. GWK-Grenswisselkantoren at Centraal Station (☎ 06-0566) is open 24 hours.

Car breakdowns   Telephone the police, or ring the ANWB Wegenwacht (road patrol), ☎ 06-0888.

Consulates

American Consulate, Museumplein 19,
☎ 70-3109209.

British Consulate, Koningslaan 44,
☎ 70-3645800

Canadian Consulate, Sophialaan, Den Haag,
☎ 70-3614111

Emergencies

Police, Ambulance, or Fire: Dial 06-11.

Hot Lines

Alcoholics Anonymous (☎ 20-6149481)

Gay & Lesbian Switchboard (☎ 20-6236565)

Narcotics Anonymous (☎ 20-6626307)

Lost Passports
Contact the **local police** (☎ 20-5599111) and your consulate immediately.

Lost Property
At Schiphol Airport, ☎ 20-6012325. On trains, ☎ 20-5578544. On trams, buses, or the metro, ☎ 20-5514408.

Medical & Dental Emergencies
Doctors and Dentists 24-hour service: ☎ 06-35032042. First-aid departments: Stichting Kruispost, ☎ 20-6249031; Academisch Medisch Centrum, ☎ 20-5669111.

Pharmacies
Pharmacies where prescriptions are filled are known as *apotheken* in Holland. Some conveniently located apotheken are **Dam,** Damstraat 2, ☎ 20-6244331; **Proton,** Utrechtsestraat 86, ☎ 20-6244333; and **Het Witte Kruis**, Rozengracht 57, ☎ 6231051. **All-Night Pharmacies**: ☎ 20-6948709.

Tourist Information
VVV Tourist Information, ☎ 06-340344066. Offices are located at Stationsplein 10, across from Centraal Station; and at Leidseplein 1. Amsterdam **Uit Buro,** Leidseplein 26, ☎ 20-6211211, is the source for information on cultural events. Another useful resource is **Amsterdam Information and External Relations,** Amstel 1, ☎ 20-552911.

Transportation Information
Schiphol Airport (☎ 20-6019111)

Airlines (TWA, ☎ 20-6274646; KLM, ☎ 20-4747747; Martinair, ☎ 20-6011222)

Taxis: Call Blokband Taxi, ☎ 6777777.

Canal Bus (☎ 20-6265574)

Water Taxi (☎ 20-6222191)

Public Transportation: Tram, bus, and metro-station, Centraal Station, and Amstelstation, ☎ 06-9292.

PORTRAITS OF AMSTERDAM

A Brief History

Legend has it that Amsterdam was founded when the crew of a storm-tossed fishing boat followed their seasick dog from marsh onto dry land. Amsterdam subsequently adopted a coat of arms showing a boat with 2 fishermen and a dog on board (which was appropriate regardless of legend since Amsterdammers love their dogs and take them just about everywhere).

The most official version, however, of Amsterdam's origins is that the city began, as its name suggests, at a dam in the Amstel River. Much of Amsterdam was originally peat bog or marsh, and its early settlers built huts on muddy river banks. They drained what land they could and built a dam in the Amstel River as protection against floods. In the following centuries, the Dutch perfected their drainage methods, which resulted in the creation of *polders*—wetlands (lakes, marshes) reclaimed from the sea and from inland waters. Dutch mastery of the sea resulted in ingenious feats of engineering (locks, dikes, windmills) and the creation of a seafaring nation that grew affluent from world trade during the golden age, which began in the late 16thC.

The Netherlands has remained one of the most affluent nations in the Western world and a center of trade and business. However, Dutch politics have undergone changes—and contained sizable contradictions. Although the Netherlands was once a colonial power that participated in slave trade and exploited its African and Indonesian colonies, the country has become a haven of tolerance and social democracy that welcomes immigrants from its former colonies (as it once welcomed Jews, Armenians, and Huguenots), offering them political and religious liberty as well as generous social programs.

Landmarks in Dutch History

c. AD 1250: Count William II of Holland built a castle at The Hague. His son, Floris V, erected the Ridderzaal within the castle walls.

1275: Count Floris V of Holland granted Amsterdam exemption from tolls—the first document to refer to Amsterdam.

Late 13thC: Conflict between Counts of Holland and Bishops of Utrecht; Count Floris V of Holland was assassinated and his son died 2 years later; Holland then passed to John of Hainault, who defeated the Bishop of Utrecht and installed his brother Gwijde as Bishop. In 1300 Gwijde granted Amsterdam its first charter.

1317: Amsterdam annexed to Holland.

1345: Count William IV of Holland died, and the county passed to the son of his sister, Margaretha, wife of Ludwig of Bavaria. This led to feuds between "Hooks" and "Cods."

Mid-14thC: Amsterdam became an important center for goods from northern Germany, the Baltic, and Flanders; especially beer and grain.

1428: Philip the Good, Duke of Burgundy, acquired Holland from his cousin Jacoba of Bavaria. Burgundy, now controlling much of the Low Countries, pursued a policy of centralization that eroded the privileges enjoyed by the cities; but the Ax brought stability and prosperity to trading cities, especially Amsterdam, which vied with the League for Baltic Trade.

1477: Death of Charles the Bold, son of Philip the Good. He was succeeded by his daughter, Mary of Burgundy, who restored the privileges to the cities in the Grotto Privilege to secure the loyalty of the Low Countries. She married Maximilian Hapsburg, later Holy Roman Emperor, who in 1489 granted Amsterdam the privilege of placing the imperial crown above its coat of arms.

1496: Philip the Fair, son of Mary and Maximilian, wed Juana the Mad, heiress to Castile and Aragon.

1500: Birth of Charles V, their son.

1515: Charles V assumed control of the Low Countries and of Spanish and German territories.

1535: A group of Anabaptists (radical Protestants), following the example of Münster (1533), seized Amsterdam town hall, but were evicted the following day and executed.

1555: Charles V abdicated in favor of his son, Philip II of Spain. Philip pursued an increasingly intolerant policy toward Protestantism and tried to assert the power of the crown over cities and nobles.

1566: The Iconoclasm (Beeldenstorm), an outburst of popular unrest, during which numerous Catholic works of art were destroyed.

1568: William of Orange led the Dutch Revolt against Spain; the Eighty Years' War began.

1576: The Pacification of Ghent briefly united 17 provinces of the Low Countries, but stalled on religious grounds.

1578: Amsterdam, previously loyal to the Catholic (Spanish) side, finally converted to the Protestant side in a peaceful revolution (Alteratie).

1579: The Union of Utrecht was signed by the seven northern provinces of the Netherlands, guaranteeing mutual assistance yet leaving provinces with considerable independence.

1581: The Northern provinces renounced Philip II as their sovereign.

1584: Assassination of William of Orange at Delft.

1585: Antwerp fell to the Spanish and Amsterdam seized the chance to attract trade; the influx of refugees from Antwerp also benefited Amsterdam economically.

1588: The defeat of the Spanish Armada eroded Spanish naval power. Beginning of Holland's golden age, a period of economic prosperity and scientific and artistic brilliance.

1594–97: Willem Barents made several unsuccessful attempts to discover a northern route to China.

1594: Nine Amsterdam merchants established the Compagnie van Verre to exploit the spice trade; Cornelis de Houtman discovered Java.

1599: The Compagnie's second expedition to the East Indies yielded 400% profits.

1602: Dutch East India Company established.

1603–11: Construction of Amsterdam's Zuiderkerk, the first Dutch Protestant church to be built.

1604: Publication of *De Jure Praedae* by Hugo Grotius proclaimed freedom of the seas.

1609: The plan of the 3 canals was drawn up for Amsterdam.

1609–21: A 12-year truce with Spain was concluded; during this period a dispute flared up between 2 Protestant factions—the Remonstrants and Counter-Remonstrants—leading to the execution of Van Oldenbarnevelt and the imprisonment of Grotius.

1620: The Pilgrim Fathers departed from Delftshaven on the *Speedwell,* bound for the New World.

1621: Dutch West India Company established.

1626: Peter Minuit purchased Manhattan from Indians for beads and other trinkets worth about 60 guilders ($24) and built a fort at the south end of the island. This became the settlement of New Amsterdam, which in 1664 ejected the Dutch governor Pieter Stuyvesant in favor of the English; the settlement was then renamed New York.

1628: Descartes settled in Amsterdam.

1632: A university, the Athenaeum Illustre, was established in Amsterdam.

1634–7: Tulip mania led to spectacular price increases, which then collapsed causing many bankruptcies.

1642: Rembrandt painted *The Night Watch;* his wife Saskia died in the same year.

1642–3: The Dutch navigator Abel Tasman, searching for a route to South America through the East Indies, discovered Tasmania and New Zealand.

1648: The Treaty of Münster concluded the Eighty Years' War; in the same year work began on a new Baroque town hall for Amsterdam.

1652: A Dutch settlement was established at Cape Town.

1652–4: The First Anglo-Dutch War broke out as a result of the English Navigation Act.

1665–7: The Second Anglo-Dutch War began, in the course of which Admiral de Ruyter sailed up the Medway and set fire to the English fleet.

1672: The "Year of Disasters." Louis XIV invaded the Netherlands, and Johan and Cornelis de Witt were murdered by an angry mob in The Hague.

1672–4: Hostilities broke out once more between the Dutch and the English in the Third Anglo-Dutch War.

1683–8: John Locke, the English philosopher, lived in Holland.

1685: The revocation of the Edict of Nantes by Louis XIV brought a flood of Huguenot refugees from France.

1688: The Glorious Revolution: Stadholder William III of Holland and his wife Mary became King and Queen of Great Britain.

1697: Czar Peter the Great visited the Netherlands to study shipbuilding.

18thC: Decline of Amsterdam's role as a center due to competition from France and England.

1747: French invasion; civil unrest in the Netherlands.

1780–4: The Fourth Anglo-Dutch War was caused by Dutch assistance given to American rebels.

1782: Persuaded by John Adams, the Netherlands was the first European government to recognize the United States.

1795: The Batavian Republic was established in the Netherlands by Dutch radicals, with the aid of French revolutionary troops.

1806: The Kingdom of the Netherlands was established with Louis Napoleon as head of state.

1813: Liberation of the Netherlands; creation of a Kingdom under William I; this briefly reunited the north and south Netherlands.

1830: The Belgian Revolt; Belgium (formerly south Netherlands) became an independent state.

1848: In the Year of Revolutions a new Dutch constitution drafted by Thorbecke was approved.

1876: Construction of the North Sea Canal brought new prosperity to Amsterdam.

1901: The Housing Act led to a dramatic improvement in the design of public housing.

1907: Completion of the Peace Palace in The Hague.

1928: Olympic Games held in Amsterdam.

1932: Completion of the *Afsluitdijk,* a dike enclosing the Zuider Zee (the South Sea), to create the IJsselmeer (a fresh water lake).

1940: Holland capitulated to the invading German army after the bombing of Rotterdam.

1941: Amsterdam dockworkers went on strike to protest the deportation of Jews.

1942: Japan occupied the Dutch East Indies.

1943: The Dutch Resistance Movement burned the Amsterdam Registry.

1944–5: Liberation of Holland.

1949: Dutch East Indies achieved independence; the Republic of Indonesia was created.

1953: Disastrous floods in Zeeland killed 1,800 people.

Mid-1960s: Provo demonstrations and happenings in Amsterdam resulted in short-lived radical policies such as free municipal bicycles (the white bicycles) and public electric cars (Witcars). The Provos were against capitalism, pollution, and traffic congestion.

1967: The Provos disband. The Kabouters (Gnomes), a group that replaced the Provos, continued the environmentalist Provo ideas and advocated progressive social policies that addressed traffic congestion, the problems of the elderly, and the housing shortage.

1970: Kabouters win 5 seats in the 45-seat city council.

1970s: Clashes in Amsterdam over metro construction, housing, squatting, and new opera house.

1975: Dutch Guiana becomes the independent Republic of Surinam.

1986–7: Completion of town hall and opera house complex in Amsterdam.

1991: Treaty of Maastricht (proposing a political and economic union of the European Community) is signed by 12 EC members.

1992: Completion of new parliament building in The Hague.

Art & Architecture
Architecture

Walking though Amsterdam is much like walking through an open-air architectural museum—if you look closely. Amsterdam is a city where subtle architectural flourishes—a graceful gable, intricately carved door, or artfully designed stained-glass window—become an art form. Wandering through almost any street in the medieval city or the 17thC canal ring (formed by the Herengracht, Keizersgracht, and Prinsengracht canals) yields architectural finds. Although some of the masterpieces are large buildings like de Keyser's Westerkerk, Cuypers's Rijksmuseum, Berlage's Exchange, and Tuschinski's Art Deco Cinema, master architects like these, and many others, also built homes for the wealthy citizens.

As befits a trading city, Amsterdam's principal buildings are merchants' homes, warehouses, shops, weigh houses, banks, exchanges, and insurance offices. Small-scale architecture has always flourished in Amsterdam and most styles are to be found here, trimmed to fit the narrow facades on the canals. What is delightful about Amsterdam is the profuse detail, from the sculpted gable tops to the witty gable stones illustrating the trade or name of the house owner. Interior design in shops, cafes, and restaurants is equally diverse, from the creaking, wooden ambiance of traditional Dutch interiors to Art Deco, De Stijl, and minimalist designs.

Gothic The street pattern of the Middle Ages is preserved in the narrow lanes around Amsterdam's 2 pre-Reformation parish churches, the **Oude Kerk** and **Nieuwe Kerk** (old and new churches). After Amsterdam's conversion to Protestantism in 1578, the numerous convents and monasteries of the old city were used for secular purposes such as orphanages, universities, hospitals, or barracks, leaving only the lovely Begijnhof on Spui and the 2 chapels south of Oude Hoogstraat as reminders of the city's Catholic origins. Stringent town-planning regulations in the 17thC also led to the virtual extinction of the picturesque wooden Gothic houses, which were a notorious fire hazard in the crowded, industrious city. Here and there, however, the odd glimpse of a jettied wall indicates a resilient medieval framework to which a more modern facade has been attached.

Dutch Renaissance Dutch Renaissance architecture was a late and rather eccentric development of Italian and French Renaissance styles. The early Dutch Renaissance emerged during the reign of the Emperor Charles V, when Dutch architects were able to travel to Italy, while Italian architects were often employed by

Dutch patrons. The Revolt of the Netherlands severed these links with Italy, however, and architects of the late Dutch Renaissance had to rely largely on books of engravings. The most influential of these source books was published by Hans Vredeman de Vries in Antwerp in 1577, illustrating a style that had much in common with the Mannerism of Michelangelo. The best examples of this style in Amsterdam are the ornate gates of the Orphanage (now the Amsterdams Historisch Museum) and the Athenaeum Illustre at Oude Zijds Voorburgwal 231.

Hendrick de Keyser (1565–1621) was city architect at just the moment Amsterdam's economy began to take off, and he was appointed to build 3 new Protestant churches, several delicate spires, the first stock exchange, and many private houses. One soon learns to spot a De Keyser building by its animated step-gabled facade of whitened sandstone set off against rosy-red brick. Amsterdam's Westerkerk, East India House, and Bartolotti House are 3 striking examples of his style.

Dutch Classicism De Keyser's Mannerism was too playful and ornamental for the austere sensibilities of the Dutch Calvinist rulers of the second quarter of the 17thC. They much preferred the sober and rational classicism of **Jacob Van Campen** (1595–1657). **Constantijn Huygens,** the powerful secretary to Prince Frederik Hendrik, put his weight behind Van Campen because he "admonished Gothic curly foolery with the stately Roman, and drove old Heresy away before older Truth." Van Campen's stately style can be seen in the house at Keizersgracht 177 built in 1624 for the Coymans brothers, and the Royal Palace (formerly Town Hall; see **Koninklijk Paleis** in "Sights & Attractions") in Amsterdam (1648–55). These simple, reserved buildings reflect the quiet dignity of the Dutch golden age.

 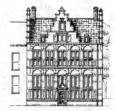

The Groenland Pakhuizen and House on the Three Canals, two elegant examples of 17thC architecture distinguished by their fine step gables.

A 1638 neck-gabled house on Herengracht.

Philips Vingboons (1608–75), known for his domestic architecture, developed a less austere classicism that retained a fondness for the Gothic gable. Vingboons's distinctive contribution to the Amsterdam skyline was the neck gable—a simplified step gable with ornate claw pieces—as in his 4 stately houses built for the Cromhout family at Herengracht 364-70. His brother **Justus Vingboons**'s 1660 Trippenhuis on Kloveniersburgwal shows an even more stately form of Dutch classicism.

Daniel Stalpaert (1615–76) had a significant impact on Amsterdam as city architect during the mid-17thC. His first task was to complete the Town Hall after Jacob van Campen mysteriously dropped out of the project, and he then went on to design a number of massive public buildings such as the austere 1656 Admiralty Arsenal on Prins Hendrikkade, the 1661 Prinsenhof on Oude Zijds Voorburgwal, the German Synagogue on Waterlooplein, and the Amstelhof on the River Amstel.

Even more sober were the residences built by **Adriaen Dortsman** (1625–82) in the 1660s and 1670s on fashionable sites close to the Amstel. Dortsman's houses (examples of the school of Restrained Dutch classicism) stand out sharply against the colorful pluralism of Amsterdam, with their gray sandstone facades purged of all decoration except for lithe sculptures of Grecian gods perched on the balustrades. Few Dortsman houses have survived intact, but a splendid pair at Keizersgracht 672-74 house the Museum Van Loon.

French Styles of the 18thC   After the decline of classicism at the end of the golden age, Dutch architecture fell under the spell of French styles introduced by Protestant refugees who fled from France after Louis XIV's Revocation of the Edict of Nantes in 1685.

Daniel Marot (1661–1752) brought the grand Baroque style of Louis XIV to Holland, carefully compressing its features to fit the modest proportions

of Dutch houses. This Dutch Louis XIV style is characterized by monumental double staircases, splendidly
decorated centerpieces, grand entrances, and cornices
laden with heavy, symmetrical decoration. A handsome example of this style is the Museum Willet-
Holthuysen at Herengracht 605. The busy tops of
Keizersgracht 244-46 illustrate the tendency at this time
for architects to be over-zealous in their work.

During the mid-18thC, the Baroque symmetry of
Louis XIV softened into the rococo style of Louis XV.
Since the Herengracht and Keizersgracht élite had
already spent their money on Louis XIV improvements, the Louis XV details tend to appear on more
modest dwellings on the less prestigious Singel,
Prinsengracht, and Kloveniersburgwal canals. The style
is characterized by capricious bell gables and other
touches of whimsy. Prinsengracht 126 shows this style
at its most flamboyant.

After the flourishes of rococo, a sober reaction set
in that reached Amsterdam from France in the 1770s.
During this period—exactly 100 years after the sobri-
ety of Dortsman and Stalpaert—necks, bells, and crests
were chopped off and replaced by flat cornices. This
resulted in the destruction of large tracts of Amsterdam's
skyline, although the consequences were far more dire
in Delft and The Hague.

The French occupation in the late 18thC and early
19thC brought the Empire style to Holland. This was a
continuation of the geometrical Louis XVI style, with
various oddities such as cushion doors and palm motifs. The economy of Amsterdam was in poor shape at
this time, however, and the Empire style had little impact beyond the decoration of fanlights with attractive
geometrical designs.

Eclecticism   A somber tone persisted through to the
Greek Revival architecture of the early 19thC, as

A stately 18thC canal house with a Louis XIV–style cornice.

An elegant example of an 18thC bell-gabled house.

seen in the austere law courts at Prinsengracht 436 and the solid 1840 Willemspoort at the west end of Haarlemmerstraat.

After the economic doldrums of the French occupation, Amsterdam's economy began to take off with the opening of the North Holland Canal in 1823 and the Amsterdam-Haarlem railway in 1839. New mansions were commissioned on the edge of the Vondelpark or overlooking the Amstel. Architects flirted with various historical styles, from Old Dutch Renaissance (favored by Protestants) to fussy neo-Gothic (favored by Catholics). Architects of public buildings tended to adopt a diplomatic compromise between these 2 styles, although **P. J. H. Cuypers** (1827–1921) could not conceal his Catholic leanings in his neo-Gothic designs for the Rijksmuseum, Centraal Station (1881–89), and numerous churches. On the other hand, **A. N. Weissman**'s Stedelijk Museum is a solid piece of neo–Renaissance design. Eventually, a compromise between neo–Dutch Renaissance touches and a more international neoclassicism was reached in **A. L. van Gendt**'s dignified 1888 Concertgebouw.

Art Nouveau architecture failed to make much headway in Amsterdam. The finest Art Nouveau work in Amsterdam was produced by the versatile **Gerrit van Arkel,** who moved deftly from neo–Renaissance (Heiligeweg 35) and neo-Gothic (Plantage Middenlaan 36) to outrageous Art Nouveau in his 1905 E.H.L.B. office building overlooking Keizersgracht at Leliegracht.

Modern Architecture   H. P. Berlage (1856–1934), the father of modern Dutch architecture, completed the Amsterdam Beurs (stock exchange) on Damrak in 1903. This building marked a decisive break with 19thC eclecticism and asserted a new architectural ethic based on rigorous proportions and a use of traditional Dutch building materials. Berlage was also responsible for drawing up the Expansion Plan for Amsterdam Zuid

(1905–17), which brought an end to the ruthless urban growth of the 19thC and a return to the harmonious ideals of the 17thC. The Plan was drawn up under the 1901 Housing Act, which required municipal authorities to subsidize and control the construction of working-class housing.

The **Amsterdam School**—with its expressionist sensibilities, its taste for decorative brickwork, and its exciting approach to housing and design—arose in reaction to Berlage. The first wave of new housing after the 1901 Act was designed by Amsterdam School architects, a group of idealistic socialist architects who developed an inventive, organic style that took its first form in the 1911 to 1916 design for the Scheepvaarthuis. This large office building on Prins Hendrikkade is expressionist in style and decorated with seafaring motifs. Blocks of workers' housing were later designed by **Michel de Klerk** (1884–1923) at Spaarndammerbuurt in west Amsterdam, one of the first social housing blocks using imaginatively designed brick, doors, and stair rails. Dageraad, a unique apartment complex designed by De Klerk with a brickwork by P. L. Kramer, brings together brick columns, internal courtyards, and fanciful decoration. In the south at Henriette Ronnerplein, **P. L. Kramer** (1881–1961) displayed similar creative energy in his matching blocks on P. L. Takstraat, and in many unusual bridge designs.

Despite its unbounded creative vitality, the Amsterdam School style lasted barely a decade. It lost much of its impetus with the early death of De Klerk in 1923, but there were other reasons for its demise, such as its high production costs and its concentration on surface decoration.

The Dutch Modern Movement architects moved away from the whimsy and romantic socialism of the

Amsterdam Beurs

Aldo van Eyck's
Moederhuis

Amsterdam School. They sought to design spacious, light-filled buildings that were crisply functional. The Cinétol at Tolstraat 154 (now a public library) is one of the best examples of Modern Movement architecture in Amsterdam, designed in 1926 by **J. A. Brinkman** and **L. C. van der Vlugt.**

A much later building in this same tradition is the Van Gogh Museum, designed by **Gerrit Rietveld** (1888–1964). A key figure in the development of post-war Amsterdam architecture is **Aldo van Eyck,** whose 1981 Moederhuis combines functionalism with a rainbow of colors. (In 1990, van Eyck won the prestigious Royal Gold Medal for Architecture.) The city council's "compact city" policy in the 1980s led to the filling in of numerous gap sites in the Nieuwmarkt and the Jordaan with small-scale housing projects, while **Cees Dam** and **Wilhelm Holzbauer**'s controversial—and monumental—Muziektheater (concert hall) and Stadhuis (town hall) complex brought international modern architecture to the old Jewish quarter. But the careful creativity that has been a hallmark of Amsterdam architecture through the centuries is perhaps best illustrated by **Tony Alberts**'s NMB Bank headquarters in Amsterdam Zuid-Oost, with its eccentric angles precisely calculated to maximize energy efficiency.

Dutch Painting

To most people Dutch painting means the art of the golden age: the peaceful landscapes of **Jacob van Ruisdael** and **Hobbema,** the quiet domestic interiors of **Vermeer** and **De Hooch,** the merry banqueting scenes of **Frans Hals,** and the vibrant portraits by **Rembrandt.**

The **Rijksmuseum** in Amsterdam holds the world's finest collection of Dutch art of the golden age, and there are also excellent collections at the **Mauritshuis** in The Hague and at the **Museum Boymans-van Beuningen** in Rotterdam. Other well-known Dutch artists are van Gogh, to whom a museum (**The Van Gogh Museum**) is devoted in Amsterdam, and the abstract painter Piet Mondrian, whose work can be studied in The Hague's **Gemeentemuseum.** For more specific information on the collections at the Rijksmuseum, Stedelijk Museum, Van Gogh Museum, and Rembrandthuis, see "Sights & Attractions."

It is also interesting while in Holland to explore some of the lesser-known areas of Dutch art, such as the exquisite Delft Masters of the 15thC, the Haarlem Mannerists of the 16thC, and the Impressionists of the 19thC.

Early Netherlandish Painting

Early Dutch painting was influenced by Flemish Masters such as **Jan van Eyck** (1385–1441) and **Rogier van der Weyden** (1399–1464), who were active in the Southern Netherlands (present-day Belgium) during the 15thC. **Van der Weyden** moved beyond the static devotional art of his time by focusing on fewer human figures and creating a less static, more emotional form of painting. Haarlem painter **Albert Outwater** continued in this new, less static and more dynamic vein as did one of the most notable Dutch artists of this period—**Geertgen tot Sint Jans** (1460s–90s), an eccentric who painted oddly expressive faces in calm, colorful, religiously symbolic settings.

Even more eccentric was **Hieronymus Bosch** (c. 1450–1516), a Flemish artist whose paintings present disturbing, surreal visions of burning cities, erotic fantasies, and fabulous beasts.

NMB Bank headquarters, Amsterdam

Renaissance

Hints of the Renaissance can be detected in early 16thC paintings by **Jan Mostaert** (c. 1475–c. 1555) from Haarlem, whose works abound in delightful detail, and **Jacob Cornelisz. van Oostsanen** (c. 1470–1533), who was influenced by Italian Renaissance art. But it was van Oostsanen's pupil **Jan van Scorel** (1495–1562) who introduced the techniques of the Renaissance to the Northern Netherlands after his return from Italy. As keeper of the Vatican art collection in Rome from 1522 to 1523 under the Dutch Pope Adriaen IV, van Scorel was able to study the works of Leonardo da Vinci and Raphael. Paintings such as his *Mary Magdalene* in the Rijksmuseum are unmistakably Italian in style, although lingering traces of Flemish realism can be detected in the group portraits he painted in Utrecht and Haarlem. His pupil **Maerten van Heemskerck** (1498–1574) displays a similar blend of Renaissance and Flemish styles in his portraits. Van Heemskerck also traveled to Italy, bringing Mannerist ideas (that art and imagination could "improve" nature rather than merely imitating it) back with him.

A particularly dynamic and fluid style was achieved by **Lucas van Leyden** (1494–1533) in works such as *The Last Judgment,* which hangs in the Lakenhal in his home town of Leiden, and the *Dance around the Golden Calf* in the Rijksmuseum. His figures are far less static than those of other 15thC paintings, and his use of color and drawing show an Italian Renaissance influence. In nearby Haarlem, an exotic form of Mannerism was being developed by artists such as **Cornelis Cornelisz** (1562–1638).

Further north, in Utrecht, a new school of painting resulted from yet another Italian influence: Caravaggio. Caravaggio's use of contrasting light and shadow, known as *chiaroscuro,* had a profound impact on **Gerrit van Honthorst** (1590–1624) and also influenced later Dutch artists such as Vermeer and Rembrandt.

The Golden Age

For most of the 17thC, artists produced the type of painting that is thought of as typically Dutch—a Protestant, down-to-earth art whose subject matter was daily life in Holland.

The golden age is characterized by its placid landscapes with grazing cattle, tranquil domestic scenes, dramatic seascapes, austere white churches, and portraits of surgeons, civic guards, and magistrates. During this period, the church ceased to be an important patron of the arts, and merchants, burgomasters, and even shopkeepers became avid collectors of paintings. This led to a shift from religious themes to simple subjects such as household tasks, banquets, breakfasts, and courtyard socializing.

The art of this period is frequently discussed in terms of category—by town (Delft, Leiden, Amsterdam), by school (Mannerists, Caravagists), or by genre (history, landscape, still life, animal, portraiture, or scenes from daily life), although sometimes these categories overlap.

The mood of the golden age is faithfully reflected in group portraits by **Frans Hals** (c.1580–1666), which range from jovial civic guards celebrating festive occasions to grim, tight-lipped governors of hospitals and senior citizens' homes.

Holland's greatest golden-age artist is **Rembrandt van Rijn** (1606–69), who in 1632 moved from Leiden to Amsterdam. He painted a number of group portraits, such as *The Anatomy Lesson of Dr. Tulp* (1632), *The Night Watch* (1642), and *The Wardens of the Amsterdam Drapers' Guild* (1661), bringing vitality and originality of form to the conservative art of portraiture. The mysterious golden light that suffuses these works is also present in his numerous individual portraits and his historical and biblical paintings. Rembrandt was also a skilled etcher, as can be seen in the remarkable collection of portraits and landscapes in the Rembrandthuis.

Numerous pupils studied under Rembrandt in his studio on Jodenbreestraat, including **Gerrit Dou, Ferdinand Bol, Nicholas Maes,** and the gifted, mysterious **Carel Fabritius** (1622–54). **Gerrit Dou** (1613–75) became one of the better-known Leiden-genre painters who painted patrician domestic interiors using some chiaroscuro techniques; his meticulous technical style contributed to the Leiden school of "fine painters." His pupil, **Gabriel Metsu** (1629–67), continued to produce fine genre paintings such as *The Sick Child,* a tender domestic painting of mother and child, which is now in Amsterdam's Rijksmuseum.

In Delft, **Jan Vermeer** (1632–75) was painting meticulous streets scenes and domestic interiors that conveyed a serene, meditative quality. Vermeer produced about 30 paintings in his lifetime, of which 6 remain in Holland. Many of his paintings are of patrician domestic interiors in which the objects on display are Turkish tapestries, silver pitchers, and luminous

pearls. One of his most extraordinary paintings is the
View of Delft (c. 1658) in the Mauritshuis, which the
French writer Marcel Proust praised as "the most beautiful painting in the world." The Mauritshuis also owns
the simple, enthralling *Head of a Girl* (c. 1660), while
the Rijksmuseum owns another fond view of Delft,
and 2 tranquil portraits—*The Kitchen Maid* (c. 1658)
and *Woman Reading a Letter* (c.1662)—that demonstrate
Vermeer's exceptional skill at capturing various quali-
ties of light. Another Delft painter of the 17thC, **Pieter
de Hooch** (1629–c.1684) painted idealized, serene
domestic interiors rich in spatial complexity.

The paintings of **Jan Steen** (1625–79) show a more
exuberant, humorous, but morally questionable side of
Dutch daily life. His painting *The Merry Family* in the
Rijksmuseum shows a family gathered around a table
having a good time drinking and playing music. But
the painting is inscribed with the maxim: "As the Old
Sing, So the Young Chirp" since the children in the
picture are learning the indulgent, intemperate ways of
their parents—which bodes ill in Calvinist 17thC Holland. Some of Steen's other erotic and playful paintings
such as *Woman at her Toilet* in the Rijksmuseum and *Girl
Eating Oysters* in the Mauritshuis (oysters were a popular aphrodisiac) also contain hidden moral warnings,
although Steen's good-natured portrayal of such merry
disorder sometimes softens his moral stance.

Landscape painting also flourished during the golden
age, when artists acquired a taste for the low horizons,
cloudy skies, and watery meadows of Holland. **Salomon
van Ruysdael** (c. 1600–70) was fond of depicting
tranquil, windless days and spacious landscapes while his
nephew **Jacob van Ruisdael** (c. 1628–82), the greatest
Dutch landscape artist, preferred stormy, changeable skies
as a romantic backdrop to his deliberately composed and
balanced scenes. **Hobbema** (1638–1709) was more
drawn by peaceful vistas, while **Jan van Goyen** (1596–
1656), a master of light and atmosphere, portrayed the
gray, desolate scenery of the eastern provinces. His *Landscape with Two Oaks* in the Rijksmuseum shows his subtle
way of handling the way light cuts through clouds and
damp air. Under the influence of the Italian-influenced
landscape painters of Utrecht such as Jan Both, **Albert
Cuyp** (1620–91) from Dordrecht produced idealized
Dutch scenes in which the mellow golden light and
the rolling landscape do not ring quite true. Much
more realistic are the joyful winter-skating scenes painted
by **Hendrick Avercamp** (1585–1634) of Kampen.

Still-life paintings came into vogue in the 17thC, reaching a peak of technical virtuosity in the works of Haarlem artists **Pieter Claesz** (c. 1597–1661) and **Willem Claesz. Heda** (1599–c. 1680). Dutch still-life painters, like the genre painters, reflected the 17thC interest in the domestic and everyday. Sometimes the everyday was simple and plain, such as in the "breakfast piece" where the subject matter was often bread and cheese. But banquet paintings of china, lovely table-settings, and expensive foods were also popular in affluent, golden-age Holland. **Abraham van Beyeren** (1620/1–90), a master of the banquet piece, painted a luxurious patrician banquet in his *Banquet Still Life* in The Hague's Mauritshuis.

Another form of the still life was flower painting. **Ambrosius Bosschaert the Elder** (1573–1621), the founding father of Dutch flower painting, created carefully composed paintings of flower arrangements that were impossible in the 17thC world since the flowers bloomed during different seasons.

Eighteenth- to Nineteenth-Century Painting

In the 18thC, art became less moralistic and more decorative. Artists such as **Gerard de Lairesse** (1640–1711) and **Jacob De Witt** (1695–1754) were employed to paint the ceilings of patrician homes and the interiors of public buildings and churches.

A fresh vitality entered Dutch art in the middle of the 19thC when the artists of The Hague School (Haagse School), inspired by French painters of the Barbizon School, turned their attention to the peculiarities of Dutch landscape and light. The leading figure of The Hague School was **Josef Israels** (1824–1911), whose paintings display a sad, pensive quality, while his son **Isaac Israels** (1865–1934) painted cheerful Impressionistic views of the dunes at Scheveningen. Other artists of The Hague School include **Hendrik Weissenbruch** (1824–1903), painter of watery meadows and luminous skies; **Hendrik Willem Mesdag** (1831–1915), a prolific and skilled seascape painter; and **Jacob Maris** (1837–99), who depicted rain-swept Dutch skies.

The Amsterdam artist **George Breitner** (1857–1923) used Impressionism to capture the bustle of Amsterdam in the heady days of the Industrial Revolution, while at other times his paintings showed the sad melancholy of the old port area, where he had a studio.

The subtly colored, cloudy landscapes of The Hague School stand in sharp contrast to the feverish vitality of **Vincent van Gogh** (1853–90), born in the village of Nuenen near Eindhoven. Van Gogh's earliest works show the same dark tones and somber mood as the works of Josef Israels, but later, after moving to Paris and falling under the spell of Impressionism, his works became increasingly colorful, intense, and unique, particularly after his move to Arles in 1888. Amsterdam's Van Gogh Museum has an impressive collection of his work, including *Vase of Irises,* van Gogh's version of flower painting, and his *Self-Portrait at the Easel at the Age of Thirty-five.*

Modern Art

A school of modern art called *De Stijl,* "The Style," influenced early 20thC Dutch art, architecture, and interior design. Modern art in the Netherlands began with **Piet Mondrian** (1872–1944), a methodical artist whose lifestyle developed in perfect harmony with his art. Mondrian inhabited a cluttered studio in Amsterdam and exhibited dreamy moonlit Symbolist paintings, but in 1912 he moved to Paris and began to develop an increasingly abstract style. After helping to set up the De Stijl (The Style) movement in 1917, he evolved his distinctive use of horizontal and vertical lines enclosing vivid blocks of primary color. Other influential De Stijl artists were **Theo van Doesburg** (1883–1931) and **Bart van der Leck** (1876–1958).

Before World War II, such modern movements as Expressionism and Magic Realism influenced Dutch art. **Jan Wiegers** (1893–1953) led the Expressionist movement. Magic Realism, with its fondness for the surreal or fantastic, influenced **Raoul Hynckes** (1893–1973), **Pyke Koch** (1901–1991), and **Carel Willink** (1900–1983).

Contemporary Dutch artists continue to experiment with a series of colors and abstractions. Their rejection of conventional forms after World War II is reflected in the delightfully colorful and childlike works of **Karel Appel, Constant, Corneille,** and **Brands,** who form the Dutch branch of the international Cobra group. The Cobra group (including artists from Copenhagen, Brussels, and Amsterdam) developed an innocent "grown-up child style" influenced by primitive art. Other modern and contemporary Dutch artists can be seen at the Stedelijk Museum in Amsterdam and in many small commercial galleries throughout the city.

INDEX

AMSTERDAM

1-2 Amsterdam Environs
3-10 Amsterdam Street Atlas
11-12 Amsterdam Region
13-14 Rotterdam

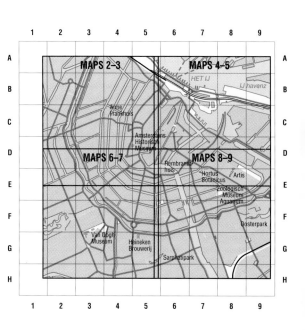

	1	2	3	4	5	6	7	8	9	

MAPS 2–3

MAPS 4–5

HET IJ

IJ havenz

Anne Frankhuis

Amsterdams Historisch Museum

MAPS 6–7

MAPS 8–9

Rembrandt huis

Hortus Botanicus   Artis

Zoologisch Museum Aquarium

Oosterpark

Van Gogh Museum

Heineken Brouwerij

Sarphatipark

KEY TO MAP SYMBOLS

Major Place of Interest	P Parking
Park	M Metro
Built-up Area	— Railroad
Other divided highway	i Information
Primary road	8 Adjoining Page No.
Secondary road	
Other road	

Landsmeer

Purmerend

Het Schouw

0   5   1 Mile

0   5   1 Kilometer

A10

KADOELENWEG

IJPLEIN

Noordhollandsch Kanaal

N247

SLOCHTERWEG

RINGWEG NOORD

Zunderdorp

Buiksloot

N10

FLORA PARK

NIEUWE LEEUWARDERWEG

IJDOORNLAAN

N10

Nieuwendam

PURMERWEG

Noord Amsterdam

N10

NIEUWENDAMMERDIJK

W.H. VLIEGENBOS

N10

A10

ZUIDERZEEWEG

Schellingwoude

MEEUWENLAAN

HET IJ

IJ TUNNEL

IJHaven

N10

Oosterdok

S100

rum

Ned. Scheepvaart Museum

S100

Artis

S113

WEESPERSTRAAT

PLANTAGE MIDDENLAAN

Lozingskanaal

S100

ZEEBURGERDIJK

ZUIDERZEEWEG

IJMeer

Tropen Museum

LINNAEUSSTRAAT

INSULINDEWEG

100

OOSTERPARK

MUIDERPOORT

FLEVE PARK

Nieuwe Diep

WIBAUTSTRAAT

Amstel

S113

Amsterdam Rijnkanaal

110

AMSTELDIJK

Watergraafsmeer

N10

A10

AMSTEL STATION

GOOISEWEG

MIDDENWEG

Ajaxstadion

DIEMEN

Diemen

0

Over Amstel

Weesper Trekvaart

S112

ersum trecht

S111

Diemen Zuid

S113

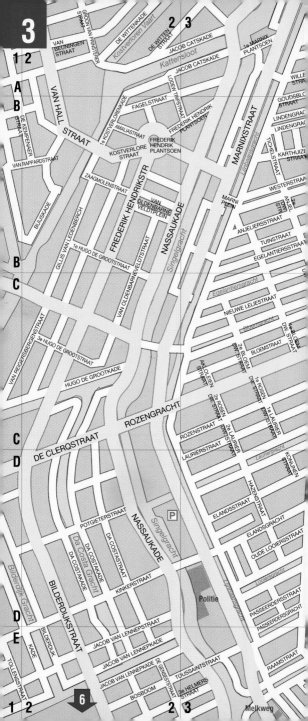

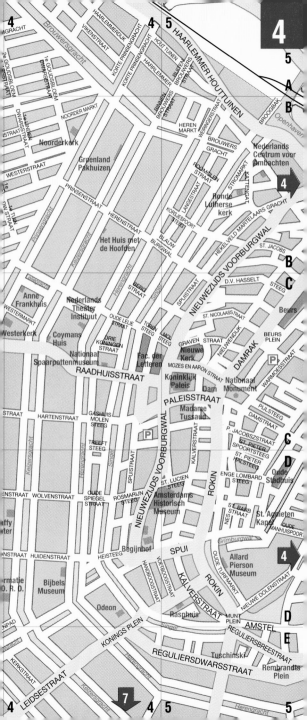

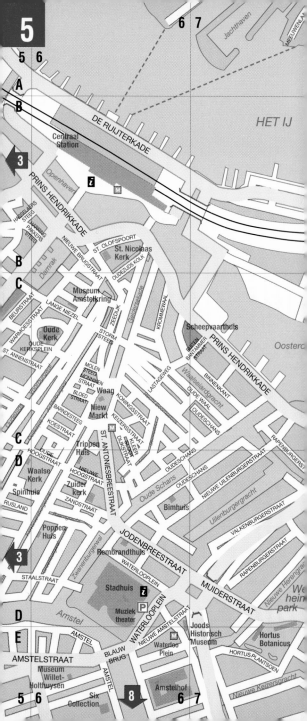

5

6 7

5 6

A

B

DE RUIJTERKADE

HET IJ

Centraal
Station

Openhaven

3

Jachthaven

MEEUWENLA

PRINS HENDRIKKADE

HASSELAERS
STEEG
WARMOESSTRAAT
JURRIAN
PLANKERS
STEEG
NIEUWE BRUGSTRAAT

ST. OLOFSPOORT

St. Nicolaas
Kerk

Damrak

B

OUDEZIJDS KOLK

C

Museum
Amstelkring

BEURSTRAAT
LANGE NIEZEL

Gelderskade

ZEEDIJK

Scheepvaarthuis

KROMMEWAAL

BINNEN
BANTAMM
STRAAT

PRINS HENDRIKKADE

Ooster

WARMOESSTRAAT

Oude
Kerk

OUDE
KERKSPLEIN

ST. ANNENSTRAAT

STORM
STEEG

MOLEN
STEEG
MONNIKEN
STRAAT
BLOED
STRAAT

Waag

Niew
Markt

KONINGSSTRAAT

KEIZERSSTRAAT

KLEER

LASTAGEWEG

Waalseilandgracht

OUDE WAAL

BINNENKANT

OUDESCHANS

RAPENBURGERS

C

BARNDESTEEG

KOESTRAAT

OUDE
HOOGSTRAAT

Trippen
Huis

ST. ANTONIESBREESTRAAT

DIJKSTRAAT

OUDESCHANS

Oude Schans

NIEUWE UILENBURGERSTRAAT

OUDESCHANS

D

Waalse
Kerk

Spinhuis

RUSLAND

NIEUWE
HOOGSTRAAT

Zuider
kerk

ZANDSTRAAT

Bimhuis

Uilenburgergracht

VALKENBURGERSTRAAT

Poppen
Huis

Zwanenburgerwal

3

Rembrandthuis

JODENBREESTRAAT

WATERLOOPLEIN

RAPENBURGERSTRAAT

STAALSTRAAT

Stadhuis

MUIDERSTRAAT

Nieuwe Herengra

We
hein
park

D

Amstel

AMSTEL

Muziek
theater

P

WATERLOOPLEIN

NIEUWE AMSTELSTRAAT

Joods
Historisch
Museum

Hortus
Botanicus

E

AMSTELSTRAAT

BLAUW
BRUG

Waterloo
Plein

HORTUS PLANTSOEN

Museum
Willet-
Holthuysen

AMSTEL

Amstelhof

Nieuwe Keizersgracht

5 6

Six
Collection

8

6 7

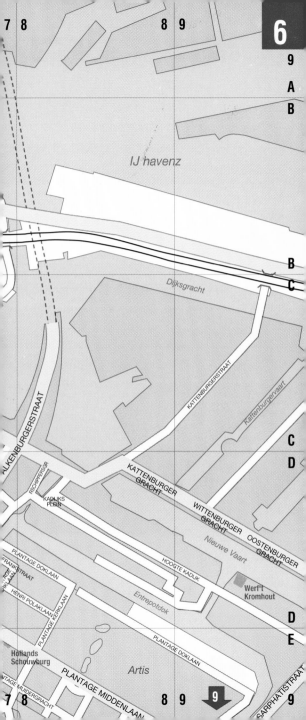

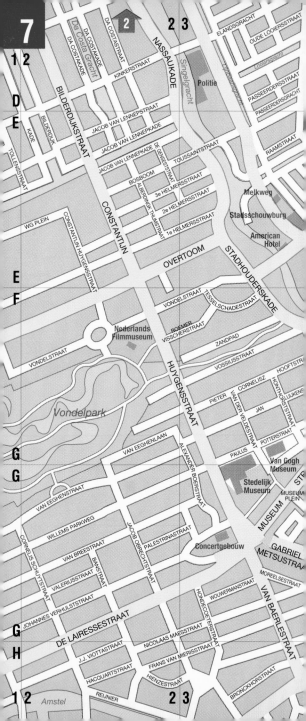

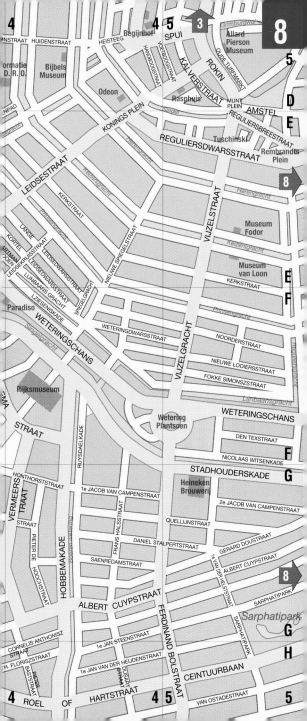

9

JODENBREESTRAAT

2 3

4

1 2

Zwanenburgerwal

Rembrandthuis

WATERLOOPLEIN

Stadhuis *i*

D

Muziek theater

WATERLOOPLEIN

NIEUWE AMSTELSTRAAT

MUIDERSTRAAT

RAPENBURGERSTRAAT

Nieuwe Herengr

W
heir
park

E

AMSTEL

Waterloo
Plein

Joods
Historisch
Museum

Hortus
Botanicus

AMSTELSTRAAT

BLAUW
BRUG

HORTUS PLANTSOEN

PLANTAGE PARK

Rembrandts
Plein

Museum
Willet-
Holthuysen

Amstelhof

Nieuwe Keizersgracht

NIEUWE KERKSTR

7

Six
Collection

AMSTEL

Amstel

NIEUWE KERKSTP

Nieuwe Prinsengr

UTRECHTSESTRAAT

MAGERE BRUG

WEESPERSTRAAT

KERKSTRAAT

watergracht

E

F

Amstel
Veld

Theater
Carré

Weesp
Plein

Amstel
Kerk

Nieuwe

UTRECHTSE DWARSSTRAAT

ACHTERGRACHT

VOORMALIGE
STADSTIMMERTUIN

M.J.
KOSTERSTRAAT

FALCKSTRAAT

HOGESLUIS

PROF. TULPPLEIN

FALCKSTRAAT

FREDERIKS
PLEIN

Amstel
Hotel

KADE

HUDEKOPERSTRAAT

WESTEINDE

Nederlandsche
Bank

OOSTEINDE

SARPHATI

TORONTO BRUG

SWAMMER

F

G

1e BOERHAAVESTRAAT

DAMSTRAAT

DEYMAN
STRAAT

7

HEMONYLAAN

GOVERT FLINCKSTRAAT

AMSTELDIJK

WEESPERZIJDE

RUYSCHSTR

ALBERT CUYPSTRAAT

2e JAN STEENSTRAAT

NIEUWE
AMSTELBRUG

BLASIUSSTR

VAN WOUSTRAAT

2e JAN VAN DER HELDENSTRAAT

1e OOSTERPARK
STRAAT

CEINTUURBAAN

Amstel

OETGEN
STRAAT

SARPHATIPARK

SARPHATIPARK

ST. WILLIBRORDUSSTRAAT

Weesp

arphatipark

VAN OSTADESTRAAT

G

SARPHATIPARK

KUIPERSTRAAT

AMSTELDIJK

H

Gemeentearchief

NINT

1 2

RUSTENBURGERSTRAAT

PIETER AERTSZSTRAAT

2 3

TOLSTRAAT

Cinetol
Library

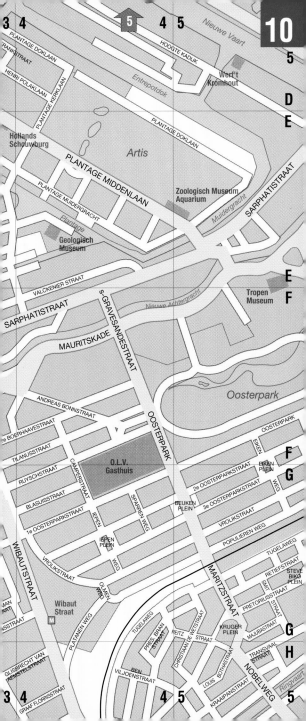

11

NOORDZEE

Heemskerk

Wijk aan Zee

Beverwijk

A8

A9

Kromm

Zaa
Sch

Zaandijk

Velsertunnel

Westzaan

Noordze
Kanaal

Zaanda

Ijmuiden

Sahtpoort

A9

Spaarndam

Nat. Park de
Kennemerduinen

Bloemendaal

Haarlem

A5

N5

Zandvoort

Zwanenbur

A9

Heemstede

Badhoevedorp

Vogelenzang

Amsterdam

Bennebroek

Hoofddorp

Hillegom

Aviodome

SCHIPI

Keukenhof

Nieuw-
Vennep

A4

Aalsm

Noordwijkerhout

Lisse

Noordwijk
aan Zee

Abbenes

Uithoorn

Sassenheim

Westeinder
plassen

Katwijk
aan Zee

A44

Kagerplassen

Rijnsburg

Roelofarendsveen

Oegstgeest

Nieuwkoop

Wassenaar

A44

Leiden

Hoogmade

Voorschoten

Oude Rijn

Alphen a/d Rijn

Zoeterwoude

Rijndijk

A4

Bodegrave

Leidschendam

Boskoop

Den Haag

Zoetermeer

A12

A12

Waddinxveen

Pijnacker

Gouda

Delft

A20

A13

IJssel

Vlaardingen

A20

A20

Capelle

Krimpen

Schiedam

Europoort

Rotterdam

12

Hoorn

sp

A7

Purmerend

Edam

Volendam

Purmerland

Monnickendam

Marken

Markermeer

anstad

Broek-in-
Waterland

Uitdam

A10

AMSTERDAM

Durgerdam

IJmeer

**ZUIDELIJK-
FLEVOLAND**

Almere-
Stad

Groningen

A6

mstelveen

A2

A1

Muiden

A6

Almere-
Haven

Gooimeer

Weesp

Haarden

Huizen

Oudekerk

A9

Abcoude

Bussum

A27

Blaricum

Amstel

Vreeland

Vecht

's Graveland

t'Gooi

Laren

Baarn

A1

Vinkeveen

A2

Loenen

Hilversum

Oud-
Loosdrecht

Apeldoorn

recht

*Loosdrechtse
plassen*

Breukelen

Hollandsch
Rading

A27

Soest

Maartensdijk

Bilthoven

De Haar

A2

Maarssen

De Bilt

Utrecht

Zeist

den

Harmelen

A12

Bunnik

A12

Oudewater

IJsselstein

Driebergen-
Rijsenburg

Nieuwegein

Amsterdam Rijnkanaal

Lexmond

Lek

A2

Culemborg

Lek

oonhover

A27

Noordeloos

udriaan

Hoornaar

Leerdam

Geldermalsen

0   5   10 Miles

0   5   10 Kilometers

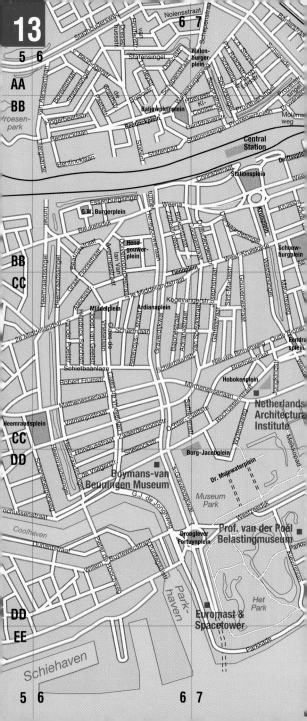